The Press of the Text

The Press of the Text

Biblical Studies in Honor of James W. Voelz

EDITED BY
Andrew H. Bartelt,
Jeffrey Kloha,
AND
Paul R. Raabe

◆PICKWICK *Publications* • Eugene, Oregon

THE PRESS OF THE TEXT
Biblical Studies in Honor of James W. Voelz

Copyright © 2017 Wipf and Stock Publishers. All rights reserved. Except for brief quotations in critical publications or reviews, no part of this book may be reproduced in any manner without prior written permission from the publisher. Write: Permissions, Wipf and Stock Publishers, 199 W. 8th Ave., Suite 3, Eugene, OR 97401.

Pickwick Publications
An Imprint of Wipf and Stock Publishers
199 W. 8th Ave., Suite 3
Eugene, OR 97401

www.wipfandstock.com

PAPERBACK ISBN: 978-1-4982-3590-7
HARDCOVER ISBN: 978-1-4982-3592-1
EBOOK ISBN: 978-1-4982-3591-4

Cataloguing-in-Publication data:

Names: Bartelt, Andrew H., editor | Kloha, Jeffrey, editor | Raabe, Paul R., editor

Title: The Press of the text : biblical studies in honor of James W. Voelz / edited by Andrew H. Bartelt, Jeffrey Kloha, and Paul R. Raabe

Description: Eugene, OR: Pickwick Publications, 2017 | **Includes bibliographical references.**

Identifiers: ISBN 978-1-4982-3590-7 (paperback) | ISBN 978-1-4982-3592-1 (hardcover) | ISBN 978-1-4982-3591-4 (ebook).

Subjects: LCSH: Voelz, James W. | Bible. New Testament—Criticism, interpretation, etc.

Classification: BS2395 P81 2017 (print) | BS2395 (ebook).

Manufactured in the U.S.A.   05/09/17

All Bible translations are the authors' own unless otherwise indicated in the text.

The following Bible versions are identified in the text:

Scripture quotations marked (CEV) are from the Contemporary English Version Copyright © 1991, 1992, 1995 by American Bible Society, Used by Permission.

Scriptures marked as (GNT) are taken from the Good News Translation—Second Edition © 1992 by American Bible Society. Used by permission.

Scripture texts marked (NABRE) are taken from the *New American Bible, revised edition* © 2010, 1991, 1986, 1970 Confraternity of Christian Doctrine, Washington, D.C. and are used by permission of the copyright owner. All Rights Reserved. No part of the New American Bible may be reproduced in any form without permission in writing from the copyright owner.

Scripture quotations marked (NASB) are taken from the New American Standard Bible® (NASB), Copyright © 1960, 1962, 1963, 1968, 1971, 1972, 1973,1975, 1977, 1995 by The Lockman Foundation Used by permission. www.Lockman.org

Scripture quotations marked (NIV) are taken from the Holy Bible, NEW INTERNATIONAL VERSION®, NIV® Copyright © 1973, 1978, 1984, 2011 by Biblica, Inc.®Used by permission. All rights reserved worldwide.

Scripture quotations marked (NRSV) are taken from the Revised Standard Version of the Bible, copyright © 1989 National Council of the Churches of Christ in the United States of America. Used by permission. All rights reserved worldwide.

Scripture quotations marked (RSV) are from the Revised Standard Version of the Bible, copyright © 1946, 1952, and 1971 National Council of the Churches of Christ in the United States of America. Used by permission. All rights reserved worldwide.

Contents

Editors' Foreword / ix
Tribute to James W. Voelz by Jack Dean Kingsbury / xi
List of Abbreviations / xiii
List of Contributors / xvii

1 Creeds as Corroborative Witnesses / *Charles P. Arand* / 1

2 A Hard Saying, with Purpose: Isaiah 6:9-10 and the Gospel of Mark / *Andrew H. Bartelt* / 19

3 Limited Government and Freedom of Religion / *Lawrence C. Brennan* / 31

4 The *Weltanschauung* of the New Testament Authors / *Chrys C. Caragounis* / 46

5 The Relevance of Authorial Language, Style and Usage in the Evaluation of Textual Variants in the Greek New Testament / *J. Keith Elliott* / 67

6 Body, Self, and Spirit: The Meaning of Paul's Anthropological Terminology in 1 Thessalonians 5:23 / *Charles A. Gieschen* / 85

7 Repent, O Lexicon, and Do not Begin to Say That You Have Bauer and Danker as Your Father / *David S. Hasselbrook* / 102

8   The Development of the Greek Language and
    the Manuscripts of Paul's Letters / *Jeffrey Kloha* / 114

9   Texts, Open Spaces, and Readers: A Brief Update on
    the Continuing Challenge of Romans 13 / *Bernard C. Lategan* / 137

10 The Christian Life and the World Series: Does How We Live Matter?
    / *Michael P. Middendorf* / 150

11 Steps for the Definition of the Lexemes in the Greek-Spanish New
    Testament Dictionary: The Lexeme δῆμος / *Jesús Peláez* / 164

12 Eye for an I: An Intertextual Reading of Matthew 5:38 and
    the Artwork of Samuel Bak / *Gary A. Phillips* / 179

13 Isaiah's Philistia Oracle and Hermeneutics: Isaiah 14:28–32
    / *Paul R. Raabe* / 200

14 From Learners to Apostles—Will We Ever Learn? The Parable of
    the Sower in Mark's Narrative World / *Dieter Reinstorf* / 218

15 Communication Models, Relevance Theory, Bible Translation,
    and Exegesis / *Vilson Scholz* / 234

16 Effective Justification and Its Hermeneutical Implications
    / *Mark A. Seifrid* / 244

17 Doubting "Doubting Thomas" / *William C. Weinrich* / 254

18 Beyond Exegesis: The Summons of Contemporary Context
    / *Gerald West* / 270

19 "Saved through Child-bearing"? Theology and Hermeneutics
    in Reading 1 Timothy 2:15 / *Thomas M. Winger* / 283

The Reverend Professor James W. Voelz:
Biography and Bibliography / 301

Editors' Foreword

The Press of the Text. It's a phrase often used by James Voelz himself to highlight the "direction of fit" *ala* Hans Frei, reminding us that we stand under and not over the text. It presses upon us, and as God's Word it presses in ways that both condemn and save. Both this *opus alienum* of God's Law and the grace-filled *opus proprium* of his Gospel are always the work *of God* upon *us*, and while we work diligently to translate and understand and teach and proclaim, we are servants of the text and not lords.

Yet it is an im*pressive* list of contributors and contributions that form the substance of this aptly-named *Festschrift* in honor of James W. Voelz. A great part of the joy of working on this project has been the connection and cooperation with a wide diversity of scholars. Twenty scholars from seven countries in four continents represent the spectrum of interests that James Voelz has engaged in scholarly and ecclesiastical circles, from Greek language and lexicography to hermeneutics and translation theory to interpretation and theology of both biblical testaments to contemporary issues in church and world. Though reflecting a range of interests and specializations, and of various theological and social views, including some that Dr. Voelz would not necessarily hold, they have all shared a common respect and appreciation for James Voelz as a scholar, interlocutor, colleague, and friend. Along with gratitude to all who contributed to this project, we would also thank Wipf & Stock publishers for their expertise and encouragement in bringing this volume through to publication.

As editors, we also share that bond of collegiality and friendship, made even closer by serving together on the faculty of Concordia Seminary for many years. It is a special privilege to work within a collegium that shares a deep common cause in serving church and world, and to do so in a way that supports, encourages, cross-pollinates, and even challenges each of us. The essays in this volume represent the kind of intellectual world that we as Confessional Lutherans need to engage with academic credibility and respect and without surrendering our own theological integrity, as Jim has shown us how to do.

As colleague and friend, Jim has long been a catalyst in such collegial interaction, whether organizing dialogues or just always ready for informal conversation, whether in classrooms and halls or on sidewalks and in the field house. Such conversations, once engaged, quickly deepen and broaden, filled with challenging insights and enquiry, analysis and application, and the inevitable analogy. His leadership and energy at our erstwhile Friday discussions (which always featured better wine when it was Jim's turn on that rota) accelerated the generative intellectual vitality that those sessions provided. This was a think-tank and incubator for new ideas, where iron was allowed to sharpen iron, and we owe much of our own critical thinking, insights, and scholarship to what Jim brought to those occasions.

Students, too, know his readiness to challenge them, both intellectually and into the other areas of pastoral, professional, spiritual, and personal life. Often the first to arrive and last to leave, Dr. Voelz will be there, in the field house, in the Commons, on the soccer field, coaching the golf team, asking the penetrating question at the convocation, holding court at the wine tasting. He frequently and regularly reminded his colleagues in faculty meetings: "It is all about the students." His teaching style is legendary, and the church has received more than a generation of pastors whose seminary formation was shaped by "taking Greek with Dr. Voelz." Likewise with graduate students, a next generation has arisen who know well Dr. Voelz as teacher, scholar, and as *Doktorvater*, and who serves church and the larger scholarly community, including the universities and seminaries of our church.

The occasion for this celebratory project is his 70th year of life. The year 2015 was also his 40th year of ordained ministry, filled with his extraordinary stewardship of God's gifts from scholarship to sports, with tireless energy and interests that have helped form countless pastors, shaped pastoral theologians, and modeled scholarship at the highest levels. To date his life's work includes three major books, a myriad of scholarly articles and other such contributions, his love and faithful care for his family, and interests that stretch from tennis, soccer, golf, and bridge to his legendary oenophilia. The year 2014 was marked by the first volume of his Mark commentary. In a coming year we anticipate the second volume. But in this time in between celebrating books *by* James Voelz, it is indeed an honor and joy to celebrate a book *for* James Voelz.

Andrew H. Bartelt

Jeffrey Kloha

Paul R. Raabe

Tribute to James W. Voelz

—*Jack Dean Kingsbury*

James W. Voelz is one of the finest New Testament scholars whether in this country or abroad. A man of extraordinary linguistic talent, he attained to a high level of sophistication in the biblical languages and especially Hellenistic Greek already as a college student and seminarian. In further pursuit of both theology and Greek, he earned his doctoral degree at Cambridge University in England under the tutelage of G. W. H. Lampe. Two books he has written chart his linguistic and literary career. The one book, now in its fourth edition, is entitled *Fundamental Greek Grammar* and attests to Voelz's goal of attaining mastery of Hellenistic Greek. The other book, in its second revised edition, bears the title of *What Does This Mean?* and, as the subtitle states, deals with the principles of biblical interpretation in the postmodern world. Having traversed the fields of grammar and hermeneutics, Voelz currently applies his expertise to the task of writing a two-volume commentary on the Gospel according to Mark. To judge from the first volume, now available, it is already apparent that the completed set will reward student, seminarian, pastor, and scholar alike with the fruits of Voelz's broad knowledge and keen mind.

Should these books provide insight into the path that James Voelz's career has taken, they constitute only a part of his scholarly accomplishments. Voelz has contributed numerous articles to scholarly journals found especially in this country but also in Europe. For years, he has held membership in organizations such as the Society of Biblical Literature (USA), the Society of New Testament Studies (Great Britain), and the International

Organization of Septuagint and Cognate Studies. By delivering papers in the seminars of these organizations or serving in a leadership role as chair or cochair of their sections, Voelz has played a prominent role in their annual conferences.

In his scholarship, James Voelz further shows himself to be a man of the church. In his books and articles, the Lutheran Confessions are never far from his mind. For example, as he explores Mark's Gospel, he refers in the footnotes to the Confessions and quotes from them. In the process, he calls attention to ways in which the Confessions stand in alignment with Mark (*sola scriptura*). Also, the very fact that Voelz has undertaken to interpret a canonical Gospel necessarily involves him in dealing with the other familiar Reformation principles regarding grace, faith, and Christ. It is noteworthy, too, that in specifying the overriding purpose of Mark's Gospel, Voelz finds that if the disciples of Jesus are to "see" him clearly and understand him rightly, they must first "believe" the promises he has given them. "Believe" Jesus' promises so as to "see" clearly who he is and what he had done is thus Voelz's construal of the powerful message of Mark.

James Voelz is not only an accomplished scholar but also the husband of Judy (nee Hayes) and the father of Jonathan. Together they enjoy the blessings that accrue to a tightly knit family. As professor and teacher, Voelz is well liked and respected in the scholarly guild and by his seminary colleagues and students. Adept at playing tennis, golf, and soccer, he coaches seminarians in these sports. He accordingly makes himself available to the seminary community and becomes well acquainted with students not only "in" but also "out" of the classroom. As he moves toward retirement, James Voelz moves toward a major project that will enable him to make use of his impressive skills and talents: the completion of the second volume of his commentary on Mark.

Jack Dean Kingsbury

Aubrey Lee Brooks Professor Emeritus of Biblical Theology
Union Presbyterian Seminary
Richmond, VA

Abbreviations

ACCS	Ancient Christian Commentary on Scripture
AE	*Luther's Works*. General editors, Jaroslav Pelikan and Helmut T. Lehmann. 55 vols. St. Louis: Concordia; Philadelphia: Fortress, 1955–1986
AHD	*The American Heritage Dictionary*
ANF	*The Ante-Nicene Fathers: Translations of the Writings of the Fathers down to AD 325*. Edited by Alexander Roberts and James Donaldson et al. 9 vols. Edinburgh, 1885–1897
BAG	Walter Bauer, William F. Arndt, F. Wilbur Gingrich. *A Greek-English Lexicon of the New Testament and Other Early Christian Literature*. Chicago: University of Chicago Press, 1957
BAGD	Walter Bauer, William F. Arndt, F. Wilbur Gingrich, and Frederick W. Danker. *Greek-English Lexicon of the New Testament and Other Early Christian Literature*. 2nd ed. Chicago: University of Chicago Press, 1979.
BBC	British Broadcasting Corporation
BDAG	Walter Bauer, Frederick W. Danker, W. F. Arndt, and F. W. Gingrich. *Greek-English Lexicon of the New Testament and Other Early Christian Literature*. 3rd ed. Chicago: University of Chicago Press, 2000
BDB	Francis Brown, S. R. Driver, and Charles A. Briggs. *The Brown-Driver-Briggs Hebrew and English Lexicon*. Boston: Houghton Mifflin, 1906; reprint, Peabody, MA: Hendrickson, 2000

BDR	Blass, Debrunner, Rehkopf. *Grammatik des neutestamentlichen Greichisch*
BETL	Bibliotheca Ephemeridum Theologicarum Lovaniensium
CBQ	*Catholic Biblical Quarterly*
CEBI	Centro de Estudos Bíblicos
CEV	Contemporary English Version
CJ	*Concordia Journal*
DDR	Deutsche Demokratische Republik
ESV	English Standard Version
ETL	*Ephemerides Theologicae Lovanienses*
FDA	Food and Drug Administration
FELSISA	Free Evangelical Lutheran Synod in South Africa
GNT	Good News Translation
HHS	Department of Health and Human Services
HUCA	*Hebrew Union College Annual*
ICC	International Critical Commentary
JETS	*Journal of the Evangelical Theological Society*
JTS	*Journal of Theological Studies*
JPS	Jewish Publication Society
JSOTSup	Journal for the Study of the Old Testament Supplement Series
KJV	King James Version
LCL	Loeb Classical Library
LCMS	Lutheran Church—Missouri Synod
LSJ	Henry George Liddell, Robert Scott, and Henry Stuart Jones. *A Greek-English Lexicon.* 9th ed. Oxford: Clarendon, 1996
LXX	Septuagint
MT	Masoretic Text
NA	Nestle-Aland, *Novum Testamentum Graece*
NABRE	New American Bible Revised Edition
NASB	New American Standard Bible
NCCS	New Covenant Commentary Series
NICNT	New International Commentary on the New Testament

NICOT	New International Commentary on the Old Testament
NIGTC	New International Greek Testament Commentary
NIV	New International Version
NKJV	New King James Version
NovT	*Novum Testamentum*
NovTSup	Supplements to Novum Testamentum
NPNF¹	*A Select Library of the Nicene and Post-Nicene Fathers of the Christian Church*. Edited by Philip Schaff. 1st ser. 14 vols. Edinburgh, 1886
NPNF²	*A Select Library of the Nicene and Post-Nicene Fathers of the Christian Church*. Edited by Philip Schaff and Henry Wace. 2nd ser. 14 vols. Edinburgh, 1890
NRSV	New Revised Standard Version
NTTSD	New Testament Tools, Studies, and Documents
NTS	*New Testament Studies*
OED	*The Oxford English Dictionary*
par.	parallel
PG	Patrologia Graeca. Edited by J.-P. Migne. 162 vols. Paris, 1857–1886
RSV	Revised Standard Version
SBL	Society of Biblical Literature
SNTS	Studiorum Novi Testamenti Societas
SNTSMS	Society for the Study of the New Testament Monograph Series
TDNT	*Theological Dictionary of the New Testament*. Edited by Gerhard Kittel and Gerhard Friedrich. Translated by Geoffrey W. Bromiley. 10 vols. Grand Rapids: Eerdmans, 1964–1976
TLG	*Thesaurus Linguae Graecae: Canon of Greek Authors and Works*
VT	*Vetus Testamentum*
VTSup	Supplements to Vetus Testamentum
WBC	Word Biblical Commentary
WTNID	*Webster's Third New International Dictionary*
WUNT	Wissenschaftliche Untersuchungen zum Neuen Testament

Contributors

Charles P. Arand, The Waldemar A. and June Schuette Professor of Systematic Theology, Concordia Seminary, St. Louis, MO

Andrew H. Bartelt, The Gustav and Sophie Butterbach Professor of Exegetical Theology, Concordia Seminary, St. Louis, MO

Lawrence C. Brennan, Professor of Systematic Theology, Kenrick-Glennon Seminary, St Louis, MO

Chrys C. Caragounis, Professor Emeritus in New Testament Exegesis, Lund University, Sweden

J. Keith Elliott, Emeritus Professor of New Testament Textual Criticism, The University of Leeds, UK

Charles A. Gieschen, Professor of Exegetical Theology and Academic Dean, Concordia Theological Seminary, Ft. Wayne, IN

David S. Hasselbrook, Pastor, Messiah Lutheran Church, Missoula, MT

Jack Dean Kingsbury, Aubrey Lee Brooks Professor Emeritus of Biblical Theology, Union Presbyterian Seminary, Richmond, VA

Jeffrey Kloha, Professor of Exegetical Theology and Provost, Concordia Seminary, St. Louis, MO

Bernard C. Lategan, Founding Director: Stellenbosch Institute for Advanced Study (STIAS), South Africa

Michael P. Middendorf, Professor of Theology, Christ College, Concordia University, Irvine, CA

Jesús Peláez, University of Cordoba, Spain

Gary A. Phillips, Edgar H. Evans Professor of Religion, Wabash College, Crawfordsville, IN

Paul R. Raabe, Professor of Exegetical Theology, Concordia Seminary, St. Louis, MO

Dieter Reinstorf, Bishop, Freien Evangelisch-Lutherischen Synode in Südafrika and Research Associate of the Department of New Testament Studies, University of Pretoria, South Africa

Vilson Scholz, Translation Consultant—Sociedade Bíblica do Brasil—and Professor of Exegetical Theology at the Lutheran University, Canoas, and Seminário Concórdia, São Leopoldo, Brazil

Mark A. Seifrid, Professor of Exegetical Theology, Concordia Seminary, St. Louis, MO

William C. Weinrich, Professor of Historical Theology, Concordia Theological Seminary, Ft. Wayne, IN

Gerald West, Senior Professor in the School of Religion, Philosophy, and Classics, University of KwaZulu-Natal, South Africa

Thomas M. Winger, Professor of Theology and President, Concordia Lutheran Theological Seminary, St. Catharines, Ontario, Canada

1

Creeds as Corroborative Witnesses

—*Charles P. Arand*

One of Jim Voelz's lasting contributions to the Lutheran church lies in his thinking on the hermeneutics of Scripture, especially within a postmodern context of reader-response approaches to Scripture.[1] What makes his work especially valuable is that Jim tackles the issue from the stance of one who is a staunch confessional Lutheran. In other words, he approaches the task of reading Scripture from the stance of a pastor and theologian who has subscribed unconditionally to the Lutheran Confessions as doctrinal expositions of Scripture.

While many in the wider biblical world may view such a stance and approach as a straitjacket or a hindrance, Jim has shown in his work that reading the Scriptures within the church's own reading is not only helpful, but a joyous guidance. To see the confessions as hindrances to the reading of Scripture results from a failure to understand the nature and function of confessions as well as a willingness to turn one's back upon the church's reading in pursuit of individualistic autonomy.

Jim already indicated as much in an article that he and I coauthored a number of years ago and which appeared as chapter 13 in his text on hermeneutics, *What Does This Mean?*[2] In that article, we explored the hermeneutical principles that underlay the confessors' treatment of Scripture, especially

1. Voelz, *What Does This Mean?*
2. It also appeared as Arand and Voelz, "The Confessions as Normative Guides."

as found in Melanchthon's response to his opponents in the Apology of the Augsburg Confession. We identified in that document a christological principle, a contextual principle, and an integrity principle for a Lutheran reading of Scripture. Here I would like to extend that article to an examination of how the confessors used the creeds as witnesses of the church to close off certain readings of Scripture and to open up fresh readings of Scripture.

Over the years, the church has constantly wrestled with the role and function of its confessional writings. In this regard, Charles Porterfield Krauth wrote about the confessional principle,[3] while C. F. Walther and Arthur Carl Piepkorn[4] explored the extent of confessional subscription and John F. Johnson[5] examined the biblical basis for confessions.

In this essay we will examine the role of the confessions for the task of theology, in regards to how they help us in our reading of Scripture and how they help us address issues in our day that they could not have foreseen. To do that, I am going to focus on the role of the three ecumenical creeds and their use by the sixteenth-century confessions. This in turn can model for us how we might utilize the sixteenth-century confessions in our own day. We will first look at the confessions as "summaries of Scripture,"[6] "boundaries" or "foul lines,"[7] or grammar[8] for reading Scripture, and then consider them as examples for helping us address the issues of our day.[9]

Creeds as Summaries of Scripture's Narrative

Just as the rule of faith[10] served to summarize the message of apostles in the early church, so the creeds that we now have provide a handy summary of

---

3. Krauth, *The Conservative Reformation and Its Theology*.

4. Walther, "Why Should Our Pastors, Teachers and Professors Subscribe Unconditionally" and Piepkorn, "Suggested Principles for a Hermeneutics of the Lutheran Symbols."

5. John Johnson, "Confession and Confessional Subscription."

6. Maxwell, "The Nicene Creed," 16–20.

7. Timothy Luke Johnson, *The Creed: Why Christians Believe*.

8. Lindbeck, *The Nature of Doctrine: Religion and Theology in a Postliberal Age*.

9. For some recent thinking on the function and role of the Lutheran Confessions, see a special issue of the *Concordia Journal* by the systematics department devoted to that question. Okamoto, "Making Sense of Confessionalism Today," 34–48; Maxwell, "The Nicene Creed in the Church," 13–22; and Kolb and Arand, "'I Make These Confessions My Own': Lutheran Confessional Subscription in the Twenty-First Century," 23–33.

10. Blowers, "The *Regula Fidei* and the Narrative Character."

the overarching narrative of the Scriptures. In this they follow the lead of Scripture itself, which provides several summaries of its own narrative.

In the Old Testament, several narratives stand out for summarizing the work of God in creation and redemption (Neh 9:6; Jer 32:17–21; and Ps 136). In the New Testament, Colossians 1:15–20 also sets forth the narrative of creation and redemption, this time telling it through Christ. Beyond these comprehensive narratives, there are numerous narrative summaries of Christ's biography that tell of his incarnation, death, and resurrection. Two of the most well-known are found in Rom 1:1–3 and 1 Cor 15:3. They focus on Christ's incarnation, death, and resurrection—the very same elements that get picked up in the Apostles' Creed and Nicene Creed.

In a similar vein, the creeds summarize the overarching narrative of Scripture. Kathryn Green-McCreight acknowledges that the Nicene Creed is not strictly a narrative, but that it contains what she calls "narrative elements."[11] Along similar lines, David Maxwell refers to the creeds as "plot summaries" of the Bible in addition to being lists of doctrines or functioning as outlines for catechesis.[12] Such summaries are very helpful when one considers how overwhelming the Bible can be in quantity of stories, the span of time over which it was written, and its numerous teachings. It can be a labyrinth of wonders, and for that very reason also very intimidating. This is even more true in an age when biblical illiteracy is on the rise and in a church where people often hear snippets of Scripture read in the lectionary but aren't sure how to locate those readings within the larger story of the Scripture. The creeds help keep one focused on what's most important and central.

Consider Jesus Christ. What do I need to know about him? What is the key to his life? Why is his life significant for my life? We have four Gospels in the New Testament that tell us a good deal about Christ's life. The creeds give us something of a thirty-second elevator speech, or a Titter tweetable summary, that focuses our attention on the keys to unlocking the significance of Jesus' life. They function like travel guidebooks that direct us to the "must see" sights of Scripture. These include the incarnation, suffering and death, resurrection and exaltation of Jesus. When one considers the Gospels, it soon becomes apparent that these are the foci of their narratives. All four Gospels devote considerable space to the death and resurrection of Christ, toward which the entire narrative moves. Matthew, Luke, and John also pick up the incarnation of Jesus. This is not to say that the rest of what they say is unimportant or insignificant. But it is to say that whatever else

---

11. Green-McCreight, "He Spoke through the Prophets," 174.
12. Maxwell, "The Nicene Creed," 16–20.

you say about Jesus, these are the key elements that make all the difference! Not surprisingly, the first half of the church year centers on these three events as well.

And what about the God of Jesus Christ? These christological summaries are embedded into the larger narrative of God's work in the world. The creed summarizes God's work from creation through the resurrection of the body into the new creation. Indeed, it could perhaps be summarized as "The Story of One True God and His Creation."[13] In other words, the entire Bible gives an account of God's very first work (directed outside the Trinity), namely, the creation of the world, and the rest of God's work all the way to God bringing that creation to its fulfillment.

Creeds as Corroborative Witnesses

As summaries of Scripture, the creeds function as corroborative witnesses for our own reading of Scripture. While the Lutheran Confessions stress in no uncertain terms that the Scriptures are the fountain of Christian theology, they also stress that the creeds are key witnesses to that theology. But they are not just anyone's witness, they are the church's witness to the teaching of the Scriptures.[14]

Here we might consider the analogy of a court of law (not surprisingly, since Melanchthon utilizes the *judicial genus* of rhetoric in constructing the Apology).[15] In that setting, we might think of a witness stand wherein someone is called to testify to the truthfulness or falsity of a defendant. In this case, we (and our reading of the Scriptures) are the defendants. We read the Scriptures and draw certain conclusions or doctrinal statements from them.[16] But did we read the Scriptures accurately? Or did we distort them in some way with our prejudices or lack of reading skills?

This is where the creeds (and, by extension, the confessions) come into play. In a sense, when we use them, we are summoning them to the witness stand to testify that our reading and proclamation of the Scriptures are congruent with the Scriptures themselves. The testimony of the confessions can confirm (or not confirm) that our reading is consistent with how others have read the Scriptures, particularly, the wider church. If my reading of the

---

13. Thanks to Joel Okamoto for this fortuitous way of stating it.
14. See Kolb and Wengert, eds., *The Book of Concord*, 527–28.
15. See Arand, "Melanchthon's Rhetorical Argument."
16. Here Melanchthon in the Apology makes a very interesting observation that one can draw not only upon the Scriptures, but upon arguments derived from the Scriptures (see Apology IV, par. 119).

Scriptures is completely idiosyncratic, then I should probably reconsider my reading. Am I the only one in the history of the church that has come up with this interpretation? If so, then this would seem to suggest a certain hubris or arrogance on my part.

Such a question was very real to the Lutherans in the sixteenth century following Luther's death. While he was alive, there was a sense that if you had a question on biblical interpretation you could write Luther and ask him for an opinion. He was seen as a trustworthy authority. But now that he is gone, where should one go to determine which reading of Scripture is sound and which is not? And so in the sixteenth century, the Lutheran theologians collected certain texts together into a single volume, namely, the *Book of Concord*.[17] These were those writings that the church had considered authoritative expositions of Scripture. That brings us to the next question, what makes such a text authoritative?

I would argue that there are two ways by which a text becomes an "authoritative witness" so as to be regarded as a creed or a confession of the church.

The first is by official action. Where has the church gathered in order to agree on the conclusions of their joint reading of the Scriptures? These would be instances where a statement was either presented in an official assembly or subscribed to by those who represented the church. For example, the Nicene Creed was prepared by the bishops of the church and presented to the emperor at the Council of Nicaea in 325 and reaffirmed at the Council of Chalcedon in 451. The Augsburg Confession was presented by the German princes (who had responsibility for the churches in their domains) to Emperor Charles V on June 25, 1530. The Smalcald League adopted the *Treatise on the Power and Primacy of the Pope* in 1537 as an appendix to the Augsburg Confession. A number of those present personally subscribed to the Smalcald Articles. And perhaps just as significantly for Lutheran unity in the second half of the sixteenth century, the Formula of Concord was adopted by more than eight thousand pastors.

Another way a text comes to be seen as an official reading of Scripture by the church is by its widespread and constant use within the church. In other words, everyone is using the text as a reliable and faithful reading of Scripture. A number of the writings in the *Book of Concord* fit this criterion. The Apostles' Creed was frequently utilized by the church for teaching and catechizing its people in the faith as well as for baptizing them into the faith.

---

17. See Dingel on the development of this idea of confessional authority following the death of Luther. See "The Preface of *The Book of Concord* as a Reflection of Sixteenth-Century Confessional Development," and "The Function and Historical Development of Reformation Confessions."

The Athanasian Creed also fits this model, as it had come to be regarded as an orthodox summary of the fourth and fifth centuries. In the sixteenth century, no more important and authoritative texts arose than Luther's Small and Large Catechisms. These provided an exposition of the creed along with other classic texts of the faith such as the Ten Commandments and the Lord's Prayer.

The Formula of Concord provides a hierarchy of authority for Lutherans. You begin with the Scriptures and then move to the creeds, followed by the Augsburg Confession (which they regard as a "pure, Christian creed").[18] The other statements are described as expositions of the Augsburg Confession.[19] But how can one statement be regarded as more authoritative than another statement if both are biblical? Doesn't the Bible give them their authority? Yes, in one sense, they are of equal weight with regard to the teaching of Scripture. But authority here is being used also with respect to their reception by the church. In this sense, the creeds are regarded as the most important witnesses, for they are received by the entire church (hence their name, ecumenical creeds). While in the sixteenth century they held this for all three creeds, of the three creeds, it is the Nicene Creed that is accepted by both the Eastern and the Western Churches. Following the creeds comes the Augsburg Confession, for all Lutherans accepted it as a reliable statement of Scripture.

How does this view of authority affect our use of them? That depends on whom we are speaking to. For that will determine which witnesses we can most effectively call to the witness stand. Are they witnesses that both sides agree upon? In this case, when speaking with non-Lutherans, we can summon the creeds to the witness stand with regard to our reading of Scripture on Trinity and Christology. But when we are speaking with Lutherans, we can also summon the distinctively Lutheran Confessions to the stand, for they define what is Lutheran (hopefully one day, others will recognize them too).[20]

How do these confessional writings function as corroborative witnesses for our reading of the Scriptures? I will suggest two things. First, they serve as a boundary or a grammar for speaking in a way that Scripture

18. Kolb and Wengert, eds., *The Book of Concord*, 525, par. 4.

19. The authors emphasized that they only have one creed of their generation in response to Rome's charge that the Lutherans kept developing new confessions.

20. In the 1970s, Joseph Ratzinger floated the idea that Rome might be able to recognize the Augsburg Confession as a Christian confession. This spawned dozens of articles and several books, including a joint commentary on the Augsburg Confession by Lutheran and Catholic theologians, entitled *Confessing One Faith : A Joint Commentary on the Augsburg Confession by Lutheran and Catholic Theologians*.

speaks, and second, they serve as generative guides for speaking that word of Scripture in our day.

The Function of the Creeds as Corroborative Witnesses

The confessions have long been recognized as a touchstone for a sound reading of the Scriptures in both theses and antitheses. That is to say, they set forth that doctrine which is considered healthy and wholesome for faith. And they warn against that teaching (and "stiff-necked teachers" of that doctrine) which causes spiritual harm.

It is most important to speak as Scripture speaks. This does not mean that we must use the identical words (in Hebrew and Greek no less) of Scripture, but that we speak in a way that conveys what Scripture says (e.g., the *homoousios* of the Nicene Creed). A couple of analogies can be considered here.

Timothy Luke Johnson, in his book *The Creed*, suggests that we think of the creed as the foul lines of a baseball field. If ball is outside the foul lines, it is out of play. In a similar way, if a reading or speaking of Scriptures goes outside the lines provided in the creeds, it is outside the way Scripture talks. But as long as the ball is in play, there are many plays that one can execute. One can use bunts, hit-and-runs, stolen bases, suicide squeezes, and the like. So also, when it comes to theology, as long as one is working within the boundaries of the creeds, there are many ways of unpacking and framing theology in an orthodox way.

George Lindbeck, in his *Nature of Doctrine*, has likened doctrine to the function of grammar. In other words, it provides the grammatical rules for speaking the word of God today in a way that is congruent with the Scriptures themselves. It is like saying, "If you speak this way, you are speaking the way Scripture speaks." Or, "if you talk about God in that way, you are not speaking the way the Scriptures speak." They do not limit the ways in which one speaks of God as long as one is following the grammatical rules. They simply exclude certain ways of speaking.[21] Do we speak in a way that conveys the truth that God wants to convey?

The creeds especially center our attention on how to speak of Christ in relationship to the Father and the Spirit, on the one hand, and in relationship to his human creatureliness, on the other hand. The distinctively Lutheran, sixteenth-century confessions then show us how to speak in a

---

21. One caveat is that Lindbeck seems to reduce doctrine to one of only function. We also need to emphasize that it has to do with content, that is, with the truth.

scriptural way about justification. In other words, they now ask, if Jesus is the Son of God, if he is both our Creator and our Lord, what does this mean for us and our restoration? We will first look at the Athanasian Creed, and then turn to the use of the Apostles' Creed in the confessions.

Examples of Creeds as Boundaries

For many readers, the Athanasian Creed seems confusing and befuddling in its construction. It may even seem as if its authors were trying to demystify the Trinity by putting God under a microscope. But nothing could be further from the truth! In point of fact, the Athanasian Creed provides the "foul lines" or grammar for speaking about the Trinity and about Christology. It is a masterpiece for providing guidelines on how to speak of the Trinity in a biblical way.

With regard to the unity of the Trinity, it simply lays down two foul lines. However you talk about God, don't talk about God as if he were three different gods and don't talk about him as if he were only one person. To speak those ways is to speak outside the way the Scriptures speak of God. What follows simply explicates the thesis with examples from God's attributes and titles. There is no attempt to "explain" the mystery of the three in one, only to confess it. With regard to the distinction of the three persons, it simply affirms that the Father is described as unbegotten, the Son as begotten, and the Spirit as proceeding. But what is the difference between being "begotten" and "proceeding"? The creed does not say. It simply affirms that, in some way, these terms distinguish the Son and the Spirit from each other (along with the referents: Son-Father; Spirit from Father and Son).

The same thing applies to Christology. The Athanasian Creed summarizes the christological debates of the fifth century and the conclusions set forth in the Councils of Ephesus (431) and Chalcedon (451). Once again, it affirms the ontological truth that Jesus is one person in two natures. How does one speak in a way that affirms that? Well, don't speak of Jesus as if he were two persons (Nestorius) and don't speak of Jesus as if he were one nature (Eutyches). He is fully God and he is a complete and genuine man. Don't speak of him as if he did not have a genuine human nature (Sabellius) or a complete human nature (Apollinarius).

How did the Lutheran confessors in the sixteenth century utilize the creeds as boundaries/grammatical rules when addressing the issues of their day?

Perhaps the best example can be found in article 1 of the Formula of Concord. There the confessors draw upon the creed as an "analogy of faith" to refute the position of Matthias Flacius. In a debate with Victor Strigel over the topic of free choice, they had addressed the question about the impact of original sin upon the human will. How extensive was the damage? Strigel relied on the philosophical categories of substance and accident and argued that sin was an accident of human nature. Flacius perceived (correctly) that Strigel used the term "accident" in order to minimize the damage caused by original sin. But rather than stressing the enormity of its impact upon us by redefining the term, he chose to stress its enormity by choosing the other term and saying that sin is the "substance" of human nature. There was no difference between being human and being sin. And so he was quickly criticized as reprising the error of Manichaeism.

The formulators rejected Flacius's teaching on the basis of the Scriptures to which statements in previous Lutheran writings (e.g., the Apology and the Smalcald Articles) witnessed regarding sin. But of special interest is the way in which they brought in the creed as the analogy of faith. They used it as a way for bringing to bear on this issue other statements and affirmations of Scripture that were not about original sin. In other words, they showed how Flacius's position on original sin violated the boundaries not only of Scripture's teaching on original sin, but also of Scripture's teaching on creation (God did not create sin), the incarnation (the Son of God did not assume a sinful human nature), redemption (Christ did not rescue sin), and the resurrection (neither Christ nor we rise with sinful bodies). So Flacius's way of speaking transgressed the boundaries for speaking about these other cardinal topics of the Christian faith. Creation is good.

Confessions as Generative Exemplars/Conversation Partners

As corroborative witnesses, the creeds not only functioned as boundaries for orthodox or nonorthodox speaking of the faith. They also provided guidance and direction for addressing issues at stake in the creeds or opening up ways for a fresh speaking to these new issues.

The most obvious example is the Nicene Creed with its use of the famous *homoousios* to speak of the deity of Jesus. The orthodox side tried hard to find a biblical expression to affirm the full deity of the Son of God—an expression the Arians could not interpret to their advantage. In the end, they had to settle on a nonbiblical term, *homoousios* (same essence/being/substance). It was not ideal in that it was not only not a biblical word, but Sabellius had also used it a century earlier to support his modalistic view of the Trinity. But that was then and this is now. *Homoousios* captured nicely that whatever the Father was, that was the Son. It gave rise to a way of speaking about the Trinity that came to be known as the immanent or ontological Trinity (as we see in the Athanasian Creed). It also opened the door for new avenues of confessing the incarnation by giving rise to the need for distinguishing between "person" and "nature" when speaking of the two natures of Christ in the one person of Jesus.

What about the Lutheran confessors' own use of the creeds? One of the goals that the princes and theologians had at Augsburg was to convince the emperor that they were faithful citizens of the empire. The Diet of Augsburg was, after all, a political assembly and not a church council. It was the princes and other secular authorities in Germany who had to give an account to the emperor of the changes they had instituted in the wake of the first diet of Speyer. For this reason, right out of the chute, they cited the Nicene Creed in order to affirm that they were in accord with the Theodosian Code.[22] Emperor Theodosius in 380/381 declared that to be a Roman citizen in good standing one had to accept the Nicene faith. At Augsburg, the question was raised whether or not the Lutheran princes were in fact entitled to that standing.

But of special interest in how the creeds also provided foundation within which they could build is article 3 of the Augsburg Confession on Christology. The entire article consists of a quotation from the second article of the Apostles' Creed. But Melanchthon inserts into the creed several statements that bring out the gospel purpose of those statements from the Apostles' Creed. Thus, after the words "crucified, dead, and buried," Melanchthon adds "in order both to be a sacrifice not only for original sin but also for all other sins and to conciliate God's wrath."[23] He then proceeds to quote the next statement of the Apostles' Creed about the exaltation of Christ. Following the clause "is sitting at the right hand of God," Melanchthon inserts the purpose statement "in order to rule and reign forever over all creatures, so that through the Holy Spirit he may make holy, purify, strengthen, and comfort all who believe in him, also distribute to them life and various gifts and benefits, and shield and protect them against the devil and sin."

So Melanchthon relies upon the creeds, not only to exclude certain teachings, but also to affirm other teachings that are not set forth explicitly in the creeds but are fully consistent and congruent with them. One of the things that the creeds did not explicitly set forth was drawing the conclusions of what their confession of the deity of Jesus meant for salvation. The Athanasian Creed sets forth how one should talk about the Trinity as well as

---

22. Schultz, "An Analysis of the Augsburg Confession Article VII, 2.
23. Kolb and Wengert, ed., *The Book of Concord*, 38.

how one should talk about the human and divine natures of Christ. It then concludes by briefly summarizing the biography of Christ.[24]

The topic of how we are justified was not the burning issue of the fourth and fifth centuries that it would become in the sixteenth century. It was enough to confess "who for us human creatures and our salvation became a human creature" (Nicene Creed) or he "suffered for our salvation" (Athanasian Creed). The Apostles' Creed really makes no reference to salvation other than by implication when it confesses "and in Jesus Christ, his only Son, OUR Lord." But the topic of justification became *the* issue in the sixteenth century. The reformers drew upon the creeds as a framework or springboard for confessing that salvation is by Christ alone and by faith alone. To do that, they started with the biography of Jesus in the creeds by asking, "What else was the purpose of that biography or work?" In this regard, Melanchthon actually draws upon the phrase "forgiveness of sins" in the third article, where it speaks of the church.

Thus in article 4 of the Apology, Melanchthon builds his case for justifying faith by drawing upon the Apostles' Creed. He writes, "It will be easy to determine what faith is if we consider the Creed where this article, 'the forgiveness of sins,' is set forth. Thus it is not enough to believe that Christ was born, suffered, and was raised again unless we also add this article, which is the real purpose of the narrative: 'the forgiveness of sins.'" He goes on, "For why was it necessary to give Christ for our sins if our merits could make satisfaction for them?"[25] With this, Melanchthon built his case that faith is not historical knowledge ("believing the facts") but is instead a desire for and reception of the promise. In this way, the Lutherans insisted that the Gospel = story + promise of forgiveness. The promise provided the purpose of the story and called forth the necessity of faith as its corollary (a promise seeks to elicit trust).

Beyond the Augsburg Confession, the richest and liveliest reception of the creeds is doubtless the Small and Large Catechisms of Martin Luther. The catechisms are remarkable on a number of counts. Luther's explication is not limited to their language or even the language of justification. Nowhere does he actually use the terminology of "Trinity" or justification. Yet few would doubt that he has them clearly in view. We will consider these two teachings.

First, in the second article of the creed, Luther never mentions the term "justification." This seems all the more remarkable when we recall that this was the issue that launched the Reformation! This was the issue at the

---

24. Ibid., 25.
25. Ibid., 128.

heart of Luther's complaint with Rome. Melanchthon would devote nearly four hundred paragraphs to the topic in the Apology of the Augsburg Confession. And yet here in Luther's two catechisms, not a word or mention of it. Why? The answer would seem to lie in the audience that Luther had in view. His audience was largely illiterate. He wrote for peasants. How many of them would ever see the inside of a courtroom to understand the legal and technical terminology related to justification?

So Luther instead draws upon the language of the creed by focusing on the phrase "our Lord." This allowed him both to connect the article to the insight of the gospel (*pro me*) and to apply it to sixteenth-century peasants. In other words, Luther takes the word "Lord" as a trajectory. He takes the word "Lord" and puts it into the language and thought world that a German farmer could understand.[26] They lived in a feudal society, in a world of kings and queens, princes and princesses, lords and ladies.

And so Luther provides a narrative of how each of us is imprisoned and enslaved under the tyranny of sin, death, and Satan. And then Jesus frees me, thereby becoming my Lord (before that, he notes, I had no lord, only jailers and tyrants). And the purpose of it all? "That I might be his own!" And that I might live under him and his kingdom, a kingdom of grace and peace. So even though Luther never uses the technical language of justification, all the elements of the gospel are here: the work of Christ, the promise of redemption, and faith, which trusts that promise.

Another example is the unity of the Trinity. Luther brings out what is only implicit in the creeds themselves. And in light of the gospel, he shows God to be one who holds nothing back from us. He is "the God who Gives Himself to Us."[27]

> But here you have everything in richest measure. For in all three articles God himself has revealed and opened to us the most profound depths of his fatherly heart and his pure, unutterable love. For this very purpose he created us, so that he might redeem us and make us holy, and, moreover, having granted and bestowed upon us everything in heaven and on earth, he has also given us his Son and his Holy Spirit, through whom he brings us to himself. For, as explained above, we could never come to recognize the Father's favor and grace were it not for the Lord Christ, who is a mirror of the Father's heart. Apart from him we see nothing but an angry and terrible judge. But neither

---

26. Nestingen, "Luther's Cultural Translation of the Catechism."

27. Thanks to Jeff Kloha for this fortuitous and succinct summary of Luther's statement.

could we know anything of Christ, had it not been revealed by the Holy Spirit.[28]

Two things are striking about this statement. First, Luther takes the creeds (which didn't say much about how the three persons relate to each other) and formulates the relationship of the three persons in terms of what has become known as the economic language (the structure of their relationship to the world) of the Trinity. Here the three persons find their unity in the Father as the source of the Trinity (*a patre ad patrem*). We have a pattern that moves from the Father through the Son to the Holy Spirit into our lives. But then just as importantly for faith and piety, we are taken by the Spirit through the Son to the Creator (and thus return to his creation). Thus we learn what kind of a Creator he is—one with a fatherly heart.

Second, Luther also relates the three persons to each other by means of their work. Again, the creeds are fairly sparse when it comes to their purpose or application. The same might even be said initially for Luther's treatment of the creed in the Small Catechism. There the Father creates, the Son redeems, and the Spirit sanctifies (the headings given each article). But here in the Large Catechism, he makes the intriguing (and somewhat enigmatic) statement: "For this very purpose he created us, so that he might redeem us and make us holy," and brings their work into an interesting relationship. "Consider it. God creates us in order to redeem and sanctify us!" With this, Luther brings out how the work of the three creeds is a unity provided with the trajectory of creation. God creates (*creatio continua*), that is, he sustains us for the very purpose of renewing and remaking his creation. Luther's approach is creative yet orthodox. The work of creation and the work of redemption are cut from the same cloth. Just as I am created and sustained apart from any merit or worthiness, so I am redeemed apart from any merit or worthiness. Instead, it is by "divine, fatherly goodness."

Our Use of the Confessions Today

The confessions also serve as a "pattern" for thinking afresh about issues of our day. Not every issue we face was addressed in the sixteenth century. Within their boundaries there is plenty of room for "playing the game of theology," so to speak. Again, remember that they serve us both as boundaries for orthodox Christian speaking congruent with Scripture and as generative templates for addressing new issues that the church encounters. We can briefly illustrate that by drawing upon the three articles of the creed.

28. Kolb and Wengert, ed., *The Book of Concord*, 439–40.

First Article

Many, if not most, of the issues facing the church within our culture pertain to the first article of the creed, namely, creation. These issues range from bioethical issues, to what it means to be male or female, to what it means to be human (where do the boundaries exist between being machine and human?), to concern for the environment. Let's consider the last one (only because I've done the most work on that so far).

The first article provides boundaries for speaking about creation in a scriptural way. God created the world. And this God is a good and gracious God (we know him as the father of Christ), not an evil or fallen deity (e.g., as in Gnosticism). What might this mean for us? First of all, the earth is not divine. The earth is God's *creation*. And so we do not worship it. The distinction between God and creation lies at the foundation of the first commandment and the confession of the Son's deity. By the same token, creation is not simply a stockpile of resources for us to use as we please. It is *God's* creation.

So how do we regard the world today? Do we see it only as bad? There is biblical warrant for "being in the world but not of the world." And, to be sure, it is easy to regard the world in purely negative terms given the Holocaust and genocides of the twentieth century, and now the terrorism of the twenty-first century. But the creeds remind us that it is still God's good world! And how do we regard people? Distinguishing the thorough corruption of our nature by sin from its createdness by God insists that we regard and treat all people (regardless of their sin) as human beings, as fellow human creatures within God's creation, and thus as part of that "world" that God so loved that he sent his only-begotten Son. They are fellow creatures and also fellow fallen human creatures for whom Christ died.

The first article also opens up avenues for addressing other issues in a positive way. For example, what is our relationship to nonhuman creatures? Luther's exposition of the first article affirms a distinction as well as a commonality between human creatures and nonhuman creatures (God made me "together with all creatures"). We are distinguished from other creatures by being made in the image of God and being given dominion. Yet when affirming this distinction we need not go to the opposite extreme (after all, the opposite of error can also be error!) and deny any connection. Both are creatures of God and thus important to him. Again, God made "me together with all creatures." There is a commonality that we share. We are both made from the dust of the ground and given the breath of life. Similarly, we need to affirm certain things about the goodness of creation.

Second Article

The second article also provides us with boundaries and guidance for speaking about Jesus today. We live in a celebrity-obsessed culture. One only need consider how many magazines and cable networks are devoted to "entertainment" news, that is, news or gossip about our favorite celebrities. We want to know the "dirt" on these celebrities (to make them more like us?). We want to know about their personal lives, their romances and marriages, their struggles and celebrations, their interests and causes. As has been noted by Stephen Prothero and others, there is no greater celebrity in America than Jesus![29] So it is not surprising over the last four decades that numerous movies and books have come out purportedly revealing something of Jesus' personality, his romances (or wife and children), etc. Americans seem to have little appetite for a discussion of two natures and one person, or a discussion of his redemptive work.

The creeds provide generative ways for speaking about Jesus. For example, what is key to understanding his significance for us? The creed does a great service by focusing our attention on who he is and what he has done. It centers our attention on the Son's incarnation, suffering and death, resurrection and exaltation. It is as if to say, "Whatever else you need to know, this is the key to understanding Christ and, with him, the message of the New Testament." This also goes to the heart of our reading of the New Testament and guides us in that reading. After all, what does Paul focus on? He is descended from David according to the flesh, died, and rose. One could argue that the Gospels center their attention on this as well. Nearly one-third of the Synoptic Gospels is devoted to the last week of Jesus' life, and nearly one-half of John. This does not mean that other matters are not important, such as his baptism, ministry, miracles, teaching, etc. But it does suggest that these are not as central as his incarnation, death, and resurrection. Or, more to the point, they are to be seen in reference to these three central acts.

Third Article

The relationship of the three articles can also help us address contemporary issues in terms of boundaries and sources with regard to the Holy Spirit and the end times. For example, what is the content of Christian hope? It is at times pictured in the popular culture as a disembodied soul floating around on clouds and carrying a harp (hardly an inspiring picture!). But for most Christians, it probably consists of dying and going to heaven (again, often

---

29. Prothero, *The American Jesus*. See also Fox, *Jesus in America*.

pictured in nonphysical terms). Now, while Christians are with Jesus when they die, this is not the end of the story.[30] It is simply the beginning of the final chapter of this present age. And what happens to the world when our souls are taken off the earth? Or after we are raised from the dead? Some suggest that the earth will then be annihilated. Namely, it will be returned to nothingness, from which it came.[31]

At this point, the creeds provide important direction for envisioning our ultimate hope. The Apostles' and Nicene Creeds each direct the believer's confession to the hope of the resurrection of the body and the life everlasting that follows. This brings the theme of creation to a culmination in the Christian story by affirming the goodness of physical existence and earthly life in the new creation. This was a radical countercultural confession in the first century (over and against Platonic and gnostic views of the word), and it is again in our day when the world and our physical life are seen as little more than malleable materials that we can choose to change or remake however we see fit. Over and against this, the creed affirms that this is God's world and we are God's creatures. This defines us and points us toward our purpose. God defines the world as his personal expression and sets its purpose.

To return to how Luther relates the three articles of the creed in the Large Catechism, I would argue that the Creator gives his Son and Spirit to us in order to open his heart to us and to bring us back to himself (as our Creator). To what end? That we might enjoy life as earthly creatures on earth in fellowship with God, who dwells with us on this earth. In other words, Jesus brings us back to the Creator (now our Father) and thus to his creation. He shows us God's loving heart that we might also see creation as an expression of that loving heart.

Conclusion

More now than in recent centuries, Christians need to rally around their creeds as the identifying banners of their Christian faith and their Christian reading of Scripture. But as we do so, we also need to make them our own in such a way that they become part of us and thus shape how we instinctively think and approach the world in which we live. And Lutherans, in turn, need to share with the wider Christian community the riches of the Augsburg Confession as a statement that continues the trajectory of the ancient

---

30. Gibbs, "Christ Is Risen, Indeed.
31. See Raabe, "'Daddy, Will Animals Be in Heaven?'"

creeds, that it might one day be received as the creed of all Christians that I believe the confessors envisioned.[32]

Bibliography

Arand, Charles P. "Melanchthon's Rhetorical Argument for *Sola Fide* in the Apology." *Lutheran Quarterly* 3 (Autumn 2000) 281–308.

Arand, Charles P., and James Voelz. "The Lutheran Confessions as Normative Guides for Reading Scripture." *Concordia Journal* 21 (1995) 366–84.

Blowers, Paul M. "The *Regula Fidei* and the Narrative Character of the Early Christian Faith." *Pro Ecclesia* 6.2 (1997) 199–228.

Confessing One Faith: A Joint Commentary on the Augsburg Confession by Lutheran and Catholic Theologians. Edited by George Wolfgang Forell and James F. McCue, in cooperation with Wenzel Lohff [and others]. Minneapolis: Augsburg, 1982.

Dingel, Irene. "The Function and Historical Development of Reformation Confessions." *Lutheran Quarterly* 26.3 (2012) 295–321.

———. "The Preface of *The Book of Concord* as a Reflection of Sixteenth-Century Confessional Development." *Lutheran Quarterly* 15.4 (2001) 373–95.

Fox, Richard W. *Jesus in America: Personal Savior, Cultural Hero, National Obsession.* San Francisco: HarperSanFrancisco, 2004.

Gibbs, Jeffrey A. "Christ Is Risen, Indeed: Good News for Him, and for Us." *Concordia Journal* 40 (2014) 113–31.

Green-McCreight, Kathryn. "He Spoke through the Prophets." In *Nicene Christianity: The Future for a New Ecumenism*, edited by Christopher Seitz, 167–75. Grand Rapids: Brazos, 2001.

Johnson, John F. "Confession and Confessional Subscription." *Concordia Journal* 66 (1980) 235–41.

Johnson, Timothy Luke. *The Creed: Why Christians Believe and Why It Matters.* New York: Doubleday, 2003.

Kolb, Robert, and Charles P. Arand. "'I Make These Confessions My Own': Lutheran Confessional Subscription in the Twenty-First Century." *Concordia Journal* 41 (2015) 23–33.

Kolb, Robert, and Timothy Wengert, eds. *The Book of Concord: The Confessions of the Evangelical Lutheran Church.* Minneapolis: Fortress, 2000.

Krauth, Charles Porterfield. *The Conservative Reformation and Its Theology as Represented in the Augsburg Confession, and in the History and Literature of the Evangelical Lutheran Church.* Philadelphia: Lippincott, 1871.

Lindbeck, George A. *The Nature of Doctrine: Religion and Theology in a Postliberal Age.* Philadelphia: Westminster, 1984.

Maxwell, David R. "The Nicene Creed in the Church." *Concordia Journal* 41 (2015) 13–22.

Nestingen, James Arne. "Luther's Cultural Translation of the Catechism." *Lutheran Quarterly* 15 (2001) 440–52.

Okamoto, Joel P. "Making Sense of Confessionalism Today." *Concordia Journal* 41 (2015) 34–48.

---

32. Kolb and Wengert, eds., *The Book of Concord*, 525.

Piepkorn, Arthur Carl. "Suggested Principles for a Hermeneutics of the Lutheran Symbols." *Concordia Theological Monthly* 29 (January 1958) 1–24.

Prothero, Stephen R. *The American Jesus: How the Son of God Became a National Icon.* New York: Farrar, Straus & Giroux, 2003.

Raabe, Paul R. "'Daddy, Will Animals Be in Heaven?': The Future New Earth." *Concordia Journal* 40 (2014) 148–60.

Schultz, Robert C. "An Analysis of the Augsburg Confession Article VII, 2 in Its Historical Context, May & June 1530." *Sixteenth Century Journal* 11 (1980) 25–35.

Voelz, James. *What Does This Mean? Principles of Biblical Interpretation in the Postmodern World.* 2nd rev. ed. St. Louis: Concordia, 2013.

Walther, Carl F. W. "Why Should Our Pastors, Teachers and Professors Subscribe Unconditionally to the Symbolical Writings." *Concordia Journal* 15 (1989) 274–84.

2

A Hard Saying, with Purpose

Isaiah 6:9–10 and the Gospel of Mark

—*Andrew H. Bartelt*

The commission of Isaiah to "make the heart of this people dull, ... lest they see with their eyes, and hear with their ears, and understand with their hearts, and turn and be healed" (ESV) provides not only a *crux interpretatum* but also a *crux theologicum*, just the kind of problem that James Voelz would want to attack with his instinctive curiosity, his careful analytic method, his concern for biblical theology, and his grasp of the use of language within a close reading of the text. It is also a study in a holistic, literary reading of texts within contexts near and far, and ultimately a study in hermeneutics and biblical theology that spans both Testaments, even as our personal friendship and academic lives have combined interests both "Old" and "New."

My goal in this short essay is not to resolve—or even address—all the issues raised in Isa 6:9–10,[1] but to use this text as a case study in reading a text, from translation to a contextual interpretation that considers both the literary and historical worlds, and from focus on the implied author and reader to any significance to the larger conceptual world signified by textual

---

1. Commentaries devote attention to this problem in this text, but rarely deal with the larger context of a holistic reading of Isa 1–66. Selected special studies include Beale, "Isaiah VI 9–13"; Beuken, "The Manifestation of Yahweh"; Evans, *To See and Not Perceive*; Beuken, "Isa 6:9–13 in the Context of Isaiah's Theology"; Robinson, "The Motif of Deafness and Blindness"; Uhlig, *The Theme of Hardening*.

signifiers, especially in texts considered to be theologically authoritative by their primary interpretive community.

Isaiah 6 is clearly a commissioning of some sort,[2] based on the model of prophetic "insight" into the throne room of Yahweh.[3] In brief overview, it is in the year of the death of King Uzziah, after a long and prosperous reign, that Isaiah sees the true king of the kingdom of God, quite alive and well and sitting on the heavenly throne. Yet the Lord of heaven and earth "comes down" to establish a presence in the midst of his people, in the temple. The tension between the "holiness" (thrice קָדוֹשׁ) and the "glory" (כָּבוֹד) of God presents a rich theological paradox between God's "otherness" in being unapproachable (*deus absconditus*) and God's sacramental presence in being manifest on earth (*deus revelatus*).

Isaiah sees and hears and responds appropriately, confessing his uncleanness as a sinner in the presence of the holy God. The holy God responds by sending a messenger to purge the lips of the prophet, restoring him personally in a way consistent with the larger theme of the purification of Zion (1:24–26; 4:3–4). Attention is then turned to the larger mission and commission to "a people unclean of lips," whose corporate guilt is recognized but not confessed by them (v. 5, see 1:4). But the command is striking (all translations are my own):

> 9 "Go and say to this people (הָעָם הַזֶּה),
>
> 'Listen ("hear") intently, but do not perceive!
>
> Look ("see") intently, but do not understand!'
>
> 10 Make fat the heart of this people;
>
> Their ears make heavy and their eyes make blinded over,
>
> Lest they see with their eyes and with their ears they hear,
>
> And their heart understands,
>
> And then they are healed again!"

---

2. Whether Isa 6 is an inaugural call or not is not a major concern for the purposes here. In my view, the position of chapter 6 is integral to the structure of the whole of chapters 2–12 that reflects a unity far more complex and convincing than even intentional redactional activity. It may well be an inaugural call, whether it sets the time frame of chapters 1–5 to the time of Uzziah (even for one year) or not. But it clearly introduces chapters 7–8, which in turn are the focal point around which 2–12 are organized. See commentaries and my own proposal for the structure of ch 2-12 in Bartelt, *The Book Around Immanuel*.

3. The revelation to Micaiah in 1 Kgs 22:19 seems a similar model, though not completely parallel in narrating a commissioning.

The Hebrew is relatively straightforward, with poetic features adding to the effect. The use of the infinitive absolute (שָׁמוֹעַ) intensifies the main verb (here the imperative שִׁמְעוּ). This infinitive appears before or after the main verb (with imperative forms it always follows), with no apparent distinction in meaning.[4] The specific nuance of "intensification" must be determined by context. More significant is the use of the verb pair "hear and see" in reverse order from how Isaiah's reaction had been described, as he "saw" Adonay (וָאֶרְאֶה) in verse 1 and then "heard" (וָאֶשְׁמַע) the voice of Adonay in verse 9.

But to the senses of sight and sound is added the heart, traditionally the seat of understanding more than emotion. Verse 10 then forms a well-worked chiasm, turning on the triad of "heart > ears > eyes // eyes > ears > heart." Detailed analysis shows more, developed by the alternation of verbs and nouns in the first and last clauses: "make fat > heart // heart > understands" (V>N//N>V). The four inner clauses show a linear but inverted pattern in the first two clauses: "ears > make heavy // eyes > make blinded over" (N>V//N>V) but a chiastic pattern in the second pair: "see > with eyes // with ears > hear" (V>N//N>V).

The verse begins and ends with the heart, as informed by ears and eyes, and the whole unit turns on the conjunction "lest" (פֶּן). But there is one more statement, which brings the force of the negative particle to conclusion: "and they turn and be healed" (וְרָפָא לוֹ, lit. "there be healing to them/it = 'this people'"). While the general translation of this clause is not debated, the force of the verb שׁוּב is not sufficiently nuanced. That it can and does mean "repent" as derived from the basic sense of "turn, return" (cf. μετανοέω) is clear (though the LXX here translates with the more literal ἐπιστρέφω). The name of Isaiah's child (in chap. 7, which follows immediately) certainly plays with that meaning (though whether a remnant "repents" or "returns" may best be left to the wordplay). But the use of שׁוּב in a hendiadys construction is also common, and this is clearly the sense in

---

4. Despite the apparent assumption of many translations, supported by older grammars (e.g., GK 113, r), it cannot be affirmed that the infinitive absolute in a postpositive position (after the main verb) implies duration (e.g., "keep on listening..."; so NRSV, ESV; NIV has "be ever hearing"). Both Waltke and O'Connor (35.3.1.d, p. 585) and Joüon (123.l, pp. 424f.) leave the nuance as unmarked and contextual, although Wildberger (250) wrongly appeals to Joüon that the postpositive position "stresses the continuation of an activity." Cf. also Bartelt, *Fundamental Biblical Hebrew*, 137–38. The simplest translation value is usually expressed with "certainly," though other adverbs may be used. The same construction occurs in 55:2, where NRSV and ESV translate "listen carefully/diligently" (NIV repeats the imperative, "listen, listen"). Cf. Job 13:17; 21:2, where NRSV and NIV have "listen carefully" and ESV has "keep listening" (cf. 37:2 for other variations).

6:13 ("and yet a tenth in it, it will again be burned"), and I propose that as the sense also in verse 10.[5]

In either case, this final line balances the opening command in verse 9 and is the intended result and even purpose of saying to this people, "Listen and look ('hear and see') intently, but do not perceive or understand!" The jarring force of the imperatives in verse 9 is softened in the LXX by the use of future indicatives (Ἀκοῇ ἀκούσετε ... βλέποντες βλέψετε, "by hearing you will hear ... seeing you will see"), each followed by the subjunctive (καὶ οὐ μὴ συνῆτε ... καὶ οὐ μὴ ἴδητε, "but you will not understand ... but you will not perceive"). Verse 10 is also rendered by the LXX with indicatives, in the third person, and aorist. But while preaching to those who "have not ears to hear" can often result in such "hearing and hearing without understanding," the actual imperatives to Isaiah have much more a sense of purpose than result.

The language of verse 10 is reminiscent of, and often compared to, the "hardening" of Pharaoh's heart. However, the more common verb for the hardening of hearts is the piel of חזק, used eight times in the exodus account (Exod 4:21; 9:12; 10:20, 27; 11:10; 14:4, 8, 17), all with God as the subject. The hiphil of כבד is used in the exodus account three times with Pharaoh as subject, Exod 8:11, 28 (ET, vv. 15, 32), 9:34, and only once with YHWH as the subject, toward the end of the account in 10:1. In the first reference to "hardening" at 7:14, the qal is used to describe the existing state of Pharaoh's heart (see also 9:7). Further, God commands Isaiah to "make heavy" their ears. Their hearts are to be "made fat."

There do appear to be similarities with Pharaoh, perhaps most notably that he needed to be brought low so that YHWH might "be glorified" ("get glory," niphal of כבד; Exod 14:4, 17, 18), and so that YHWH might show himself the true king also of Egypt, so that God's people would know that "I am YHWH" (Exod 10:2). These themes certainly lie in the background in Isa 6, also in connection to Isa 2, where the elevation of Zion and Yahweh is contrasted to the arrogant "lifting up" of the self-proclaimed high and mighty (2:2-4, 9, 11, 12-17). But the theme of being brought low is not the language of Exodus. Conversely, the "glorification" of YHWH is not the language of Isaiah or the goal of Isa 6. The parallels to Pharaoh and exodus are not as clear as they may seem in this regard. But what is a parallel and important theologically, is that any such "hardening" by God is

---

5. This may seem to "soften" the harshness of the entire verse, removing the explicit mention of "turning" or "repentance," which would seem to be the goal of Isaiah's preaching and which, in turn, makes this commission statement so difficult theologically. But in fact, the effect is the same: God will "heal" them (note that the LXX translates the verb expressing healing [רפא] with ἀφίημι [ἀφεθῇ, "it will be forgiven").

in fact purposeful. It is also focused on a particular moment and not to be understood as paradigmatic for the way God operates in any time and place. As with Pharaoh, so also with Isaiah in his time and message, God's commission even to "harden hearts" has a specific goal within a specific circumstance and context.

More helpful is the immediate context of Isa 6, which continues into verses 11-13. Again, we can only summarize, but the message of these verses is that things will get even worse for Judah before they get better. If the remnant motif was to be represented by the "tenth" that would remain, it, too, would be destroyed. Isaiah is commissioned to bring Judah, Zion, her king, and her people to a point where there is no more option for any escape from the judgment of God. The people and especially their leaders described in chapters 2-3 are beyond simple reform; they must be completely removed. God will restore Zion by a spirit of judgment and burning (Isa 4:2-6). The vineyard in chapter 5 is already condemned for destruction. The "woes" in 5:8-30 describe those who are completely turned around, calling "good evil and evil good" (5:20).[6] These were people who were "wise in their own eyes" (5:21) and who dared God to "speed up his work that they might see" (5:19). Their assumption was that God would not act upon his threatened judgment, that he would relent from his punishment and instead spare them. What had been described in Isa 1:3 as "my people" in rebellion, had now shown themselves to be "this people."[7] But the time had come for even the people of God to realize and recognize the true result of sin and refusal to humble themselves in confession, as Isaiah properly modeled in 6:5.

Isa 6:11-13, despite the difficulties in translation, makes clear that God's judgment would be complete. The presence of God's holiness to fill the earth can leave no room for unholiness or uncleanness. It is as though the land must be purged and cleansed for God's holiness to fill it (cf. 1:25, 27-31, with its own reference to cultic oaks). There would not be another "sparing" of Zion, but even the "tenth" that might remain would be "for burning."

But this is not the end of the story, either. It is necessary, in the same sense that absolution cannot come without confession, and in the same sense that new life, especially resurrection, cannot come without death. The

---

6. This list of "seven woes," including 10:1, is chiastically ordered, with the threefold chiasm in 5:20 as the fourth or middle woe, clearly making the point that at the center is a complete inversion of God's will for human ways. See Bartelt, "Isaiah 5 and 9," 167-68.

7. The phrase (הָעָם הַזֶּה) first occurs in chapter 6, and then again in 8:6, 11, 12, and in 9:15 (ET: 9:16). The phrase is used elsewhere in Isaiah only in chapters 28-29, where the context again is pejorative (against Ephraim in 28:11, 14; against those in Jerusalem in 29:13-14).

final line of Isa 6:13, often dismissed as a later gloss, precisely because it seems even more jarring and inconsistent than the command to "harden hearts" in verse 10, is in fact not to be ignored.[8] Whatever is meant by the reference to a cultic *maṣṣebah*,[9] there is a sense of hope in the "holy seed," small though it may seem, that stands in clear contrast to the basis for the current worship practices of the people of Judah. Yet Yahweh will remain faithful to his long-range plan and purposes, which now must include a full accounting for judgment on sin in order to proceed with new life.

The "seed as descendant" motif is carried forth in Isaiah's children in Isa 7–8, as Isaiah seems to be demonstrating to Ahaz that, in spite of the king's apostasy, God's word embodied in Isaiah will continue to at least the next generation. And so also the seed will continue for the house and lineage of David in the royal son as the sign of God's presence in Isa 7:14, played out in 8:4 and 8:8. Isa 9 continues the motif of a royal son, yet with a description that almost expands the scope beyond just another "son of David." Isa 11:1 speaks of new growth from the rootstock of Jesse, not another davidic son but another David. God's promise continues, but with a sense of discontinuity and a new beginning.

That even "Isaiah of Jerusalem"[10] might have foreseen not only judgment but also redemption and restoration (so Isa 1:27; 2:2–4; 4:2–6) is an interpretive insight gradually being restored within the academy of Isaiah scholarship, now much more focused on reading the book holistically, even in spite of a host of redactional hypotheses.[11] Theologically, Isa 6 is consistent with the biblical pattern of condemnation and salvation, of judgment

---

8. The omission in the LXX (though not in the Qumran scrolls) seems clearly due to haplography in confusion from the use of מַצֶּבֶת in 13b to the use of מַצַּבְתָּהּ as the final word in 13c. Yet this is all too readily assumed to be evidence for the line as secondary.

9. מַצֵּבָה is elsewhere a sacred standing stone and only here glossed as "stump," suggested by the context of the trees in 6:13Ba. However translated, the word brings a cultic overtone from the high places. There may well be sarcastic wordplay here, in which the cutting down of trees yields just another object of pagan worship.

10. The identification can refer to the historical person of the eighth century or, as is the trend in much contemporary readings, as a literary presentation of the prophet, "as though" it is attributed to the prophet himself. See especially the seminal article by Ackroyd, "Isaiah i–xii."

11. The literature is vast, and much recent scholarship revolves around the SBL Formation of Isaiah Group, formed as a consultation in 1990, and out of which was published Melugin and Sweeney, *New Visions of Isaiah*, and, more recently, Mathews McGinnis and Tull, *"As Those Who Are Taught*. Also see, *inter alia*, Ackroyd, "Isaiah i–xii"; Beuken, "The Unity of the Book of Isaiah"; Clements, "The Unity of the Book of Isaiah"; Conrad, *Reading Isaiah*; Gitay, *Isaiah and His Audience*; Hayes and Irvine, *Isaiah the Eighth-Century Prophet*; Leibreich, "The Position of Chapter Six"; Rendtorff, "Zur Komposition"; Rendtorff, "Jesaja 6."

and restoration, of tearing down and building up (Jer 1:10), of killing in order to make alive (Hos 6:1–2; Ezek 37:1–14). The harsh command to Isaiah to "make fat the hearts of this people" should not be softened; it is, in theological jargon, the "alien work" (*opus alienum*) of a God who condemns in order to save (which is his "proper work," *opus proprium*). Thus any text must be read within its context, not only the literary and historical context of the text itself, but within the larger structure and scheme of the canonical process that brought these texts and these collections of texts into a larger collection of texts.[12] However one views the process by which the "Vision of Isaiah" came to be the prophetic collection of sixty-six chapters that it is today, the implied author is stated in the single superscription, presumably governing the whole book, in 1:1, so that the whole book is to be read from the point of view of a single author and unified message.

A most unclean and unholy people cannot stand in the presence of the Holy One of Israel, but the only one who can rectify that situation is in fact the Holy One of Israel, who alone can make the unclean clean, the unholy holy, and the sinner forgiven as a saint. Isaiah will contrast the darkness of the end of chapter 5 with the light in chapter 9. But in even greater measure, the blind and deaf will be specifically addressed as those who will later come to see and to hear.

Isaiah 29 moves toward a turning point in the book, as the theme of blindness is highlighted and heightened. Chapter 29:9–10 reports that God himself has closed the eyes of the (false) prophets. What is worse is that the "vision" has become "words in a sealed scroll," which is sealed to those who can read (scribes), and ironically then given to those who cannot read. Not surprisingly, they cannot read it, either, because they cannot read (vv. 11–12)! "This people" is then accused of vain worship (v. 13). God will show his true wisdom and wonder (v. 14), and the wisdom of the wise and the understanding of the discerning (וּבִינַת נְבֹנָיו, חָכְמַת חֲכָמָיו, cf. 3:3;5:21) will be undone. Such people who love darkness are further described as those who "turn things upside down" (הֶפֶךְ, cf. 1:7) and as clay telling the potter what to do (cf. the theme of the inversion of good and evil in 5:20).

However, in 29:17 the great reversal is announced, "in a very short time." The land will be rejuvenated, and in that day "the deaf will hear the words of the scroll, and from darkness the eyes of the blind will see." Chapter 35 speaks of the new creation, following the cosmic destruction of chapter 34, and announces that when "your God will come and save you" (35:4), "then the eyes of the blind will be opened, and the ears of the deaf

---

12. While hardly a full statement of the assumptions and methods of "canonical criticism," this is a basic assumption of reading not just texts or books but the canon itself "holistically."

unstopped." Isa 53:5 speaks of the servant by whose wounds there will be healing for us (וְרִפָא לָנוּ).[13]

Clearly with Isa 6 in mind, God announces in 42:7 and 16 that he will "lead the blind ... and turn the darkness into light," and then he proclaims in 42:18, "hear you deaf, look to see, you blind!" This is the major theme of Isa 42–44[14] and testifies that the commission of 6:9–10 has been carried out. God's "servant" Israel is even more blind and deaf than the nations; they have seen many things but not observed; they have had ears opened, and they still do not hear. But God would lead out "those who have eyes but are blind, who have ears but are deaf" (43:8).

Thus the "blinding" or even "hardening" of God's people served a greater goal: those walking in darkness would actually see—and appreciate, and know—the light (9:1 [ET=9:2]). When, and how, that would take place remains within the ways and means of God, whose thoughts and ways are not "ours" (Isa 55:8–9). In 63:17, it is asked, "why do you make us err from your ways, and harden our heart so that we fear you not?" (although the verb is the rare קשח, used only here in Isaiah).

So also the "germination" of the holy seed is beyond human comprehension, yet purposeful within the economy of God's larger plan (Isa 55:10–11).[15] In the longer and larger literary context, this seed would include the next generations of God's people, gathered after exile from east and west (Isa 43:5; see also 44:3), who will be righteous and even possess the nations (45:25; 54:3). They will be known among the nations as a people blessed by Yahweh (61:9), bearing children for generations to come (65:23), and be heirs of the new creation (66:23). And the suffering servant, even in his own death as an offering for sin, would "see his offspring" (53:10).

Indeed, the seed provided by the Holy One would accomplish what Isaiah could only see by faith. God's Word, like the seed that springs forth, would not return void. Indeed, the land that would become a desolation and forsaken (שְׁמָמָה and עֲזוּבָה, Isa 6:11c–12) would no more be called forsaken (עֲזוּבָה) or desolation (שְׁמָמָה, Isa 62:4).

In the time of Ezra, well into the postexilic era, there was renewed concern for the holiness of God's people. The issue at that time was intermarriage with the "peoples of the lands with their abominations" (Ezra 9:1). Whether the reference to "the seed of holiness" (translated "holy race" [ESV, NIV, NASB] or "holy seed" [NRSV]) is directly influenced by or a

---

13. This connection is even suggested by Rendtorff, "Jesaja 6 im Rahmen der Komposition des Jesajabuches," 78.

14. See Lessing, *Isaiah 40–55*, 286.

15. For a discussion of the connection of Isa 55:10–11 to the sower parable, see Evans, "On the Isaianic Background," 466.

recollection of Isa 6:13 cannot be known for certain, but it is the only other use of this phrase in the Hebrew Bible. If so, it is a reminder that the fundamental problem was not solved or resolved even by the destruction of Jerusalem and exile, with a return and restoration that signaled renewed life and a new beginning. The "holy nation" of Exod 19:6 still had within it the seeds of the old fallen creation, continually at war and with enmity between the seed of the serpent and the seed of the woman (Gen 3:15). It would not be until the fully "holy seed" would come as the embodiment of all Israel and all nations (Gal 3:16) that the holiness of God's people would be confirmed once for all, in the new creation.

In Isa 6, the prophet received a commission not only to proclaim God's word to those who had not ears to hear but even, by his very preaching, to make them blind and deaf and unresponsive. So it can be that the Word of God only seems to confirm those who are obdurate in their hard-heartedness. But this was not simply the sad result of proclamation; it was purposeful. Throughout his ministry Isaiah would no doubt have dealt with a sense of failure and fatigue, though he did not share his personal confessions in the manner Jeremiah did (e.g., see Jer 20). But God's plan, revealed in the heavenly council of the King of kings and Lord of lords, had a future and a hope that extended beyond Isaiah's lifetime. From the vantage point of Isa 6:13c, it may have looked small and insignificant, less like an oak or terebinth and more like a mustard seed, perhaps. But so it is with the mystery of the kingdom of God.

And so it is with reading texts as part of a larger construct, first within Isa 6, then chapters 1–12, 1–39, and 1–66. Any one expression of theological thought needs to be connected to the larger patterns that link texts together as parts form a whole.[16] But there is more. As is well known, the "hardening" motif of Isa 6 is cited five times in the New Testament.[17] We shall here consider only one. That the motif of God's purposeful "hardening" and his

16. This hermeneutic assumes, of course, some sense of unity to the whole of Scripture, which admittedly is a theological assumption about the nature of Scripture itself, including the historical processes and contexts reflected in its parts.

17. The Synoptics all cite the hardening with reference to why Jesus began to teach in parables, within the parable of the sower (Matt 13:14–15; Mark 4:12; Luke 8:10). John cites Jesus in linking the passage with Isa 53:1 as explanation for the lack of belief in him (John 12:37–40). John's Gospel also develops the motif of being blind in order to see clearly, though without direct reference to the Isaiah texts. The Acts of the Apostles concludes with Paul citing Isa 6 (Acts 28:25–28) in the indicatives/subjunctives (versus MT imperatives) of the LXX to explain both the unbelief of many of the Jews and the opening of the Gentile mission. This hardening likely lies behind Paul's excursus in Rom 9–11 as well, though he never cites Isa 6 directly, in spite of at least six citations from Isaiah. Romans 11:7 cites God's "hardening" in Isa 29:10, which seems to be a development of Isa 6 within the book of Isaiah.

motif of a "holy seed" come together may further inform the use of Isa 6 in the context of the parable of the sower, the soils, and the seed. Here we do well to turn to the commentary of our honoree himself, who argues for the very purposeful use of the ἵνα clause in Mark 4:12, against those "bridling at the idea that for those outside all things confront them in parables 'in order that' they might not see and understand."[18] Mark's citation follows the LXX in reading the initial imperatives as indicatives,[19] but his use of the ἵνα clause would seem to compensate for the change in the LXX from the imperatives, indicating that the "seeing without seeing" and "hearing without understanding" was actually the intent of what Isaiah was commissioned to do.

Eschewing all efforts to soften the force, Voelz is well aware of the original sense in Isa 6, and his ability to transfer the biblical pattern from Isaiah to the application and fulfillment in the words and deeds of Jesus is a key in his own understanding of the interpretive task as guided by his hermeneutical assumptions.[20] He is also guided by a holistic reading of both Isaiah and Mark, and by the interpretive manner in which New Testament authors (not to mention our Lord himself) engage Old Testament texts, by which citations "serve as 'hooks' into the larger OT context."[21] In sum, he is able to understand Isa 6 in light of the near and far contexts within Isaiah, and then to understand that Jesus is "here applying Isaiah's 'full text,' so to speak, to himself and describing himself and his career with the description that Isaiah was given of his own person and career. Such a description involves having a mission to God's people (Is 6:8), delivering a message that has a negative purpose and effects (Is 6:9–10), enduring a period of time with no positive results (Is 6:11a), producing the destruction of God's people (Is 6:11b), resulting in devastation (Is 6:12), but leaving a remnant centered in the Holy Seed (Is 6:13)."[22]

What is more, Voelz captures the larger agenda of the vision of Isaiah, that God's "hardening" is not the "first move" in God's action, but "follows

---

18. Voelz, *Mark*, 284.

19. Mark seems to cite the LXX, though the change from second to third person may be influenced by the Targum (see Evans, *To See and Not Perceive*, 92; Evans also concludes that the ἵνα clause must be a final clause, 95). The order of "hearing . . . seeing" is also reversed to "seeing . . . hearing."

20. Voelz is well aware of the importance of transparency of one's assumptions in bringing the "second text" of the interpreter within one's own community to the task of interpretation; see Voelz, *What Does This Mean?* 19-20.

21. Voelz notes the importance and influence of both C. H. Dodd (*According to the Scriptures*) and C. F. D. Moule (in his Cambridge lectures, many of which we attended together), see Voelz, *Mark*, 141–43.

22. Ibid., 285.

upon persistent rejection by Israel of her gracious God"[23] (as we have observed in Isa 1–5). Nor is it the last move, either. We have seen how God's purposes in making hearers blind and deaf is a step toward opening their eyes and ears to see and hear anew. Voelz's ability to put Isa 6 into the larger construct of the whole book of Isaiah is only a piece of his larger understanding of a biblical narrative that is fulfilled in Christ, and especially in the crucified and risen Christ.[24] Or to state it in thoroughly "Voelzian" style, "Furthermore, as he [Jesus] embraces the description of Isaiah's ministry as his own, Jesus is 'saying' (on level 2) [footnote to excursus on interpretation on levels 1, 2, and 3] not only that (vis-à-vis Isaiah) the same God is working in the same way for the same purposes, but also and especially that his ministry will bring the prior divine visitation in BC times to its final end and fulfillment."[25]

As scholar and theologian, James Voelz has engaged his understanding of Greek and biblical studies in the service of a biblical theology that understands not just "intertextuality" but especially the unity of the one great story. As friends who seek to engage an understanding of both Greek and Hebrew in the greater service of the same biblical theology, our work together gives witness to the unity of God's testament in Christ, old and new, as complementary, even as this essay seeks to be most complimentary in honoring the ministry of James W. Voelz.

Bibliography

Ackroyd, P. "Isaiah i–xii: Presentation of a Prophet." In *Congress Volume: Göttingen 1977*, 16–48. VTSup 29. Leiden: Brill, 1978.

Bartelt, Andrew H. *The Book around Immanuel: Style and Structure in Isaiah 2–12*. Winona Lake, IN: Eisenbrauns, 1996.

———, and Andrew E. Steinmann. *Fundamental Biblical Hebrew / Fundamental Biblical Aramaic*. St. Louis: Concordia, 2004.

———. "Isaiah 5 and 9: In- or Interdependence?" In *Fortunate the Eyes That See: Essays in Honor of David Noel Freedman in Celebration of His Seventieth Birthday*, edited by Astrid B. Beck, et al., 157–74. Grand Rapids: Eerdmans, 1995.

Beale, W. K. "Isaiah VI 9–13: A Retributive Taunt against Idolatry?" VT 41 (1991) 257–78.

---

23. Ibid., 292.

24. Many personal conversations have revolved around the key "hermeneutical" (actually, "dia-hermeneutical"!) statement of Luke 24:27, which depends upon Christ's first being killed and then raised from the dead, καὶ ἀρξάμενος ἀπὸ Μωϋσέως καὶ ἀπὸ πάντων τῶν προφητῶν διερμήνευσεν αὐτοῖς ἐν πάσαις ταῖς ραφαῖς τὰ περὶ ἑαυτοῦ.

25. Voelz, *Mark*, 292, italics in original.

Beuken, Willem A. M. "The Manifestation of Yahweh and the Commission of Isaiah: Isaiah 6 Read against the Background of Isaiah 1." *Calvin Theological Journal* 39 (2004) 72–87.

———. "The Unity of the Book of Isaiah: Another Attempt at Bridging the Gorge between Its Two Main Parts." In *Reading from Right to Left: Essays on the Hebrew Bible in Honour of David J. A. Clines,* edited by J. C. Exum and H. G. M. Williamson, 50–62. JSOTSup 373. Sheffield: Sheffield 2003.

Clements, R. E. "The Unity of the Book of Isaiah." *Interpretation* 36 (1982) 117–29.

Conrad, Edgar W. *Reading Isaiah.* Minneapolis: Augsburg Fortress, 1991.

Evans, Craig A. "On the Isaianic Background of the Sower Parable." *CBQ* 47 (1985) 466–468.

———. "Isa 6:9–13 in the Context of Isaiah's Theology." *JETS* 29 (1986) 139–46.

———. *To See and Not Perceive: Isaiah 9.9–10 in Early Jewish and Christian Interpretation.* JSOTSup 64. Sheffield: Sheffield Academic, 1989.

Gitay, Yehoshua. *Isaiah and His Audience: The Structure and Meaning of Isaiah 1–12.* Studia Semitica Neerlandica 30. Assen: Van Gorcum, 1991.

Hayes, John H., and Stuart A. Irvine, *Isaiah the Eighth-Century Prophet.* Nashville: Abingdon, 1987.

Kautsch, E. ed. *Gesenius' Hebrew Grammar.* Revised by A. E. Cowley. Oxford: Clarendon, 1910.

Joüon, Paul, SJ. *A Grammar of Biblical Hebrew.* Translated and revised by T. Muraoka. Subsidia Biblica 27. Rome: Editrice Pontificio Istituto Biblico, 1996.

Leibreich, L. "The Position of Chapter Six in the Book of Isaiah." *HUCA* 25 (1954) 37–40.

Lessing, R. Reed. *Isaiah 40–55.* St. Louis: Concordia, 2011.

Mathews McGinnis, Claire, and Patricia K. Tull, eds. *"As Those Who Are Taught": The Interpretation of Isaiah from the LXX to the SBL.* SBL Symposium Series 27. Atlanta: SBL, 2006.

Melugin, Roy F., and Marvin A. Sweeney, eds. *New Visions of Isaiah.* JSOTSup 214. Sheffield: Sheffield Academic, 1996.

Rendtorff, Rolf. "Jesaja 6 im Rahmen der Komposition des Jesajabuches." In *The Book of Isaiah—Le livre d'isaie,* ed. J. Vermeylen, BETL 8, 73–82. Leuven: Leuven University Press, 1989.

———. "Zur Komposition des Buches Jesaja." *VT* 34 (1984) 295–320.

Robinson, Geoffrey D. "The Motif of Deafness and Blindness in Isaiah 6:9–10: A Contextual, Literary, and Theological Analysis." *Bulletin for Biblical Research* 8 (1998) 167–86.

Uhlig, Torsten. *The Theme of Hardening in the Book of Isaiah: The Analysis of Communicative Action.* Forschungen zum Alten Testament 2/39. Tübingen: Mohr/Siebeck, 2009.

Voelz, James W. *Mark 1:1—8:26.* Concordia Commentary. St. Louis: Concordia, 2013.

———. *What Does This Mean? Principles of Biblical Interpretation in the Post-Modern World.* 2nd ed. St. Louis: Concordia, 2013.

Waltke, Bruce K. and M. O'Connor. *An Introduction to Biblical Hebrew Syntax.* Winona Lake, IN: Eisenbrauns, 1990.

Wildberger, Hans. *Isaiah 1–12.* Translated by Thomas H. Trapp. Continental Commentaries. Minneapolis: Fortress, 1991.

3

Limited Government and Freedom of Religion

—Lawrence C. Brennan

I no longer remember when we started the dialogue, but I first met Dr. James Voelz in a series of informal meetings between members of the faculties of Concordia Seminary and Kenrick-Glennon Seminary in St. Louis. I was impressed with his knowledge of the Roman Catholic tradition and his commitment to what he has called an "evangelical Catholicism." It reminded me of how much our respective traditions hold in common, even as it clarified the nature of our divergences. Of course, his knowledge of the Bible and of the biblical languages was without compare. I was on assignment to the Catholic Diocese of Colorado Springs from 2010–2016, where I directed a small program of permanent diaconal formation. In 2012, Dr. Voelz was gracious enough to join me in a regional deacon conference on the subject of new interpretations of Saint Paul. As I fully expected, his presentations and interactions were sterling. I am happy to be a part of this Festschrift to honor him.

My topic is limited government and freedom of religion. I will be relying on the thought of Father John Courtney Murray, the American Jesuit theologian of the twentieth century whose thought influenced the document *Dignitatis Humanae*, the declaration on religious freedom produced by the Second Vatican Council in 1965. His book *We Hold These Truths: Catholic Reflections on the American Proposition*, published in 1960, is one of the most important ever written on the subject of religious freedom. It is still in print and is available at the websites of Amazon and Barnes and Noble.

I would like to address my topic under four headings: the notion of ordered liberty, the notion of civic virtue, the role of mediating institutions in society, and the constitutional relationship of church and state. After this, I would like to apply these thoughts to two contemporary controversies about religious liberty: the Department of Health and Human Services (HHS) insurance mandate requiring church coverage of contraception, and the recent Supreme Court decision in the *Obergefell* case, creating a new right to same-sex marriage.

The Notion of Ordered Liberty

I am using the expression "ordered liberty" in a wide sense. The constitutional structure of American government is sometimes referred to as an experiment in ordered liberty, in contrast to the other Western offspring of 1789, the French Revolution, which is an example of liberty run riot. Ordered liberty is a true instance of freedom, but freedom limited by the need for order in society. At its core, it is an oxymoron, since we ordinarily think of freedom as the absence of limit or constraint, but it is an oxymoron that works, not a contradiction in terms. If in the end there were no constraints on freedom, only the most powerful would really be free; the lack of order in society would function as a constraint on everyone else. An analogy is the classical notion of art, the merging of form with creative impulse. If I want to write a sonnet, it can have only fourteen lines. I can, if I like, write a poem of thirteen lines or fifteen lines, but I may not call it a sonnet. The remarkable thing about the poems that we do call sonnets is how much creativity and variety are contained within that limit of fourteen lines. They are what we might call a literary version of ordered liberty. Or conversely, if you will, we might call our lived experience of ordered liberty a constitutional sonnet.

It is important to understand the notion of limits correctly. For instance, tyranny limits freedom, but tyranny imposes such limits from outside the moral order. Tyranny is always a denigration of the dignity of the human person and the human community, and for this reason cannot stand for any length of time. In modern times, tyranny often leads to revolution, but in the process, sadly, one tyranny is often simply replaced by another. The most remarkable thing about the American Revolution is that it did not do this. It created what the Great Seal of our nation calls a *novus ordo seclorum,* "a new order of the ages." In this new order the people are corporately sovereign, and like any of the sovereigns of the old order, they institute a government, in the words of the Declaration of Independence, "laying its foundation on such principles and organizing its powers in such form, as to them shall seem most likely to effect their safety and happiness." The people are the larger entity in the equation, not only in the sense that there are more people than officers of government, but in the deeper sense that government is subservient to its sovereign and therefore limited in whatever way the sovereign chooses to limit it. I will return to this theme shortly.

Another element of the notion of limits is contained within the notion of order itself. The order of society is part of a larger order, a moral order, that of the natural law. This is an innate sense of right and wrong that is wired into the human species and that reveals itself in the universal phenomena of either a good conscience or a bad conscience, a sense of satisfaction or a sense of guilt about a given moral act. Governments are not free to ignore the natural law, and a good deal of the Declaration of Independence explains why the tyranny of George III was incompatible with "the laws of nature and nature's God." By the same measure, neither societies nor individuals may ignore the natural law. The price for doing so is a sense of guilt borne of a bad conscience, which leads to self-correction, or failing that, to rationalization or moral indifference. A good deal of the acrimony and incivility of the contemporary political conversation can be traced to unwillingness of bad conscience to acknowledge itself or to change course. As we hear in the Gospel, "Everyone who does wicked things hates the light and does not come toward the light, so that his works might not be exposed" (John 3:20 NABRE).

Morality is discovered, not invented. Its sanctions are spontaneous and not imposed. As a people we are free to refashion our constitution if we so choose: France has done it five times; some of the American states, almost as frequently. But we are not free to change the natural law. It is an essential limit from which we cannot escape, and any attempt to change it will result in personal unhappiness and societal discord on a massive scale.

Perhaps the best expression of the meaning of ordered liberty is Lord Acton's famous dictum: "Liberty is not the power of doing what we like but the right of being able to do what we ought." Every element here deserves comment. Liberty is not about a power but about something more fundamental, namely, a right, something to which we have a just claim. And *what* we have a just claim to is not primarily about our likes but about our duties. It is hard to imagine a definition that more squarely cuts across the sentimentality and silliness of what passes for moral reflection in our popular culture. "Ought" is more important than "like." Value is more important than feelings. For centuries the realization of that truth was what marked the passage from adolescence to adulthood. Our societal rejection of that truth does not mark a great step forward in the inevitable progress of the West but a reversion to a permanent societal adolescence. There is no such thing as freedom without responsibility.

The Notion of Civic Virtue

Benjamin Franklin once said, "Only a virtuous people are capable of freedom." In this he was calling on a tradition of morality that was much older than the American founding, even much older than the Christian West. The notion of virtue goes back to the ancient Greeks, and to the famous academy that produced Socrates, Plato, and Aristotle. Later the Roman orator Cicero took up the same theme. These great figures devoted a great deal of thought to what constituted a responsible citizen, in democratic Athens and republican Rome, respectively. The clearest formulation can be found in Aristotle's treatise the *Nicomachean Ethics,* which begins with the universal desire for happiness, shows its relation to the various virtues, and ends by placing them in the context of friendship and citizenship.

In the High Middle Ages, Thomas Aquinas took up this ancient tradition and placed it in the context of charity rather than citizenship. Since this is the context more familiar to a Catholic audience, allow me to elaborate in these terms—on the assumption that charity makes for good citizenship. For Thomas, virtue was a question of habit, as was its opposite, vice. A habit is a fixed and stable disposition within us that orders our abilities and desires well or poorly. Good habits are what we call virtues; bad habits, vices. Our habits, good or bad, accumulate in us through the course of countless repeated decisions, great or small, and that accumulation is what we refer to as character. The virtues work together to make it easier for us to practice charity; in a similar way, the vices make it more *difficult* for us to practice charity.

The principal virtues are prudence, justice, fortitude, and temperance. Prudence puts abstract principles into concrete practice; it translates the great law of love into concrete decision making. Justice renders to persons and communities their due; it is a minimum form of charity. Fortitude allows us to act when doing so involves fear or difficulty; it allows us to make the sacrifices that charity sometimes demands. And temperance moderates the enjoyments of our body; it enables us to be balanced and unselfish.

The principal vices, called capital vices, are pride, envy, anger, sloth, gluttony, avarice, and lust. Pride is a distorted sense of the self; it detracts from charity by putting the self before others. Envy is a resentment of the excellence or the achievements of another; it detracts from charity by reinforcing a lack of self-respect and by lending itself to rivalry, backbiting, and gossip. Anger is a desire for vengeance; it detracts from charity by unkind thoughts, words, or deeds. Sloth is a sorrow or depression that fails to accept the self as a good gift from a loving God; it detracts from charity by either withdrawal from others or by the driven behaviors that lead to various addictions. Gluttony can be either an eating disorder or a problem with alcohol; it detracts from charity as a failure of self-respect and self-care. Avarice is an excessive attachment to wealth or possessions; it detracts from charity by putting things before people. Lust is the disordered desire for sexual pleasure; it detracts from charity as a failure of respect for the other, respect for the self, and respect for the plan of the Creator in human conjugal love.

A psychologist friend of mine, who is not a Catholic, once observed to me that the capital vices are the behaviors of depressed people. Christians would certainly agree that in the end these behaviors are joyless. More importantly, though, Christians would assert that these behaviors are not really free. None of them deliver on their promises, and the soul that is trapped in any of them seeks an ever-increasing dose of an ever-diminishing payoff. It is the devil's bargain.

A virtuous people are a free people. They may not be perfect, but they seek to live in harmony with one another, with their best self, and ultimately with God. These are truths of the natural law, and they are accessible to the unbiased mind. However, if I may paraphrase G. K. Chesterton, it is not that they have been tried and found wanting; they have been found difficult and left untried. For reasons too numerous to explore here, the culture of the West no longer commonly uses the language of virtue, although it has generated no substitute language. As a result, when the subject is morality, or still more, morality and law, the public conversation quickly descends into a Babel. There is no common reference to a possible truth that can command universal assent on the basis of its inherent reasonableness. Absent such a truth, there is little left to democracy than "might makes right."

This is distressing enough, but there are also powerful forces in Western society engaged broadly in an effort that Daniel Patrick Moynihan once called "defining deviancy down." It is not simply the case that we lack a common language for talking about morality or values; some are actively distorting and devaluating the language we have. The sexual revolution has been consciously redefining the institution of marriage since the end of World War I. Within that effort, and abated by the advent of artificial contraception in the 1960s, it has redefined the purposes of sexuality itself. As a result, in popular culture lust is no longer considered a vice but a birthright, and chastity is something at least quaint and probably unhealthy.

This devaluation is accompanied by another phenomenon that lends itself to the acrimony of the current cultural and political conversation, the phenomenon that philosophy identifies by the French loanword *ressentiment*. This phenomenon, though only recently named, is age-old. The book of Wisdom (contained in the Orthodox and Catholic canon but not in the Jewish or Protestant) gives testimony to it in these words, on the lips of the wicked:

> Let us beset the just one, because he is obnoxious to us;
>> he sets himself against our doings,
>
> Reproaches us for transgressions of the law
>> and charges us with violations of our training.
>
> He professes to have knowledge of God
>> and styles himself a child of the Lord.
>
> To us he is the censure of our thoughts;
>> merely to see him is a hardship for us,
>
> Because his life is not like that of other men's,
>> and different are his ways.
>
> He judges us debased;
>> he holds aloof from our paths as from things impure.
>
> (Wis 2:12–16 NABRE)

Ressentiment[1] is an elaborate form of the capital vice of envy, and like envy it begins in an adverse comparison of the self to another or others. More specifically, it is a comparison of one's *values* to those of others, in which one perceives a put-down of the self along with an inability to do anything about it. Here is the point of applicability for Chesterton's dictum: the values or virtues in question have been found difficult and left untried. The comparison leads to a hostility, anger, or indignation that requires an attack on the values in question, an attack that issues in hatred and a continuous belittling of the values themselves and the people who hold them.

And the problem does not stop there. The rejection of one value usually involves a distortion of the whole scale of values. And the worst part of *ressentiment* is that this distortion can spread through a whole social class, a whole people, a whole epoch. Does that sound familiar? Does it not explain the invective directed to cultural conservatism by the liberal elites of the nation? And what exactly is their distortion of the whole scale of values? In a word, tolerance. This is their supreme virtue, although it is little more than

---

1. See Lonergan, *Method in Theology*, 33.

a mask for their philosophical and moral relativism. "Tolerate everything but intolerance," they say. But why stop at intolerance? If there is no such thing as truth, what is the basis for excluding intolerance? Please do not misunderstand here; this is not to argue in favor of intolerance. But contemporary liberalism sees the whole tradition of Western moral reflection as an instance of intolerance, and there is little more to their argument than the bumper sticker Mean People Suck.

The important thing to remember is that I can do nothing about another person's envy—or that of another group. The fact that some of our fellow citizens consider chastity to be beyond them and that therefore the whole notion of virtue must be discarded does not invalidate either chastity or virtue. As someone who is seriously committed to the moral reality of virtue and who strives to eliminate personal vice, I must avoid situations in which I might *inflame* envy or *ressentiment*; I must avoid personal sanctimony and self-righteousness. But by the same token, I must not allow envy a *veto* over my words or actions. In this, we must stand our ground together. Virtue is the key to personal happiness and societal cohesion. It is the foundation of democracy, and without that foundation the American republic will collapse.

Mediating Institutions and Limited Government

Alexis de Tocqueville was a French aristocrat and political thinker who visited the United States in the early 1830s and later published his observations in a famous book, *Democracy in America*. One of the things he noted was the robust presence of voluntary associations in American culture. He wrote:

> Americans of all ages, all conditions, and all dispositions constantly form associations. They have not only commercial and manufacturing companies, in which all take part, but associations of a thousand other kinds, religious, moral, serious, futile, general or restricted, enormous or diminutive. The Americans make associations to give entertainments, to found seminaries, to build inns, to construct churches, to diffuse books, to send missionaries [abroad]; in this manner they found hospitals, prisons, and schools.
>
> As soon as several of the inhabitants of the United States have taken up an opinion or a feeling which they wish to promote in the world, they look out for mutual assistance; and as soon as they have found one another out, they combine. From

that moment they are no longer isolated men, but a power seen from afar, whose actions serve for an example and whose language is listened to.

If it is proposed to inculcate some truth or to foster some feeling by the encouragement of a great example, they form a society. Wherever at the head of some new undertaking you see the government in France, or a man of rank in England, in the United States you will be sure to find an association.[2]

Although these associations today are sometimes derided as "special interest groups" in the political process (usually by their opponents), they remain a fundamental means by which American society operates, cooperates, and makes cultural, societal, and economic progress. They are a part of the fabric of life in the United States, and it is important to understand their role.

In 1977 sociologist Peter Berger and then-Lutheran pastor and commentator Richard John Neuhaus (an alumnus of Concordia Seminary) coauthored a book entitled *To Empower People: From State to Civil Society*. In this book, the authors argued vigorously for the crucial role in society of what they called "mediating institutions," such as neighborhoods, the family, church, and voluntary associations. These institutions interpose layers of social organization between the individual and the government, and in this way serve to protect the individual from governmental overreach. Actually, this could be better stated. They are an organic phenomenon into which the individual is embedded, an extension of the primordial "we" that precedes the distinction of "you" and "me," or of "us" and "them." Their organicity is what creates civil society. Their purpose is to empower the individual and to link him or her to mutual societal supports for growth and perfection.

Totalitarian government actively militates against such organicity and the mediating institutions that support it. In totalitarian society, there *are* no mediating institutions, and the individual is directly at the disposal of the state. It is part of what makes such societies so inhumane, so contrary to human dignity. Against totalitarianism, Catholic social teaching since Pope Leo XIII (1810–1903, elected pope in 1878) has enunciated a principle of subsidiarity, the idea that government should have a subsidiary function, performing only those tasks that cannot be performed effectively at a more immediate or local level. To paraphrase a contemporary saying, all politics should be as local as possible. If a complex function can be performed equally well by a local government or a higher level of government, the preference of subsidiarity is for the local option. In American terms, this is sometimes referred to as federalism.

---

2. Tocqueville, *Democracy in America*, book 2, chapter 5.

As noted earlier, in the American constitutional order, society is superior to the state, the people to their government. The people, through the wisdom of the Founders, have created a system of limited government and limited governmental power. This is expressed within the text of the Constitution by the checks and balances among the three branches of governmental power—legislative, executive, and judicial. More importantly, it is expressed in the Bill of Rights, which restricts the power of government against any of the specified rights. The Ninth and Tenth Amendments then give the clearest statement of American federalism: the central government possesses only those functions enumerated in the Constitution, with all other powers reserved to the people and the states.

Henry David Thoreau gave currency to an expression that is sometimes attributed to Thomas Jefferson: "That government is best which governs least." He went on to explain: "Government is at best but an expedient; but most governments are usually, and all governments are sometimes, inexpedient." The Bill of Rights, and in particular the Ninth and Tenth Amendments, is a constitutional device meant to *keep* government an expedient, a tool of the sovereign people of the United States, and not a totalitarian, all-consuming Leviathan.

After the family, the church is the most formative and most vital of the mediating institutions of society. In the American context it has flourished, and that flourishing has only strengthened the American people and the American state. Any attempt to compromise the integrity of this mediating institution must be seen as unconstitutional and unjust.

The Constitutional Relationship of Church and State

The First Amendment to the Constitution of the United States of America restricts government power in the realm of religion: there is to be no established religion, and there is to be no governmental interference in the free exercise of religion. This is popularly interpreted to mean a separation of church and state, but that phrase does not occur in the Bill of Rights. If there is no established religion, there are no religious leaders seated ex officio in the chambers of Congress; conversely, neither Congress nor the president has any right to name religious leaders to their religious offices. If the free exercise of religion is to be respected, the government may not encumber that right with taxes, penalties, or prohibitions.

In the late nineteenth century, when the states began to exercise a reserved power, namely, to educate their citizenry, they created a system of public education that necessarily involved them in matters of religion, since a key function of education is the transmission of values, and the most fundamental basis of values is religion. In the 1940s, the United States Supreme Court began to adjudicate this situation in a series of cases that has had the net effect of establishing irreligion in public education—that is to say, a positive hostility to religion—and unjustly encumbering the rights of citizens who wish their children to be educated away from the corrosive irreligion of public schools. The Catholic Church can be justly proud of the educational system it established in order to transmit its values to its younger generations. The fact that Catholic parents must support the irreligion of public education with their taxes, and additionally pay for their children's tuition in private schools, amounts to a financial penalty on their free exercise of religion. The Court's decisions in this matter amount to an arbitrary and irrational animus against religion and ultimately must be corrected, although the path to that correction remains unclear.

This series of cases formed part of the background for the work of John Courtney Murray. He began his reflection with the simple historical observation that the First Amendment was "an articles of the peace," not an establishment of religious indifferentism. The latter holds that one religion is as good as another, but is itself a religious idea. An articles of peace, however, engages the political question of how might citizens agree on practical issues of the common good while disagreeing on ultimate issues of meaning. This is the genius of Anglo-American government. It is not necessary for all citizens to agree that salvation is through faith and works in order to agree that the sidewalk should be on the west side of the street. This example, of course, is trivial, but it establishes the point with relative clarity. Until the advent of public education, the enumerated functions of American government—functions such as national defense, regulation of the currency and commerce, a highway system, a postal service—were relatively practical and did not engage the great religious debates of sixteenth-century Europe. Indeed, the practicality of the Founders' solution was born of the historical uniqueness of the United States: from its very beginnings it was a religiously pluralistic society; there had never been a time when there was one established American religion like the Christendom of medieval Europe, nor a later time when that religious unity was sundered by theological divisions and warfare.

As the federal government has expanded beyond the enumerated powers of the Constitution, that is to say, beyond the relatively practical matters on which it is easier to attain political consensus, the issue of religion has come more and more to the fore. I have already visited the question of public education, originally a state question now federalized by an overreaching US Supreme Court. The question of welfare and the social safety net also falls beyond the scope of the original enumerated powers of the federal government. This was a question of social policy that touched religious concerns like care for the poor, but by and large revolved around the practical question of how best to exercise this care—and we have gone through several different versions of this policy. The current debate about health care has little to do with the enumerated powers of the Constitution. Because it involves questions of life and death, questions of medical ethics, questions of the dignity of the human person and the integrity of human sexuality—ultimate questions in life—it necessarily entangles itself with the question of religion.

It is important for believers to insist that unbelief, secular humanism, or, as it likes to call itself, liberalism, is a religion in its own right. It is a coherent set of answers to the ultimate questions of life, even when it alleges that there are no ultimate questions of life. Simply stated, it is impossible to be neutral on the question of religion; the idea that it is indeed possible is itself religious in nature. The core beliefs of liberalism are as unverifiable as the core beliefs of any other religion; therefore these beliefs are held on faith, even though the people who hold them think they are too sophisticated for faith. An established religion of secularism is no more consistent with the First Amendment than any other establishment of religion. Religious believers must make this clear. They must make clear to every branch of government that an established secularism has nothing to do with the genius of the American founding and that it will not be tolerated. If government continues to entangle itself with unenumerated functions that compromise religious liberty, then either those functions must be rethought or they must be assigned to another institution in society.

Two Contemporary Controversies

HHS Insurance Mandate

In August 2011, the US Department of Health and Human Services (HHS) issued a mandate that all group health plans, including those of religious institutions, must cover FDA-approved contraceptive methods, sterilization procedures, and patient education and counseling for all women with reproductive capacity. The mandate includes abortion-inducing contraceptives and so-called morning-after pills, or emergency contraceptives that prevent implantation and are thus also abortion inducing. Since contraception, sterilization, and abortion are incompatible with the principles and values of the Catholic community, the mandate requires Catholic institutions and individuals to violate their consciences. Liberals hold that this is a matter of women's health, not of religious liberty, illustrating their insensitivity and profound ignorance on matters religious. Religion is insignificant to them; *of course* it cannot be permitted to trump the sexual revolution.

Despite strong protests, HHS has remained adamant in its position. It has offered a number of "accommodations" in which the cost of the mandate would be shifted to insurers rather than imposed on the institutions themselves, but the accommodations strike many as a distinction without a difference. What is just as troubling is that in the current discussion the administration has begun speaking of "freedom of worship" rather than freedom of religion, thereby attempting to restrict First Amendment protections to houses of worship only, not to the churches' vast outreaches of educational and social service.

The US Conference of Catholic Bishops has found both the mandate and the HHS accommodations unacceptable and has demanded that the mandate be rescinded in its entirety. Popular opinion as measured in polls has been running against the mandate, but just this past July (2015) the administration finalized the mandate in its objectionable form.

In June 2014, in the case *Burwell v. Hobby Lobby*, the Supreme Court found in favor of Hobby Lobby, exempting closely held private companies from compliance with the mandate. The decision was unusual in that it allowed for the first time a for-profit corporation to claim religious rights. This development somewhat eased the government's pressure on small-business owners who felt compromised by the HHS mandate. To other opponents of the mandate it offered hope.

According to the Becket Fund for Religious Liberty (www.becketfund.org), there are currently fifty-six cases being litigated against the HHS mandate; plaintiffs include thirty-seven universities, forty religious charities, and fifteen dioceses. Additionally, sixteen states have filed *amicus curiae* briefs in support of the plaintiffs. These cases are at varying levels of resolution by the courts, but it is hoped that the Supreme Court will offer a definitive clarification of the matter, possibly by the summer of 2016. Its interventions to date have favored the objectors more than the administration.

Obergefell v. Hodges

This past June (2015) in the *Obergefell v. Hodges* case, the Supreme Court created a right to same-sex marriage based on the Fourteenth Amendment. The majority opinion, authored by Justice Anthony Kennedy, has been criticized as much for its purple prose as for its lack of legal merit. Here are two passages from the opinion:

> The First Amendment ensures that religious organizations and persons are given proper protection as they seek to teach the principles that are so fulfilling and so central to their lives and faiths, and to their own deep aspirations to continue the family structure they have long revered. The same is true of those who oppose same-sex marriage for other reasons. In turn, those who believe allowing same-sex marriage is proper or indeed essential, whether as a matter of religious conviction or secular belief, may engage those who disagree with their view in an open and searching debate. The Constitution, however, does not permit the State to bar same-sex couples from marriage on the same terms as accorded to couples of the opposite sex. (p. 32)

> As some of the petitioners in these cases demonstrate, marriage embodies a love that may endure even past death. It would misunderstand these men and women to say they disrespect the idea of marriage. Their plea is that they do respect it, respect it so deeply that they seek to find its fulfillment for themselves. Their hope is not to be condemned to live in loneliness, excluded from one of civilization's oldest institutions. They ask for equal dignity in the eyes of the law. The Constitution grants them that right. (p. 33)

Kennedy admits that the debate will continue, but nonetheless asserts that "the Constitution" has settled the matter. However, the Constitution, as written, says nothing about love enduring past death, about the idea of marriage, about fulfillment, or about loneliness.

In *Obergefell* the majority has not created a new right; nor has it discerned a right that already exists. Only God creates rights, the same God who created the order of marriage between a man and a woman and who made it the origin of the family, the basic unit of society. What the majority did in *Obergefell* is to evacuate the word "marriage" of any significant meaning in American law. As a legal precedent, it will be the source of much moral mischief.

Forty-two years ago, in the still-controversial *Roe v. Wade* decision, dissenting Justice Byron White characterized the majority opinion as "an exercise of raw judicial power." Similarly, it would be easy to characterize the majority opinion in the *Obergefell* case an exercise in raw judicial fantasy. Neither of these court cases has a basis in the text of the Constitution or in the precedents of the Court itself. The majorities simply decided the outcome they desired and imposed that outcome on the nation without regard for the limits of their power.

Religious believers are still appraising the new legal landscape. Although the Court claims to respect the religious viewpoints of those who hold for traditional marriage, it cannot hold back the power of popular culture to shame and vilify those viewpoints. Religious traditions that defend heterosexual marriage will remain free to do so within their church buildings, but in the conversations that form culture they will be increasingly marginalized. They can expect litigation against their charitable and social works, where these involve the question of same-sex marriage and parental issues. Indeed, in March 2006, anticipating just such litigation, Archbishop Sean P. O'Malley and leaders of Catholic Charities of Boston stunned the state of Massachusetts by ending the agency's adoption work—deciding to abandon its founding mission rather than comply with state law requiring that homosexuals be allowed to adopt children. One senses that more such announcements will be coming from other corners of society.

Religious educational institutions that sponsor residences for students will be required to respect the new rights of students in same-sex relationships. Presumably, religious senior care facilities will be required to do the same. It can be expected that religious agencies who provide insurance policies for their workers will be required to extend benefits to same-sex couples. Similarly, it can be expected that insurance agencies or reinsurance agencies will seek to end religious institutional coverages where same-sex litigation may arise.

An interesting question arises on the matter of rabbis, priests, or ministers signing state marriage certificates after religious wedding ceremonies. Currently in the United States these clergy act on behalf of the state in witnessing marriages. If they are members of religious traditions that do not recognize or perform same-sex marriages, will they be allowed to continue to act in this way? There will almost certainly be litigation against the practice, resulting at least sometimes in its dramatic withdrawal. Some members of the clergy, anticipating this development, argue that the religious bodies should proactively refuse to witness in the name of the state, since what the state believes about marriage is incompatible with what they believe.

In sum, President Ronald Reagan once said, "Freedom is never more than one generation away from extinction. We didn't pass it to our children in the bloodstream. It must be fought for, protected, and handed on for them to do the same." This is our time to protect religious freedom. Our children deserve to inherit the Constitutional order that we inherited from our forebears, an order of liberty supported by virtue, an order of the common good supported by organic mediating institutions, an order of the flourishing of religion within a democratic and pluralistic society. The Constitution of the United States was a noble experiment when it was written, and the great, free republic that it created has been a source of hope for mankind. Whether it remains so depends to a large extent upon our vision, our courage, and our cooperation with Providence.

Bibliography

Lonergan, Bernard J. F. *Method in Theology.* New York: Herder, 1972.
Tocqueville, Alexis de. *Democracy in America.* http://xroads.virginia.edu/~HYPER/DETOC/ch2_05.htm.

4

The *Weltanschauung* of the New Testament Authors

—*Chrys C. Caragounis*

Introductory Remarks

Every New Testament exegete ought to be interested in the worldview that was rife in the countries around the eastern Mediterranean during New Testament times and whether the New Testament authors were influenced by it. Naturally, given the progress in ancient studies in classical and Hellenistic literature, in epigraphy and papyrology, in sociological and anthropological investigations, as well as the many specialist studies in various areas of related research, some of the ancient positions on such matters have undoubtedly come to the attention of New Testament scholars. On the other hand, the absence of sustained presentations of the relevant data applicable to the time of the New Testament is liable to create only fleeting impressions in the mind of the modern NT scholar, which do not provide him with a sound basis for a correct evaluation of the situation in the writings with which he is concerned.

For my part—unless I have missed the whole thing altogether—I am not aware of any investigations into these matters relevant to the New Testament. I recall how in my doctoral student days I chanced upon commentators' and, in general, theologians' comments on various NT passages that appeared to be strange to me, that is, out of harmony with impressions I had received from my reading of the classics. In other words, these comments seemed to be uninformed. For example, Rudolf Bultmann was happy to dismiss certain NT utterances as representing the worldview of the ancient Near East. A saying such as Phil 2:10: πᾶν γόνυ . . . ἐπουρανίων καὶ ἐπιγείων καὶ καταχθονίων, would be a typical passage that revealed the so-called ancient worldview of a three-flat-disk or three-story universe. Accordingly, in reference to this text, Hawthorne says, "In antiquity people believed in a three-storied universe and universality was thus often expressed by phrases that embraced all three (cf. Hom. *Od.* 5. 184–86). It is possible therefore that when Paul wished to proclaim the universality of worship due from creation to Jesus, he used the phaseology of his day."[1]

It is obvious here that Hawthorne is unaware of the great progress that had been made since Homeros's time and of the actual state of scientific insights into the universe in Paul's time. Similarly, in commenting on John 8:23: ὑμεῖς ἐκ τῶν κάτω ἐστέ, ἐγὼ ἐκ τῶν ἄνω εἰμί, Barrett presents it as the formulation of "a primitive 'three-storey' universe."[2]

This "three-story universe" was in fact the worldview of ancient Sumer,[3] Babylonia,[4] and Egypt.[5] Thus, too, in his commentary on Revelation, the master of apocalyptic, R. H. Charles, writes: "This threefold division is found already in Ex xx 4 [i.e., heaven above, the earth beneath, the waters under the earth]. This . . . agrees exactly with the Babylonian division of the world into heaven and earth and water (*apsu* = water) under and around the earth."[6] But was it also the worldview of the NT authors?

These few examples show beyond any reasonable doubt that the same view that obtained in ancient Babylonia and Egypt is assumed by many NT scholars to be the worldview of the New Testament.

In the light of these facts, it might not be out of place to set forth a few relevant scientific facts obtaining in the days of the apostles. Those scholars already acquainted with these data can simply overlook my audacity, while those for whom these data constitute new information will not be any worse

---

1. Hawthorne, *Philippians*, 93.

2. Barrett, *Gospel according to St. John*, 341.

3. See, e.g., the Sumerian creation myth, which speaks of heaven, earth, and the underworld, in Beyerlin, *Near Eastern Religious Texts*, 74.

4. On the Babylonian epic of creation, *Enuma Elish*, according to which Marduk, on having slain Tiamat, splits her carcass to create heaven and earth, see Tablet IV 138-146; Tablet VI 40-46, in Pritchard, *Ancient Near Eastern Texts*, 67–68; Thomas, *Documents from Old Testament Times*, 10, and notes on 14–16; Beyerlin, *Near Eastern Religious Texts*, 83–84.

5. On ancient Egyptian creation myths, see the texts in Pritchard, *Ancient Near Eastern Texts*, 3–8, and Beyerlin, *Near Eastern Religious Texts*, 5–7.

6. Charles, *A Critical and Exegetical Commentary*, 1:139.

off for becoming acquainted with them. Such an investigation, I dare hope, will be quite germane in a Festschrift honoring a scholar who has always maintained a deep interest in the ancient world: its language, its literature, and its achievements.

Which Worldview Was Current in New Testament Times?

The worldview current in New Testament times was neither the Mesopotamian nor the Egyptian worldview. It was the Hellenic worldview. This view formed over many centuries and, by the time of the New Testament, bore hardly any similarity to the worldview represented in the works of Homeros[7] and Hesiodos,[8] and even less to that of the Near East.

The Hellenic worldview was transmitted to Palestine when Palestine was incorporated in Alexander's empire. Of crucial importance here is Alexander's vision. Alexander did not merely wish to conquer the ancient world for the sake of conquest or self-glory as conqueror, nor merely to punish the Persians for their burning of Athens. Above all, Alexander believed that the Hellenic culture was superior to all other cultures and wished to civilize the barbarians and make them partakers of the blessings of the civilization that the Hellenic states had developed and were enjoying.

This, at once, meant that the peoples conquered, or rather, liberated from their backward despotic regimes, would need to be educated in the Hellenic language and way of life; to be raised above the level of the brute and to be humanized in the full sense of the word: to think and act as free men according to principles of freedom, justice, equality, and dignity. To achieve that they should participate in Hellenic παιδεία.

This παιδεία could be acquired only through learning the Hellenic language, studying Hellenic literature, and becoming acquainted with the progress of Hellenic research in the various departments of science.

This was achieved through the Hellenic *polis*, with its institutions for the cultivation of the mind (i.e., schools for language and literature, rhetoric, and philosophy), artistic education (e.g., architecture, sculpture making, painting, theatrical spectacles, etc.), exercise to produce a healthy and strong body (*gymnasia* and *palaestrae*), as well as hippodromes. As the Jewish scholar Victor Tcherikover expresses it, "The most important channel through which Hellenism penetrated into Palestine was furnished by

---

7. Homeros's view can be extracted from his epic works, *Ilias* and *Odysseia*.

8. Hesiodos's view can be extracted mainly from his seminal work on the Hellenic pantheon, creation, and Hellenic mythology: *Theogonia*.

the Greek cities."⁹ For this purpose, hundreds of *poleis* were founded or refounded by Alexander and his *diadochoi* in the vast empire.¹⁰ In the Gospels we read, in particular, of the district of Ten Cities (*Dekapolis*) in Palestine. In his history, Schürer discusses some thirty-three cities in Palestine and nearby regions, some of which were indeed founded by Herod and his successors, although they, too, were constituted as Hellenic *poleis*.¹¹ "The cities were constituted after the model of the Greek *polis*, and were equipped with all the necessary apparatus—schools, gymnasia, palaestrae, theaters, stadia, hippodromes —for an uninhibited Greek existence in all departments of life: political, civil, social, commercial, religious, educational, athletic, aesthetic, recreational."¹²

This policy was soon crowned with success. As for Jerusalem, the initiative to Hellenize it came from the Jews themselves. First Maccabees 1:11–15 expresses the matter thus:

Ἐν ταῖς ἡμέραις ἐκείναις ἐξῆλθον ἐξ Ἰσραὴλ υἱοὶ παράνομοι καὶ ἀνέπεισαν πολλοὺς λέγοντες Πορευθῶμεν καὶ διαθώμεθα διαθήκην μετὰ τῶν ἐθνῶν τῶν κύκλῳ ἡμῶν, ὅτι ἀφ᾽ ἧς ἡμέρας ἐχωρίσθημεν ἀπ᾽ αὐτῶν, εὗρεν ἡμᾶς κακὰ πολλά. καὶ ἠγαθύνθη ὁ λόγος ἐν ὀφθαλμοῖς αὐτῶν, καὶ προεθυμήθησάν τινες ἀπὸ τοῦ λαοῦ καὶ ἐπορεύθησαν πρὸς τὸν βασιλέα, καὶ ἔδωκεν αὐτοῖς ἐξουσίαν ποιῆσαι τὰ δικαιώματα τῶν ἐθνῶν. καὶ ᾠκοδόμησαν γυμνάσιον ἐν Ιεροσολύμοις κατὰ τὰ νόμιμα τῶν ἐθνῶν καὶ ἐποίησαν ἑαυτοῖς ἀκροβυστίας καὶ ἀπέστησαν ἀπὸ διαθήκης ἁγίας καὶ ἐζευγίσθησαν τοῖς ἔθνεσιν καὶ ἐπράθησαν τοῦ ποιῆσαι τὸ πονηρόν.¹³

Hellenism must have exerted an irresistible fascination upon the Jews, if a high priest (Jason) was prepared to pay such a high price to Antiochos

9. Tcherikover, *Hellenistic Civilization and the Jews*, 91.

10. Alexander was said to have founded some 70 cities. Seleukos Nikator founded 58 cities, according to Appian, *Syria* 57. See the Ἱστορία τοῦ ἑλληνικοῦ Ἔθνους, 4:473, for a map dotted with newly founded Hellenistic or Hellenized cities. Tcherikover, *Hellenistic Civilization and the Jews*, 22, calculates the number of such Hellenistic cities to about 350. See the lists in Josephos, *Antiqvitates* 14.75ff., and *Bellum* 1.155ff.

11. Schürer, *History of the Jewish People*, 2:85–183. This is not certain in the case of Antipatris, Phasaelis, Julias, and Livias.

12. Caragounis, "Greek Culture and Jewish Piety," 299 and n. 117 (for bibliography).

13. English translation: "In those days certain renegades came out from Israel and misled many, saying, 'Let us go and make a covenant with the Gentiles around us, for since we separated from them many disasters have come upon us.' This proposal pleased them, and some of the people eagerly went to the king, who authorized them to observe the ordinances of the Gentiles. So they built a gymnasium in Jerusalem, according to Gentile custom, and removed the marks of circumcision, and abandoned the holy covenant. They joined with the Gentiles and sold themselves to do evil." (NRSV)

Epiphanes to achieve the honor of civilizer of Jerusalem.[14] In this he had the aristocracy and the youth on his side. As Applebaum points out, entrance into the gymnasium "must have been purchased with the betrayal of Judaism."[15] As I commented: "It was, in fact, not uncommon for members of the priestly class to espouse the new culture and style of life with enthusiasm. As the gymnasium was erected close by the temple [2 Macc 4:12], at the sound of the gong, the priests, abandoning their despised and neglected temple duties, ran with eagerness to take part in the palaestra [cf. 2 Macc 4:14]. Since the habit of the Greeks was to wrestle and exercise naked, these 'servants' of Yahweh with their aristocratic compatriots submitted themselves to operations in order to disguise their circumcision for which they were ashamed."[16]

E. Bevan's remarks here are quite telling: "The conversion of Hellenic cities was not something which the king compelled ancient communities to undergo, it was something which he conceded as a favour.... There was enough force and attraction in Hellenism to render compulsion, had Antiochus contemplated it, superfluous."[17]

The Maccabean revolt came as an answer to the threat of obliterating national Jewish distinctiveness.

There is an enormous amount of evidence for the Hellenization of Palestine and even for the much coveted title Ἀντιοχεῖς ἐν Ἱεροσολύμοις, "Antiochenes in Jerusalem" (i.e., Jews who were so Hellenized that they were permitted to call themselves "citizens of Antioch" [although they lived in Jerusalem]).[18] The noblest of the Jerusalem youth, the high priest, the *gymnasiarch,* and the *archon* of "the Antiochenes in Jerusalem" all came at once under the *petasos,* the distinctive broad-rimmed hat of the *ephebes.*[19]

The impact of the Hellenic language and culture on the peoples of the Near East in general and on Palestine and the Jews in particular is well attested. Such evidence comes from archaeological excavations of Hellenic establishments, such as Marisa, and papyri and inscriptions, from synagogues

---

14. Cf. 2 Macc 4:8-14. Cf. also, Bevan, *The House of Seleucus,* 2:168ff.

15. Applebaum, review of *Hellenistic Civilization and the Jews,* XIII Summary.

16. Caragounis, "Greek Culture and Jewish Piety," 301. See 1 Macc 1:15; 2 Mac 4:11-17; Josephos, *Antiqvitates* 12.241. Further, Schürer, *History of the Jewish People,* 1:148-49, and n. 28, for rabbinic references to these operations. Also, Goldstein, *1 Maccabees,* 200.

17. Bevan, *The House of Seleucus,* 2:153-54.

18. See Schürer, *History of the Jewish People,* 2:123; see two examples in Caragounis, "Greek Culture and Jewish Piety," 300n118.

19. The *ephebes* were the young men (eighteen to twenty years old) who exercised in the gymnasium or *palaestra.* See also Hengel, *Judaism and Hellenism,* 1:73.

as well as from other historical sources and authors like Josephos and Philon, Aristoboulos of Alexandria, and perhaps Menippos of Gadara.

Speaking the language was a *sine qua non* for anyone who wished to succeed in life: to find worthy employment, to rise in status in social circles, and to find fulfillment: "Impeccable command of the Greek language was the most important qualification for taking over Greek culture."[20] We thus find that Hellenic eclipsed Aramaic in communication and business transactions. For example, almost the entire corpus of the Zenon papyrical correspondence, with approximately two thousand items, is written in Hellenic.[21] Hengel points out that apart from Jewish tomb, ossuary, and synagogue inscriptions, written—naturally—in Aramaic, almost all Palestinian inscriptions from the third century BC are in Hellenic.[22] Such evidence comes from all parts of Palestine.[23] Schürer devotes some 230 pages to "Jewish literature composed in Greek,"[24] with ample bibliographies.[25] The correspondence of the Jew Tobias, a commander of a cleruchy, with the Hellenistic authorities was in excellent Hellenic. His grandsons were sent to famous Hellenic schools, and they and their sons made up the hard core of those Jews who applied to the king of Antioch for permission to make Jerusalem a Hellenistic city and grant Hellenic citizenship to Jews who met the necessary requirements—a move that finally led to the Maccabean revolt.[26]

The great number of Jews bearing Hellenic names is another indicator of how deeply Hellenism had influenced the Jews.[27]

Finally, the Hellenic language made deep inroads into the languages used by the Jews. Jewish rabbis strew their teaching with innumerable

---

20. Ibid., 1:58.

21. A few are written in Egyptian demotic but none in Aramaic; ibid., 1:58.

22. Ibid., 1:58. See also, 2:42nn4 and 5 for references.

23. See the long presentation of evidence in, e.g., Hengel, *Judaism and Hellenism*, particularly 1:58–106; Sevenster, *Do You Know Greek?* passim; and Schürer, *History of the Jewish People*, as above.

24. E.g., *history*: Demetrios, Eupolemos, Aristeas the Exegete, Jason of Cyrene, Thallos, Josephos, Justus of Tiberias, Philon the Elder, Theophilos; *historical romance*: Artapanos, Kleodemos; *romance*: Joseph and Aseneth; *epic poetry*: Philon the Epic Poet, Theodotos, Ezekiel the Tragedian; *philosophy*: Aristoboulos and Philon Judaeus. The above are only a few of the authors discussed in Schürer, to whom must be added the Septuagint as well as various apocryphal and pseudepigraphic writings. Finally, there are also many Jewish writings under Gentile pseudonyms, e.g., *Letter of Aristeas, Sibylline Oracles*, Pseudo-Hekateus, Pseudo-Phokylides, etc.

25. Schürer, *History of the Jewish People*, 3:1, 470–700.

26. Cf. Hengel, *Judaism and Hellenism*, 1:59. See especially 1 Macc 1:11–15.

27. Ibid., 1:61–65.

Hellenic words, which found their way into the Mishnah and the later Talmuds.[28] L. H. Feldman actually computes these loans to be as many as 1,500 terms.[29]

In this brief account it is impossible to discuss all the evidence for the Hellenization of Palestine and of the Jews in particular. But such evidence can be found in greater abundance in the literature referred to. Even though the Maccabean revolt and the ensuing Jewish rule over parts of Palestine checked to a certain extent many of what Hasidic Jews considered the most provocative elements of Hellenism, the Hellenization process was not totally canceled. The Maccabean rulers themselves and their successors continued to use the Hellenic language; King Herod took great pleasure in beautifying cities and towns in Palestine with Hellenic architectural styles, and he did this even in the buildings around the temple within the temple precinct! Indeed, at this time we have to deal with what Hengel calls *interpretatio graeca*, that is, interpreting things Jewish from a Hellenic perspective.

In sum, it is impossible to learn a language without at the same time becoming imbued at least with some of the content of the language: the thought patterns, the concepts, the subject matter relevant to the language. When, therefore, the peoples of the Near East, including the Jews, submitted themselves to the Hellenization process, they at the same time adopted the outlook and worldview of the Hellenes. The Jews did not merely learn to make Hellenic sentences; they learned to write literary works, to philosophize, to discuss and argue in the Hellenic way. This is how they came to share the Hellenic worldview. And this Hellenic worldview became the possession of even the simple people, much in the way that ordinary people today, although lacking qualified knowledge in the various departments of science, are nevertheless aware in a popular way of the progress in scientific discoveries, outlook, and thinking.

Areas Affected by the Hellenic Worldview

The Hellenic worldview affected all departments of life, public as well as individual. Consequently, a proper discussion of this worldview should cover the various expressions of the human soul and mind.

The establishment of democracy was a basic presupposition. It formed the matrix within which the new developments could find their place. Thus, our inquiry, ideally, ought to address philosophical, ethical, existential,

---

28. See Schürer, *History of the Jewish People*, esp. 2:52–80.

29. Feldman, *Josephus*, 9:527, n. g., and reference to Lieberman, *Greek in Jewish Palestine*, esp. 1–57.

social, and scientific questions. How did the Hellen apprehend existence, the world around him, and his particular place in the universe? Then, again, what meaning did this life have for him, and what happened at death and after death? What was his reaction to psychological as well as natural phenomena?

This investigation could go on to discuss and analyze the various philosophers and their teachings. These were the first true scientists. They observed and described natural phenomena. They formed hypotheses and theories and tested them to the extent that it was feasible. In addition, the study should include not least the empirical scientists during classical and postclassical times and their many discoveries as well as contributions to thought and technology that they left to posterity.

Such a task would necessitate a whole volume.[30] Within the limits available to me here, I can only offer a bare summary of Hellenic science.

Even though we know of thousands of ancient authors, their works are preserved very imperfectly, and in most cases extremely fragmentarily. Most of their technological discoveries are lost to us. This is superbly exemplified by the astounding Antikythera mechanism, of which we knew nothing until a century or so ago.

In the following brief discussion, I intend to take up a few highlights in the teaching of some philosophers/scientists concerning the universe, the earth, and *materia* with a few examples from the area of medicine. In the final section, I shall endeavor to discuss some NT passages in the light of these positions.

The Hellenic Worldview

The Universe

The *Aufklärung*, as M. P. Nilsson expressed it, that was initiated by the philosophers from the sixth century BC onward wrought deep changes

---

30. Those who would like to follow a connected account of the teachings of the main philosophers are referred to the recent book by G. E. R. Lloyd, *Greek Science* (London, 2012). In spite of the great service Lloyd has done us, his book fails to satisfy entirely, because he compares the various scientists not with what was there before them, to indicate the difference each made, but often with modern positions, which invariably turn out to the disadvantage of the scientists he discusses. Moreover, he often emphasizes their mistaken positions. This approach I deem to be historically incorrect, not least because all modern scientists have put forward mistaken positions, but because what always counts are not the mistakes, but the correct hypotheses.

in the outlook of the Hellenes.[31] That the universe did not consist of three flat disks, as was believed earlier in Mesopotamia and Egypt, but was conceived as spherical, full of spheres, some fixed and others in motion, was a widespread position that began already in preclassical times.[32] Thales of Miletos (fl. 600 BC), the earliest recorded philosopher/scientist, believed in a spherical universe.[33] On that basis, he was able to predict an eclipse of the sun, which, according to modern science, took place on May 28, 585 BC.[34] Such a fete presupposes extraordinary insights into planetary movements and precise mathematical calculations. His slightly younger compatriot Anaximandros (b. 610 BC) regarded the earth as a sphere[35] and the sun as a pure fire,[36] while the Pythagorean school (from the sixth century BC on) taught that not only the earth but all heavenly bodies were spheres.[37] Aristoteles[38] and Platon (429–347 BC),[39] like Thales and Anaximandros, taught that the universe was spherical. In fact, Anaximandros actually constructed a globe to aid him in teaching.[40]

The revolution of the earth around a central fire (i.e., the sun) appears to have been a fairly early position. For example, Aristoteles (384–322 BC) informs us that many philosophers/scientists up to his time, particularly the Pythagoreans (fifth century BC), placed the fireball (i.e., the sun) rather than the earth at the center (that is, as stationary), around which the earth revolved.[41]

One of the philosophers/scientists who taught that the earth revolved around its axis was the Pythagorean Hiketas (fifth–fourth century BC) of

---

31. On this, see Caragounis, "Greek Culture and Jewish Piety," esp. 295.

32. Liritsis and Coucouzeli, "Ancient Greek Heliocentric Views," 39–49, go so far as to actually argue for belief in a spherical universe already in Mycenaean times through hints in the Orphic fragments (whose dates are, however, uncertain).

33. According to Aëtios (second century AD), Περὶ ἀρεσκόντων ξυναγωγή, 340, 11–19. Cf. also, Platon, *Timaios* 31–34.

34. Thales, frg. 2.10: 5.1: τὴν γενομένην ἔκλειψιν τοῦ ἡλίου προειπεῖν φησι, . . . βασιλεύοντος Κυαξάρους . . . Μήδων, Ἀλυάττου δὲ τοῦ Κροίσου Λυδῶν.

35. Anaximandros, frg. 1.1 (= Diogenes Laertius 2a1-2): τὴν γῆν . . . οὖσαν σφαιροειδῆ.

36. Anaximandros, frg. 1.1: τὸν ἥλιον . . . καθαρώτατον πῦρ.

37. See, e.g., Aristoteles, *On the Heavens* 293a20ff.; 293b16ff.; 293b33–34.

38. See Aristoteles, *On the Heavens* 2.4: σχῆμα δ' ἀνάγκην σφαιροειδὲς ἔχειν τὸν οὐρανόν.

39. See Platon, *Phaidon* 110b, and Proklos, *In Platonis Timeaum* 3.141.22.

40. See Anaximandros, frg. 1.2: καὶ σφαῖραν κατεσκεύασε.

41. Aristoteles, *On the Heavens* 2.13 (= 293a20ff.). Cf. also, Platon, *Timaios* 40b: γῆν . . . ἰλλομένην δὲ τὴν περὶ τὸν παντὸς πόλον τεταμένον.

Syracuse,⁴² and possibly his compatriot Ekphantos. Going further, Herakleides (c. 390-310 BC) of Pontos specified that the earth's revolution about its axis took twenty-four hours;⁴³ the sun was stationary.⁴⁴

In spite of the often fragmentary nature of our sources, sufficient evidence has been preserved for us to form not merely a plausible but a well-founded opinion. For example, Philolaos (470-390 BC) was one of the first to make the earth a planet, orbiting the central fire.⁴⁵ Herakleides of Pontos not only believed the earth to be turning around its axis, but may also have been the first to hold the heliocentric view, that is, that the earth revolves around the sun.⁴⁶

If there is any doubt about Herakleides being the first propounder of the heliocentric view, there can be no doubt that Aristarchos of Samos (310-230 BC) held the view. In his work *Psammites* 1.4-7, the renowned mathematician and scientist Archimedes of Syracuse (c. 287-212/211 BC), writing in his Doric dialect, presents Aristarchos's hypothesis thus: Ὑποτίθεται γὰρ τὰ μὲν ἀπλανέα τῶν ἄστρων καὶ τὸν ἅλιον [= ἥλιον] μένειν ἀκίνητον, τὰν δὲ γᾶν [= τὴν δὲ γῆν] περιφέρεσθαι περὶ τὸν ἅλιον κατὰ κύκλου περιφέρειαν, ὅς ἐστιν ἐν μέσῳ τῷ δρόμῳ κείμενος.⁴⁷ Aristarchos maintained that the earth made one revolution around the sun each year, as did the other planets.

It may sound surprising that Aristarchos's revolutionary theory was not better preserved or that others, who preceded or followed him, have not left behind them any traces. From Aristoteles's information (*On the Heavens*, e.g., 2.13 [293a-296a]), we know that many other philosophers/scientists held similar views. Why, then, are they not mentioned by name and their writings not preserved? There are excellent reasons for this. The geocentric view went hand in hand with very old and sacred traditions.

42. Hiketas, frg. 1: "quae cum circum axem se summa celeritate convertat et torqueat, eadem effici omnia quae si stante terra caelum moveretur."

43. Herakleides, frg. 108: τῆς δὲ γῆς ... ἀπὸ δυσμῶν κινουμένης ἑκάστης ἡμέρας μίαν ἔγγιστα περιστροφήν. See Gottschalk, *Heracleides of Pontus*, passim; Guthrie, *History of Greek Philosophy*, 5:484.

44. Herakleides, frg. 110: ὅτι καὶ κινουμένης πως τῆς γῆς, τοῦ δὲ ἡλίου μένοντός πως.

45. Philolaos, frg. 21 (Aëtios 3.13.1-2): οἱ μὲν ἄλλοι μένειν τὴν γῆν· Φιλόλαος δὲ ὁ Πυθαγόρειος κύκλωι περιφέρεσθαι περὶ τὸ πῦρ. See also *Oxford Classical Dictionary*, 3rd ed., 1166, and Guthrie, *History of Greek Philosophy*, 1:285-86.

46. Cf. Herakleides, frg. 110: κινουμένης ... τῆς γῆς τοῦ δὲ ἡλίου μένοντός. There has been a lot of debate on this, for which, see Guthrie, *History of Greek Philosophy*, 5:485n1.

47. "[Aristarchos's] hypothesis is that the fixed stars and the sun remain unmoved and that the earth revolves around the sun in the circumference of a circle, with the sun lying in the middle of the orbit."

These could not be violated with impunity. Moreover, the geocentric view seemed to better explain the phenomena, that is, as things appeared to the ordinary observer: for example, the sun *rose up* in the morning, during the day *moved westward,* and in the evening *went down.* The heliocentric view, on the other hand, could not explain the phenomena, since no one had reason to think that the earth moved. In fact, a special phrase was created: "saving the phenomena" (σώζειν τὰ φαινόμενα), that is, "explaining the phenomena."[48] Thus, philosophers and astronomers who brought untraditional teachings to the Athenians, contrary to received hollowed traditions, were often prosecuted or condemned to death for impiety. As examples, I may mention: Anaxagoras (in 432 BC, saved by Perikles);[49] Protagoras (in 416 BC);[50] Sokrates (in 399 BC);[51] Aristoteles (in 323 BC);[52] Diagoras of Melos (fifth-fourth century BC);[53] Theodoros of Kyrene (340-250 BC?);[54] Theophrastos (in 316 BC);[55] and finally Aristarchos of Samos.[56]

The fear of prosecution would seem to explain why heliocentric scientists were careful in propagating this view or why their writings were not more numerous or better preserved. In addition, Aristoteles's taking sides for the geocentric view, adding to it his enormous authority, seemed to have decided the issue. At all events, it appears from various sources that the advocates of the heliocentric view were not few. Accordingly, to self-complacently dismiss ancient man as crudely holding to the geocentric view without mentioning the advocates of the heliocentric view and without any qualifications, is to misrepresent the historical facts.

---

48. This expression is older than Ploutarchos (*pace* Liritsis and Coucouzeli, "Ancient Greek Heliocentric Views," 45). It is found already in, e.g., Eudemos (fourth century BC) and Herakleides of Pontos (390-310 BC). Liritsis and Coucouzeli give sufficient evidence for the fact of prosecution on account of ἀσέβεια (see 42-45).

49. Ploutarchos, *Perikles* 32.

50. Diogenes Laertius 9.54; Philostratos, *Lives of the Sophists* 1.10.3 (494), whose books, according to Eusebios, *Praeparatio evangelica* 14.19.10, were publicly burned (but see Platon, *Menon* 91e)!

51. See, e.g., Platon *Apology,* passim, and *Phaidon,* passim.

52. Diogenes Laertius 5.5; *Anthologia Palatina* 3.48 (= *Anthologia Graeca* 7.107).

53. Diodoros Sikolos 13.6.7: Τούτων δὲ πραττομένων Διαγόρας ὁ κληθεὶς ἄθεος, διαβολῆς τυχὼν ἐπ' ἀσεβείᾳ καὶ φοβηθεὶς τὸν δῆμον, ἔφυγεν ἐκ τῆς 'Αττικῆς· οἱ δ' 'Αθηναῖοι τῷ ἀνελόντι Διαγόραν ἀργυρίου τάλαντον ἐπεκήρυξαν.

54. He was actually surnamed the Atheist.

55. Diogenes Laertius 5.36 (indited but freed).

56. Ploutarchos, *On the Face of the Moon* 6.923a. On such charges, see Caragounis, "Greek Culture and Jewish Piety," 290-91; Liritsis and Coucouzeli, "Ancient Greek Heliocentric Views," 42-44; and Lloyd, *Greek Science,* 191. On atheism in general, see Drachmann, *Atheisme i den Antike Hedenskab.*

And thus, it is generally thought today that Nicolas Copernicus is the founder of the heliocentric view. It is not generally known, however, that Copernicus was a prolific reader of ancient Hellenic literature, which in his day, thanks to the art of printing, was becoming increasingly available. There is evidence that Copernicus had read Aristarchos and, accepting his theory, first thought of crediting it to him, but later decided to remove the reference to Aristarchos and take the credit to himself.[57] But enough of this.

In the second century BC, Hipparchos established mathematical astronomy and applied trigonometry, and improved and invented a number of astronomical instruments.[58] Although he taught that the earth rotated around its axis, he seems to have held the geocentric view. Studying a lunar eclipse, he calculated the distance of the moon from the earth as fifty-nine times the length of the earth's radius (i.e., 6,371 km x 59 = 375,889 km). The figure accepted as correct today is roughly sixty times (i.e., 384,400 km). He reckoned the moon's diameter to be one-fourth that of the earth. The correct figures today are, for the earth, 12.742 kilometers, and for the moon, 3,474 kilometers. Moreover, he mapped 1,080 starts, an enterprise that led to his discovery of the precession of the equinoxes. This meant that there was a certain wobbling in the orientation of the rotation of the earth's axis, which required 25,772 years for the earth's return to the same point.[59] Further, Hipparchos refined the length of the solar year from 365 days and 6 hours, as was reckoned by his predecessors, to 365 days, 5 hours, and 55 minutes. The correct figure today is 365 days, 5 hours, 48 minutes, and 6 seconds. Thus, Hipparchos's calculation of the duration of the year was less than 7 minutes off the value accepted today! His "calculation of a 'great year' gives for the mean lunar month a figure differing by less than one second from

---

57. E. M. Antoniadis, one of the directors of the British Astronomical Society ("Copernicus," in Μεγάλη Ἑλληνικὴ Ἐγκυκλοπαίδεια, 24 + 4 vols. [1926–1963; 2nd ed. 1956], 14:849), after presenting a long list of early Hellenic scientific positions, which Copernicus adopted without acknowledgment, points out that also with respect to the heliocentric view, he deleted his original acknowledgment to Aristarchos: "credibile est hisce similibusque causis Philolaum mobilitatem terrae sensisse, quod etiam nonnulli Aristarchum Samium ferunt in eadem fuisse sententia." Similarly, J. Mau, in *Der Kleine Pauly*, 1:553, is conscious of this: "Copernicus (*De rev. cael.* ed. Thorum, 1873, 34, Anm., auch S. 30 ZELLER) nennt ihm als Zeugen, strich den Passus jedoch vor der Drucklegung."

58. Ptolemaios, *Syntaxis mathematike* (= *Almagest*) 5.4; Proklos, *Outline of the Astronomical Hypotheses* 4; Pliny, *Natural History* 2.24.95.

59. Cf. Hipparchos, Περὶ τῆς μεταπτώσεως τῶν τροπικῶν καὶ ἰσημερινῶν σημείων, cited by Ptolemaios, *Syntaxis mathematike* 7.2 (1.2.13). See also, Lloyd, *Greek Science*, 202ff., who gives the figure as circa 26,000 years.

the present accepted value"![60] There can be no doubt here, that in spite of the prevailing geocentric view, astronomy was far advanced.[61]

Hipparchos's work was utilized with great appreciation by Ptolemaios (*Syntaxis mathematike* or *Almagest*), whose work became the definitive view down to Copernicus and Galileo.

Among astronomical instruments, a place of pride must now be assigned to the Antikythera mechanism, discovered in 1900-1901. This complex instrument, to which many international scientists have devoted their skills in the past few decades, has been hailed as "an ancient analog computer designed to calculate astronomical positions."[62]

That the moon had no light of its own but reflected that of the sun was probably first put forward by Anaximandros (610/609-547/46 BC),[63] or Anaximenes (585-525 BC),[64] or at the latest by Anaxagoras (500-428 BC),[65] and was held all down the line to Aristarchos.[66]

The Earth

Already by the sixth century BC, the earth was conceived of as a sphere (e.g., by Anaximandros and the Pythagoreans). It was divided into latitudes and longitudes (Aristoteles, Dichaiarchos, Eratosthenes). The last named, one of the directors of the Alexandrian library, divided the earth into two hemispheres. Hipparchos, presumably following Babylonian number leads,

---

60. *Oxford Classical Dictionary*, 1st ed., 429.

61. The above information of Hipparchos's work is based on Ptolemaios's frequent citations of Hipparchos, in his *Syntaxis mathematike*.

62. See "Antikythera Mechanism" in Wikipedia. Prof M. Edmunds of Cardiff University, one of the scientists who investigated the mechanism, writes: "This device is just extraordinary, the only thing of its kind. The design is beautiful; the astronomy is exactly right. The way the mechanics are designed just make your jaw drop. Whoever has done this has done it extremely carefully" ("Mysteries of Computer from 65 B.C. Are Solved").

63. E.g., Anaximandros, frg. 1 (= Diogenes Laertius 2.1): τήν τε σελήνην ψευδοφαῆ καὶ ἀπὸ ἡλίου φωτίζεσθαι. The same view is ascribed to Parmenides (c. 500 BC) in frg. 42: καὶ γὰρ ἀπ' αὐτοῦ [sc. τοῦ ἡλίου] φωτίζεται, and even to Thales (frg. 17): Θαλῆς πρῶτος ἔφη ὑπὸ τοῦ ἡλίου φωτίζεσθαι. Πυθαγόρας, Παρμενίδης ὁμοίως, but this is doubted by modern scholars.

64. Anaximenes, frg. 16 (= Theon Smyrnaios 198.14): Ἀναξιμένης δὲ ὅτι ἡ σελήνη ἐκ τοῦ ἡλίου ἔχει τὸ φῶς.

65. Cf. Platon, *Kratylos* 409a: ὅτι ἡ σελήνη ἀπὸ τοῦ ἡλίου ἔχει τὸ φῶς.

66. Aristarchos, *The Magnitude and Distances of the Sun and the Moon* 1: τὴν σελήνην παρὰ τοῦ ἡλίου τὸ φῶς λαμβάνειν.

divided the longitudes (or meridians) into 360 degrees and each degree into sixty minutes and each minute into sixty seconds.

To Eratosthenes goes the honor of having accurately calculated the circumference of the earth. On hearing that in the summer solstice the sun cast no shadow from a perpendicular gnomon in Aswan, Upper Egypt, which he reckoned to be 5,000 stadia from Alexandria, he discovered that in Alexandria the rays of the sun had an angle of 7 degrees 12 minutes. This was one-fiftieth of the circle (360 degrees) and gave 50 x 5,000 = 250,000 stadia. The length of the stadium differed from one Hellenic state to another, but if we assume 10 stadia per mile, then 250,000 stadia equals 40.233 kilometers. The figure for the earth's circumference today is 40.072 kilometers!

Eratosthenes's work is lost, but we are indebted to Strabon's *Geography* for summaries of it. Strabon described Europe, Asia, and Africa. This work was extended by Ptolemaios, who made ten maps for Europe, twelve for Asia, and four for Africa.

Materia

Hellenic philosophers/scientists made it their life's interest to investigate the world around them, to ask for rational answers about its origin, its parts, as well as the purpose of life. These philosophers were at the same time scientists and theologians.

Thus, in their effort to explain matter, Leukippos (fifth century BC)[67] and particularly his pupil Demokritos (b. 460 BC)[68] taught that all matter, including the bodies of men and beasts, are composed of atoms. The word "atom" means "indivisible" or "uncuttable," and denotes the smallest possible particle. The atoms move within a vacuum, in comparison with which their size is infinitesimal. The atoms are invisible, and have various sizes, shapes, and weights.

These insights into the nature and composition of things led these atomic philosophers to postulate an evolution of worlds that exhibited an increasing complexity in organization. This complexity was to be found also in human cultures.

---

67. On Leukippos, see Diogenes Laertius 9.6; Diels and Kranz, *Fragmente der Vorsokratiker*, no. 67; and Guthrie, *History of Greek Philosophy*, 2:383–86.

68. On Demokritos, see Diogenes Laertius; Diels and Kranz, *Fragmente der Vorsokratiker*, no. 68. Demokritos's teaching is found in fragments preserved by various authors, comprising circa 150 pages. See also Guthrie, *History of Greek Philosophy*, 2:386–89, and on the atomic theory of Leukippos and esp. Demokritos, 389–507.

Teachings like these, though far short of present-day positions (to take an example, the atom is split), must be deemed quite advanced. This shows that the worldview current in NT times was far different from the primitive outlook that had often been assumed for the NT.

Medicine

In that there is a medical doctor among the NT authors, it would not be out of place to include a few words on the state of the medical sciences at the time of the NT.

Even though Hippokrates is regarded as the father of medical science, medicine had a long history in Hellas before him. While all the writings ascribed to Hippokrates are not accepted as genuine today, there can be no doubt that he had a truly scientific approach in his varied work: natural causation; observation and diagnosis; the application of medicine, diet, and climate; and not least, the importance of the organism in the healing process. The famous Hippocratic code urges an elevated ethical and professional approach and values. His research was taken further by his professional successors, so that by the first century AD medicine was a highly developed science.

Herophilos was the first scientist to dissect human bodies rather than merely animals, as had been done up to his time. He composed a manual of anatomy. His work on the parts and functions of the human body was momentous; he discovered the nervous system and its sensor and motor functions, as well as the brain as the faculty of thinking; he accurately described the eye and the genitals; and he discovered the pulse.[69]

Erasistratos (early third century BC) contributed to physiology, pathology, and pathological anatomy. He also described the heart chambers (the circulation of the blood was known long before) and held that the body was composed of atoms moving in a vacuum.[70]

Soranos (first–second century AD), the famous gynecologist, concentrated on gynecology and obstetrics.

Surgery was also greatly advanced. For example, Archigenes (first–second century AD) worked with amputations; Hegetor (second century BC) specialized on hip operations.[71] Skull operations were carried out by,

---

69. On Herophilos, see von Staden, *Herophilus*.

70. On Erasistratos, see the fragments (from various sources) collected under his name in *TLG*, making up some 100 pages. See also Lloyd, *Greek Science*, e.g., 213–22.

71. On Hegetor, see von Staden, *From Andreas to Demosthenes Philalethes*.

for example, Heliodoros (first-second century AD), while Antillos (second century AD) performed eye cataract operations.[72]

The Roman Aulus Cornelius Celsus (fl. first century AD) wrote an encyclopedic work, of which only *De Medicine* survives.[73] In this he summarizes Hellenic medicine, taking up, for instance, operations for goiter, stones in the bladder, and perhaps tonsils; facial operations; and dentistry.

The last of the most important physicians in antiquity, Galenos of Pergamos (AD 129-199), is attributed an enormous number of writings, which deal with practically every conceivable aspect of medicine.[74] Galenos was the private doctor of Marcus Aurelius and the incomparable physician of his day, who added his own researches to the earlier medicine. As was the case with Ptolemaios's astronomy and geography, Galenos's medicine became standard for Europe until the close of the Middle Ages.

It is difficult to sufficiently emphasize the immense advances of modern science over the state of research in antiquity in the areas that have occupied us in this study: astronomy, geography, physics, medicine, etc. This fact, however, does not predicate as irrelevant or primitive the achievements of ancient scientists. It is also a fact that in no area of research have modern scientists started from scratch. In each discipline they have built on Hellenic science. This alone shows that the worldview current when Christianity was born was a truly scientific worldview, just as there is no doubt that today's view is scientific, although we know—from past experience—that our worldview a hundred years from now will be appreciably different from what it is today.

The Hellenic Worldview and the New Testament Authors

The NT does not contain any detailed indications that might be compared with the Hellenic worldview discussed above. The few statements that have often been interpreted as divulging the ancient Mesopotamian view, that is, Phil 2:11: ἐπουρανίων καὶ ἐπιγείων καὶ καταχθονίων, as well as John 8:23: ὑμεῖς ἐκ τῶν κάτω ἐστέ, ἐγὼ ἐκ τῶν ἄνω εἰμί, simply present matters as we would today in nontechnical writing. They are "saving the phenomena" in precisely the same way as we speak today of the sun *rising up* or *going down*,

---

72. Of Antillos, only a brief text survives. On his work and that of Heliodoros, see *Oxford Classical Dictionary*, 3rd ed., "surgery," 1457-58.

73. See Marx, *Cornelii Celsiquae supersunt*.

74. Only a third of Galenos's medical writings survive, comprising twenty-two volumes and containing 3 million words, published by Kühn, *Claudii Galeni opera omnia*.

instead of specifying how many degrees the earth has rotated on its axis. This "saving the phenomena" has been the practice of man throughout history. Thus, to explain such statements as evidence that the NT authors held to old, outmoded views about the world is quite simplistic and uninformed.

However, there is one piece of information in the NT that betrays the NT authors' awareness of Hellenic scientific astronomy.

We saw above that the fact that the moon derives its light from the sun was well known, if not already in the sixth century BC, then at least by the fifth century. Matthew and Mark provide a rare glimpse into this question. At Matthew 24:29 and Mark 13:24, the Evangelists quote the OT. The OT text that comes closest is Isaiah 13:10: חָשַׁךְ הַשֶּׁמֶשׁ בְּצֵאתוֹ וְיָרֵחַ לֹא־יַגִּיהַּ אוֹרוֹ, "The sun will be darkened and the moon shall not give its light."

Ezekiel 32:7 is also fairly close: שֶׁמֶשׁ בְּעָנָן אֲכַסֶּנּוּ וְיָרֵחַ לֹא־יָאִיר אוֹרוֹ, "I will cover the sun with a cloud and the moon shall not give its light."

Although the English renderings of the above texts use the same wording, the Hebrew texts use two different verbs: the hiphil of the verb נגה ("to shine," "to illuminate") and the hiphil of the verb אור ("to give light," "to shine," respectively). The LXX translates the Isaiah passage with καὶ σκοτισθήσεται τοῦ ἡλίου ἀνατέλλοντος, καὶ ἡ σελήνη οὐ δώσει τὸ φῶς αὐτῆς, and the Ezekiel passage with ἥλιον ἐν νεφέλῃ καλύψω, καὶ σελήνη οὐ μὴ φάνῃ τὸ φῶς αὐτῆς.

What in the Hebrew and the LXX text may be only implicit, becomes quite explicit in Matthew and Mark: ὁ ἥλιος σκοτισθήσεται, καὶ ἡ σελήνη οὐ δώσει τὸ φέγγος αὐτῆς. The LXX translates the Isaiah text with οὐ δώσει τὸ φῶς αὐτῆς ("shall not give its light") and the Ezekiel text with οὐ μὴ φάνῃ τὸ φῶς αὐτῆς ("shall not [let] shine its light"). Thus, in both texts the LXX, as does also the Hebrew, uses the ordinary Hellenic word for light: φῶς. Matthew and Mark, on the other hand, when quoting (freely) the LXX OT texts, both of which use φῶς, exchange the LXX word φῶς for φέγγος.

The word φέγγος has been used in Hellenic from Homeros to the present day. Its meaning is "light," "shine," "reflection." Both φῶς and φέγγος can in certain contexts be used with the sense of "light," though there is a difference between the kind of light that each word denotes. Ever since Platon's time, the word φέγγος has been used especially of the moonlight as opposed to the daylight.[75] The φέγγος is a weak light, which is quite appropriate in describing the reflected light of the moon, rather than the strong, direct light of the sun.

---

75. Platon, *Republic* 508c: τὸ ἡμερινὸν φῶς . . . νυκτερινὰ φέγγη ("the light of the day . . . the shine of the night").

In due time the word φέγγος gave us the diminutive form φεγγάρι[ον]. This word has been used since Byzantine times, all the way to the neo-Hellenic, with the meaning of "moon" and its reflected light!

From the above discussion, it must be obvious that the NT authors in this text reflect the knowledge that the moon derived its light from the sun. That is why they modified the LXX expression, to give a more qualified and exact description of the relation of the moon to the sun. Accordingly, when the sun is darkened, a natural and necessary consequence is that the moon ceases to shine its φέγγος—its reflected light.

The connection between the writings of Luke and Hellenic medical science is evidenced also in the medical vocabulary Luke uses. Thus, for example, Luke 4:38 uses the technical ἦν συνεχομένη πυρετῷ μεγάλῳ in place of the nontechnical expressions in Matthew (βεβλημένην καὶ πυρέσσουσαν) and Mark (κατέκειτο πυρέσσουσα). Though the verb συνέχω occurs often in nontechnical writing, it also occurs frequently in the *medicus* Galenos in the technical medical sense, as in Luke.[76]

As for Luke 13:11-13, although the verb συγκύπτω occurs in non-medical senses, the verb ἀνακύπτω occurs repeatedly in Galenos and other medical writers in the technical medical sense.[77] In Luke 14:2 the condition of "dropsy" is expressed by ὑδρωπικός. This term is very infrequent in ancient literature, but occurs regularly in medical contexts.[78] In other words, the term belonged to the medical vocabulary.

Acts 3:7 relates the story of the cripple sitting at the Beautiful Gate of Jerusalem, whose βάσεις and σφυρά[79] were made firm and he could stand. The term σφυρά was a technical term for "ankles," while the unusual word in this connection, βάσεις, is often used in medical contexts for "feet," as in the Acts passage.[80]

Finally, in Acts 28:8 Poplios's father is said to suffer from πυρετοῖς and δυσεντερίῳ. The plural πυρετοῖς belonged to the medical jargon of the times,

---

76. E.g., Galenos, *Anatomicis administrationibus* 2.221; *De usu partium* 3.56; *De compositione medicamentorum* 7.525.

77. Galenos, 4.80 (2x); 6.147; Oribasios, *Collection* 6.14; 48.8; 74.2; Aëtios, 5.11; 5.12; 12.1; 12.70; etc.

78. E.g., Hippokrates, *Epidemiai* 5.1.106; 7.1.20 (2x); 7.1.21; Physiologos (second-fourth century AD), 46.2.

79. Some of the older MSS have the nonstandard form σφυδρά, which is preferred in NA.

80. For σφυρά, see Hippokrates, *De officina medici* 12.20; *De fracturis* 11.15; *De articulis* 68.9; Aristoteles, *Physiognomonica* 810a24: Galenos, *De curandi ratione per venae sectionem* 11.303; etc. For βάσεις, see Galenos, *Anatomicis administrationibus* 2.641; *De usu partium* 4.307; Soranos, *Gynaeciorum* 3.17.4; *De morborum differentis* 6.856; etc.

indicating the recurrent onslaught of fever, while δυσεντέριον was an acute, contagious disease accompanied by painful bloody diarrhea, caused by ulcerous damage of the intestinal mucous mebrane, and was regularly used as a technical medical term.[81]

From these few examples, it becomes obvious that NT authors were acquainted with the scientific progress of the times, and that interpreting their various statements in the light of ancient Near Eastern cosmogony and *Weltanschauung* reveals lack of acquaintance with the true historical facts.

Bibliography

Texts

Aëtios. Περὶ ἀρεσκόντων ξυναγωγή.
Anaximandros. Fragments.
Anthologia Palatina (=*Anthologia Graeca*).
Appian. *Syria*.
Aristarchos. *The Magnitude and Distances of the Sun and the Moon*.
Aristoteles. *On the Heavens*.
———. *Physiognomonica*.
Aulus Cornelius Celsus. *De Medicine*.
Diodoros Sik.
Diogenes Laertius. *Lives of Philosophers*.
Erasistratos. Fragments.
Eusebios. *Praeparatio evangelica*.
Galenos. *Anatomicis administrationibus*.
———. *De compositione medicamentorum*.
———. *De curandi ratione per venae sectionem*.
———. *De usu partium*.
Hegetor. Fragments.
Herakleides. Fragments.
Heliodoros.
Herophilos. Fragments.
Hesiodos. *Theogonia*.
Hiketas. Fragments.
Hipparchos. Περὶ τῆς μεταπτώσεως τῶν τροπικῶν καὶ ἰσημερινῶν σημείων.
Hippokrates. *De articulis*.
———. *Epidemiai*.
———. *De fracturis*.
———. *De officina medici*.
Homeros. *Ilias*.
———. *Odysseia*.
Josephos. *Antiqvitates*.
———. *Bellum*.

---

81. See, e.g., the many occurrences in Hippokrates's and Galenos's works.

Letter of Aristeas.
Oribasios. Collection.
Parmenides. Fragments.
Philolaos. Fragments.
Philostratos. Lives of the Sophists.
Physiologos.
Pliny. Natural History.
Platon. Apology.
———. Kratylos.
———. Menon.
———. Phaidon.
———. Republic.
———. Timaios.
Ploutarchos. On the Face of the Moon.
———. Perikles.
Proklos. In Platonis Timeaum.
———. Outline of the Astronomical Hypotheses.
Pseudo-Hekataios.
Pseudo-Phokylides.
Ptolemaios. Syntaxis mathematike (= Almagest).
Sibylline Oracles.
Soranos. Gynaeciorum.
———. De morborum differentis.
Thales. Fragments.
Theon Smyrnaios. De utilitate mathematicae.

Literature

Antoniadis, E. M. "Κοπέρνικος." In Μεγάλη Ἑλληνικὴ Ἐγκυκλοπαίδεια, 24 + 4 vols. Athens, 1926–63.
Applebaum, S. Review of *Hellenistic Civilization and the Jews*, by V. Tcherikover. *Tarbiz* 28.3–4 (1958–59).
Barrett, C. K. *The Gospel according to St. John*. 2nd ed. Philadelphia: Westminster, 1978.
Bevan, E. R. *The House of Seleucus*. 2 vols. London: Arnold, 1902.
Beyerlin, W., ed. *Near Eastern Religious Texts Relating to the Old Testament*. Old Testament Library. Philadelphia: Westminster, 1978.
Caragounis, C. C. "Greek Culture and Jewish Piety: The Clash and the Fourth Beast of Daniel 7." *ETL* 65.4 (1989) 281–308.
Charles, R. H. *A Critical and Exegetical Commentary on the Revelation of St. John*. 2 vols. ICC. Edinburgh: T. & T. Clark, 1920.
Diels H., and W. Kranz. *Fragmente der Vorsokratiker*. 6th ed. 1952.
Drachmann, A. B. *Atheisme i den Antike Hedenskab*. Copenhagen: Universitetsbogtrykkeriet, 1919.
Edmunds, M. "Mysteries of Computer from 65 B.C. Are Solved." *Guardian*, November 30, 2006.
Feldman, L. H. *Josephus: Jewish Antiquities*. LCL. Cambridge: Harvard University Press, 1969.

Goldstein, J. *1 Maccabees*. Anchor Bible. Garden City, NY: Doubleday, 1977.
Gottschalk, H. B. *Heraclides of Pontus*. Oxford: Clarendon, 1980.
Guthrie, W. K. C. *History of Greek Philosophy*. 6 vols. Cambridge: Cambridge University Press, 1978–93.
Hawthorne, G. F. *Philippians*. WBC. Waco: Word, 1983.
Hengel, M. *Judaism and Hellenism*. 2 vols. London, 1974.
Ἱστορία τοῦ Ἑλληνικοῦ Ἔθνους. 16 vols. Athens, 1970–2000.
Kühn, C. G. *Claudii Galeni opera omnia*. Leipzig: Cnoblochii, 1821–33.
Lieberman, S. *Greek in Jewish Palestine*. New York: Jewish Theological Seminary of America, 1942.
Liritsis, I., and A. Coucouzeli. "Ancient Greek Heliocentric Views Hidden from Prevailing Beliefs." *Journal of Astronomical History and Heritage* 11.1 (2008) 39–49.
Lloyd, G. E. R. *Greek Science after Aristotle*. Ancient Culture and Society. London: Chatto & Windus, 2012.
Marx, F. *Cornelii Celsiquae supersunt*. 1915.
Mau, J. *Der Kleine Pauly*. 5 vols. Munich, 1979.
Oxford Classical Dictionary. 1st ed. Oxford: Clarendon, 1957.
Oxford Classical Dictionary. 3rd ed. Oxford: Clarendon, 1996.
Pritchard, J. B., ed. *Ancient Near Eastern Texts Relating to the Old Testament*. Princeton: Princeton University Press, 1969.
Schürer, Emil. *The History of the Jewish People in the Age of Jesus Christ (175 B.C.–A.D. 135)*. 4 vols. Edinburgh: T. & T. Clark, 1973–87.
Sevenster, J. N. *Do You Know Greek? How Much Greek Could the First Christians Have Known?* Leiden: Brill, 1968.
Tcherikover, V. *Hellenistic Civilization and the Jews*. Translated by S. Appelbaum. New York: Atheneum, 1975.
Thomas, D. W., ed. *Documents from Old Testament Times*. 1961. Reprinted, Ancient Texts and Translations. Eugene, OR: Wipf & Stock, 2006.
von Staden, H. *From Andreas to Demosthenes Philalethes*. 1995.
———. *Herophilus: The Art of Medicine in Early Alexandria*. Cambridge: Cambridge University Press, 2007.

5

The Relevance of Authorial Language, Style, and Usage in the Evaluation of Textual Variants in the Greek New Testament

—*J. Keith Elliott*

It is with great pleasure that I offer this small contribution to Professor James Voelz's Festschrift. I have known Jim for many years; we meet regularly at the annual meetings of the international professional New Testament society, Studiorum Novi Testamenti Societas (SNTS), and of the Society of Biblical Literature. It has also been my pleasure to be Jim's guest twice at his auld sod, Concordia Seminary in St. Louis. I well recall one occasion when he took my wife and me to the ballpark to watch a match (sorry, game) where the St. Louis Cardinals were playing the Arizona Diamondbacks, during which he attempted to explain to me the intricacies of the action, utilizing analogies from cricket!

My contribution concerns a number of textual variants in the manuscripts of the Greek New Testament where I have tried to resolve the differences using criteria based on the authors' styles and New Testament usage. These are criteria Jim himself applies, as we readily see in his recent commentary on Mark.[1] His commentary invests much space on features of Mark's distinctive and sophisticated use of language—vocabulary, word

---

1. Voelz, *Mark 1:1—8:26*; hereafter *Commentary*.

order, Semitisms—and his style. (In his judgment[2] the famous Codex Vaticanus [B 03] predominantly maintains these idiosyncratic or distinctively Markan features where textual variation occurs within the manuscript heritage.)

I have no hesitation using features such as these in the examples below written in his honor, even when he and I may sometimes choose to differ in our conclusions. I begin my selection of variants with Mark but then move on to show how my principles of textual criticism, often dubbed "thoroughgoing criticism," may be applied to the rest of the New Testament. We end with two general excursuses. But first, to Mark.

Mark

1:1-3

If we analyze the language and style of these verses, it soon becomes obvious that we are reading a piece of text that differs significantly from Mark 1:4—16:8, and soon may collect a greater number of features alien to the *echt* Mark than are located proportionately in the spurious longer ending (Mark 16:9-20). These include:

1. The names Ιησου Χριστου found joined only here.
2. ευαγγελιον, which occurs eight times in Mark (seven of which relate to Jesus' sayings); only here at 1:1 does it refer to messianic *action*. Αρχη is temporal elsewhere in Mark. It is not temporal in 1:1. Jim has a fascinating "take" on 1:1 in his commentary; he draws our attention to αρχη ευαγγελιου in Phil 4:15 ("when I started preaching"). According to him, here in 1:1 the "beginning (of the preaching)" is *John the Baptist's* teaching in 1:4-8.
3. καθως always follows a main clause in Mark proper (4:33; 9:13; 11:6; 14:16, 21; 15:8; 16:7), and it is improbable that it can refer here to the "title" (v. 1). Also, this is the only quotation in Mark prefaced by the words καθως γεγραμμενον. There are admittedly very few biblical citations in Mark, but those that we meet elsewhere in this Gospel occur within speech; this is the only one within the words of the narrator.
4. The composite quotation is made up of two elements. The two stages are most readily understandable only if the first three verses are seen as a later addition to Mark: (a) Isaiah 40:3 is taken from the Matthean

---

2. For example, on 25-26, 97.

parallel (Matt 3:3) and (b) the second part of the quotation comes from Q (= Luke 7:27, par. Matt 11:10) and applies to the Baptist. The attribution of all to Isaiah is then wrong, although pedantic scribes subsequently altered the attribution to "the prophets." On the normal assumption that 1:2–3 comes from Mark, one would have to say that, later, Matthew and Luke independently unraveled Mark's citations, putting one in a Markan context but the other, composite, citation into a Q context—and that seems unlikely.³

All these problems—and several more besides—make me conclude that Mark 1:1–3 was not written by Mark, and that these three verses should be relegated to the footnotes as a later, secondary, addition. Arguing for that position means we lose the original opening words of Mark, that is, everything prior to Mark 1:4, and I am aware that I am proposing as a reading an omission that belongs to that dangerous territory of "conjectural emendation."⁴ (We turn below at Rev 2:1ff. to other such emendations, that is, proposed readings lacking Greek manuscript support.)

1:4; 6:14, 24, 25; 8:28

What name does Mark give John the Baptist? Our editions usually call him βαπτίζων at Mark 6:14 (v.l.⁵ βαπτιστης D S W Θ) and 24 (v.l. βαπτιστου A C D W) but βαπτιστης at 6:25 as well as at 8:28. Variants exist at 6:25 giving a form of the participle (in L 700 892) and at 8:28 (in 28 565); these variants are ignored in the *apparatus* of NA28. Consulting the text of NA28, we may well ask why Mark changed the substantive in two contiguous verses (6:24–25). But thanks to the variants, we can restore a consistent usage throughout Mark.⁶ The newly coined Christian noun βαπτιστης is found in Matthew, in Luke, and in later writers. The earlier form, based on the verb βαπτιζω, should stand throughout Mark. The change to the name, albeit made erratically, comes from scribes encouraged by later and normal church usage.

Our decision here may help resolve the more important variations at Mark 1:4 where John, at first mention, may naturally be defined by his distinctively Markan name, ο βαπτίζων. If so, that would allow us to read

---

3. Against the normal arguments for Markan priority, Jim Voelz argues that Mark comes after Matthew and Luke, but it is not clear to me from his commentary at this point how he thinks Mark worked with his predecessors' quotations here.

4. See my article "Mark 1:1–3."

5. Here, and throughout, I use the standard abbreviations for *varia lectio* (v.l.) and *variae lectiones* (v.ll.).

6. Nestle²⁸ shows the *v.ll.* at 6:14, 24 but not at 6:25; 8:28!

εγενετο κηρυσσων with this name as its subject, giving us either a periphrastic "John the baptizing one was preaching . . ." or, probably better in this context, "John the baptizing one appeared, preaching . . ." (cf. Mark 9:7). The reading with the article should be accepted as the *Ausgangstext* (this is a recently coined jargon term meaning the initial text from which all subsequent text-critical changes derive); we also follow the reading of B 33 in omitting και before κηρυσσων. Jim Voelz removes ο but he allows και to remain within brackets, albeit with "some doubt" (according to his commentary, p. 26). If ο is omitted, Voelz claims that we have a predicative position participle and the meaning "baptizing," observing that in 1:5-8 John first baptizes and then he preaches; but if ο βαπτιζων is read, it is John's title. Then we have an attributive position participle followed by a predicative position participle (see *Commentary*, 100).

At Mark 6:25 Voelz does not accept *v.l.* βαπτιζων (see *Commentary*, 94n14: it is "likely" that the text reads βαπτιστης). Part 1 ends at 8:26, that is, two verses before the name recurs in verse 28.

1:27

How do we translate Mark 1:27, "What is this?" One way is with the answer following, "(It is) a new teaching(, one) with authority"; this is based on NA28 with ℵ B L 33. Not all manuscripts read that. Alternatively, is it: "What is this? Is it a new teaching (τις η διδαχη η καινη αυτη;), for he commands . . . ?," giving the explanation why the bystanders raise their questions? (Κατ' εξουσιαν would then belong with the explanation.) That reading, found in manuscripts C K Γ Maj, should be accepted here as the *Ausgangstext*. The distinctive Semitic word order, article + noun + article + adjective + demonstrative (not noted by Voelz here), is found in Mark 12:43 *v.l.* η χηρα η πτωχη αυτη, and see also Luke 21:23 *v.l.*; 27:24 *v.l.*; Acts 2:40; 6:13, 14; 21:28, and frequently in the LXX, and that usage should determine what is printed as the text at Mark 1:27. The use of οτι (= γαρ) is also common to Mark, and is another feature often avoided by scribes (see Mark 8:24 *v.l.* omit οτι); it also poses a double question, one introduced by τι, the other by τις—Mark's style has many such examples (2:7, 8-9; 4:13, 21, 40; 6:2; 7:18-19 etc.), although this feature is also not referred to at 1:27 by Voelz. All in all, the variant in C K Γ Maj commends itself.

6:22

There is a problem with the translation of Mark 6:22,[7] which can also be resolved by an appeal to the variants and a recognition of our author's usage. Is the dancing girl Herod's daughter,[8] or Herodias's daughter with the same name as the mother,[9] or an unnamed daughter of Herodias? If we follow A C K Θ reading θυγατρος αυτης Ηρωδιαδος, meaning not necessarily "the daughter of Herodias herself" but "her daughter, that is to say, Herodias's (daughter)," such a usage agrees with Markan style; Mark frequently inserts similar explanatory parentheses (e.g., at 2:10, 15, 21; 6: 14–15; 7:2, 3–4, 19, 26; 8:14; 13:14; 14:36). Scribal attempts to remove the parenthesis or to delete what may have been seen as a redundant pronoun were probably responsible for the other readings. Markan usage should be determinative: the girl is the anonymous daughter of Herodias.

10:1

Jim will be familiar with this example—I often use it! We read in NA28 that "crowds," not "a crowd," approach Jesus. That is a unique occurrence of the plural of this noun in Mark. But there is a variant (not included in NA28) giving the singular. We are looking not only at οχλος/οχλοι, either of which terms could have been written accidentally for the other by an inattentive scribe, but also at its associated verb. Rather, this is a *deliberate* change: συμπορευονται ... οχλοι read by ℵ B and συμπορευεται ... οχλος read by D Θ W fam.13 *pauci* Lvt aur k q. From what I observe, most commentaries on Mark fail to discuss this variant.[10] (I eagerly await Jim's notes on this verse when part 2 of his commentary appears—especially as B 03 reads the plural!) In looking for consistency, we see that οχλος (singular) occurs elsewhere about thirty-eight times in Mark, and nearly all of them are firmly established. In Luke, Acts, John, and Revelation the noun is also singular; in

---

7. This section and the one following (on Mark 10:1) were used in the main paper at the SNTS meeting in 2014 in Szeged, Hungary, and now has appeared in *NTS*, see "Using an Author's Consistency of Usage and Conjectures."

8. We discount Voelz's argument in his commentary that αυτου is the adverb meaning "just there," as at Matt 26:36; Luke 9:27; Acts 15:34 *v.l.*; 18:19; 21:4 and cf. Mark 6:33 *v.l.* in D 05 and 565.

9. As found, for example, in the apocryphal text *The Life and Martyrdom of John the Baptist*.

10. Vincent Taylor's *Gospel according to St. Mark* is a rare commentary to note *v.l.* singular, although he does not accept it as original. The *v.l.* is shown in Aland, *Synopsis*15. Heinrich Greeven and Eberhard Güting discuss it in their *Textkritik des Markusevangeliums*. G. D. Kilpatrick's *Mark* correctly has the singular as its text.

Matthew it is frequently plural (he has thirty plurals and twenty singulars, with *v.ll.* at Matt 8:18; 15:31). As an indication that there is no inherent difference in the meanings, we may see from our synopses that the singular at Mark 4:1*pr.* parallels the plural in Matthew 13:2; cf. similarly at Mark 3:9 // Matthew 12:15 plural and *v.l. om.*; Mark 5:24 // Luke 8:42 plural; Mark 5:31 // Luke 8:45 plural; etc.

I suggest we read the singular noun and verb at Mark 10:1 as being consistent with Mark elsewhere, and especially comparable with Mark 3:20. The plural form at Mark 10:1 is likely to have arisen as a scribal harmonization to the parallel in Matthew 19:2 or *ad sensum* (picking up from αυτους). Once this change was made, few readers thereafter would have noticed the inconsistency with the rest of Mark thereby created.

John 21:8 (with Revelation 21:17 and 1 Timothy 1:10)

We turn now to the issue of Atticism versus Hellenism, which may be used to determine a first-century author's consistency in language. A basic tenet of the type of textual criticism I espouse is that the biblical authors were more likely to write non-Attic than Attic Greek. Prof. Chrys Caragounis of Lund, Sweden (who for many years co-chaired with Jim the seminar on Greek language at the annual meetings of SNTS), wrote a long and important chapter on Atticism in his book *The Development of Greek and the New Testament*. Using the Nestle text, he observes that both Attic and non-Attic equivalents coexist in the New Testament. In so doing, he draws on the lists surviving from the second-century grammarians Moeris and Phrynichus.[11]

From the selections listed by Caragounis we pick on just two: (a) Phrynichus paragraph 217 declares πηχων to be Hellenistic and πηχεων is commended as the preferred Attic form. Not surprisingly, both spellings appear in different manuscripts as variants at John 21:8 and Rev 21:17. What do we print? I suggest the Hellenistic word, as this is appropriate for a first-century writing and is a word condemned by later stylists. (b) εφιορκοις *v.l.* επιορκοις at 1 Tim 1:10. The variant should again be resolved by Phrynichus (here paragraph 279): εφιορκους Τουτο δια του π λεγε επιουρκους. We therefore would print the "condemned" form with φ.

---

11. See Caragounis, *Development of Greek and the New Testament*, 136, for listing of 407 units containing 513 phrases and constructions that Phrynichus, the neo-Atticist grammarian, recommends. Of these, some 204 are New Testament words; 111 of them are condemned by Phrynichus. Caragounis includes a comparable list of words commended or condemned by Moeris, another of the second-century neo-Atticist grammarians.

Caragounis uses the Nestle *text*, but he does not refer to its *apparatus*, nor that of any other. Had he done so, he would have noted what I have, namely, that there are variants in our New Testament manuscripts in many such places, and these need resolution. When such *v.ll.* occur, I think it unlikely that a scribe would ever have sought consciously to archaize an author's style by eliminating an original Atticism and replacing it with a Hellenism merely because he had cleverly observed that the author in question may use such popular confections.[12] In our day we may be able to spot these stylistic features because we possess concordances, grammars, and lexicons. I doubt if the average scribe was more than a mere hack copyist, determined to get his task of reproducing a text done as briskly as he could; he would not have had the time or inclination—or ability—to attend to the niceties of the text's language and style with such a degree of precision. The neo-Atticist grammarians like Moeris and Phrynichus, however, did find willing readers among learned literati who wished to emulate the precision and felicities of the grammarians. That is why many of their pronouncements that have a bearing on the vocabulary of the Bible found a place in some New Testament manuscripts. Change in that direction could have been relatively automatic. Thus we can obviously see where a word deemed offensive or nonclassical is replaced occasionally with the preferred classical alternative.[13]

Acts 7:56

At Acts 7:56 Stephen refers to the Son of *Man* standing at the right hand of God. Apart from the verb "standing," much ink has been spilled over this

---

12. Places where deliberate scribal change is readily detectable include (a) the harmonizing of one Gospel to wording more familiar to the copyist from another Gospel, possibly one more regularly used in the church, say Matthew, or one already recently copied in a fourfold Gospel codex; (b) the avoidance of an unfamiliar word or expression, say a Semitism or other non-Greek term; (c) the introduction of a preferred Atticism as opposed to a Koine word that may have seemed jarring to an educated scribe. Obviously, other types of deliberate scribal changes are identified, such as the (rare) inserting of a marginal gloss to clarify the text, or a theological change to defend a currently acceptable theological position.

13. Tommy Wasserman recognizes the relevance of Atticism in investigations into textual criticism (in his article "Criteria for Evaluating Readings in New Testament Textual Criticism," 590), but he, like Caragounis, and before him G. D. Fee, is prepared to see change from an original Atticism to a scribal non-Attic equivalent as occasionally possible. So too does Flink, *Studies in the Second Century Text of the New Testament*, who accepts Atticism as a reason for change in New Testament textual history but argues that the opposite tendency may occasionally also have played a part. I do not share those opinions.

erratic use of the term "Son of Man." This is the only occurrence of the title outside the Gospels.[14] But there is a variant reading "Son of God" by P74 491 and 614. We may legitimately argue that the New Testament writers were consistent in reserving the term "Son of Man" to the Gospels and used it only on Jesus' lips. Further, I would argue that the title Son of God in Acts was altered on stylistic grounds precisely to avoid a fourfold use of the name God in two contiguous verses, 55 and 56. (Scribes were often sensitive to repetition.) If so, "Son of *God*" is original to Acts 7:56; our author conforms to New Testament practice.

Pastoral Epistles

1 Timothy 4:9; 2 Timothy 2:11; Titus 3:8

A distinctive usage in the Pastorals is the expression πιστος ο λογος, found in each letter (1 Tim 4:9; 2 Tim 2:11; Titus 3:8), a usage that, among other such examples, emphasizes the common authorship of the three letters.[15] There are no variants in those places. Two further occurrences appear as variants at 1 Tim 1:15, where Old Latin witnesses b dmon r, and a number of Latin patristic witnesses[16] read *humanus* (i.e., ανθρωπινος), and at 1 Tim 3:1 where the reading ανθρωπινος is read by D* supported by Lvt (b g m) Ambst Spec. It is unlikely that we should accept the reading ανθρωπινος at 1 Tim 1:15 based on only the Latin—there *humanus* may have been an inner-Latin assimilation to the word found in some Latin manuscripts at 3:1. Nor is this word appropriate in the context.

The main problem is the reading at 3:1. Ανθρωπινος (probably meaning "human" or "true to human needs") is found in the LXX, Josephus, and Philo and occurs in the New Testament at only Acts 17:25; 1 Cor 2:13; 4:3; 10:13; Jas 3:7; and 1 Pet 2:13, and significantly at Rom 6:19, where ανθρωπινον λεγω is comparable to the context at 1 Tim 3:1. There are no *v.ll.* in those places. (φιλανθρωπια is used at Titus 3:4.) At Rev 21:5 and 22:6 a comparable linking of πιστος and λογος is found, but the expression πιστος ο λογος is not used there. Πιστος, as one may expect, is common in the New Testament. But used as a predicate to an arthrous noun, πιστος occurs without variant at 1 Cor 1:9; 10:13; 2 Cor 1:18—all with reference to God; see also at 2 Thess 3:3 with reference to Κυριος.

---

14. Obviously the anarthrous and different use of "Son of Man" in Rev 1:13; 14:14 is not relevant here.

15. See Marshall, *Pastoral Epistles,* excursus 9, "The Trustworthy Sayings," 326–30.

16. E.g., Ambrosiaster, Augustine, Julian-Eclanum, Vigilius.

The term in the Pastorals seems to underline and confirm the truth of an accompanying statement and is additionally found alongside και πασης αξιος αποδοχης at 1 Tim 1:15 and 4:9. The main issue here is vocabulary. Did the author claim that the λογος was πιστος or ανθρωπινος?

A resolution to the text-critical variant is related to a question of structure and exegesis, that is, whether the opening words of what is commonly numbered 3:1a belong to what precedes (i.e., 2:15) or to what follows (3:1bff.). Πιστος points backward at 1 Tim 4:9 and Titus 3:8, but forward at 1 Tim 1:15 and 2 Tim 3:8. It is usually claimed that the phrase, be it with πιστος or ανθρωπινος, applies better to the more personal message to follow than to what is the more theologically significant passage at the end of chapter 2. And which statement is the more likely to be called a λογος? Certainly ανθρωπινος seems to apply better to what follows.

From the point of view of thoroughgoing eclectic principles, one should note that our author uses the phrase with πιστος four times. Should we expect him to be consistent in the way he describes a λογος? Or may one argue that πιστος is secondary to ανθρωπινος here, having been introduced by a scribe who was familiar with the author's usage elsewhere and therefore conformed this verse to the usage in those other passages? One cannot convincingly claim, as some have done, that the other four occurrences seem to apply to salvation, whereas here, however one may punctuate the ending of chapter 2 and the opening of chapter 3, that is not the case. On balance, we should probably read ανθρωπινος at 1 Tim 3:1. For once, our preferred reading is not based on preserving consistency in the author.

2 Timothy 4:22

There are two main variant units in the verse.

1. The reading ο Κυριος μετα του πνευματος σου is read by NA[28] and has the following variants: after Κυριος A 104 614 Lvg add Ιησους and ℵ C D K L P Maj add Ιησους Χριστος; these are likely to be examples of a common liturgical expanding of the divine names. The titles would not have been deliberately expunged were they original (although accidental omissions could perhaps be contemplated even—or especially—if all were contracted, as *nomina sacra* regularly were).

2. η χαρις μεθ' υμων as in NA28 has *v.ll.*:

- η χαρις μεθ' ημων 614 Lvg copt (boh)
- η χαρις μετα σου 263 sy[p] copt (sah (ms.), boh (ms.))

- *om.* 330 sah (mss.) eth Ambst Pel Ps-Jer (the omission was probably made because a scribe felt the greeting was superfluous after the preceding farewells)
- ερρωσ' εν ειρηνη D*, 1 Lvt (ar b)

The greeting with the 2 pers. plu. is found in the concluding greetings in 1 Tim 6:21 (*v.l.* 2 pers. sing. read by D K L 048 Maj) and Titus 3:15 (*v.l.* 2 pers. sing. read with an expanded greeting by 33 only, and cf. 81). In those places *v.l.* 2 pers. sing. is an obvious if pedantic correction in letters ostensibly addressed to an individual. But here 2 Tim 4:22a is actually directed to this individual (σου is without variant), so may σου be original in 22b also? (Cf. Titus 3:15a also and note there ασπασαι *v.l.* ασπασασθε.) Ought one expect our author, or any author, to be consistent in his greetings? If the answer is in the affirmative, then perhaps the wording in 2 Timothy could determine that σου should be original in all three letters, including the longer farewell greeting of Titus with 33, with the 2 pers. plu. being substituted once the letters were being read generally. (The fluctuation ημων/υμων is universal throughout the New Testament.)

Hebrews 11:37

Nouns in lists are often subjected to textual change. On the one side, vigorously inventive scribes may have been tempted to increase the elements in the list; on the other side, lazy and careless copyists may have removed words accidentally. In most cases the omission, once made, would not have been readily detectable. Shuffling the order of the words in a list is also a common cause of differences between manuscripts. Such rearrangements may be deliberate in order to have words placed in a particular sequence, perhaps to produce a desired crescendo, or they may be accidental, where the scribe commits a string of words to memory but writes them down in a new order.

Here at Heb 11:37 we find the following variants:

- επρισθησαν P[46] 1241 sy[p] Eus
- επειρασθησαν 0150 Lvg (mss.)
- επρισθησαν επ(ε)ιρασθησαν P[13vid] D[1] K 104 365 Maj
- επιρασθησαν επιρασθησαν D*
- επειρασθησαν επρισθησαν ℵ L P 048 33 81 326 1505 επρησθησαν επειρασθησαν Ψ[vid] 1923

Misreading, haplography, and dittography may all be invoked to explain these variants. The itacistic reading of D*, επιρασθησαν επιρασθησαν, is a clear instance of dittography. Επρησθησαν by Ψ^{vid} 1923 may be a legitimate reading ("they were burnt") or, as in P^{13vid} Maj, an itacistic spelling of επρισθησαν. Metzger lists a large number of ingenious conjectures by scholars who adapted the apparently incongruous longer reading that includes επειρασθησαν.[17]

In a list that begins with capital punishments, the apparent inappropriateness of the middle of πειραω may have caused its deletion. That favors its originality. However, its differing locations (in, say, ℵ compared with Maj) could suggest secondariness—fluctuating locations are often a sign of unoriginality. Zuntz[18] considered επειρασθησαν to be a "corrupt dittography."

Thus we have two opposing yet plausible conclusions. On balance, I would accept the longer reading, that is, to include επειρασθησαν, but without a clear reason to place it either before or after επρισθησαν.

Revelation

1:6

Do we read εις τους αιωνας των αιωνων or only εις τους αιωνας? NA^{28} brackets των αιωνων, leaving the poor reader to decide for him/herself whether to ignore the bracketed words and accept the shortened phrase or to ignore the brackets. We need to ask if the longer reading, despite its being a relatively common biblical expression, may be secondary, the influence of a liturgical formula perhaps, or whether the author of Revelation or New Testament authors more widely prefer the longer phrase that afterward may have been truncated accidentally or even deliberately. Here at Revelation 1:6 we see that the manuscript support for both readings may be described as balanced. The same *v.l.* occurs in the doxology at Rom 16:27, and see also 1 Pet 5:11.

A concordance reveals the following statistics: the longer phrase occurs in doxologies at Rom 11:36; Gal 1:5; Eph 3:21; Phil 4:20; 1 Tim 1:17; 2 Tim 4:18; Heb 1:8; 13:21; 1 Pet 4:11; 5:11; 2 Pet 3:18 (read by 623 *pauci*); and Jude 25, but in some of these verses as a *v.l.* with other manuscripts supporting the shorter reading.[19] The longer form is not found in the Gospels save as a *v.l.* in the additions to one form of Matthew's *Paternoster*. When we locate firm examples of the shorter text (i.e., with no known *v.l.* reported)

---

17. Metzger, *Commentary, ad loc.*
18. Zuntz, *The Text of the Epistles.*
19. At 1 Tim 1:17 only minuscule 623 (again) supports the shorter text.

at Rom 1:25 and 9:5 within a doxology, is it safe to use that as definitive not just for Romans but for Paul more generally?

Apart from its occurrence in doxologies, the shorter form stands firm six times in the Synoptics, twelve times in John, and commonly in the epistles (although not all these are firm; *v.ll.* reading a longer form may be seen at, *inter alia*, 2 Cor 9:9; Heb 1:8). Outside this verse, Revelation 1:6, the shorter form is not in Revelation; all other examples are the longer form and those are firm (Rev 1:18; 4:9, 10; 5:13; 7:12; 10:6; 11:15; 14:11; 15:7; 19:3; 20:10; 22:5). That certainly seems definitive for Revelation, but elsewhere I leave it to readers to judge the extent to which we may impose a criterion of consistency to resolve the apparent irregularity of practice found in the manuscripts, and through them in our printed editions.

2:1ff.

It is here where we encounter our second conjectural emendation (cf. Mark 1:1–3). This is a variant I chose for my SNTS main paper delivered in Szeged, Hungary, in 2014, at which Jim was present, so this example is no surprise to him!

The introductory words to each of the seven letters to churches in Revelation are formulaic (Rev 2:1, 8, 12, 18; 3: 1, 7, 14), and the wording is identical in NA²⁸, namely, τω αγγελω της εν (Εφεσω) εκκλησιας γραφον, but at 2:1 (A C), 6 (A), 12 (2050), 18 (A); 3:1 (046), the manuscripts within my brackets here, some highly respected by many text-critics because of their age, read τω, not της. Versional evidence seems to support τω² at 3:7 and at 3:14. It is reasonable to expect an author to be consistent in such stereotypical formulae. Scribes, though, are clearly erratic here. Manuscript A throughout the seven formulae has της four times, τω thrice! The usage της . . . εκκλησιας to mean "to the angel of the church at . . ." (rather than "to the angel who is of the church at . . .") looks right, but is that what later scribes thought as they, admittedly irregularly, changed the texts in that direction, that is, from τω to της? Grammar should help us, and it favors the originality of τω throughout. The rule is that prepositional phrases such as εν Εφεσω may precede anarthrous nouns, but ought not to stand between an article and its noun. That ruling would militate against της in all seven places. If such a phrase were in an attributive position, as here, it must *follow* the noun and the appropriate article (which would be τω) has to be repeated. See also Revelation 11:19 *v.l.* ηνοιγη ο ναος του θεου ο εν τω ουρανω.

May grammar and a recognition that this author has been consistent be determinative for the originality of τω here, despite the alleged thinness of the Greek support in five places and its absence in the other two? If a version be deemed an inappropriate witness when discussing Greek articles, then we would be obliged to conjecture τω at 3:7, 14. If one goes along with my arguments here, one may lay oneself open to accepting a reading with no Greek witnesses. Are we allowing conjectural emendation in pursuit of this Holy Grail of consistency? At the very least, the barrenness of the manuscript attestation for τω from the earliest Christian centuries permits the opinion that an original form of the wording has not survived 100 percent of the time. Admittance of a conjecture as the *Ausgangstext*, though, requires careful thought.

5:12

The NA[28] *apparatus* shows the following variant: τον πλουτον 046 1006 1611 1841; πλουτον ℵ A C *cett*. The repetition of the article before a second—but not any subsequent—member in a sequence seems to be characteristic of our author, and so should be preserved here as the *Ausgangstext*. The removal of the article may be attributed to a scribe's imitating the anarthrous nouns following, or could be accidental because of homoioteleuton.[20]

Excursus 1

As an appendix, two brief excursuses may now be in order. The first concerns the relevance of consistency as a guiding principle. Conservative scholars are often willing to justify and explain theological change or indeed ecclesiastic and social change, for example, within the Pauline corpus, in their attempts to preserve at all costs the unity of *all* the letters written under Paul's name as genuinely from this one writer. Any changes are then routinely claimed to reflect different times, different motives, different moods, and even a development of his thinking as Paul grew older, matured, or adapted to new circumstances. But where such a line of argument begins to look insecure is when one analyzes changes in the language, style, usage, and grammar. Those skeptical of the conservatives' arguments readily—and rightly—point out that authors cannot change their lifelong writing styles completely. By "writing style" I mean that unself-conscious use of the distinctive minutiae of an individual's text, particles, prepositions, word-order preferences, and so on, which are a constant; such features are ingrained

---

20. Cf. Rev 3:17, where *v.l.* o before ελεεινος should similarly be read with A Maj., and see also the single repetition of επι as a *v.l.* at Rev 10:11, which should be accepted. Likewise, see *v.l.* + εις την at Rev 9:15.

and never likely to change. Any literary figure may mature and express himself with an increased clarity and confidence, but I cannot believe that a Goethe, a Dickens, or a Dostoevsky changed from the basic structures of his language as he aged, with the consequence that the work of that writer when mature is unrecognizable from writings from the same pen of, say, thirty or forty years earlier. If such observations are correct, then any significant linguistic changes within an author's alleged oeuvre are more likely to indicate different authorship. The Pastorals are always useful to refer to in this context. The near consensus view is that the language and style of these letters differ from the language of the undisputed Pauline epistles and indicate a different author.

To argue that sometimes Paul employed an amanuensis and allowed him to use his own language and style rather than reproducing Paul's own is specious, and is probably used only by those who reluctantly have to admit the occasional existence of non-Pauline language but who, nonetheless, cannot bear to conceive of deceit and forgery camouflaged as pseudonymity playing any part in the composition of Holy Writ.

Rather, I argue that an author's style remains a constant throughout his lifetime and for the criterion of using that constant style to determine the *Ausgangstext* or "original" text when discussing variations in our extant manuscripts, as well as, of course, when assessing matters of authorship and pseudonymity.

The definition of this word "original" is regularly questioned. It has been an issue ever since Eldon Epp wrote his now classic essay "The Multivalence of the Term 'Original Text' in New Testament Textual Criticism" fifteen years ago.[21] There he attempted to define that weasel word "original." *Inter alia*, it can refer to a predecessor text behind a composition, the authorial writing published, the subsequent consensual canonical text, or the interpretative text promulgated by a church, and one must recognize that not all these stages need be, nor may be, recoverable at each unit of variation. As a result, text critics today hesitate to bandy about "original text" as the primary purpose of their research.

This recent hesitation to use the term "original," arising from Epp's timely warnings, is in contrast with the nineteenth century when Westcott and Hort could entitle their edited text "The New Testament in the *Original* Greek." I do, however, note that even as recently as 2005 Maurice Robinson and William Pierpont, two "majority text" promoters, were bold enough to give their edition of the Byzantine text-type that same title! A similar

---

21. Most recently reprinted in Epp, *Perspectives on New Testament Textual Criticism*, 551–93.

arrogance was also found only one generation ago in Münster, which unashamedly trumpeted the then-current Nestle edition as the *Standardtext!*

Such overweening confidence has no place in the textual criticism of today. I too acknowledge a change in my own writing. When I first pronounced on these matters, I was confident that, with the 5,000 or so Greek New Testament manuscripts at our disposal, we were well equipped to locate at virtually every point the original, *authorial* text. Now such an aim is chimeric, and the definition of our function and purpose needs nuancing. Nonetheless, I maintain that for much of the New Testament text we are able, thanks in part to the evidence provided by undisputed areas of text, to proffer a relatively stable *Ausgangstext*, which in large measure *may* represent the authorial Greek of its creative composer. Using as touchstones a proven literary and linguistic style and usage in any given book provides demonstrable and helpful aids for resolving textual variation and (just as importantly) for explaining the origins and, perhaps, motives for subsequent scribal alterations. In most cases that consistency of style will go back to the creative author of the composition.

In an earlier time and culture, when all that the text critic was apparently trying to achieve was one indubitably original text, variations from that gold standard were often rejected and ignored as "secondary"; now these alternatives are to be seen not as mere blunders or the consequences of maverick rewritings. Rather, much church history and Christian theology may be exposed in an *apparatus*, in the recognition that the manuscripts supporting even what may commonly be agreed are secondary, later readings were once the canonical, authorized texts of the communities or individuals who used, read, and revered the manuscripts containing their Scriptures. The current shift away from trying primarily to establish the author's published text comes alongside an allied recognition that *all* alternatives merit attention as stepping-stones in the dense and varied history of the New Testament.

Even those whose academic interests seldom concern matters text-critical regularly appeal to a writer's style establishing patterns of expression or vocabulary. But to collect together what those regular features are requires us to work not from any one particular manuscript, nor even from one critically edited text—be that an edition prepared by a single scholar or, as is now inevitably and increasingly the case, by a committee of editors meeting in solemn conclave to produce a running line of text underneath which they can display the alternatives to those who have eyes to see and the will to make use of what they find there—but from as full an *apparatus criticus* as possible.

Excursus 2

Our second excursus looks at the sources of the New Testament books, many of which have a prehistory prior to their "publication." We now need to ask: Is it reasonable to expect to be able to uncover the authors' consistency in language and style, especially in the Synoptic Gospels, because they have written, and have oral sources behind them on which they drew and which, in theory, they then may have reproduced, despite differences from their sources' own preferred usage?

By contrast, the results of studies in the language and style of Mark (in particular), but also legitimately in Johannine, Matthean, and Lukan language and style, suggest that, despite later authors' having used, copied, and adapted their predecessors' works, the Evangelists nonetheless imprinted on the new writing their own distinctive fingerprints. Each writer has his own DNA. Even when one argues that Matthew read and used Mark, any Markan sources detectable in the later writing do not permit a scholar examining verses from Mark used in Matthew to produce a grammar of Markan style[22] that replicates the *echt* Mark as found within his own Gospel. The earlier written sources have been adopted and adapted.[23] The same is of course true of theological perspectives.

Similar conclusions may be made *mutatis mutandis* were one to be arguing, as does Jim Voelz, for a different solution to the Synoptic problem and another sequencing of the Gospels. Even when it is agreed that a literary, written source has been used, this conclusion does not enable one to re-create from the later writing the precise language and text of any of its sources. In addition, if one accepts a text as usable, and applies the text-critical principle that wherever variation occurs one should accept as "original" a reading that makes parallels *more dissimilar*, given that scribes are more likely to harmonize parallels than make them differ, then the resultant texts will appear even more different from the other(s) than is normally the case.

We may apply that principle to other alleged sources behind the canonical Gospels. As far as Q is concerned, can one indeed do what the Leuven series Documenta Q tries to do and reconstruct the distinctive language of Q as found in Matthew and Luke, or to ask if Q is camouflaged by Matthew's or Luke's own writing? As we see from the meticulous studies of distinctive Q passages in the Documenta Q volumes, a decision about

---

22. Elliott, *The Language and Style of the Gospel of Mark*.

23. C. H. Turner and others successfully plotted Markan language from an edition of Mark itself, wisely (but, unfortunately, not often enough) referring to the occasional textual variant. They did not turn to Mark in Luke or Mark in Matthew to complete or nuance what was in Mark itself.

which of the two canonical books has preserved anything from the original Q language (as opposed to Q's theology) is often open to dispute. To expand our examples, we may note that *logia* in the *Gospel of Thomas*, which parallel canonical sayings, are seldom identical to them. Similarly, patristic citations of biblical passages (even lemmata in commentaries) rarely follow the New Testament text as we possess it in all its particulars. Again, the secondary author's own style comes into play, and, of course, the context and intention will also cause differences.

Biblical scholarship has invested much energy—with profitable results—in investigating the likely sources behind the "published" books, especially the fourfold New Testament Gospels. The interrelationships of these Gospels are concerned with who copied, or rather used, what and from whom. Study of the sources and texts behind the Gospels (or behind Acts, or the contents and composition of Paul's epistles) is an ongoing fascination for many. So too is the growing recognition that the "published" version of the constituent parts of the New Testament also then generated a life of its own, as scribal copies were adapted *and used* over the centuries. There a watershed has been defined: the prehistory of a published text (which may be labeled "literary criticism") and the scribal copying to which much ancient literature was subjected. The latter is "textual criticism." Both stages recognize change. If we examine language and style and see that Matthew and Luke improved on Mark's style, such an examination is, however, not dissimilar to our plotting what scribes were to do later with their copies of Mark, also sometimes changing his vocabulary and language. One, of course, needs to bear in mind that a creative Gospel writer made deliberate changes to his source(s) in more than just its language; he made changes to its contents, sequences of pericopae, even dominical sayings on a scale not seen in scribal copyings. A distinct feature of *scribal* activity, on the other hand, is that copyists were responsible for much assimilation between parallels. As is well known, many variants in the Gospels are deliberate scribal harmonizations.

What the first Evangelist did with his possible sources and what a later writer did with his predecessors' work are legitimate questions in Gospel criticism. Synoptic studies seek the distinctive characteristics of each final composition, including its linguistic features. When we move to textual criticism, we ask comparable questions. Where, why, and how did deliberate changes occur? Answers to both may, however, be similar, such as the need to enhance or clarify the wording or meaning or theology, to expand, to correct.

Those are among the principles of thoroughgoing textual criticism with its tools and questions that I seek to apply when studying the biblical texts. Many of these are shared by our honoree, whom I now toast (with his favorite *Rotwein*) with the words: "Ad multos annos!"

Bibliography

Aland, Kurt. ed. *Synopsis quattuor evangeliorum*. 15th ed. Stuttgart: Deutsche Bibelgesellschaft, 1996.
Caragounis, Chrys. *The Development of Greek and the New Testament*. Tübingen: Mohr/Siebeck, 2004; Grand Rapids: Baker, 2006.
Elliott, J. Keith. "Mark 1:1–3: A Later Addition to the Gospel?" *NTS* 46 (2000) 584–88.
———, ed. *The Language and Style of the Gospel of Mark: An Edition of C. H. Turner's "Notes on Marcan Usage" Together with Other Comparable Studies*. NovTSup 71. Leiden: Brill, 1993.
———. "Using an Author's Consistency of Usage and Conjectures as Criteria to Resolve Textual Variation in the Greek New Testament." *NTS* 62 (2016) 122-135.
Epp, Eldon Jay. *Perspectives on New Testament Textual Criticism*. NovTSup 116. Leiden: Brill, 2005.
Flink, Timo. *Studies in the Second Century Text of the New Testament*. Joensuu, Finland: University of Joensuu, 2009.
Greeven, Heinrich, and Eberhard Güting. *Textkritik des Markusevangeliums*. Theologie: Forschung und Wissenschaft 11. Münster: Lit, 2005.
Kilpatrick, G. D. *Mark: A Greek-English Diglot for the Use of Translators*. London: BFBS, 1958.
Marshall, I. H. *The International Critical Commentary on the Pastoral Epistles*. London: T. & T. Clark, 1999.
Metzger, Bruce. *A Textual Commentary on the Greek New Testament*. 2nd ed. Stuttgart: United Bible Societies, 1994.
Taylor, Vincent. *Gospel according to St. Mark*. London: Macmillan, 1952.
Voelz, James W. *Mark 1:1—8:26*. Concordia Commentary. St. Louis: Concordia, 2013.
Wasserman, Tommy. "Criteria for Evaluating Readings in New Testament Textual Criticism." In *The Text of the New Testament in Contemporary Research: Essays on the Status Quaestionis*, edited by Bart D. Ehrman and Michael W. Holmes, 579–612. 2nd ed. NTTDS 42. Leiden: Brill, 2013.
Zuntz, Günther. *The Text of the Epistles: A Disquisition upon the Corpus Paulinum*. Schweich Lectures, 1947. London: British Academy and Oxford University Press, 1947.

6

Body, Self, and Spirit

The Meaning of Paul's Anthropological
Terminology in 1 Thessalonians 5:23

—*Charles A. Gieschen*

Besides Paul's proclamation of resurrection in 1 Cor 15:1–58, 1 Thessalonians contains his most significant teaching about eschatology, especially Jesus' triumphal coming (παρουσίᾳ) on the last day and the resurrection of "those who are asleep" (1 Thess 4:14).[1] Paul introduces eschatology prominently already at the close of the letter's thanksgiving: "and also to await his Son from the heavens, whom he raised from the dead, Jesus, who delivers us from the wrath that is to come" (1:10).[2] He punctuates this letter several times with short proclamations of eschatology (2:13–16; 2:17–19; 3:11–13). His more extensive discussion of Jesus' triumphal coming in 4:13–18 is probably his response to one of the primary situations that prompted Paul to write this letter: confusion among these new Christians about whether their brothers and sisters in Christ who died before Jesus'

---

1. This study results from my current work on the 1–2 Thessalonians volume in the Concordia Commentary series. It is offered here in honor of James W. Voelz, my esteemed mentor and friend, with sincere appreciation for the profound manner in which his teaching during my studies at Concordia Theological Seminary, Fort Wayne (1980–1984), has shaped my own study and teaching of the New Testament in the subsequent decades.
  See especially Luckensmeyer, *The Eschatology of First Thessalonians*. For a terse introduction, see Gieschen, "Christ's Coming and the Church's Mission in 1 Thessalonians."

2. All English translations of biblical texts are my own.

return would miss out on the blessings of that day. Finally, Paul concludes this letter with a blessing in 5:23–24 that contains this very intriguing eschatological summary:

> Αὐτὸς δὲ ὁ θεὸς τῆς εἰρήνης ἁγιάσαι ὑμᾶς ὁλοτελεῖς, καὶ ὁλόκληρον ὑμῶν τὸ πνεῦμα καὶ ἡ ψυχὴ καὶ τὸ σῶμα ἀμέμπτως ἐν τῇ παρουσίᾳ τοῦ κυρίου ἡμῶν Ἰησοῦ Χριστοῦ τηρηθείη. πιστὸς ὁ καλῶν ὑμᾶς, ὃς καὶ ποιήσει.

> Now may the God of peace himself sanctify you completely, and may your spirit, self, and body as a whole be kept blameless at the triumphal coming of our Lord Jesus Christ. The one who calls you is faithful, who also will do it.

This blessing, limited though it is, provides important evidence of Paul's understanding of anthropology (i.e., what makes up *anthropos*).[3] Here Paul testifies that each Christian is, in some sense, τὸ σῶμα, ἡ ψυχή, and τὸ πνεῦμα. But what exactly is Paul signifying with these terms? Does he use σῶμα here as a more inclusive term instead of σάρξ (flesh), a term he uses frequently when speaking of the flesh and Spirit dichotomy in Christian anthropology?[4] What is the nature of the σῶμα that Paul states will be sanctified completely and kept until the triumphal coming of Jesus at the last day: physical, spiritual, or ethereally material? It is especially difficult to determine the meaning of ἡ ψυχή, which is translated typically as "soul" in English. But that translation raises its own challenges of what exactly is being signified in English by "soul." "Soul" is popularly understood to be a Christian's "spiritual nature" that separates from the body after death, but how does one then understand "soul" in relation to "spirit"? It is also difficult to determine the meaning of τὸ πνεῦμα here, which is usually translated "spirit" but could be understood as "the [Holy] Spirit" in light of the change in anthropology that happens through baptism. First Thess 5:23, in fact, has prompted debate about so-called bipartite (body and spirit) versus tripartite (body, soul, and spirit) anthropology in Paul and the rest of the Scriptures.[5]

---

3. See esp. Stacey, *The Pauline View of Man*, and Jewett, *Paul's Anthropological Terms*. Jewett's work is somewhat flawed by his tendency to postulate a conflict on every page of Paul's epistles, including early manifestations of Gnosticism.

4. Bultmann made popular the understanding that Paul uses σῶμα to mean "the whole person." See Bultmann, *Theology of the New Testament*, 1:192. Contrast Gundry, *Sōma in Biblical Theology*.

5. For a brief discussion of this debate that favors a bipartite understanding, see Pieper, *Christian Dogmatics*, 1:476–77. For a brief history of research on the understanding of these three anthropological terms, see Weima, *1–2 Thessalonians*, 421n10.

Recognizing that "Paul's use of anthropological terms is neither original, systematic, nor consistent," Abraham Malherbe states:

> This is the only place in Paul's letters where the tripartite division of human nature into spirit, soul, and body appears, and this particular division appears nowhere before him. Plato speaks of mind or intelligence (nous) in the soul, and of the soul in the body (*Timaeus* 30B), and the Stoic Marcus Aurelius a century after Paul has the division body, soul, and mind (*Meditation* 3.16), but Paul's trichotomy in 1 Thessalonians is the earliest occurrence of that precise formulation. Scholars have been divided since antiquity over whether this trichotomy represented Paul's view of human nature or whether he held to the more traditional dichotomist view of body and soul.[6]

Most commentators argue that Paul is not defining *parts* of anthropology here, but primarily emphasizing that the *complete* person will be sanctified and kept unto the triumphal coming of Christ. M. Eugene Boring offers what can be seen as a representative example of this position: "'Spirit, soul, and body' is a rhetorical expression for 'completely,' not a tripartite analysis of human being, as though Paul were here presenting doctrinal teaching on the nature of human selfhood. Nor is he consistent in his ways of speaking about the nature of human being; note the variety of ways in which he used *kardia* (heart), *psychē* (soul, life, self), *nous* (mind), *sōma* (body), *sarx* (flesh), *pneuma* (spirit), as aspects of human being (e.g., Rom 13:1; 16:4; 1 Cor 16:18; 2 Cor 2:13; 7:1, 5, 13; Gal 6:18; Phil 4:23; 1 Thess 2:4, 8; 5:28; Phlm 25)."[7] Although Paul uses a variety of language to express anthropology, the three terms in 1 Thess 5:23 are more than rhetorical flourish; they are teaching anthropology in some manner. It is important to attempt to understand how they should be understood in light of Paul's broader expression of anthropology in his various letters.

An examination of the Pauline corpus leads to the conclusion that Paul understands man—whether one believes in Christ or not—primarily as a dichotomy, rather than a trichotomy, made up of the inner *anthropos* and the outer *anthropos*: "Although our outer man [ὁ ἔξω ἡμῶν ἄνθρωπος] is wasting away, yet our inner man [ὁ ἔσω ἡμῶν] is being renewed day by day" (2 Cor 4:16). A. T. Robertson offers the following explanation of this basic understanding of Paul's anthropology that includes the distinguishing feature of the anthropology of one who has been united with Christ by faith through the Holy Spirit: "Both believers and unbelievers have an inner man

---

6. Malherbe, *Letters to the Thessalonians*, 338.

7. Boring, *I and II Thessalonians*, 201.

(soul *psuchē*, mind *nous*, heart *kardia*, the inward man *ho esō anthrōpos*) and the outer man (*sōma, ho exō anthrōpos*). But the believer has the Holy Spirit of God, the renewed spirit of man (I Cor. 2:11; Rom. 8:9-11)."[8]

What does Paul mean by "the inner man"? Robert Gundry speaks of "the inner man" as "the human spirit, the center of psychical feelings," but this explanation seems to fall far short of Paul's understanding.[9] For Paul, the "inner man" of the person who has been united with Christ can no longer be understood apart from the person of Christ: Christ enlivens and defines the "inner man" of all who are "in Christ" (Rom 7:22; 2 Cor 4:16; Eph 3:16; Col 3:9-10), whom Paul also identifies as the "new man" (Eph 4:22-23).[10] To express it pointedly: "I [Paul] have been crucified with Christ. It is no longer I who lives, but Christ who lives in me" (Gal 2:20). After conversion, Paul does not understand his "inner man" or "new man" as the "new Paul," but as Christ in Paul through the Holy Spirit (Rom 8:9-11). Thomas Winger draws a similar conclusion when he argues that the "new man" discussed in Eph 4:23 is "not simply the old one renovated," but "Christ himself," who is also identified as "the inner man" (Eph 3:16) and "the complete man" (Eph 4:13).[11]

Given Paul's broader understanding of the anthropology of one who is in Christ expressed over the course of his thirteen letters, it is reasonable to postulate how the three anthropological terms expressed in his first letter (1 Thessalonians) function within his basic dichotomy of the inner and outer man.[12] Although this remains to be supported in what follows below, Paul's understanding of the outer man is expressed in 1 Thessalonians with τὸ σῶμα, and his understanding of the inner man is expressed with the terms ἡ ψυχή and τὸ πνεῦμα. From the perspective of this triad, the distinctive

---

8. Robertson, *Word Pictures*, 4:38.

9. Gundry, *Sōma in Biblical Theology*, 137.

10. The manner in which Christ is identified with and defines the "inner man" and "new man" after conversion is not made clear in Middendorf, *The "I" in the Storm*, 106, and Middendorf, *Romans 1:1—8:39*, 569-70. I have argued for a more christological understanding of the "inner man" and "new man" previously; see Gieschen, "Paul and the Law," 137n83, and Gieschen, "The Son as Creator and Source," 136-37. It is worthy to note that the ESV translations of these terms are not helpful. For example, Eph 4:22-24 has the translations "old self" for παλαιὸν ἄνθρωπον and "new self" for καινὸν ἄνθρωπον. The ὁ ἔσω ἡμῶν ἄνθρωπος of 2 Cor 4:16 is translated in the ESV as "our inner self." Such translations make the christological identification of the "new man" and the "inner man" even more difficult for the reader.

11. Winger, *Ephesians*, 518.

12. There is some debate about Galatians possibly having been written earlier, but 1 Thessalonians is widely recognized to have been written in early AD 50 from Corinth; see Malherbe, *Letters to the Thessalonians*, 71-74.

aspect of anthropology for one who is in Christ is τὸ πνεῦμα. Because of τὸ πνεῦμα, the inner man is both alive and new while the outer man (τὸ σῶμα), after decay and death, will be raised in glory at the triumphal coming of Christ.

The questions posed above demonstrate that this simple triad of anthropological terms is filled with complexities. This study will argue that the meaning of this terminology is best expressed in English with the terms "body," "self," and "spirit," while also demonstrating that Paul's primary purpose in using this triad is to emphasize the totality of the human and prevent confusion that some part of the human will not be sanctified completely and participate in resurrected glory upon the triumphal coming of Jesus. Furthermore, a unique contribution of examining this triad in its first-century Greco-Roman context will be to demonstrate that if Paul did not mention ψυχή (self) in his understanding of eschatological anthropology, then most of the listeners to his letter in Thessalonica would have naturally wondered, "What will happen to my ψυχή in the afterlife?"

σῶμα in Paul's Epistles and the Thessalonian Context

Paul's understanding of σῶμα (body) is grounded in the foundational testimony in Israel's Scriptures to YHWH's creation of all that is visible and invisible (Gen 1:1), especially the creation of man and woman followed by the pronouncement that it was "very good" (Gen 1:26–31). It is this big-picture understanding of creation that shaped Paul's understanding of "body," not one particular term in the Hebrew Scriptures. This is clear from the fact that the Hebrew term for body, גְּוִיָּה, occurs only fourteen times.[13] In the Septuagint, however, σῶμα is used to translate a number of Hebrew terms, especially בָּשָׂר (flesh), when the terms signify the physical body alone.[14] Against the tendency of twentieth-century scholarship, especially Rudolf Bultmann, to argue that Paul used σῶμα to signify the whole or total person, Robert Gundry has demonstrated that Paul continued to understand the term in line with its use in the Septuagint to signify the outer, material, or physical aspect of man that is distinct from the spirit or inner man. "Paul fully personalizes *sōma* as a necessary part of the human constitution and of authentic existence. However, he neither dematerializes *sōma* in theological usage nor makes it comprehend the total person. To do either would lay upon the term a burden heavier than it can bear. Rather, without having

---

13. Stacey, *Pauline View of Man*, 181.
14. Gundry, *Sōma in Biblical Theology*, 23.

to do double duty for the spirit, *sōma* gains theological significance as the physical body, man's means of concrete service for God."[15]

A significant problem that Paul faced in his first-century context was the denigration of the "outer man" or "body" in wider Greco-Roman thinking, including that of a first-century Roman city like Thessalonica.[16] Unlike Homer's appreciation for the physical life, the elevation of the value of the soul and the denigration of the body as the prison for the soul began to be seen in the Orphic mysteries of the sixth century BC, then in the Pythagorean school, and continued to be strong in later Hellenistic philosophy such as that of Plato.[17] One of the features of Orphism was the conception of "disincarnate immortality" as the ultimate destiny of the soul.[18] Within some expressions of Hellenistic philosophy, evil and irrationality were part of the outer man or body.[19] In such thinking, the stated desire is for the individual soul to escape the body and, after migrating to various bodies in order to be purified, eventually to ascend to be part of the collective spirit.[20] Such thinking was even embraced by some Jews as they were influenced by Hellenization. For example, Wisdom of Solomon (c. first-century BC in Alexandria) states, "For a perishable body [σῶμα] weighs down the soul [ψυχήν], and this earthly tent burdens the thoughtful mind" (Wis 9:15) and "A good soul [ψυχῆς] fell to my lot; or rather, being good, I entered a defiled body [σῶμα]" (Wis 8:19–20).

As with Israel's Scriptures that were the foundation for his understanding, Paul has no such negative understanding of the outer man or body. For Paul, the "old man" or "flesh" signifies the sinful condition that dominates both the outer and inner man before conversion, and continues to have an impact after conversion.[21] The body itself, however, is a creation of God, an essential aspect of what makes up human life, and "very good" apart from its corruption by sin. This understanding of the body is the theological

---

15. Gundry, *Sōma in Biblical Theology*, 244. See also Bultmann, *Theology of the New Testament*, 1:192–203.

16. See the extensive discussion of the variety of Hellenistic ideas about the body in Stacey, *Pauline View of Man*, 59–81. Because it was thoroughly impacted by first-century Roman religion and thought, it is reasonable to conclude that these ideas would be present in Thessalonica.

17. Stacey, *Pauline View of Man*, 64–65.

18. Ibid., 64.

19. Ibid., 73.

20. An example of this idea in Vergil is quoted and discussed below.

21. "Sin" is still present "in" man as well as still causing the outer man to age and decay, even though Christ is the dominant reality of the inner man and new man (Rom 7:7–25). See Gieschen, "Original Sin," 359–75, esp. 365–72.

foundation for Paul's confession of the incarnation and birth of the Son in a body as well as the body of Jesus being raised by the Father. It is also the foundation for his abundant testimony to the resurrection of the body unto glory for all who believe in Christ (e.g., 1 Cor 15:1–58; 1 Thess 4:13–18). Gundry provides this very substantive summary of the theological significance of Paul's understanding and use of σῶμα.

> In sum, the consistently substantival meaning of the term *sōma* protects the functional element proper to the term. That element consists in the instrumental function of the physical body, a function necessary to human existence. Consequently, *sōma* bars asceticism and mysticism, withdrawal from history and society. Spiritualizing idealism, romanticism, introvertive existentialism—somatic anthropology excludes them. Positively, the physicalness of *sōma* affirms life in a material world and our responsibility for it. . . . By assuring the importance of materiality in the future through physical resurrection, *sōma* insures the importance of materiality in the present. Thus theology retains its this-worldly relevance along with its other-worldly hope.[22]

What about the σῶμα of a Christian after resurrection? Although it has been argued above that Paul understood σῶμα in a material/physical manner, is it possible that Paul understood that there would be a substantive change in the resurrected body of those in Christ so it would no longer be a material/physical body?[23] Some scholars have argued that Paul taught such a substantive change in the resurrected body based upon his use of the adjectives ψυχικός and πνευματικός in 1 Cor 15:44. James Ware's recent study has carefully and convincingly countered those holding this position.[24] He notes that "the σῶμα ψυχικόν describes the present body as given *life by the soul*, the life given by the very breath of God (1 Cor 15:45a, ἐγένετο ὁ πρῶτος ἄνθρωπος Ἀδὰμ εἰς ψυχὴν ζῶσαν, 'the first man, Adam, became *a soul that is living*' [echoing Gen 2:7]), but in Adam subject to mortality and decay (1 Cor 15:21–22)."[25] He then states that the σῶμα πνευματικός describes "the resurrected body as given life by the Spirit (cf. 1 Cor 15:45b, ὁ ἔσχατος Ἀδὰμ

---

22. Gundry, *Sōma in Biblical Theology*, 202–3.
23. See especially, Martin, *The Corinthian Body*.
24. Ware, "Paul's Understanding of Resurrection," 809–35. For a brief history of interpretation concerning 1 Cor 15 that reviews the positions he counters, see 810–17.
25. Ware, "Paul's Understanding of Resurrection," 835 (underlining and italics original). Although I would differ from Ware on translating forms of ψυχή as "soul" due to confusion about what this term signifies in English (see below), I agree with his argument here.

εἰς πνεῦμα ζῳοποιοῦν, 'the last Adam became *a Spirit who is life-giving*')."[26] Based upon this understanding, a possible paraphrase of 1 Cor 15:44a is: "It is sown a soul-given-life body; it is raised a Spirit-given-life body." Finally, Ware draws the conclusion that Paul understood resurrection "as the miraculous reconstitution of the mortal body of flesh and bones and its transformation so as to be imperishable."[27] As Paul wrote to the Christians in Thessalonica who had previously held negative understandings of the body, he affirms the value of the physical body as God's creation that is essential to what man is, he encourages living sanctified lives in the body, and he confirms the sure hope that the body will be raised in glory at the triumphal coming of the risen and living Jesus.

ψυχή in Paul's Epistles and Thessalonian Context

Considering the widespread Hellenistic conceptions about ψυχή being the immortal and immaterial soul or inner being that is found in each person, it is striking that ψυχή appears only thirteen times in the Pauline corpus.[28] What it signifies in these few occurrences has to do with individual life or self and is quite distinct from the typical Hellenistic conceptions.[29] Stacey observes that "it is patent that the Greek view of soul cannot be found in Paul."[30] Paul's limited use of this term appears to be related to the use of ψυχή in the Septuagint to translate נפשׁ (vitality, life, self), a term that appears with great frequency in the Hebrew Scriptures.[31] Robert Jewett explains the three basic connotations of ψυχή in Pauline usage as well as what it does not connote:

> It can bear the sense of one's earthly life as it is publically observable in behavior; the sense of the individual's earthly life which can be lost in death; or the sense of the individual person. The particular sense of the word depends upon the context in which is it is used rather than upon a development within Paul's

26. Ware, "Paul's Understanding of Resurrection," 835 (underlining and italics original).

27. Ibid., 835.

28. See Rom 2:9; 11:3; 13:1; 16:4; 1 Cor 15:45; 2 Cor 1:23; 12:15; Eph 6:6; Phil 1:27; 2:30; Col 3:23; 1 Thess 2:8; 5:23. For a history of research, see Jewett, *Paul's Anthropological Terms*, 334–40.

29. The definitions listed in BDAG, 1098–100, all have to do with "life" or "individual life/person," yet the English term "soul" is also glossed unhelpfully as another word for "inner human life."

30. Stacey, *Pauline View of Man*, 125.

31. It occurs 756 times according to ibid., 121.

thought. From the first to the last letter, Paul remains basically within the Judaic tradition in his use at this point. There are, however, several connotations of ψυχή within popular Judaic usage which Paul appears to avoid. *He never uses it in the strict sense of the "soul," i.e. the God-related portion of man which survives after death.* Furthermore, Paul avoids the interchangeability between πνεῦμα and ψυχή which was the mark of the Rabbinic usage, related as it was to the question of the fate of the soul after death.[32]

Because of what the English term "soul" has come to signify (e.g., "our immaterial spiritual being that exists beyond death," as well as the problematic conceptions about the soul from Hellenistic philosophy that impacted Christianity in different ways), "soul" is not a helpful English term to use in translating the Pauline uses of ψυχή. "Life," "individual person," or "self" are translations that communicate more clearly and prevent the confusion that arises from what is being signified with the English term "soul." Because Paul is writing about the ψυχή being kept blameless until the last day in 1 Thess 5:23, "life" is not a viable translation here. Because he is clearly distinguishing ψυχή from πνεῦμα, the translation "self" may communicate this distinction in the best manner. One of the most important texts in the Pauline corpus for understanding Paul's usage of ψυχή in 1 Thess 5:23 is his earlier usage of the term in 1 Thess 2:8, "We desired to share with you not only the gospel of God but also *our own individual selves* [τάς ἑαυτῶν ψυχάς]." For Paul, each human has a unique, individual self, or personhood, created by God, which will be sanctified and kept unto the resurrection of the body on the day of the triumphal coming of Jesus.

In contrast to Paul's usage, ψυχή was widely understood within Hellenistic philosophy after the sixth century BC to be a godlike, immaterial, immortal reality that had been imprisoned in the body and soiled by contact with the flesh.[33] The teaching of the immortality of the soul led to the prominent teaching of the transmigration of souls after death in order to accomplish purification. An example from Vergil's *Aeneid*, written in the first century BC, explains that the soul is part of the universal spirit, with the so-called immortal soul seeking escape from the physical body and then purging corruption through a thousand-year cycle of punishment:

> In the first place a spirit within sustains the sky, the earth, the waters, and the shining globe of the moon, and the Titan sun and stars; this spirit moves the whole mass of the universe, a

---

32. Jewett, *Paul's Anthropological Terms*, 448-49 (emphasis added).
33. See esp. Stacey, *Pauline View of Man*, 59-81.

mind, as it were, infusing its limbs and mingled with its huge body. From this arises all of life, the race of men, animals and birds, and the monsters that the sea bears under its marble surface. The seeds of this mind and spirit have a fiery power and celestial origin, insofar as the limbs and joints of the body, which is of earth, harmful, and subject to death, do not make them full and slow them down. Thus the souls, shut up in the gloomy darkness of the prison of their bodies, experience fear, desire, joy, and sorrow, and do not see clearly the essence of their celestial nature. Moreover, when the last glimmer of life has gone, all the evils and all the diseases of the body do not yet completely depart from these poor souls and it is inevitable that many ills, for a long time encrusted, become deeply engrained in an amazing way. Therefore they are piled with punishments and they pay the penalties of their former wickedness. Some spirits are hung suspended to the winds; for others the infection of crime is washed by a vast whirlpool or burned out by fire. Each of us suffers his own shade. Then we are sent to Elysium and we few occupy these happy fields, until a long period of the circle of time has been completed and has removed the ingrown corruption and has left a pure ethereal spirit and the fire of the original essence. When they have completed the cycle of one thousand years, the god calls all these in a great throng to the river Lethe, where, of course, they are made to forget so that they might begin to wish to return to bodies and see again the vault of heaven.[34]

Given the fact that most of the members of the church in Thessalonica would have been familiar with such teaching about the soul, is it any wonder that Paul writes a comforting message of peaceful falling asleep and then embodied resurrection to them (1 Thess 4:13–18)? Given the focus on ψυχή in Hellenistic understandings of man, is it any wonder that Paul specifically includes this term, with a meaning of "individual self" distinct from Hellenistic understandings of the soul, in his description of the whole person who will be sanctified and kept to the triumphal coming of Christ? If Paul would not have included this term, the Christians at Thessalonica would have posed the question: "But what will happen to my ψυχή in the afterlife?"

Certainly ψυχή is present in the Pauline corpus, but why was it not used more frequently? Paul gives very limited attention to ψυχή largely because of the dominant attention he gives to πνεῦμα in his anthropology of the believer in Christ. Stacey explains this shift as resulting from Paul's own

---

34. Vergil, *Aeneid*, 700–751. This translation is from Morford and Lenardon, *Classical Mythology*, 246.

religious experience of the Spirit. "In [Paul's] Christian experience, ψυχή, the term for purely human vitality, became unimportant. πνεῦμα, the term that began with God but proceeded into man, became central. The infrequency of the use of ψυχή in Paul is the key to the understanding of it. This fact points us away from Jewish and Greek ideas to the third factor, Paul's religious experience. Paul's knowledge of the Holy Spirit set the basis of his anthropology and πνεῦμα took the leading role."[35]

πνεῦμα in Paul's Epistles and Thessalonian Context

It is clear that τὸ πνεῦμα plays the leading role in Paul's anthropology: it is used some 146 times in his letters.[36] As a first-century Jew, Paul's understanding of πνεῦμα is grounded in the rich testimony in the Hebrew Scriptures to the divine רוּחַ (breath, spirit), as expressed here by W. David Stacey: "Between Paul and the Old Testament there are no striking differences, only development and a variation of emphasis. The framework of Paul's belief about the Spirit is exactly the Old Testament framework. It begins with the Divine Nature, passes on to divine activity, to the power that invades men, to the element in regenerated man that receives it, and to the results in belief and practice that ensue from the spirit invasion. This common pattern is too clear, too complete, to be accidental."[37]

While the background for Paul's usage may be clear, Paul's actual use of πνεῦμα is complex and varied.[38] Stacey notes six different uses of πνεῦμα in Paul: Holy Spirit, the Spirit at work in the believer in Christ, evil spirits, evils spirits at work in unbelievers, the Christian spirit as a result of the Holy Spirit, and the individual spirit of each human.[39] This brief discussion will not attempt to analyze this broad testimony to πνεῦμα, but will simply address three important questions. Does Paul teach that all individuals, apart from being in Christ, have πνεῦμα as an aspect of their anthropology? If so, what is the relationship between this πνεῦμα and the πνεῦμα of a Christian? Finally, what can be said about Paul's understanding of the relationship between "the spirit" of a Christian and "the Holy Spirit"?

The fact is that Paul wrote very little about πνεῦμα as constituting the inner man of every human being. First Corinthians 2:10–12 implies that

---

35. Stacey, *Pauline View of Man*, 126–27.
36. Ibid., 121.
37. Ibid., 138.
38. To confirm this conclusion, one only needs to examine the section on Paul in Eduard Schweizer, "πνεῦμα, πνευματικός."
39. Stacey, *Pauline View of Man*, 128–29.

each human has a πνεῦμα who knows the inner thoughts of his or her own person. Paul also states there that Christians have not received "the spirit of the world" (τὸ πνεῦμα τοῦ κόσμου) but "the Spirit from God" (τὸ πνεῦμα τὸ ἐκ τοῦ θεοῦ) so that Christians can understand the thoughts of God. The implication of this is that one's individual spirit has received and is impacted by either "the spirit of the world" or "the Spirit from God." Stacey notes that in Paul's letters the Spirit is "the key to the understanding of man's spirit . . . but one does not shade off into the other."[40]

Paul understands that man's spirit is re-created, transformed, and made new by the Holy Spirit so that the Christian possesses a spirit different from an unbeliever because of indwelling of the Holy Spirit. This understanding is reflected when Paul writes about "my spirit" or "our spirit" as distinct but not separated from the Holy Spirit. An example of this is Rom 8:16, "The Spirit himself (αὐτὸ τὸ πνεῦμα) bears witness with our spirit (τῷ πνεύμα ἡμῶν) that we are children of God." Paul is telling each of the Roman Christians that the Spirit and their spirit (e.g., because their spirit had been enlivened and defined by the indwelling of the Spirit) both testify to their status as children of God. Another example is when Paul writes about praying and praising with "my spirit" (1 Cor 14:14–15); his spirit here is distinguished from the Spirit who indwells Paul even though it is not separate from the Spirit. Such an understanding is also reflected in Paul's statement that when the Corinthians would assemble for church discipline, "my spirit is present" (1 Cor 5:3–5).

What is the relationship between the spirit of the Christian and the Holy Spirit? While some distinction remains, the very close relationship between the two has led James Frame to conclude about the texts discussed immediately above: "it is evident that 'my spirit' is that portion of the divine Spirit which is resident in the individual."[41] Robert Jewett states that "Paul thought of the human spirit simply as the apportioned divine spirit . . . thought to so enter human possession that it could be referred to as 'mine' and yet at the same time retaining its character as divine."[42] In spite of the objections of some scholars, Paul's understanding of the Christian's spirit cannot be easily distinguished from the presence of the Holy Spirit in the Christian.[43] It is precisely the Spirit's close union with the Christian's spirit that is the "firstfruits" of the redemption of the body (Rom 8:23).

---

40. Stacey, *Pauline View of Man*, 132.

41. Frame, *Critical and Exegetical Commentary*, 212.

42. Jewett, *Paul's Anthropological Terms*, 451; see also 175–83.

43. For example, Fee states that "this suggestion will simply not hold up"; see *First and Second Letters to the Thessalonians*, 228.

Because of the close relationship, even union, between "spirit" and "Spirit" in Paul's anthropology, it must be emphasized that "spirit" in the triad of 1 Thess 5:23 should always be understood in light of the presence of "the Spirit." Even as Christ has redefined Paul's understanding of the "inner man" and "new man" so that Christ dominates his understanding of the *anthropos* in the Christian, so the Spirit profoundly dominates the individual spirit in Paul's anthropology of the Christian. There can be little doubt that Paul spent time teaching the Thessalonians about τὸ πνεῦμα, probably in part to correct their Hellenistic misunderstandings of ψυχή, but especially to fill out their understanding of πνεῦμα, especially the Holy Spirit (cf. 1 Thess 1:5, 6; 4:8; 5:19). In fact, such teaching is assumed by the imperatival exhortation that comes shortly before this triad: "Do not quench τὸ πνεῦμα" (5:19).

Conclusion: The Meaning and Function of 1 Thessalonians 5:23

Drawing on the understanding of the three anthropological terms proposed above, a terse interpretation of 1 Thess 5:23 will now be set forth, beginning with a brief overview of the structure of this blessing. It is made up of two major clauses that are divided as follows:

> First Clause: May the God of peace himself sanctify you completely,
>
> Second Clause: and may your spirit, self, and body as a whole be kept blamelessly at the triumphal coming of our Lord Jesus Christ.

Within these two clauses, elements of parallel structure are also visible between the two verbs, two pronouns, and two adjectives in what amounts to a chiastic structure.[44]

> Optative Verb: ἁγιάσαι ("may he sanctify")
>
> Recipients: ὑμᾶς ("you")
>
> Adjective: ὁλοτελεῖς ("completely")
>
> Conjunction: καὶ ("and")
>
> Adjective: ὁλόκληρον ("whole")

---

44. Weima, *1–2 Thessalonians*, 418.

Recipients: ὑμῶν τὸ πνεῦμα καὶ ἡ ψυχὴ καὶ τὸ σῶμα ("your spirit, self, and body")

Optative Verb: τηρηθείη ("may it be kept")

Paul begins this blessing by using a reassuring and comforting title for God: ὁ θεὸς τῆς εἰρήνης ("the God of peace"). The powerful Roman Empire promised peace through its *Pax Romana*, but cannot deliver from divine judgment (cf. 1 Thess 5:3). It is God who delivers us from the wrath of judgment through Jesus (cf. 1 Thess 1:9; 5:9). In light of the anxiety caused by suffering (e.g., 2 Thess 1:4), it is not surprising that a similar blessing comes at the close of 2 Thessalonians: "May the Lord of peace himself give you peace" (2 Thess 3:16). The optative mood verb ἁγιάσαι with the pronoun ὑμᾶς expresses the blessing of the first phrase: "May he sanctify you." The adjective ὁλοτελεῖς is a *hapax legomenon* in the New Testament and rare in other literature, but is found used with physiological terminology.[45] Although an adjective, ὁλοτελεῖς is translated adverbially here ("completely"); it is describing "the totality of sanctification."[46] Malherbe notes that ὁλοτελεῖς is used in tandem with the similar sounding ὁλόκληρον in the second clause as "synonymous adjectives denoting entirety."[47] The use of the personal pronoun αὐτός prior to the title for God serves as an intensifier: "May the God of peace *himself* sanctify you completely."

The second clause has an epexegetical function: it explains further the meaning of the first clause about being sanctified completely. The optative mood verb of this clause, τηρηθείη, is used with the adjective ἀμέμπτως to express the blessing of the second clause: "may . . . be kept blameless." The passive voice of τηρηθείη without an expressed agent implies that this is a divine action (i.e., kept blameless by "the God of peace"). This understanding is confirmed in the statements that follow: "The one who is calling you is faithful, who also will do it." There is a virtually synonymous relationship between the verbal actions of these two clauses: "sanctify" and "keep blameless." The object of this divine "keep blameless" action is the "whole" person, as is clear from both the adjective ὁλόκληρον, which modifies all three nouns that follow, and the triad: ὁλόκληρον ὑμῶν τὸ πνεῦμα καὶ ἡ ψυχὴ καὶ τὸ σῶμα ("your spirit, self, and body as a whole"). Gordon Fee notes that "whatever distinctions he may have understood are quite secondary to the greater

---

45. Malherbe notes that it was used by Aetius (first or second century AD) of the fully formed human embryo in *Compendium of Tenets* (see Ps.-Plutarch, *On the Opinions of Philosophers* 5.21); see *Letters to the Thessalonians*, 228.

46. Malherbe, *Letters to the Thessalonians*, 228.

47. Ibid.

concern of completeness."[48] The use of the triad may reflect completeness in a way similar to the language of "heart, soul, and might" in the Shema (Deut 6:4)[49] and "heart, soul, mind, and strength" in Jesus' summary of the law (Matt 22:37; Mark 12:30; Luke 10:37).[50] Given the fact that one of the issues that Paul addresses is the misunderstanding that the death of fellow Christians prior to Christ's coming means those Christians will miss out on blessings brought at the parousia, Jeffrey Weima posits that this triad may be a final word of assurance that addresses this misunderstanding: "By closing the letter with a prayer that God may keep their spirit and soul and body 'whole' (holoklēron) at the second coming of Christ, Paul responds one last time to such fears by assuring his readers that a believer's *whole* person will be involved in the day of Christ's return. Thus those who die before the Parousia of Christ will neither miss that vindicating and magnificent eschatological event, nor will they be in any way at a disadvantage compared to believers who are still living."[51]

Although Paul is emphasizing the complete human being with this triad, nevertheless each anthropological term is important, as emphasized above. πνεῦμα (spirit) is put in first position because it reflects Paul's own anthropological priority on the Spirit. For Paul, any talk about the spirit of one who is in Christ is talk of the Spirit who has enlivened and transformed the individual spirit. Paul uses ψυχή not in the sense of Hellenistic conceptions of the soul, but to signify the unique individual self with which each human has been created. It is conceivable that Paul could have written about the whole person in terms of just πνεῦμα and σῶμα (cf. 2 Cor 7:1). If he would not have mentioned ψυχή to the Thessalonians in this context, however, some of them, because ψυχή was central in their understanding of man, would have been left wondering what would happen to their ψυχή in the afterlife, especially at the triumphal coming of Jesus. Paul anticipates this question by including ψυχή in his triad that emphasizes the whole person participating in the last day deliverance, not merely a disembodied ψυχή. Finally, Paul mentions σῶμα (body) because, unlike the denigration of the body as a prison for the soul in Hellenistic philosophy, the human body is a creation of God that will be resurrected and restored to glory; for Paul, σῶμα is essential to what it means to be an *anthropos*. The eschatological thrust of this blessing is made explicit in its closing words. The blessing is for the whole person to be kept blameless ἐν τῇ παρουσίᾳ τοῦ κυρίου ἡμῶν Ἰησοῦ

48. Fee, *First and Second Letters to the Thessalonians*, 230.
49. Ibid., 228n79.
50. Weima, *1–2 Thessalonians*, 422.
51. Ibid.

Χριστοῦ ("at the triumphal coming of our Lord Jesus Christ"). παρουσίᾳ is a comforting and frequent subject in the Thessalonian letters, signifying the visible and public triumphal coming of Jesus on the last day in deliverance and judgment (1 Thess 2:19; 3:13; 4:15; 5:23; 2 Thess 2:1, 8).[52]

Paul follows up this blessing with confident assurance: "The one who is calling you is faithful, who also will do it." There is to be no doubt in the Thessalonian congregation that the God of peace will sanctify them completely, and keep their spirit, self, and body as a whole blameless until the last day. Paul had already expressed the firm basis for this certain hope: "Because we believe that Jesus died and rose again" (1 Thess 4:14; cf. 5:9–10).

Bibliography

Boring, M. Eugene. *I and II Thessalonians: A Commentary*. New Testament Library. Louisville: Westminster John Knox, 2015.
Bultmann, Rudolf. *Theology of the New Testament*. Translated by Kendrick Grobel. New York: Scribner, 1951, 1955.
Fee, Gordon D. *First and Second Letters to the Thessalonians*. New International Commentary on the New Testament. Grand Rapids: Eerdmans, 2009.
Frame, James Everett. *A Critical and Exegetical Commentary on the Epistles of St. Paul to the Thessalonians*. Edinburgh: T. & T. Clark, 1912.
Gieschen, Charles A. "Christ's Coming and the Church's Mission in 1 Thessalonians." *Concordia Theological Quarterly* 76 (2012) 37–55.
———. "Original Sin in the New Testament." *Concordia Journal* 31 (2005) 359–75.
———. "Paul and the Law: Was Luther Right?" In *The Law in Holy Scripture*, edited by Charles A. Gieschen, 113–47. St. Louis: Concordia, 2004.
———. "The Son as Creator and Source of New Creation in Colossians." In *The Restoration of Creation in Christ: Essays in Honor of Dean O. Wenthe*, edited by Arthur A. Just Jr. and Paul J. Grime. St. Louis: Concordia, 2014.
Gundry, Robert H. *Sōma in Biblical Theology with Emphasis on Pauline Anthropology*. SNTSMS 29. Cambridge: Cambridge University Press, 1976.
Jewett, Robert. *Paul's Anthropological Terms: A Study of Their Use in Conflict Settings*. Arbeiten zur Geschichte des antiken Judentums und des Urchristentums 10. Leiden: Brill, 1971.
Luckensmeyer, David. *The Eschatology of First Thessalonians*. Novum Testamentum et Orbis Antiquus 71. Göttingen: Vandenhoeck and Ruprecht, 2009.
Malherbe, Abraham J. *The Letters to the Thessalonians*. Anchor Bible 32B. New York: Doubleday, 2000.
Martin, Dale. *The Corinthian Body*. New Haven: Yale University Press, 1995.
Middendorf, Michael P. *The "I" in the Storm: A Study of Romans 7*. St. Louis: Concordia, 1997.
———. *Romans 1:1—8:39*. Concordia Commentary. St. Louis: Concordia, 2013.
Pieper, Francis. *Christian Dogmatics*. St. Louis: Concordia, 1950.
Robertson, A. T. *Word Pictures in the New Testament*. Grand Rapids: Baker, 1950.

52. BDAG, 780–81.

Schweizer, Eduard. "πνεῦμα, πνευματικός." In *TDNT* 6 (1968) 415–37.
Stacey, W. David. *The Pauline View of Man: In Relation to Its Judaic and Hellenistic Background*. London: Macmillan, 1956.
Vergil. *Aeneid*. In *Classical Mythology*, by Mark P. O. Morford and Robert J. Lenardon, 2nd ed., 700–751. London: Longman, 1977.
Ware, James. "Paul's Understanding of Resurrection in 1 Corinthians 15:36–54." *Journal of Biblical Literature* 133 (2014) 809–35.
Weima, Jeffrey A. D. *1–2 Thessalonians*. Baker Exegetical Commentary on the New Testament. Grand Rapids: Baker, 2014.
Winger, Thomas M. *Ephesians*. Concordia Commentary. St. Louis: Concordia, 2015.

7

Repent, O Lexicon, and Do Not Begin to Say That You Have Bauer and Danker as Your Father

—David S. Hasselbrook

Other studies have pointed out the flaws of New Testament lexicons in detail.[1] The current essay will focus on a few examples relative to BDAG (2000)[2] that further demonstrate that the New Testament lexicon has not reached a state of perfection or of being "finished."

The Adjective Εὐάρεστος and the Corresponding Adverb Εὐαρέστως

In the foreword to BDAG, Frederick Danker discusses the traditional format of New Testament lexicons. He notes that typically word definitions have taken the form of a series of words or glosses intended to cover "a variety of possibilities for translation." Revealing a lexicographical insight with which many users of New Testament lexicons may be unfamiliar, he indicates that unfortunately "an unwary reader may think that a given word bears all the content expressed by a series of synonyms." Danker states

---

1. E.g., Lee, *A History of New Testament Lexicography*; Roberts, "A Review of BDAG"; and Hasselbrook, *Studies in New Testament Lexicography*.
2. Bauer et al., *Greek-English Lexicon of the New Testament*.

that, in an attempt to overcome this hazard, BDAG "builds on and expands Bauer's use of extended definition," except when the glosses are sufficient to convey the meaning of a given word.³

For εὐάρεστος Danker gives the following definition: *"pleasing, acceptable."*⁴ Apparently he assumed here that the glosses were sufficient to convey the meaning of this adjective. Since an extended definition is not given in this instance, are we to assume that εὐάρεστος "bears all the content expressed by" these glosses? According to *The American Heritage Dictionary (AHD)*, published in 1982, "pleasing" has the definition of "giving pleasure or enjoyment; agreeable," while "acceptable" can have the following senses: "1. Worthy of being accepted. 2. Adequate enough to satisfy a need, requirement, or standard; satisfactory. 3. Designating an amount or level that can be endured or allowed."⁵ Based on this information, one would think that εὐάρεστος can range in meaning from "that which gives pleasure" to "that which is satisfactory or tolerable," two very different senses. This range seems to be supported by the additional information given in the entry for the word, which suggests that the "pleasing" sense pertained to the Greco-Roman world and the "acceptable" sense generally to the New Testament (i.e., for the use of the word in Rom 12:1, 2; 14:18; 2 Cor 5:9; Eph 5:10; Phil 4:18; Col 3:20; Heb 13:21).⁶ If "pleasing" and "acceptable" are intended as synonyms, it would seem that they intersect in meaning in describing something that is satisfactory to a greater or lesser extent, where the latter would be "satisfactory" or "barely satisfactory" and the former "very or extremely satisfactory."

In BDAG the corresponding adverb, εὐαρέστως, is defined as *"in an acceptable manner"* (applicable for the use of the word in Heb 12:28).⁷ Here, the sense of "in a way which gives pleasure" appears to be absent. But is it?

An examination of the history of the Bauer series of New Testament lexicons reveals that the definitions given for εὐάρεστος and εὐαρέστως in BDAG have been carried over from the previous editions of the English stream, namely, BAGD (1979) and BAG (1957).⁸ BAG is essentially

---

3. Ibid., viii.
4. Ibid., s.v. εὐάρεστος, ον.
5. *American Heritage Dictionary*, s.v. "pleasing" and s.v. "acceptable."
6. BDAG, s.v. εὐάρεστος, ον, where initially it is stated of the word that "in the Gr-Rom. world commonly said of things and esp. of pers. noted for their civic-minded generosity and who endeavor to do things that are pleasing." This is followed by the statement that "[i]n our lit. gener. w. ref. to God, to whom someth. is acceptable."
7. Ibid., s.v. εὐαρέστως.
8. From here on, unless otherwise noted, the reader is referred to Hasselbrook, *Studies in New Testament Lexicography*, xiii–xxvii, for full bibliographic information of

a translation of Bauer⁴ (1952).⁹ However, in Bauer⁴, εὐάρεστος is defined as *"angenehm, wohlgefällig,"* and εὐαρέστως as *"in wohlgefälliger Weise."*¹⁰ These German glosses have the sense of "that which gives pleasure" for the adjective and "in a pleasing way" for the adverb.¹¹ The idea of "that which is merely satisfactory or tolerable" or "in a satisfactory or tolerable way" is absent. So, apparently BAG translated *angenehm* as "pleasing" and *wohlgefällig* as "acceptable." The former case makes sense, but the latter one doesn't really seem right. Or does it?

In *Webster's Third New International Dictionary (WTNID)*, published in 1966, the following definitions are given for "acceptable": "1: capable or worthy of being accepted . . . : satisfactory . . . : conforming to or equal to approved standards . . . 2. a: welcome, pleasing < compliments . . . are always ~ to ladies—Jane Austen > b: barely satisfactory or adequate."¹² A definition of "welcome, pleasing" is given to the word, with an occurrence of this sense in the usage of Jane Austen, whose writings date in the early part of the nineteenth century. *The Oxford English Dictionary (OED)*, published in 1991, also lists this sense for the word, supporting it with usages in sources dating from 1386 to 1861.¹³ While *OED* does not indicate that this sense of "pleasing" is obsolete, the *AHD* reveals that, at least in American usage and as early as 1982, such a meaning for "acceptable" is no longer current or common, a situation that is also confirmed by the experience of this author.

The conclusion of the matter is that when BAG translated *wohlgefällig*, the English word "acceptable" was used because it still conveyed the sense of "that which pleases" and was not intended to be understood in the sense of "satisfactory" or "barely satisfactory." In addition, the word "acceptable" may have been chosen due to the precedent of its use to define εὐάρεστος (and "acceptably" for εὐαρέστως) by previous Greek-to-English New Testament or ancient Greek lexicons,¹⁴ which themselves were likely influenced

---

the lexicons referenced.

9. In the foreword to the first English edition, Arndt and Gingrich state, "our departures from the general sense of Bauer's work have been few and far between." See BAG, vi.

10. Bauer4 (1952), s.v. εὐάρεστος, ον and s.v. εὐαρέστως.

11. *Langenscheidt New College German Dictionary*, s.v. *angenehm* and s.v. *wohlgefällig*. The other lexicons of the Bauer series in German, from Preuschen1 (1910) to BRAA (1988), have essentially the same senses.

12. *Webster's Third New International Dictionary*, s.v. "acceptable."

13. Simpson and Weiner, *The Oxford English Dictionary*, s.v. "acceptable."

14. E.g., Cokayne (1658); Cokayne (1661); Williams, *Conc.* (1767); Parkhurst1 (1769); Ewing (1801); Laing (1821); Parkhurstnew (1822); Wahl-Robinson (1825); Greenfield (1829); Parkhurst-Rose (1829); Bass2 (1829); Robinson (1836); Robinson-Bloomfield (1837); Robinson-Robson (1839); Bloomfield1 (1840); || LS1 (1843);

by the usage of the King James Version (KJV) that employed this translation of the word.[15] Also, the editors of BAG indicate that they had their eyes on the Revised Standard Version (RSV), which was likewise influenced by the KJV.[16] Moreover, Danker, whose life span (1920-2012) includes the time when "acceptable" conveyed the sense of "pleasing," probably still thought of this meaning when he allowed the gloss of "acceptable" to remain.

Further support for understanding εὐάρεστος as "that which pleases" (and by association, εὐαρέστως as "in a pleasing manner") is found in the lexicons of the Greeks. The *Great Lexicon of the Greek Language* defines this adjective as "the one who pleases, the one who brings forth pleasure, the pleasing one, the pleasant one," indicating that this sense of the word attains from Cleanthes (270 BC), through the time of the New Testament, all the way into medieval and finally modern Greek.[17] The *Lexicon of the Greek Language: Ancient-Medieval-Modern* and the *Epitome of the Lexicon of the Medieval Greek Popular Literature 1000-1669 of Emmanouil Kriaras* confirm this sense of the word.[18]

Parkhurst-Rose-Major (1845), Greenfield (1848), Robinson (1850), Robinson, *Condensed* (1851), Wigram (1852), Gall, *Conc.* (1863), Bassnew (1868), Green, S.G. (1871), Hudson, *Conc.*2 (1871), Bullinger, *Conc.* (1877), New Plan (1877), Robinson-Negris-Duncan (1879), Green, T.S. (1880), Green, S.G.new (1880), Hudson, *Conc.*5 (1882), Wilke-Grimm2-Thayer (1887),\\ Sophocles (1887), Hudson, *Conc.*8 (1891), Hickie (1893), Young [1895], Wilke-Grimm-Thayer4 (1896), Berry (1897), Green, S.G.rev. (1912), Abbott-Smith1 (1922), Abbott-Smith3 (1936), Vine, *Conc.* (1939-1941), || LSJ (1940), Smith, *Conc.* (1955), Gingrich, *Shorter*1 (1965), Newman (1971), Moulton (1978), Perschbacher (1990), Mounce (1993), FFM (2000), LEH (2003), and Danker with Krug, *The Concise Greek-English Lexicon*. For all these lexicons, the gloss "acceptable" is given with "pleasing," "well pleasing," "pleasing well," "grateful," and/or "pleasant" for εὐάρεστος. For Muraoka, *A Greek-English Lexicon of the Septuagint*, the gloss of "acceptable" stands alone. In the above lexicons, for εὐαρέστως, if information is provided, the gloss "acceptably" is usually given alone, although sometimes it is accompanied with "so as to please," "in a pleasing manner," or "in a manner well-pleasing to." Cokayne (1658) and Cokayne (1661), while glossing the adjective with "acceptable, pleasing," define the adverb with "to the delight, that we may please" and "delightfully, pleasingly."

15. The KJV translates εὐάρεστος with "acceptable" (Rom 12:1, 2; 14:18; Eph 5:10), "be accepted" (2 Cor 5:9), "well-pleasing" (Phil 4:18; Col 3:20; Heb 13:21), and "please" (Titus 2:9), while it translates εὐαρέστως with "acceptably" (Heb 12:28).

16. In the foreword the editors state, "In the spelling of proper names we have generally followed the usage of the Revised Standard Version." See BAG, viii. Following the KJV, the RSV (1946/1971) translates εὐάρεστος with "acceptable" in Rom 12:1-2 and 14:18 and εὐαρέστως with the same in Heb 12:28. The ESV (2001) maintains the RSV translation of the respective words in these verses.

17. "ὁ ἀρέσκων, ὁ προκαλῶν εὐαρέσκειαν, ὁ ἀρεστός, ὁ τερπνός." Zervos, *Great Lexicon of the Greek Language*, s.v. εὐάρεστος (-η) -ο(ν) 1.

18. *Lexicon of the Greek Language: Ancient-Medieval-Modern*, s.v. ευάρεστος -η, -ο,

The Noun Ἀρετή

The NIV (1984) translation of 1 Peter 2:9 is: "But you are a chosen people, a royal priesthood, a holy nation, a people belonging to God, that you may declare the praises of him who called you out of darkness into his wonderful light." Here the accusative plural of ἀρετή is translated as "praises." Danker seems to express some doubt about this translation in the entry for ἀρετή in BDAG. He says:

> In accordance w. a usage that treats ἀ. and δόξα as correlatives (ἀ. = excellence that results in approbation and therefore δόξα = renown), which finds expression outside the OT (Is 42:8, 12) in juxtaposition of the two terms . . . , the LXX transl. הוֹד majesty, high rank (Hab 3:3; Zech 6:13 . . .) and also תְּהִלָּה praise sg. (Is . . .) with ἀ. pl. The latter sense 'praise' (pl. = laudes) has been maintained for 1 Pt 2:9, which is probably influenced by Is 42:12; 43:21. It is poss. that Semitically oriented auditors of 1 Pt interpreted the expression along such lines, but Gr-Rom. publics would in the main be conditioned to hear a stress on performance, which of course would elicit praise.[19]

As can be seen, Danker indicates that the use ἀρετή in 1 Peter 2:9 is influenced by Isaiah 42:12 and 43:21, where others have maintained that the plural of ἀρετή is used to translate the singular of תְּהִלָּה in the sense of "praise." He goes on to suggest that this, however, would be a Semitic rendering and not a normal sense of the word in Greco-Roman usage.

At this point two observations will be made. First, the use of תְּהִלָּה for ἀρετή is not necessarily a Semitic, as opposed to Greco-Roman, usage.

---

and Kazazis and Karanastasis, *Epitome of the Lexicon of the Medieval Greek Popular Literature 1000–1669 of Emmanouil Kriaras*, s.v. εὐάρεστος. The former lexicon, which covers all periods of the Greek language, confirms the sense for Ancient, Hellenistic, and Modern Greek; the latter lexicon, which pertains to the vernacular literature of the medieval period from 1100 to 1669, confirms the sense for Medieval Greek. See also Louw and Nida, *Greek-English Lexicon of the New Testament*, 2:300, where εὐάρεστος, ον and εὐαρέστως are defined as "pertaining to that which causes someone to be pleased—'pleasing to, pleasingly.'" As was mentioned, many previous New Testament lexicons that provide definitions or glosses in English use the word "acceptable" to define εὐάρεστος. Similarly, most older New Testament lexicons that give glosses in Latin (e.g., Complutensian [1514], Lubin [1614], Pasor1 [1621], etc.) use words like *acceptus*, *gratus*, and *placitus*, that is, words that are often defined in English as "acceptable" (with the archaic sense of the word intended?). The previous New Testament lexicons that give meanings in German are generally better in this regard (e.g., Bahrdt [1786], Oertel [1799], Schirlitz1 [1851], Kuhne [1892], etc.), more clearly revealing the sense of "that which is pleasing."

19. BDAG, s.v. ἀρετή, ῆς, ἡ 2.

According to *The Brown-Driver-Briggs Hebrew and English Lexicon* (BDB), while הלהת can have the sense of "praise," it may also have the sense of "qualities, deeds, etc., of [Yahweh], demanding praise," in either the singular or the plural.[20] This latter meaning not only fits the sense of "a performance or action which elicits praise," which Danker gives for the second sense of ἀρετή in his entry (to which the above quote applies), but also fits his first sense that he attributes to the word of "uncommon character worthy of praise."[21] The meaning of "qualities, deeds, etc., of [Yahweh], demanding praise" for תְּהִלָּה seems especially applicable where תְּהִלָּה is the object of a verb of speaking. This would apply to the use of the word in Isaiah 42:12, 43:21, and 63:7, where it is translated with ἀρετή in the Septuagint.[22]

The KJV translates ἀρετή in 1 Peter 2:9 with "praises." According to *OED*, an archaic sense of the word "praise," supported by sources ranging from 1526 to 1894, is "That for which a person or thing is, or deserves to be, praised; praiseworthiness; merit, value, virtue."[23] Such a sense would fit with the meaning of תְּהִלָּה and ἀρετή as "qualities, deeds, etc., demanding praise." It seems that the RSV recognized this reality to a degree, translating ἀρετή in 1 Peter 2:9 as "wonderful deeds." The NIV, however, returns to the "praises" of the KJV, but in a time when the archaic sense of the word may be mostly lost to the average English speaker and may not even have been in the minds of the translators themselves. Furthermore, the NIV translation of "declare the praises" is somewhat awkward in English, having the sense of something like "express the expressions" or "declare the declarations of honor/worthiness."

---

20. Brown et al., *Brown-Driver-Briggs Hebrew and English Lexicon*, s.v. 1 הלהת. and 4.

21. BDAG, s.v. ἀρετή, ῆς, ἡ 1.

22. In support of תְּהִלָּה with the meaning of "qualities, deeds, etc., of [Yahweh], demanding praise," BDB lists Exod 15:11; Pss 9:15; 35:28; 78:4; 79:13; 102:22; 106:2, 47; Isa 43:21; 60:6; and 63:7. The only other place in the Septuagint, besides Isa 42:12; 43:21; and 63:7, where תְּהִלָּה is translated with ἀρετή is in Isa 42:8. Although the word is not a direct object to a verb of speaking, it still could have the sense we are considering here. For the passages where ἀρετή is used to translate תְּהִלָּה, see Hatch and Redpath, *Concordance to the Septuagint*, 156. For the actual passages in the Septuagint for ἀρετή or other words considered in this essay, unless otherwise noted, see *Septuaginta: Vetus Testamentum Graecum*.

23. *OED*, s.v. "praise, sb" 3.a. See also *AHD*, s.v. "praise n." 3., which gives as an archaic sense: "A reason for praise; merit."

The Verb Ἐξαγγέλλω

The ESV renders 1 Peter 2:9 as "But you are a chosen race, a royal priesthood, a holy nation, a people for his own possession, that you may proclaim the excellencies of him who called you out of darkness into his marvelous light." In this version, ἀρετή is rendered as "excellencies," which is a fairly good translation in that it can refer to either qualities or actions that are excellent or praiseworthy.[24] The ESV translates the verb ἐξαγγέλλω in this passage as "proclaim," to which we now turn.

BDAG defines ἐξαγγέλλω as "proclaim, report." Again, since an extended definition is not given here, are we to assume that ἐξαγγέλλω "bears all the content expressed by" these glosses? The verb "proclaim" conveys the meaning of "to announce openly, publicly, and/or officially," while the verb "report" conveys the sense of "to relate, tell about, or give an account of," which may or may not be done in an open, public, or official way.[25]

The entry in BDAG notes that, in relation to the New Testament, ἐξαγγέλλω occurs in the intermediate ending of Mark and 1 Peter 2:9. In the former, Mary Magdalene, Mary the mother of James, and Salome had just seen the young man clothed in white at the tomb, who announced to them that Jesus was risen and would go before the disciples into Galilee. After the women flee the tomb and say nothing to anyone because they are afraid (Mark 16:8), the intermediate ending picks up with the following: Πάντα δὲ τὰ παρηγγελμένα τοῖς περὶ τὸν Πέτρον συντόμως ἐξήγγειλαν, "And all the things that they had been told to do they reported immediately to Peter and those around him."[26]

In this use of ἐξαγγέλλω, the reporting of the women was not done in an official/formal way. Neither, it seems, was it done in an open and public way, since they apparently say nothing to anyone else at this time, except to Peter and those gathered around him.

The information given in BDAG for this verb appears to list the Septuagint as supporting the meanings of "proclaim, report." In the Septuagint, ἐξαγγέλλω is most often used to translate the Hebrew verb סָפַר.[27] In all these instances, which occur in the Psalms, the meaning of ἐξαγγέλλω

---

24. Although "excellencies" is not a very common English usage today, the average English speaker can figure out the meaning merely by the etymological connection with the word "excellence."

25. *AHD*, s.v. "proclaim" and s.v. "report"; *WTNID*, s.v. "proclaim" and s.v. "report."

26. Unless otherwise noted, biblical translations are my own.

27. In the piel form in Pss 9:14[15]; 70[71]:15; 72[73]:28; 78[79]:13; 106[107]:22; 118[119]:13, 26. In the qal form in Ps 55[56]:8[9]. For the passages where ἐξαγγέλλω is used in the Septuagint, see Hatch and Redpath, *Concordance to the Septuagint*, 483.

is to "recount,"²⁸ where what is recounted includes the deeds and qualities of God, the law of God, or the life and ways of the psalmist.²⁹ The setting where the deeds and qualities of God are recounted is "in the gates of the daughter of Zion," that is, among the people of God, in Psalms 9:14[15] and 72[73]:28; likely among the assembly gathered at the temple in Psalm 106[107]:22 (cp. v. 32); or unspecified in Psalms 70[71]:15 and 78[79]:13. The recounting of the law of God in Psalm 118[119]:13 possibly occurs in the home and to one's children (cp. Deut 6:7). The relating of the psalmist's life and ways to God in Psalms 55[56]:8[9] and 118[119]:26 seems to have been done in private.

Ἐξαγγέλλω also occurs in Sirach, which has no Hebrew *Vorlage*. In 18:4 it has the sense of "making known" the works of God, where no particular setting is implied. In 39:10 and 44:15, the verb is used of the assembly or congregation "recounting" the praiseworthy deeds or qualities of certain men, which appears to occur in a congregational setting. In these latter verses, ἐξαγγέλλω is used in parallel with διηγέομαι, which has the sense of "to set out in detail, to describe, to tell."³⁰

The final occurrence of ἐξαγγέλλω in the Septuagint is in Prov 12:16. In this passage the verb translates the niphal of יָדַע. The Hebrew text followed by the Greek translation is as follows for this verse:

אֱוִיל בַּיּוֹם יִוָּדַע כַּעְסוֹ וְכֹסֶה קָלוֹן עָרוּם׃

With respect to a foolish one, at once is made known his anger, but a sensible one is covering a disgrace.

ἄφρων αὐθημερὸν ἐξαγγέλλει ὀργὴν αὐτοῦ, κρύπτει δὲ τὴν ἑαυτοῦ ἀτιμίαν πανοῦργος.³¹

A foolish one immediately makes known his wrath, but a wise one covers the disgrace of himself.

Here ἐξαγγέλλω has the sense of "making known." This "making known," moreover, can occur either through words *or actions*. While the setting is not specified, the context suggests that the "making known" could occur in a private or public setting.

28. BDB, s.v. סָפַר Pi. 1. It seems that the translator also intended this meaning where the Hebrew had the qal form in Ps 55[56]:8[9].

29. In Pss 9:14[15]; 72[73]:28; and 78[79]:13 the object of the verb is either the singular or plural of αἴνεσις. In Pss 9:14[15] and 78[79]:13, αἴνεσις translates תְּהִלָּה with the sense "qualities, deeds, etc., of [Yahweh], demanding praise." See BDB, s.v. 4 תְּהִלָּה. This finds support in Ps 72[73]:28, where αἴνεσις translates מַלְאֲכָה.

30. Lust et al., *Greek-English Lexicon of the Septuagint*, s.v. διηγέομαι.

31. From Rahlfs and Hanhart, *Septuaginta*.

A similar sense for ἐξαγγέλλω, that is, where the "making known" is not confined to words as the means of accomplishing the action of the verb, is found in the usage of Aristotle:

> ἐπεὶ γάρ ἐστι μιμητὴς ὁ ποιητὴς ὡσπερανεὶ ζωγράφος ἤ τις ἄλλος εἰκονοποιός, ἀνάγκη μιμεῖσθαι τριῶν ὄντων τὸν ἀριθμὸν ἕν τι ἀεί, ἢ γὰρ οἷα ἦν ἢ ἔστιν, ἢ οἷά φασιν καὶ δοκεῖ, ἢ οἷα εἶναι δεῖ. ταῦτα δ' ἐξαγγέλλεται λέξει ἐν ᾗ καὶ γλῶτται καὶ μεταφοραὶ καὶ πολλὰ πάθη τῆς λέξεώς ἐστι. (Poetica 1460b.8–12)[32]

> For since the poet is an imitator like a painter or another portrait-sculptor, it is necessary for him to represent always one certain thing with respect to the number of the three things which are being, namely, things such as they were or are, things such as they are said or thought to be, or things such as they ought to be. And these things [in the case of the poet] are expressed (ἐξαγγέλλεται) by diction among which are rare words and metaphors, and there are many modifications of diction.

In this passage, it is clear that while the poet will express one of the three given categories by his choice and usage of words, the painter or sculptor will express these same possibilities via his choice or usage of figures, color, shapes, images, etc. In other words, with the use of ἐξαγγέλλω in this passage, the act of "expressing" or "making known" "things as they were or are," "as they are said or thought to be," or "as they ought to be" is not, in the implied case of the painter or sculptor, confined to the use of words.

Having considered the usage of ἐξαγγέλλω in the Septuagint and in Aristotle, we now return to the use of the verb in 1 Peter 2:9. Translating the word as "proclaim" in this verse appears to assume too much and limits the way that it can be understood. The context does not specify the situation in which the action of the verb is carried out. Therefore, limiting the translation to an open, public, or official announcement seems unwarranted. The "recounting" or "making known" (ἐξαγγείλητε) of "the virtuous qualities or deeds" (τὰς ἀρετὰς) of God can occur at the gathering of the congregation through recitation of psalms, confession of creeds, and speaking/singing of the liturgy; it can occur in the home among the family; it can occur in conversations in the workplace and elsewhere (cp. 1 Pet 3:15); it can occur in personal prayers of thanksgiving to God; etc. Moreover, the "making known" of the virtuous qualities of God can occur not only through words, but also through the life and actions of the Christian (cp. 1 Pet 1:15–16;

---

32. From the *Thesaurus Linguae Graecae (TLG)*, copyrighted by Thesaurus Linguae Graecae and the Regents of the University of California.

2:11–12).³³ In 1 Peter 2:12 the Gentiles glorify God for the good conduct of Christians because the virtues they display come from God and reveal him. In line with this is the emphasis in 1 Peter that a Christian makes Christ known by the act of enduring suffering for doing good, revealing nonverbally the virtue that Jesus manifested to accomplish our salvation (1 Pet 2:18–25; 3:9, 17; 4:1, 12–16, 19). There are times when the virtues of God are to be made known with actions *instead of words* (e.g., 1 Pet 3:1–5).

Conclusion

The cases addressed herein have demonstrated that the New Testament lexicon has not reached a state of perfection or of being "finished." In particular, we have seen that the "definitions" of the lexicon are at times based on undetected obsolete English meanings that are now hiding behind, or lost from, words that still convey other current and seemingly applicable meanings in the English language. Such a situation reveals that not only does the lexicon need to be based on an accurate understanding of a given word in the source language (i.e., Greek), but it also must convey this understanding in *current usage* of the target language (i.e., modern English in the case of BDAG). That means that the lexicon will always need to be reviewed and updated to deal with the changing nature of the target language.

In addition to fluctuations related to the target language, the lexicon is still lacking in its understanding of word usage in the source language. A more thorough consultation or consideration of Greek usage outside of the New Testament is needed to accurately assess the meaning(s) a word may signify in the then-current Greek language, of which the New Testament is a part.

This essay has pointed to some of the fruits that are produced when the New Testament lexicon is brought to "repentance." For instance, in terms of εὐάρεστος, we know that in Rom 12:1, when Christians by the mercies of God offer their bodies as a living sacrifice to him, this is viewed by God as not just acceptable (ESV) or tolerable, but as truly pleasing. We know that in Rom 14:18, when Christians in faith seek to not cause their brothers to stumble by what they eat or drink, they are not just acceptable

---

33. According to *OED*, s.v. "proclaim" 4, the word "proclaim" can be used figuratively where something is nonverbally made known. See also *WTNID*, s.v. "proclaim" 1b and c. However, given the ingrained ecclesiastical usage of this word in its more normal, verbal sense, a reader of such a translation in a religious context is not likely to think of nonverbal possibilities with the choice of this word. For this reason, "make known" seems to be a more preferable way to convey nonverbal possibilities in such a situation.

(ESV) or satisfactory, but are pleasing to God. Also, in relation to ἀρετή and ἐξαγγέλλω, we have come to see that in 1 Peter 2:9, the spiritual sacrifices that Christians offer to God through Christ (1 Pet 2:5)[34] can consist not only of making known his virtuous qualities and deeds through words in their various stations of life, but also of making known his virtues, often without words, through their actions and endurance of suffering for doing good.

Bibliography

The American Heritage Dictionary, Second College Edition. Boston: Houghton Mifflin, 1982.
Bauer, Walter, et al. *A Greek-English Lexicon of the New Testament and Other Early Christian Literature.* 3rd ed. Chicago: University of Chicago Press, 2000.
Brown, Francis, et al. *The Brown-Driver-Briggs Hebrew and English Lexicon.* Boston: Houghton Mifflin, 1906; reprint, Peabody, MA: Hendrickson, 2000.
Danker, Frederick, with Kathryn Krug. *The Concise Greek-English Lexicon of the New Testament.* Chicago: University of Chicago Press, 2009.
Hasselbrook, David S. *Studies in New Testament Lexicography: Advancing toward a Full Diachronic Approach with the Greek Language.* WUNT 2/303. Tübingen: Mohr Siebeck, 2011.
Hatch, Edwin, and Henry A. Redpath. *A Concordance to the Septuagint and the Other Greek Versions of the Old Testament.* 2nd ed. Grand Rapids: Baker, 1998.
Kazazis, I. N., and T. A. Karanastasis, eds. *Epitome of the Lexicon of the Medieval Greek Popular Literature 1000–1669 of Emmanouil Kriaras.* Thessaloniki: Center of Greek Language, 2001.
Langenscheidt New College German Dictionary. Berlin: Langenscheidt, 1995.
Lee, John A. *A History of New Testament Lexicography.* Studies in Biblical Greek 8. New York: Lang, 2003.
Lexicon of the Greek Language: Ancient-Medieval-Modern. 20 vols. Athens: Papiros, 2013.
Louw, Johannes P., and Eugene A. Nida. *Greek-English Lexicon of the New Testament: Based on Semantic Domains.* 2 vols. 2nd ed. New York: United Bible Societies, 1989.

---

34. What has been said for εὐάρεστος also applies to the adjective εὐπρόσδεκτος, which in 1 Pet 2:5 is translated as "acceptable" in the phrase "spiritual sacrifices acceptable to God" by the KJV, RSV, ESV, and NIV. The word in this verse, Rom 15:16 and 31, and 2 Cor 8:12 has the sense of "pleasingly accepted (by)." See Zervos, *Great Lexicon of the Greek Language,* s.v. εὐπρόσδεκτος -ον; *Lexicon of the Greek Language: Ancient-Medieval-Modern,* s.v. ευπρόσδεκτος -η, -ο; Kazazis and Karanastasis, *Epitome of the Lexicon of the Medieval Greek Popular Literature 1000–1669 of Emmanouil Kriaras,* s.v. ευπρόσδεκτος. BDAG, s.v. εὐπρόσδεκτος, ον 1, gives the following definition for the use of this word in these verses: "pert. to being capable of eliciting favorable acceptance, *acceptable.*" Here the definition is fairly good, but the gloss of "acceptable," which is apparently meant in the more archaic sense of the word, can be misleading. This definition supports the assumption that Danker was viewing the word "acceptable" as "pleasing" in his mind.

Lust, Johan, et al. *Greek-English Lexicon of the Septuagint*. Rev. ed. Stuttgart: Deutsche Bibelgesellschaft, 2003.
Muraoka, Takamitsu. *A Greek-English Lexicon of the Septuagint*. Louvain: Peeters, 2009.
Rahlfs, Alfred, and Robert Hanhart, eds. *Septuaginta: Id est Vetus Testamentum graece iuxta LXX interpretes*. Rev. ed. Stuttgart: Deutsche Bibelgesellschaft, 2006.
Roberts, Terry. "A Review of BDAG." In *Biblical Greek Language and Lexicography: Essays in Honor of Frederick W. Danker*, edited by Bernard A. Taylor et al., 53–65. Grand Rapids: Eerdmans, 2004.
Septuaginta: Vetus Testamentum Graecum. Göttingen: Vandenhoeck & Ruprecht, 1931–.
Simpson, John A., and Edmund S. C. Weiner, eds. *The Oxford English Dictionary*. 2nd ed. 20 vols. Oxford: Clarendon, 1991.
Webster's Third New International Dictionary of the English Language, Unabridged, with Seven Language Dictionary. 3 vols. Chicago: Benton, 1966.
Zervos, Ioannis S., ed. *Great Lexicon of the Greek Language*. 9 vols. 1936–1950. Reprint, Athens: Piroga.

8

The Development of the Greek Language and the Manuscripts of Paul's Letters

—Jeffrey Kloha

The Pauline Letters were copied over a period of some fifteen hundred years, a time span that saw significant development of the Greek language. To what extent are these developments reflected in the individual manuscripts of *Corpus Paulinum*? To those of us in the English-speaking world, the language of the four-hundred-year-old King James translation sounds archaic, and its English has been "updated," for example, in the 1979–1982 *New King James Version*. While this kind of wholesale revision did not occur in the case of the Pauline Letters, individual manuscripts demonstrate certain types of alterations that reflect linguistic developments in Greek.[1]

Thorough revision of the texts of the Pauline Letters should not be expected, however, for several reasons. First, because the extant copies are

---

1. A note of personal appreciation: Jim Voelz is well known to fellow scholars, colleagues, and students as a meticulous scholar and very close reader of the Greek text. While to some individuals this close reading can devolve into what appears to be pedantism, it in fact reflects Jim's love of the New Testament, of Greek, and his earnest desire to know, understand, and teach both in every detail, no matter how small. This paper is derived from a conference presentation made to the Greek Language seminar of the Sixty-Sixth Annual meeting of the Studiorum Novi Testamenti Societas, Annandale, NY, August 2–5, 2011; Jim Voelz is longtime co-chair of this seminar.

just that: copies, and not new editions of the texts. Copyists are attempting, with greater or lesser success, to produce a transcription of the text in front of them. Second, because the Greek language itself, in spite of certain simplifications and influence from neighboring languages, remained essentially a unified language. This is so even today, in particular its written form.[2] Third, the New Testament manuscripts were used not only for personal reading and study, but even more so for liturgical reading. This formal use of the text resulted in a stabilization of the text, even a "static" register that resisted the changes that were happening in everyday, less formal usage of Greek. Nevertheless, some readings in the Pauline manuscripts are recognizable as developments within the Greek language, in particular in areas of morphology.

This study begins not as a study of the Greek language itself, but with the problem of the various readings now found in the manuscripts of the Pauline Letters. Do readings in these manuscripts reflect developments in the Greek language? This approach reflects what has been labeled "narrative textual criticism,"[3] whereby the readings are viewed as part of the narrative history of the text of the New Testament. Manuscripts are tangible, historical artifacts produced at specific times and places by specific individuals. The copying and editing process took place within individual settings and contexts, which, at least on occasion, led to alterations to the text being copied. Not only does textual scholarship seek, therefore, to reconstruct the text (whether the "original text" or the *Ausgangstext* or some other presumed archetype), it also attempts to account for the history of the text as it was passed on. To be sure, what have been traditionally labeled "transcriptional errors" account for the vast majority of readings.[4] However, recent study of the text of the New Testament has moved in the direction of also examining the contexts for the manuscripts themselves and their resultant alterations.[5]

This study, therefore, seeks to account for some of the readings that are now found in manuscripts of the Pauline Letters as reflections of the development of Greek.

---

2. See the volume edited by Caragounis, *Greek*, especially the essays by Adrados ("The Greek Language: Its Oneness and Its Phases," 67–83) and Caragounis ("Atticism: Agenda and Achievement," 153–76). The latter point, the conservatism of literary Greek, is especially emphasized by Horrocks, *Greek*.

3. For the terminology, see Epp, *Perspectives*, xxxix–xl.

4. Classically described in Westcott and Hort, *Introduction*, 22–30.

5. Two recent collections of essays that assess and apply narrative textual criticism are Kraus and Nicklas, *New Testament Manuscripts*, and Houghton and Parker, *Textual Variation*.

Complications

An immediate complication in a diachronic study such as this is the exact form of the "original" Pauline text. What is presented in the "standard text" (now the Nestle-Aland 28th edition and United Bible Societies 5th revised edition) is, as the editors themselves acknowledge, only a "begründeten Arbeitstext / well-founded working text."[6] In particular, in matters of orthography the editions are heavily reliant on predecessor editions, themselves based on the great pandects of the fourth century. Therefore, the "original" or "archetypical" text (Ausgangstext) cannot be assumed to be represented in the standard printed editions, but each reading must be evaluated within the larger picture of the history of the text.

A second complication is the potential differences in usage in the authorial text itself. Should we expect standardization of spelling across all of Paul's letters (as we would expect in modern, edited texts)? Were examples of potential hiatus or crasis dealt with in the same way in every case, or were these, at times, idiosyncratic choices of the author—or even Paul's secretary (e.g., Rom 16:22)? The extant manuscripts do not provide enough data to draw firm conclusions on these matters, though there are some tantalizing clues that different parts of the collection were handled differently.[7] Modern editions do not appear to have taken these issues into account. Rather, as will be demonstrated below, the "best manuscripts"—meaning א B—have been followed, even where they are idiosyncratic. Therefore one cannot be entirely confident that the standard printed text unfailingly represents "the text of Paul," and that as a result the "variant readings" found in the manuscripts can be assumed to be later "corruptions" that may tell us something of the development of the Greek language. Rather, all readings from all manuscripts must be assessed and placed into a firm history of both the manuscript tradition and the history of the language.

A third complication is the matter of access to the full range of readings, including orthographical readings and readings attested by one or only a handful of manuscripts. Due to their nature as hand editions, the critical apparatus of the standard texts provides only the "most important variants

---

6. NA[27], 3*, 45*–46*. NA[28] removes this description, though the text of the Pauline epistles is unchanged from the 27th edition to the 28th.

7. For example, there is far less variation in the letters to individuals than in the letters to churches, perhaps indicating that these were either a later part of the collection, or simply that they were less used. Hebrews, as will be demonstrated below, is certainly a later addition to the thirteen-letter collection, since there are consistent orthographical differences from the other letters.

/ wichtigen Varianten."⁸ This is not a criticism, for the goal of the edition is clearly stated. Nevertheless, several complications arise for the study of both the Greek and its history. First, are fourth-century manuscripts used as the primary sources for the establishment of such issues as the orthography of first-century texts? Might other manuscripts have preserved first-century readings? And where are those readings to be found? The *Editio Critica Maior* has been completed only for the Catholic Letters.⁹

A fourth complication is the lack of early evidence for the text. The earliest fairly complete extant Greek manuscript of the Pauline Letters is 𝔓⁴⁶. While perhaps a dozen and a half other pre-fifth-century papyri contain portions of Paul, these are so fragmentary that they can only rarely be cited for the readings discussed in this study.¹⁰ This further erodes confidence in the reconstruction of the archetypical text. It been generally accepted that, in the words of H. Vogels, "Alle bewußte Korrektur ist alt. Nichts von derartigem geht, soweit ich sehe, über das 4. Jahrhundert hinaus, und das weitaus meiste, wenn nicht geradezu alles, wird ins 2. Jahrhundert hinabreichen."¹¹ Since today we have no manuscript of the Pauline Letters that was produced prior to this second-century window, all manuscripts and all readings must be considered, and each must be placed into a history of transmission, even (and for the purposes of this study) especially those readings that are not "significant" or "well attested."

For example, frequently there are several potential accounts of a reading that conflict, and the competing explanations must then be weighed, rather than a manuscript's reading dismissed simply because the manuscript has not been regarded as "important." For example, at 1 Cor 14:5, D (06) reads θέλω δὲ πάντας ὑμᾶς λαλεῖν γλώσσαις, μᾶλλον δὲ προφητεύειν, where the rest of the tradition reads ἵνα προφητεύητε in place of the infinitive. Already in the Hellenistic period, ἵνα + subjunctive began to be used where previously the infinitive would be the norm.¹² One might therefore posit that D retains the earlier form, of which ἵνα προφητεύητε is the corruption. However, a more likely explanation is that the infinitive in D at this place is simply written to correspond to the near context: προφητεύειν matches the form of λαλεῖν earlier in the sentence (whether this was an intentional

---

8. NA²⁷, 8*, 50*.

9. The most recent information on the progress of the project and completed sections is available at http://www.uni-muenster.de/INTF/ECM.html.

10. By date, these mss are: III: 𝔓12 𝔓13 𝔓27 𝔓30 𝔓32 𝔓46 𝔓65 𝔓87 III/IV: 𝔓15 𝔓16 𝔓49 𝔓92 IV: 𝔓10 𝔓17 𝔓51 𝔓89 𝔓123. Dates cited from the *Kurzgefaßte Liste* online at http://intf.uni-muenster.de/vmr/NTVMR/ListeHandschriften.php.

11. Vogels, *Handbuch der Textkritik des Neuen Testaments*, 162.

12. Cf. Horrocks, *Greek*, 129.

alteration cannot be determined, nor is that question of consequence for this point).

Furthermore, knowledge of the proclivities of the text as found in individual witnesses is essential. Similar to the variation between the infinitive and the subjunctive seen in 1 Cor 14:5, described above, are two places where F (010) G (012) shift away from the infinitive against the rest of the tradition.

1 Cor 7:39   ἐλευθέρα ἐστὶν ᾧ θέλει γαμηθῆναι] θέλει γαμήθη F G

1 Cor 7:40   δοκῶ δὲ κἀγὼ πνεῦμα θεοῦ ἔχειν] δοκῶ ἔχω F G

However, the shift from the infinitive form should not be considered a later corruption due to the development of Greek. Instead, F G are Greek-Latin diglot manuscripts that are heavily edited to conform with the corresponding Latin text (as also is D, but in different places). In nineteen other places in 1 Corinthians, the Latin text uses an indicative or subjunctive to render the Greek complementary infinitive; only in these two places is the Greek of F G altered to match the Latin: θέλει γαμήθη = *vult nubat* and δοκῶ ἔχω = *puto habeo*. Hence, the F G readings are Latinisms,[13] not the archetypical text from which the rest of the tradition reflects a development in Greek.

A final complication is the nature of the Greek of Paul and whether his writings were of sufficient literary quality to avoid improvement from literary-minded copyists, readers, and editors. While recent discussion of the Atticistic movement has tended to regard their efforts in a more positive light,[14] the question that must be answered in cases where the manuscripts attest both a "more Greek" and a "less Greek" reading is whether the "more Greek" reading is from Paul or, instead, from the users of his texts over the centuries.

Examples of Readings That Reflect the Development of Greek

Middle Verb Forms

One development reflected in the manuscripts is the use of the middle form in place of the active, a shift encouraged by the Atticistic grammarians.[15] Codex Vaticanus (B 03) prefers the middle form, reading it alone at 1 Cor

---

13. Cf. the discussion of this type of Latinism in Horrocks, *Greek*, 129.
14. Especially Caragounis, "Atticism: Agenda and Achievement."
15. Caragounis, *Development*, 108–12.

13:11 (ἐγενόμην; γέγονα rell; 𝔓⁴⁶ lac). B. Weiss proposes that this alteration may be the result of assimilation to the aorist ἔλθῃ at 1 Cor 13:10.¹⁶ Another, more likely possibility is that the shift to the middle was motivated by Atticism. B makes the same voice shift at Gal 3:24 (ἐγένετο 𝔓⁴⁶ B; γέγονεν rell) and 1 Cor 10:2 (ἐβαπτίσαντο 𝔓⁴⁶ᶜ B K L P 056 0142 0150 1739; ἐβαπτίσθησαν 𝔓⁴⁶* rell). The standard text prints the aorist form at 1 Cor 10:2.

The Pauline manuscripts use two forms of the present imperfect form of εἰμί in first-person plural (ἤμεθα and ἦμεν). In later Greek, the middle form becomes commonplace.¹⁸ ἦμεν occurs without variation at Rom 7:5, Gal 4:3 (1); 1 Thess 3:4; 2 Thess 3:10; and Titus 3:3. ἤμεθα is printed in the standard text, however, in two places:

Gal 4:3 ἤμεθα 𝔓⁴⁶ ℵ D* F G 33 1319 1573

Eph 2:3 ἤμεθα 𝔓⁴⁶ ℵ B 33 1735 1739 1881

Elliott proposes that ἤμεθα is the form that should be read, with ἦμεν representing an editorial alteration toward a more classical form, even going so far as to suggest that ἤμεθα "has been completely eradicated and ἦμεν alone remains in extant mss."¹⁹ The example of ἤμεθα at Gal 4:3 raises issues of consistency once again; since the editors of the standard text adopt the reading of the "best manuscripts," ἦμεν is printed in the second clause and ἤμεθα in the third. The presumption may have been that ἦμεν at Gal 4:3c has been assimilated to the same form at 4:3b, but if that were the case, why would Paul have used two different forms for the same verb in the same sentence? Could it have been a desire for variety? But then, how does one explain the example of ἤμεθα at Eph 2:3? It must either be viewed as an improvement to the "correct" form, or a reflection of a later adaptation to the increasingly common use of the middle for this verb (already in 𝔓⁴⁶ of the early third

---

16. Weiss, *Textkritik der paulinischen Briefe*, 43.

17. The most thorough study of the tendencies of the scribe of B is Voelz, "The Greek of Codex Vaticanus in the Second Gospel and Marcan Greek." Among his conclusions (pp. 212–16) are that B prefers καί to δέ (212), simple verbs to compounds, reflexive pronouns to personal pronouns, weak aorist terminations on strong aorist stems, and ἄν rather than ἐάν in general clauses. While this study examines only Mark, the tendency toward simple verbs and the use of ἄν have been observed also in the text of B found in the Pauline Letters. A fruitful line of inquiry would be to compare the singular readings of B's text of the Gospels with those of its text of Paul, to determine if those singular readings can be traced to a single scribe for both sections. Were different kinds of singular readings found in the two sections, it would suggest that B's text of the Gospels has a different ancestry than that of its text of Paul.

18. Blass, Debrunner, Rehkopf, *Grammatik des neutestamentlichen Greichisch*, §981 (hereafter BDR); Moulton and Howard, *Accidence and Word-Formation*, 203.

19. Elliott, "The Atticist Grammarians," 71.

century). The latter seems more likely, another example of the inconsistent, perhaps unintentional, writing of more familiar forms by scribes/editors of the manuscripts.

Modern commentaries on Paul's Letters rarely notice that the development of Greek is a likely cause of corruption, and so argue solely on the rhetorical context to decide between readings. For example, an understanding of Paul's argument is helpful in deciding between the active (ὑστεροῦντι) and middle (ὑστερουμένῳ) forms at 1 Cor 12:24. The antecedents of the participle are the "weak" and "unpresentable" parts discussed in 12:22–23. These characterizations of certain parts as inferior are, according to Paul, incorrect perceptions (δοκέω is used twice in 12:22–23). 12:24a concludes with the (again false) perception that the Corinthians had of the "presentable" parts: they do not have need of the "greater honor we bestow" (the implied object stated in the parallel at 12:23a). Paul encourages the adoption of God's perspective, who himself gives greater glory even to those perceived to be of lower status. How does this help clarify the variant? Pauline usage of ὑστερέω is consistent. The active form refers to something lower in status while the middle/passive form is used to indicate a lack or deficiency in something.[20] Since the false perception being addressed is that the "weaker" are lower in status (not that they lack something), the active form is that which best suits the context.[21] God gives glory to those parts that are perceived to be of less value.[22] Furthermore, the reading ὑστεροῦντι has the additional benefit of being the earliest attested, found in 𝔓[46] D F G, Origen, and the Peshitta,[24] although the Latin tradition likely translates ὑστερουμένῳ.[25]

20. BDAG, s.v. ὑστερέω (4) and (5b), with references.

21. Zuntz, *Text of the Epistles*, 128. Thiselton, *First Epistle to the Corinthians*, 1009–10, adopts the argument of Robertson and Plummer (p. 276), that the middle form best suits the context because it conveys "feel inferior" whereas the active implies "be inferior." This argument, however, does not match the usage of ὑστερέω described in BDAG (see previous note). Schrage (*Der Erste Brief an die Korinther*, 228n684) argues that there is little difference in meaning between the middle and active forms.

22. Fee, *First Epistle to the Corinthians*, 614, argues that the sentence is saying that God gives glory to the parts that lack it, hence the need for the middle form. However, he admits that his understanding results in a lack of clarity: "It is less clear, however, what Paul had in mind by 'greater honor.' Most likely he means that the parts that appear to be weak and less worthy are in fact accorded the greater honor of having important functions or receiving special attention." It should be noted that his explanation is precisely what the text says if the present form ὑστεροῦντι is read.

23. *Commentarii in evangelium Joannis* 10.36.238.

24. ܗܘ ܕܒܨܝܪ = "to the part which is least."

25. VL 77 78 89 Vg read *ei cui deerat* (of which *si cui deerat* in 75 is an obvious corruption); 61 AMst SED-S read *ei cui deest*. Cf. 2 Cor 12:11, where *minus fui* or *minus feci* renders the active ὑστέρησα, and 2 Cor 11:5, where *minus fecisse* renders ὑστερηκέναι

And, most convincingly, the shift to the middle form in later Greek explains the corruption. The standard text's ὑστερουμένῳ at 1 Cor 12:24 should be changed to ὑστεροῦντι.

Hellenistic Contraction

All four Pauline examples of the present infinitive of πίνω show variation in spelling. While the differences are not significant in terms of meaning, the consistency of the witnesses that use the form πεῖν reflects an older tradition than those that use πιεῖν. The four examples in the epistles are:

Rom 14:21	πεῖν B*[26] D*; πίνειν F G] πιεῖν B^c D² *rell* (𝔓⁴⁶ *lac*)
1 Cor 9:4	πεῖν 𝔓⁴⁶ B* D*; πῖν ℵ* F G] πιεῖν ²ℵ (πιεῖν) B² D² *rell*
1 Cor 10:7	πεῖν 𝔓⁴⁶ ℵ B* D* F G] πιεῖν B² D² *rell*
1 Cor 11:22	πεῖν F G 876] πίνειν *rell*

Before assessing the difference between πεῖν and πιεῖν, the readings in F G must be explained. At Rom 14:21, πίνειν is likely the result of a misunderstood correction in the predecessor of F G. The correction ιν was intended to signal a substitution for ειν (which would produce πῖν). This was misread, however, as an addition, resulting in πίνειν. A similar misunderstood correction of vowels appears at 1 Cor 9:8, where F G read η ει και ο νομος ταυτα λεγει, a nonsense reading. The πῖν at 9:4 can therefore be explained as a "successful" (i.e., sensical) interpretation of the same correction made at that place. As a result, F G may be cited at all three places in indirect support for the reading of D* (which stems from the same ancestor manuscript as F G). There is, therefore, remarkable consistency among these witnesses (𝔓⁴⁶ ℵ B D* F G) in reading πεῖν.

The other readings can be attributed to a development in Greek itself. A "Hellenistic contraction" developed around 100 BC that substituted a single *i*-sound where two occur consecutively.[27] Moulton and Howard suggest that the later NT writings are more likely to use the contraction than the earlier. For Paul they believe that inconsistency is the rule, perhaps reflective

---

(but *inferiorem esse* 77; *inferiorem fuisse* AMst; and *inferiorem* SED-S).

26. B is cited incorrectly by the editions of Tischendorf and von Soden as reading πιεῖν. The original hand was retraced as πεῖν, to which a corrector added a small superscript iota (πιεῖν).

27. See Schwyzer, *Griechische Grammatik* I, 194; Mayser, *Grammatik der griechischen Papyri* I,1, 64; Gignac, *Grammar of the Greek Papyri*, 64–65; and BDR §31(2).

of the amanuenses of the individual letters.[28] However, they are working with incorrect information regarding the reading of B at Rom 14:21, and so accept (against Westcott-Hort) πιεῖν at that place. The additional witness of 𝔓[46] and clarifying the reading of B now show the consistency of these witnesses. The standard text likewise prints πιεῖν at Rom 14:21; πεῖν at 1 Cor 9:4; 10:7; and the present-tense πίνειν at 1 Cor 11:22.

However, the Atticistic movement, beginning in the second century, rejected the Hellenistic contraction by urging again the use of ιει in place of ει. Pseudo-Herodian specifically rejects πεῖν:

> Ἁμαρτάνουσιν οἱ λέγοντες πεῖν βούλομαι μονοσυλλάβως, δέον λέγειν πιεῖν δισυλλάβως· μόνως γὰρ οὕτως καὶ παρὰ τοῖς ἀρχαίοις πᾶσιν εἴρηται, καὶ παρὰ τῷ ποιητῇ· πιεῖν οὕτω θυμὸς ἀνώγοι [reference to *Iliad* 4.263; 8.189; *Odyssey* 8.70].[29]

Similar concerns about this collocation of vowels are expressed by Moeris, who rejects ὑγεία (υ 11).[30] While "merely" an alteration in spelling, it does show that Atticism is a genuine cause of corruption in some cases. Only B D F G and, where extant, 𝔓[46], avoid this corruption.

Specific Forms Approved by Atticising Grammarians

Elliott[31] has already noted that both Phrynicus (6) and Moeris (189:7: ἄχρι ἄνευ τοῦ σ Ἀττικῶς, ἄχρις Ἑλληνικῶς) rejected μέχρις and ἄχρις. Frequently the Pauline manuscripts show variation when μέχρι and ἄχρι are followed by a vowel. Elliott proposes that the forms with final -ς preceding a vowel should be adopted as the archetypical reading, with the omission of final -ς to be regarded as an Atticising improvement. Elliott notes the following examples:

> Rom 11:25 (followed by οὗ)
> ἄχρι 𝔓[46] B* 218 1505 2495
> ἄχρις ℵ A B^c C D F G K L
>
> 1 Cor 11:26 (followed by οὗ)
> ἄχρι 𝔓[46] ℵ* B* 326 1739 1827

---

28. Moulton and Howard, *Accidence and Word-Formation*, 65.

29. *De locutionem pravatatibus*, cited from Cramer, *Anecdota Graeca*, 261. Reference provided by BDR §312.

30. Hansen, *Das attizistische Lexicon des Moeris*.

31. Elliott, "The Atticist Grammarians," 68–69.

ἄχρις ℵᶜ A Bᶜ C D F G K L Ψ 33

1 Cor 15:25 (followed by οὗ)

ἄχρι 𝔓⁴⁶ ℵ* A B* P 33 1739

ἄχρις ℵᶜ Bᶜ D F G K L □

Phil 1:6 (followed by οὗ)

ἄχρι 𝔓⁴⁶ ℵ A B

ἄχρις D F G K L

Additional examples, though found only in later witnesses, include:

Gal 3:19 ἄχρις (followed by οὗ)] ἄχρη 1243

Gal 4:19 (followed by οὗ; *lac* 𝔓⁴⁶)

μέχρις ℵ* B 0278

μέχρι 1739

ἄχρις ℵᶜ A C D F G K L ⊠

ἄχρι 2495

Only a very bold editor would consider adopting ἄχρι or μέχρι at these two passages. The reading ἄχρη (ἄχρι) of 1243 at Gal 3:19 is ruled out since it also substitutes ἄχρη at Rom 1:13 and 2 Cor 3:14.

μέχρι is used as a conjunction at Eph 4:13, where the addition of οὖν attested by a few witnesses (263 1319 1573) results in μέχρις οὖν; no witness reads μέχρι οὖν, indicating that at least in the text of these witnesses μέχρι / ἄχρι will invariably add -ς when followed by a vowel. That later witnesses come to favor -ς, regardless of whether or not a vowel follows, is seen in the following examples.[32]

Rom 1:13	ἄχρι (ἄχρη 1243; followed by τοῦ)] ἄχρις 1
Rom 15:19	μέχρι (followed by τοῦ)] μέχρις 1900
2 Cor 3:14	(ἄχρη 1175 1243; followed by γὰρ)] ἄχρις Ψ 1505 1611 2495
2 Cor 10:13	ἄχρι (followed by καὶ)] ἄχρις Ψ 6 326 1505 1611 1837 2400 2495
2 Cor 10:14	ἄχρι (μεχρι 1827; followed by γὰρ)] ἄχρις Ψ 1505 1611 2495
Gal 4:2	ἄχρι (followed by τοῦ)] ἄχρις L
Heb 4:12	ἄχρι (followed by μερισμοῦ)] ἄχρις D 2495

32. F G also substitute ἕως for ἄχρι (followed by τοῦ) at 1 Cor 4:11.

Note that Ψ (ninth-tenth century) in particular favors this form, evidence of the proclivities of a single copyist.

Two trends can therefore be observed in the manuscripts. The fourth-century pandects avoid hiatus, likely an improvement, in three places. However, by the time of the Byzantine witnesses, ἄχρις / μέχρις becomes so entrenched that it is used even in places where hiatus is not an issue. This clearly reflects a later development, albeit one that does not alter the meaning of the passages.

Another example of Atticism is the reading πλείους (K L P Ψ 6 424) in the Byzantine witnesses at 1 Cor 15:6. However, Moeris (π 8) rejects πλεόνες, the noncontracted comparative form of πολύς, as a Hellenism. He also rejects other noncontracted forms, such as ἀμείνονα, βελτίονες, and ἥσσονα. As Kilpatrick points out, most manuscripts move to the Hellenistic form at John 4:41 (πλεῖον only 𝔓75). The Hellenistic form is otherwise consistent in Paul (1 Cor 9:19; 10:5; 2 Cor 2:6; 4:15; Phil 1:14); the only other place where the Attic spelling replaces it is 2 Cor 9:2 (πλείους 919). Pauline usage suggests that πλείονες (ℵ A B D F G 048vid 0150 0243 88 915 1739) is archetypical, with πλείους an Atticising replacement, here again seen in the later witnesses.

Atticism also played a role in several variations involving the spelling of comparative adjective and adverbs. Moeris favors ἥττω as the Attic form and rejects ἥσσονα as Hellenistic.[34] The manuscripts read as follows (with the addition of examples of the interchange in verb forms for the sake of comparison):[35]

Rom 1:32	πράσσοντες] πράττοντες 1881
Rom 1:32	πράσσουσιν] πράττουσι 1 76 945 1628 1768
Rom 2:2	πράσσοντας] πράττοντες 2815
Rom 2:3	πράσσοντας] πράττοντες 1738 (πράτγοντες 618)
Rom 2:21	κηρύσσων] κηρύττων 1827
Rom 7:15	πράσσω] πράττω 1738 (πράτγω) 460 618
Rom 9:12	ἐλάσσονι] ἐλάττονι 6 205 209 323 796 945 1242 1827
Rom 13:5	ὑποτάσσεσθαι] ὑποτάττεσθε 1243

33. See Kilpatrick, "John iv. 41 πλεῖον or πλείους."

34. Moeris, *Atticista* (η 10). See also Elliott, "The Atticistic Grammarians," 75.

35. For the purposes of this list, only variations involving -σσ- / -ττ- are noted; differences in spelling involving vowels are not noted.

1 Cor 7:9	κρεῖσσον A C F G K L P Ψ 056 0142 0150 0151 614 1834
	κρεῖττον 𝔓⁴⁶ ℵ B D 33 69 81 206 321 429 1175 1739 1758
1 Cor 7:17	διατάσσομαι] διατάττομαι 1448
1 Cor 7:38	κρεῖσσον] κρεῖττον 69
1 Cor 11:17	κρεῖσσον ℵ A B C D* F G P 0150 33 81 104 181 917 1175 1241ˢ 1739
	κρεῖττον D² K L Ψ 056 0142 0151 5 6 88 326 424 614 876 915 1834
1 Cor 11:17	ἧσσον ℵ A B C D* 0150 33 81 181 917 1739 1834 1836 1875 1898
	ἧττον D² K L P Ψ 056 0142 0151 5 6 88 104 326 424 614 876 915
	ἔλαττον F G Theodoret
1 Cor 14:9	γλώσσης] γλώττης 547 629 945 2495 (γλώτης 1646)
2 Cor 12:13	ἡσσώθητε 𝔓⁴⁶ ℵ* B D*]
	ἡττήθητε ℵᶜ A D* L P 1 1241 (ἡτγήθητε 517 910 1175 1243 1424)
	ἐλατωθήται F G
2 Cor 12:15	ἧσσον 𝔓⁴⁶ ℵ* A B D* P 104* 181 630 1175 1573 2464
	ἧττον D² K L Ψ 075 6 88 424 614
	ἔλασσον Fᶜ G (λάσσον F*)
2 Cor 12:21	ἔπραξαν] ἔπραττον 76
1 Cor 12:31	μείζονα 𝔓⁴⁶ᵛⁱᵈ A B C 33 69 424ᶜ 1739 1881 (μίζονα ℵ)
	κρῖσσονα (D* F G (κρεῖσσονα D²)
	κρείττονα Ψ 1 76 209 424* 489
1 Thess 4:11	πράσσειν (πράσσιν D)] πράττειν F G 945
Heb 9:11	μείζονος 𝔓⁴⁶ ℵ
	κρείττονος 1739 (κρείττωνος 1881)

The manuscripts, and their users, are hardly consistent. Several examples in 1 Corinthians are instructive. At 7:38 the standard text simply follows the "best manuscripts" by printing -ττ- at 1 Cor 7:9, even though -σσ- is printed at 7:17. However, again in the two examples at 11:17, the standard text prints -σσ-. In fact, only in five places the standard text prints -ττ-:

Rom 11:12	ἥττημα (ἥτγ-) 33 131 326 517 2147
1 Cor 6:7	ἥττημα (ἥτγ-) 33 88 131 517 618 910 1175 1243 1735 1739 1891 2147
1 Cor 7:9	κρεῖττον (lac 𝔓⁴⁶)
2 Cor 8:15	ἠλαττόνησεν (ἠλατγ- K 33 517 1243 1424 1836* 1891 21215 2147 pc)
1 Tim 5:9	ἔλαττον (ἔλατγον 1720 1874 1880 1900 1962)

The situation is entirely opposite in Hebrews, where -σσ- is never found in the manuscripts:

> 1:4 κρείττων; 1:16 κρείττονος (κρείττονος 𝔓⁴⁶ ℵ D); 2:7 ἠλάττωσας; 2:9 ἠλαττωμένον; 7:7 ἔλαττον, κρείττονος; 7:19 κρείττονος; 7:22 κρείττονος; 8:6 κρείττονός, κρείττοσιν; 9:23 κρείττοσιν; 10:34 κρείττονα; 11:35 κρείττονος; 12:24 κρεῖττόν

On the sole basis of this evidence, one might conclude that the author of Hebrews is different from the author of the rest of the letters in the *Corpus Paulinum*, and of course, Hebrews is known to be a later addition to the collection. Nevertheless, no manuscript of Hebrews replaces -ττ- with -σσ-. Likewise, no manuscript shows later correction from -ττ- to -σσ-, though the reverse occurred in witnesses such as D. The "Byzantine" text prefers -ττ- in each case where there is variation, suggesting again that these readings are later and the product of revision. Even the Byzantine witnesses, however, do not make the shift consistently, indicating both the seemingly random nature of the changes and the persistence of -ττ- once introduced in a given passage.

Further evidence of later Greek intruding into Pauline manuscripts is a unique reading of D F G at Gal 4:17, joined by the Latin witness 89 and virtually the entire Latin commentary tradition (Marius Victorinus, Ambrosiaster, Sedulius Scottus, and the B recension of Pelagius): following ζηλοῦτε, these witnesses add a positive command: ζηλοῦτε (F G ζηλοῦται) δὲ τὰ κρίττω χαρίσματα / *aemulamini autem meliora dona*. While the Latin form of the insertion closely parallels 1 Cor 12:31 (*aemulamini autem dona meliora* 61 75 77 78 89),³⁶ the Greek text found at Gal 4:17 is significantly different from the Greek of D F G at 1 Cor 12:31, which reads ζηλοῦτε δὲ τὰ χαρίσματα τὰ κρῖσσονα. This reading cannot be derived from the Greek of D F G for three reasons. First, the group D F G never uses the spelling -ττ- when it departs from the rest of the tradition. Second, the form κρίττω, which uses the Attic termination, is found nowhere else either in Paul or in the bilinguals. Third, a different attributive position is used for the adjective at Gal 4:17 than at 1 Cor 12:31, one which is not found at that place in any Greek manuscript but does correspond to the Latin. The most likely origin of this reading, then, is a retroversion from Latin into Greek, based on a glossary available to the editor. Although a specific source has not been identified, several other examples of unique Greek readings in D F G can be traced to the use of such a lexicon.³⁷ It would not be surprising that such a tool, intended as it was for linguistic study, would read the Attic κρίττω as the gloss for *meliora*.

Hellenistic and Attic Verb Forms

Two different types of alterations made to "improve" the Greek of Paul are seen at 1 Cor 7:28, where the standard text prints καὶ γαμήσῃς, οὐχ ἥμαρτες, καὶ ἐὰν γήμῃ ἡ παρθένος, οὐχ ἥμαρτεν. The first use of the verb, γαμήσῃς, involves the form of the aorist active stem of γαμέω, which circulated in two different forms in the manuscripts.³⁸ The Hellenistic form, -γαμησ-, is consistently used in the *Corpus Paulinum*. It stands without variation at 1 Cor 7:33, 34, but at 7:9 γαμησάτωσαν is replaced with γαμείτωσαν (F G γαμή-; 323 2815 pc) and γαμῆσαι with γαμεῖν (ℵ* A C* 0150 33 pc), both of which shift to the present tense. The Attic form, -γημ-,³⁹ never occurs in the NT without variation. G. D. Kilpatrick, in a discussion of variation involving this stem, notes that -γαμησ- is firm in seven passages. After discussing the examples of variation, he concludes, "the Attic form is extremely unlikely in the NT." He then argues for the non-Attic reading at Matthew 22:25, where both γαμήσας (D W Y Π Z Γ Δ) and γήμας (ℵ B L Θ Σ Φ) are attested, and at Luke 14:20, where γυναῖκα ἔγημα is the most widely attested reading. There D, supported by the early Syriac tradition, reads γυναῖκα ἔλαβον.⁴⁰

36. The Vulgate of 1 Cor 12:31 reads *aemulamini autem charismata maiora*, which cannot have been the source for the insertion in Galatians.
37. Kloha, "A Textual Commentary," 624–32, 663–68.
38. Moulton and Howard, *Accidence and Word-Formation*, 231.
39. BDR §10116; Veitch, *Greek Verbs*, 146–47.
40. Kilpatrick, "The Aorist of γαμεῖν in the New Testament."

The manuscript variation between the Attic and the Hellenistic forms at 1 Cor 7:28 is as follows:

γαμήσῃς 𝔓¹⁵ 𝔓⁴⁶ ℵ B P Ψ 6 33 43 69 81 101ᵐᵍ 181 917 1739 1834 1836 1838 1875

γήμῃς   K L 056 0142 0150 0151 104 326 424 614 1175
           Or Chr Thret Dam Photius

γαμήσῃ A

λάβῃς γυναῖκα D F G syᵖ

    acceperis uxorem 75 77 78 89 Vg AMst SED-S

    duxeris uxorem Te

γάμῃ D* F G

γήμῃ rel

In the first example, γήμῃς may have been created unintentionally due to haplography: ΓΑΜΗCΗC, with a subsequent interchange of the initial α to η. It is more likely, however, to represent an intentional correction away from the Hellenistic form.[41] This example, as well as the tendency of the tradition as a whole to replace the Hellenistic forms with the Attic, argues also for the direction of alteration to move from γάμῃ to γήμῃ. The variation may have arisen accidently due to a common vowel interchange.[42] Nevertheless, the pattern of variation discussed here suggests that the alteration was influenced by the trend toward the Attic stem seen throughout the NT manuscript tradition.

The reading λάβῃς γυναῖκα, however, presents a completely different problem. The reading cannot be dismissed as a Latinism, as several commentators argue,[43] for the standard Latin idiom would be *duxeris uxorem*.[44] This is the way Tertullian twice renders the phrase in citations of this passage.[45] The rest of the Latin tradition, however, including the Vulgate, uses *acceperis*, which is equivalent to λάβῃς. Because this departs from typical

---

41. Note that for the identical variation at Matt 22:25 the manuscript support for the readings is virtually reversed, with the "Alexandrian" witnesses attesting the shorter, Attic form and the "Byzantine" witnesses the longer, Hellenistic form. Yet no editor in the last two centuries has printed the same reading both there and at 1 Cor 7:28.

42. Mayser, *Grammatik der griechischen Papyri aus der Ptolemäerzeit* I,1 §5(α3), 38.

43. As is done by Zuntz, *Text of the Epistles*, 88-89, and Fee, *First Epistle to the Corinthians*, 325n10.

44. Lewis and Short, *Latin Dictionary*, s.v. *duco* (I B 4).

45. *De monogomia* 11.12 and *De exhortatione castitatis* 4. In the latter passage, only *duxeris* is stated, but *uxorem* is clearly implied from the context.

Latin idiom, it can only have been based on a Greek reading, so that the Latin tradition reflects a Grecism, rather than D F G attesting a Latinism. It is also read in the Peshitta, which uses the masculine form of the verb to render the phrase. D F G therefore cannot be dismissed as a Latinism here, and represents an early form of the text.

But is it the archetypical reading? The reading γυναῖκα ἔλαβον is found also in Codex Bezae at Luke 14:20,[46] and similar forms are found, without variation, at Luke 20:28, 29, 31, for all of which the Latin consistently uses forms of the standard idiom *uxorem duxi*. This expression is clearly preferred in the LXX, which is reflecting the Hebrew idiom, with approximately ninety examples. Therefore, although found nowhere else in Paul, the idiom is certainly part of the vocabulary of the first-century Christian communities.

It is likely the archetypical reading, since adaptation to the near context appears to have given rise to the other readings. In the previous verse Paul gives the instruction: "Are you free of a wife? Do not seek a wife (μὴ ζήτει γυναῖκα)." Then follows immediately our variant: "But if you marry (λάβῃς γυναῖκα) you are not sinning." This Semitic idiom, however, misunderstood as "take a wife" rather than "marry," appears to be a contradiction with the preceding instruction: Why would one not be sinning if he "took a wife," since Paul had just instructed them not to "seek a wife"? However, recognizing that the idiom simply means "to marry" allows it to be read, properly, with verse 28: "If you (male) marry you do not sin,[47] and if a female marries, she does not sin."[48] The second clause of verse 28 in fact provided the solution to the perceived difficulty: the replacement of λάβῃς γυναῖκα with a form of γαμέω. Thereby the Semitic idiom used by Paul was replaced with the more Greek form, γαμήσῃς. This corruption was further improved with the Attic γήμῃς now found in the Byzantine witnesses. The identical kind of corruption occurs in the next clause: the Hellenistic γάμῃ is replaced with the Attic γήμῃ.[49]

---

46. Kilpatrick ("The Aorist of γαμεῖν," 188) argues that this is the archetypical reading based on its replacement in the rest of the tradition with an Attic form.

47. The context makes clear that it is the male who is discussed in the first clause of 7:28.

48. On the meaning of παρθένος see Caragounis, *The Development of Greek*, 299–316.

49. Kilpatrick ("The Aorist of γαμεῖν," 188) also argues that γαμήσῃς is Hellenistic and γήμῃς is Attic, but that λάβῃς γυναῖκα "is both Hellenistic and Attic."

Syllabic and Temporal Augment

Variation between the syllabic augment η- and temporal augment ε- for δύναμαι, βούλομαι, θέλω, and μέλλω may be simply orthographical, or may have been caused by stylistic interests. BDR claims that, in the NT, η- is always found with θέλω and ε- with βούλομαι, which is due to the word having been "borrowed from literary language," but that the examples of δύναμαι and μέλλω show inconsistency. It is often noted that ε- is Attic, and η- a later development.[50] However, Moeris rejects ε- as Hellenistic,[51] and there appears to be a movement toward the temporal augment after the period of the Greco-Roman papyri, so that it comes to dominate by the Byzantine period. It has, however, again fallen away in favor of the syllabic augment in Modern Greek.[52] This makes it difficult to decide what Pauline usage should be and which form later users would prefer; all the more so since examples of the augmented forms of these verbs are rare in Paul.

Augmented forms of θέλω appear six times in the Pauline epistles with the syllabic augment, all without variation.[53] Βούλομαι occurs once with variation (Phlm 13) and once without,[54] while μέλλω does not occur with an augment. In both examples of augmented δύναμαι, however, there is variation:

1 Cor 3:1	ἐδυνήθην C Ψ] ἠδυνήθην rel.
1 Cor 3:2	ἐδύνασθε 𝔓⁴⁶ ℵ A B C F G P 048 056 0142 0150 0185 0289] ἠδύνασθε rel.
Phlm 13	ἐβουλόμην rel.] ἠβουλόμην 1245 547 ℵ

One is tempted to opt for the temporal augment in all three places, but the limited number of examples precludes final judgment. Again, note that the standard text prints two different forms in consecutive verses.

Similar uncertainty remains at 1 Cor 3:14 in the variation between ἐποικοδόμησεν (temporal augment) and ἐπῳκοδόμησεν (syllabic augment; B² C 049 0142 6 424 1739). Comparison to other examples involving this stem

---

50. So BDR §66(3); Moulton and Howard, *Accidence and Word-Formation*, 189, which dates ἠ- to "since 300 B.C."

51. Moeris, *Atticista* (η 5): ἤμελλον ἠβουλόμην ἠδυνάμην ηὐξάμην διὰ τοῦ η· δὶ δὲ τοῦ ε Ἕλληνες.

52. See Jannaris, *An Historical Greek Grammar*, §722; Mandilaris, *The Verb in the Greek Non-Literary Papyri*, §§245-49.

53. 1 Cor 12:18; 15:38; Col 1:27; 1 Thess 2:18; Phlm 14 (all aorist); Gal 4:20 (imperfect).

54. 2 Cor 1:15 (imperfect).

cannot be made, since this is the only Pauline instance where (ἐπ)οἰκοδομέω could have been so altered.[55] Nevertheless, the preference of later users of the text suggests that ἐπῳκοδόμησεν is the corruption.

Use of Thematic Stems in Place of Athematic

The use of thematic stems in place of athematic, such as ἵστημι and τίθημι, was taking place already in the classical period.[56] This practice is condemned by Moeris.[57] Of the twenty-six occurrences in the *Corpus Paulinum* of the infinitive form of verbs based on the athematic stems,[58] twenty-four use the athematic stem without variation. This is strikingly different from the situation involving the participle forms of -ἵστημι, where six of thirteen occurrences involve the same type of variation (discussed below). The two passages where variation of stem occurs are:

1 Cor 13:2	μεθιστάναι 𝔓⁴⁶ B D F G 33 1739
	μεθιστάνειν A C K L *etc*
2 Cor 3:1	συνιστάνειν ℵ A C K L P *etc* (συνιστάνω)
	συνιστάναι F G; (συνίστημι)
	συνιστάν 𝔓⁴⁶ B D* 33 (συνιστάω)

Atticism may be suspected to have created the reading -στάναι in both passages. However, two factors argue against this. First, Paul nowhere else uses the thematic stem for the infinitive. Second, the manuscripts behave similarly when participle forms of -ιστημι are involved. The -ιστημι stem is firm in six passages.[59] Where there is variation, some witnesses fare better than others.[60] ℵ reads the thematic stem in four of six places, three alone or

---

55. Moulton and Howard, *Accidence and Word-Formation*, 191–92, where examples of the exchange in Gospels are listed.

56. Moulton and Howard, *Accidence and Word-Formation*, 202–5. BDR §93 discusses the issue in the NT, but does not distinguish indicative from infinitive or participle forms (as does Moulton and Howard).

57. *Atticista* (ι 17) ἱστάναι Ἀττικοί· ἱστάνειν Ἕλληνες.

58. The stems used in the Pauline epistles are δίδωμι, ἵστημι, ἵημι, and τίθημι; approximately fifty compounds based on these stems occur in the NT.

59. Rom 8:38; 13:2; 15:12; 1 Cor 3:22; 7:26; 1 Tim 3:12.

60. Rom 12:8 προϊστάμενος (προΐστημι); προϊστανόμενος ℵ (προιστάνω); 2 Cor 4:2 συνιστάνοντες ℵ C D* F G (συνιστάνω); συνιστάνοντες 𝔓⁴⁶ B P 075 0243 (συνιστάνω); συνιστῶντες K L Ψ (συνιστάω); 6:4 συνιστάντες 𝔓⁴⁶ ℵ* C D* F G 0225 0243 (συνίστημι); συνιστῶντες K L Ψ 048 (συνιστάω); συνιστάνοντες B P (συνιστάνω); 10:12 συνιστανόντων (συνιστάνω); συνιστάντων 𝔓⁴⁶ 0243 (συνίστημι); 10:18 συνιστάνων 𝔓⁴⁶ ℵ B D* F G

nearly alone; A is legible for only four passages, but reads the thematic stem twice (see also 1 Cor 7:3), which is similar to the "Byzantine" witnesses (K L etc) and B, which read the thematic stem three times in six passages. The witnesses that most frequently preserve the athematic stem for the participle are 𝔓⁴⁶ C D, in five of six passages, and F G in four of six. Therefore, ℵ A K L and even B should be considered unreliable for variation involving the thematic stem both for participles and infinitives. Given the proclivity away from the athematic toward the thematic stem, the reading μεθιστάνειν at 1 Cor 13:2 should be considered an alteration prompted by increasing use of the thematic stem in Greek.

This leaves the reading συνιστάν at 2 Cor 3:1. Moulton and Howard suggest that it "has good claim."[63] However, while the -αν termination is common in the LXX,[64] it occurs nowhere else in Paul. The fact that several early fathers read the same form at 1 Cor 13:11,[65] without any manuscript support, suggests that the use of this thematic form is also influenced by the development of the Greek language itself. Hiatus may have played a further role in both passages. Only one of the twenty-four firm examples of the infinitive is followed by a word beginning with an ε, α, or η (Eph 6:13 ἀντιστῆναι ἐν). However, at 1 Cor 13:2 μεθιστάναι is followed by ἀγάπην, and at 2 Cor 3:1 συνιστάναι is followed by η (or the v.l. ει). Avoidance of hiatus may have therefore led to the termination -ειν in the A C and the typical "Byzantine" witnesses at both 1 Cor 13:2 and at 2 Cor 3:1 as well as the otherwise un-Pauline -αν at 2 Cor 3:1.

That development in the Greek language accounts for the use of thematic forms is shown by another unique reading of F G, this at Rom 14:15. Here these witnesses do read a thematic termination for ἀπόλλυειν, the only Greek manuscripts to read the infinitive (ἀπόλλυε / ἀπόλυε cet). This reading results, however, from adapting the Greek to the Latin text, here the

---

H Ivid P 0121 0150 0243 (συνιστάνω); συνίστων K L Ψ etc (συνιστάνω); 1 Thes 5:12 προϊσταμένους (προΐστημι); προϊστανομένους ℵ A (συνιστάνω); 1 Tim 3:4 προϊστάμενον (προΐστημι); προσϊστάμενον F G (προιστάνω); προϊστανόμενον ℵ (προιστάνω). It may be observed that in three places ℵ alters to the -στανω stem, as with the infinitive at 2 Cor 3:1.

61. For this reason, at 2 Cor 10:12 συνισταννυτων (𝔓⁴⁶ 0243 pc) may be correct in place of συνιστανόντων.

62. προσιστάμενον at 1 Tim 3:4 may simply be an error for προϊστάμενον, a calque based on the Latin equivalent praepositum.

63. Moulton and Howard, Accidence and Word-Formation, 205.

64. BDR §933.

65. Μεθιστᾶν in Methodius, Symposium 9.4.249; Basil, Epistulae 204.1; Ephraem, Institutio ad monachos 320; Sermones paraenetici ad monachos Aegypti 26; 46 (both in Greek).

equivalent *perdere*, a common phenomena in F G. Recognizing the cause of this corruption is not only helpful in clarifying that F G adapts its Greek text to the Latin, but also that this adaptation took place relatively late in the transmission of the Greek text, for it took place after the widespread use of thematic terminations in Greek.

The alternative forms of the nasal stem verb κερδαίνω have caused confusion in the manuscripts. According to BDR,[66] Hellenistic Greek typically uses the termination -ανα in the aorist; it also notes that the Attic termination -ησα is also found in the NT. Other grammars do not see a preponderance of one form over the other.[67] In addition, both Attic and Hellenistic Greek use -ανω and -ησω as future forms. Modern editors distinguish the future form from the subjunctive by means of accents,[68] a device not used by the earliest copyists.

In the Pauline epistles the verb occurs only four times, in 1 Corinthians 9 and at Phil 3:8. The latter passage shows no variation in the manuscripts, though Cyril shifts from κερδήσω to κερδάνω in two citations.[69] In 1 Corinthians, neither example at 9:20 shows variation; at 9:22 some patristic citations read κερδήσω in place of σώσω; and at 9:19 σώσω replaces κερδήσω in only a single witness (241). At 9:21, however, the manuscript tradition splits between κερδήσω 𝔓⁴⁶ ²ℵ D K L Ψ *056 0142 0150 0151 5 6 104 296 429 436 467 1912 2298 etc* and κερδάνω ℵ* A B C F G P 33 69 181 296 630 917 1175 1739 1836 1875 1881 1898. A decision based on Pauline usage would see κερδάνω as the corruption, but it would be difficult to explain why it took place only here among the four examples that occur so closely together. On the other hand, assimilation to the near context would account quite easily for the shift from κερδάνω to κερδήσω, but it would be difficult to account for Paul's unique use of this form for the third of four parallel examples. The alternative would be to conjecture the use of κερδάνω in all four of the occurrences in this context, with only the third example preserved in the tradition. Given the propensity toward both assimilation and the general improvement in style evident in the manuscripts, the reading κερδήσω is most likely secondary. Whether Paul used κερδάνω elsewhere, however, cannot be determined from the manuscripts.

---

66. BDR §721.

67. Cf. Moulton and Howard, *Accidence and Word-Formation*, 243; for classical Greek, see Veitch, *Greek Verbs Irregular and Defective*, 364–65.

68. E.g., Westcott and Hort text prints κερδανῶ at 1 Cor 9:21, indicating a future indicative form; von Soden's text prints κερδάνω, indicating an aorist subjunctive.

69. *Thesaurus de sancta consubstantiali trinitate* (PG 75, p. 468) and *Commentarii in Ioannem* 3.6 (on John 6:32–33).

Results

The copyists and editors of the manuscripts of Paul's letters were, in limited ways, influenced by the development of Greek. This has taken place, exclusively it appears, in cases of spelling, verbs forms, and specific lexical items. Alterations of syntactical features (such as ἵνα + subjunctive in place of the infinitive) do not occur, or, where they do occur (e.g., 1 Cor 14:5), they can be accounted for as normal scribal variation. Furthermore, much later forms such as θά and νά are never, so far as I can determine, introduced into the manuscripts of Paul. This highlights the remarkable tenacity of the manuscript tradition, and demonstrates that copyists and editors did not see their role in transmitting the text as involving thorough "revision" or "updating."

Nevertheless, when individual readings are examined, language development is the only way to account for the existence of some readings in the manuscripts. Standard explanations of influence of the near context or sight/sound error cannot explain, for example, πλείους in the manuscripts at 1 Cor 15:6, or ἤμεθα at Gal 4:3 and Eph 2:3, or the seemingly random alteration to the middle form ἐβαπτίσαντο at 1 Cor 10:2.

Some general conclusions may be drawn regarding the traditional groupings of manuscripts. In general, 𝔓[46] and the fourth-century pandects show a desire to "improve" or "restore" a more literary form of Greek. Nevertheless, at times they preserve "less literary" (but nevertheless clearly "Greek") readings, such as ἤμεθα at Gal 4:3 and Eph 2:3, and ἄχρι at Rom 11:25 and 1 Cor 11:26, 15:25 (but ἄχρις by ℵ at Rom 11:25). Notably, each of these is "improved" to ἄχρις in the Byzantine witnesses.

The bilingual group D F G shows a great amount of inconsistency. The influence of the corresponding Latin text on the Greek is a constant issue (e.g., ἀπόλλυειν at Rom 14:15 = *perdere*). Some readings are undeniably influenced by literary editing (κρίττω in the addition at Gal 4:17). Nevertheless, in some places these witnesses alone preserve the "less literary" reading (λάβῃς γυναῖκα and γάμῃ at 1 Cor 7:28).

The Byzantine witnesses are the most prone to both literary improvements and influence from later forms. These witnesses never, for example, read -σσ- where the rest of the tradition reads -ττ-. In variation involving verb stems, these witnesses inevitably attest the more literary form (e.g., γήμῃς at 1 Cor 7:28; πιεῖν at Rom 14:21; 1 Cor 9:4; 10:7).

A lingering problem remains the decision of which reading is prior, and which manuscripts were influenced by the different phases of the Greek language. Does Paul favor Attic spellings and forms, or do copyists of the second to fourth centuries, or copyists of the ninth century and beyond?

Further complicating matters is the fact that the extant manuscripts are mere tradents of the texts they preserve; F G preserve a Greek text far earlier than their ninth-century date of production, and certainly the great pandects of the fourth century reach back, in many places, to readings traceable to the first collections of Paul's letters. However, the manuscripts are frustratingly inconsistent. The variation between κερδήσω and κερδάνω in 1 Corinthians 9, or the variation in spelling between -σσ- and -ττ-, does not allow for firm conclusions based on present-day manuscript evidence. In the types of morphological issues noted in this study, it may be that "conjecture," judiciously applied, is necessary. The problem is more acute because our modern editions reflect the forms used in the fourth-century manuscripts even where these witnesses reflect later developments in Greek. Study of the development of Greek cannot take the New Testament writings into account solely on the basis of present-day critical editions. Paul's Greek in particular cannot be categorized with certainty until all readings in all the manuscripts have been assessed within the context of the developments of Greek itself. Textual scholarship cannot be isolated from diachronic study of the Greek language, nor can study of the language of the New Testament be isolated from the individual manuscripts that carry the text.

Bibliography

Adrados, F. F. "The Greek Language: Its Oneness and Its Phases." In *Greek: A Language in Evolution*, edited by C. Caragounis, 67–83. Hildesheim: Olms, 2010.

Aland, Barbara, and Kurt Aland, et al. *Novum Testamentum Graece*. 27th ed. Stuttgart: Deutsche Bibelgesellschaft, 1993.

Blass, Friedrich, Alfred Debrunner, and Friedrich Rehkopf. *Grammatik des neutestamentlichen Greichisch*. 18th ed. Göttingen: Vandenhoeck & Ruprecht, 2001.

Caragounis, Chrys. "Atticism: Agenda and Achievement." In *Greek: A Language in Evolution*, edited by C. Caragounis, 153–76. Hildesheim: Olms, 2010.

———. *The Development of Greek and the New Testament*. WUNT 167. Tübingen: Mohr/Siebeck, 2004.

———, ed. *Greek: A Language in Evolution*. Hildesheim: Olms, 2010.

Cramer, J. A., ed. *Anecdota Graeca e codd. manuscriptis bibliothecarum Oxoniensium*. Vol. 3. Oxford: Oxford University Press, 1836.

Elliott, J. Keith. "The Atticist Grammarians." In *Essays and Studies in New Testament Textual Criticism*. Estudios de Filología Neotestamentaria 3. Cordoba: el Almendro, 1992.

Epp, Eldon J. *Perspectives on New Testament Textual Criticism: Collected Essays, 1962–2004*. NovTSup 116. Leiden: Brill, 2005.

Fee, Gordon D. *The First Epistle to the Corinthians*. NICNT. Grand Rapids: Eerdmans, 1987.

Gignac, Francis. *A Grammar of the Greek Papyri of the Roman and Byzantine Periods*. Milan: Istituto Editoriale Cisalpin-La Goliardica, 1981–1983.

Hansen, Dirk U., ed. *Das attizistische Lexicon des Moeris*. Sammlung griechischer und lateinischer Grammatiker 9. Berlin: de Gruyter, 1998.

Horrocks, Geoffrey. *Greek: A History of the Language and Its Speakers*. 2nd ed. Chichester: Wiley-Blackwell, 2010.

Houghton, H. A. G., and D. C. Parker. *Textual Variation: Theological and Social Tendencies?* Theological Studies 3, 6. Piscataway, NJ: Gorgias, 2008.

Jannaris, A. N. *An Historical Greek Grammar*. New York: Macmillan, 1897.

Kilpatrick, George D. "The Aorist of γαμεῖν in the New Testament." *JTS* 18 (1967) 139–40.

———. "John iv. 41 πλεῖον or πλείους." *NovT* 28 (1976) 131–32.

Kloha, Jeffrey. "A Textual Commentary on Paul's First Epistle to the Corinthians." PhD diss., University of Leeds, 2006.

Kraus, Thomas J., and T. Nicklas, eds. *New Testament Manuscripts: Their Texts and Their World*. Texts and Editions for New Testament Study 2. Leiden: Brill, 2006.

Lewis, C. T., and C. Short. *A Latin Dictionary*. Oxford: Clarendon, 1896.

Mandilaris, Basil. *The Verb in the Greek Non-Literary Papyri*. Athens: Hellenic Ministry of Culture and Sciences, 1973.

Mayser, Eduard. *Grammatik der griechischen Papyri aus der Ptolemäerzeit*. Berlin: de Gruyter, 1923–1924.

Moulton, J. H., and W. F. Howard. *Accidence and Word-Formation: A Grammar of New Testament Greek*. Vol. 2. Edinburgh: T. & T. Clark, 1929.

Schrage, Wolfgang. *Der Erste Brief an die Korinther*. Vol. 3, 1 Kor 11,17—14,40. Evangelisch-Katholishcer Kommentar. Zürich: Benziger, 1999.

Schwyzer, Eduard. *Griechische Grammatik*. Munich: Beck, 1939–1953.

Thiselton, Anthony. *The First Epistle to the Corinthians*. NIGTC. Grand Rapids: Eerdmans, 2000.

Veitch, W. *Greek Verbs Irregular and Defective*. Oxford: Clarendon, 1871.

Voelz, James W. "The Greek of Codex Vaticanus in the Second Gospel and Marcan Greek." *NovT* 47 (2005) 209–49.

Weiss, Bernard. *Textkritik der paulinischen Briefe*. Texte und Untersuchungen XIV,3. Leipzig: Hinrichs, 1896.

Westcott, B. F., and F. J. A. Hort. *Introduction to the New Testament in the Original Greek*. New York: Harper, 1882.

Zuntz, Gunther. *The Text of the Epistles: A Disquisition upon the Corpus Paulinum*. London: Published for the British Academy by Oxford University Press, 1953.

10

Texts, Open Spaces, and Readers
A Brief Update on the Continuing Challenge
of Romans 13

—*Bernard C. Lategan*

In the course of many discussions on serious matters like exegesis and golf, James Voelz always brought two important assets to the table that invariably enriched the conversation. The first was his linguistic expertise, displayed in his intimate knowledge of Greek coupled with the rigor and discipline required for mastering a classical language. The second was an inborn curiosity to know more about things and the world, to understand them more thoroughly, that is, an openness to explore and to expand his hermeneutical horizons.

This was especially the case in the hermeneutics seminar of the Studiorum Novi Testamenti Societas (SNTS), the international New Testament society where we investigated hermeneutical issues during the 1980s. James was an active participant in these annual sessions, and a much-appreciated contributor to the work of the seminar. It is a privilege to contribute to his Festschrift and to honor his friendship and outstanding scholarly achievements over so many years. I would like to do so by returning briefly to a passage we discussed at length over the years, namely, Rom 13:1–7. This section poses a perennial challenge to readers from all traditions and from all walks of life. At the 1988 session of the SNTS seminar, James read an important paper on the ambiguities contained in the text. I would like to revisit his views in light of some of the latest readings of the pericope.

The Issue

The *crux interpretationis* posed by this enigmatic passage is well known: How can Paul be so unqualifiedly positive in his attitude toward authority? Is he referring to the secular Roman state? Can an oppressive and destructive regime really be described as a "servant of God"? Is rebellion against authority under all circumstances forbidden for believers? Are Paul's statements meant only for his time, or do they have universal validity? Does his oblique reference to the "good" and the "conscience" contain an implied critique of the state?

The problems associated with this passage have as much to do with the historical situation of Paul and his social location as with the experience of subsequent readers in their own dealings with governing authorities. It is one of the most pertinent examples of how the predisposition of the reader influences the understanding of a text. In fact, it is one of those texts that throughout the long history of its interpretation has spilled over into an astounding variety of fields, many of these far removed from its original biblical or theological context. These include law, political philosophy, public administration, education, politics, and many other fields. Often its effect has been indirect. Luttikhuizen and Havelaar, for example, show how it found its way into the constitutions of political parties.[1] But the main area where pragmatic consequences of this text remain a hotly debated issue is the relationship between church and state. In any situation where the state exerts its power over institutions and individuals, the potential for conflict exists. How does the church interpret Romans 13 when it finds itself in disagreement with the policies and actions of the government of the day? How should the individual understand this passage when conscience forbids the person to obey a specific law? On the other hand, this is one of the most frequently quoted passages by those in authority when their own legitimacy and authority are being questioned.

No innocent reading of the passage is therefore possible. However, when we set ourselves the task of analyzing some of these readings, it is necessary to be clear about the methodological constraints of such an undertaking. All empirical research takes place within a specific theoretical framework.[2] Basically, the actual reading of a text can be analyzed from two perspectives—that of the text and that of the reader. Both should be kept in mind when we try to understand what happens when Romans 13

---

1. Luttikhuizen and Havelaar, "The Interpretation of Romans 13:1-7."
2. Cf. Groeben, *Rezeptionsforschung als empirische Literaturwissenschaft*; Schmidt, *Grundriss der empirichen Literaturwissenschaft II*; and Lategan and Rousseau, "Lk. 12:35-48."

is read. From the perspective of the text, what are the instructions given to the reader? How open or closed is the text? Whose interests are served by the text? From the perspective of the reader, how are these instructions followed? What are the presuppositions of the reader? Why does he or she actualize the text in a certain way?

A Return to the Text?

Given the plurality of actual readings, should we not concentrate on the text itself, that is, keep a sharp distinction between exegesis and application? Is the basic problem not that we confuse what the text says with how readers read it? Are the differences in interpretation not due to the difference in readers? There can be little doubt that the attitude, experience, and presuppositions of the reader do affect the result. But even if we confine ourselves to the text, not all issues are resolved. Here James Voelz made an important contribution by showing that we have to deal with different kinds of ambiguities in the text itself. In his 1988 paper he distinguishes three types of ambiguities:

1. Ambiguity of breadth of semantic range of words—"furniture" includes both "chair" and "table." In the case of Romans 13, examples of these "broad" terms would be "authority," "evil," "good," and "servant."
2. Ambiguity of the referent of words, which can be the result of the first kind of ambiguity. Here the question is not what is included in a specific word, but to what it refers.
3. Ambiguity of macrostructural arrangement. What is the central thought of a specific paragraph? What is the pivotal statement or statements? These are the types of questions procedures like discourse analysis try to answer, but a degree of ambiguity still remains.

What we are dealing with here are different forms and different degrees of indeterminacy within the text itself. It is this indeterminacy that necessitates the participation of the reader—the "gaps" or "open spaces" that need to be filled, in the terminology of Iser.[3] The focus on the text does not relieve us from the obligation to include the role of the reader when considering the various possible interpretations of the text.

---

3. Iser, "The Reading Process."

Filling Open Spaces

When we look in which way the imaginative cooperation of the reader is required in the realization of Romans 13, the text reveals some interesting features.

The first of these is the remarkably open or unmarked character of many of the words in our passage. "Authority," "all," "good," "evil," "servant," "submit," "conscience," and "fear" are all open and can be "filled" in a wide variety of ways. For example, "authority" in verse 1 is so unmarked that it is not even clear what form or what level of authority is included in this reference. Louw and Nida list at least eight nuances in the New Testament alone, all referring to "authority" or "power" in an unspecified way.[4] The same trend is continued in verse 3, where "rulers" is also without further qualification. But also the addressees are totally open: the statement concerns *everyone* (v. 1).

There are clear indicators that encourage an open reading of our passage. But this trend—remarkably enough—is countered by a movement in the opposite direction, one of narrowing down the concept of authority by a series of qualifications—it is a *servant* of God and intended to do you *good*.

The plurality in the form of marked/unmarked reference is related to a plurality of semantic possibilities, which leads to a remarkable series of bifurcations in the passage. The linking of God with the powers that be has a double effect. First, authorities are sanctioned as instituted by God and should therefore be obeyed. Second, this linkage not only sanctions authorities, but at the same time relativizes them, by implying that they are accountable to God. This linkage provides the textual basis and stimulus for two diametrically opposed readings. The one insists on the divine right and obligation to obey authorities. The other insists on relativizing the power of authorities by making them accountable to God. Examples of both approaches can be found in actual recorded readings.

Types of Reading Strategies

To recap what emerged from previous analyses of actual readings,[5] a basic distinction between what can be called "affirmative" and "resistant" readings becomes clear.

---

4. Louw and Nida, *Greek-English Lexicon*, 92.

5. See Lategan, "Reading Romans 13 in a South African Context"; and Lategan, "Romans 13:1–7."

Affirmative Readings[6]

Affirmative readings exhibit a positive attitude toward authority on the basis that it has its ultimate origin in God and should therefore be obeyed. The basic assumption is that the passage is universal in scope and provides fundamental guidelines for the relationship between subject and authority, between church and state. Although the text addresses in the first place believers who are subjected to authority, inferences are drawn for the conduct, powers, and responsibilities of authority in general.

The exponents of affirmative readings normally are—as could be expected—people in positions of power and authority. Following the global restructuring of power after 1989 and the rise of terrorism, Romans 13 has again become the source of both pro- and antipower readings. The former insist on the right of the state to defend itself. With reference to the "war on terrorism" of the Bush administration, Collins states that "Romans 13,4-6 affirm that rulers have the right to 'bear the sword' against evildoers."[7] This affirmative reading continues to inform the "just war" theory.[8]

Resistant Readings

Resistant readings try—in a variety of ways—to qualify, restrict, or undermine the apparently generic approval of authority—what Moo calls the "plain meaning" of the text.[9] Exponents of these readings are either victims of the abuse of power or uneasy with its unqualified call to obedience. Various strategies are employed:

1. *The interpolation move.* A drastic measure is to declare the passage as so un-Pauline in spirit or so incompatible with the rest of his theology that it could only be a *Fremdkörper* that was inserted into the text at a later stage.

2. *The intertextual move.* Romans 13 is relativized by placing it in the wider context of the letter, for example, the different nature of the paraenetic sections in Romans 12 and 13:8 and following. It is also relativized by the apostolic authority of Paul himself; by other sections of the New Testament such as Acts (which expects obedience to God rather than to man) and

---

6. In a recent contribution, Marshall, "Hybridity and Reading Romans 13," 169, uses "affiliation" and "resistance" to distinguish between these two types of readings. However, "affiliation" is too weak to capture the real essence of what is at stake here, namely, the basic affirmation of authority.

7. Collins, "Christian Faith and Military Service," 34.

8. See Holmes, "The Just War."

9. Moo, *The Epistle to the Romans*, 806.

Revelation 13 (which shows the demonic side of the state); and by the message of the Bible as a whole.

3. *The restrictive move.* This is in a certain sense the opposite of the intertextual move. Instead of widening the scope of the passage, it is restricted to a specific situation (the circumstances of the Christian community in Rome) or a specific problem (revolutionaries contemplating the overthrow of the regime or enthusiasts disregarding worldly authorities).

4. *The evaluative move.* The hegemony of "the state" is broken by introducing criteria to distinguish between good and bad government.

The first criterion is drawn from 13:4, that is, whether the authority in question acts as a servant or promotes the common good. Only those authorities that meet these criteria are worthy of obedience. The reference to the conscience in 13:5 is of great significance, because it carries with it the potential for criticism and resistance to the state.

The second criterion is based on the fact that all authority is instituted by God and, by implication, accountable to him. Those who do not fulfill this responsibility themselves cannot claim obedience.

5. *Reading under different presuppositions.* A novel way to escape the restrictions of the passage is to emphasize the horizon of the contemporary reader and to read "under democratic presuppositions."[10] This enables the reader to bring different questions to the text and to draw different conclusions regarding its contemporary implications.

6. *Redefining the authorities.* Taking the reading under democratic presuppositions even further, Nürnberger comes to the conclusion that the sword of authority ultimately belongs to the ruled.[11] They are the ones who have to judge whether the government of the day really rules for the common good. By redefining the authorities of Romans 13 in this way, Nürnberger is in fact affirming the call to obedience. But that also leads him to accept the possibility of a just revolution.

7. *The reversal move.* Hurley suggests that the passage should not be taken at face value at all.[12] By using the rhetorical tools developed by Booth and following the internal clues of the text, it becomes possible to construct an *ironic* reading that intends the opposite of the surface text and brings a new dimension to the relationship between the emerging church at Rome and the oppressive regime it faces. Herzog goes further and sees Romans 13 as an example where the ambiguous and coded political speech of the weak

---

10. Jüngel, "Jedermann sei untertan der Obrigkeit."

11. Nürnberger, "Theses on Romans 13," 40–47.

12. Hurley, "Ironie dramatique dans la mise en intrigue de l'empire en Romains 13, 1–7."

appears to support the dominant power but in actual fact is subverting it.[13] The Jews of the diaspora have a long tradition living under domination and have developed ways to survive under such circumstances. Paul uses what Herzog calls "dissembling," that is, the technique of masking the hidden transcript of resistance to Roman rule by couching it in language of submission. He sounds like an obedient and loyal Roman citizen, but in actual fact he signals to his readers the limits of state power and how to deal with it.[14]

8. *The pragmatic move.* A growing number of readings understand the passage as nothing more than sound practical advice to the Roman believers in a difficult situation. The text is overextended if it is made the basis of a comprehensive political philosophy regarding the relationship between church and state. Despite internal variations, these readings all assume that Paul accepts the reality of the Roman state and its power and that he is giving pragmatic advice to his readers on how to cope with this reality—for a variety of reasons. For Dunn, this is proof of Paul's "political realism." The apostle does not idealize the situation and is well aware of the fickleness of political power. His advice does not depend on Roman benevolence. "It is simply a restatement of the long-established Jewish recognition of the reality and character of political power."[15] This "policy of political prudence"[16] was not confined to Rome, but was widespread among Christian congregations of the time. According to Du Toit, the church in Rome was still in a very vulnerable position at the time Paul was writing to them.[17] They were still associated with the Jewish community, which was already in disfavor with Rome. Christians should therefore do nothing that can discredit the gospel. Gielen interprets the passage as instructions for cooperating with the Roman imperial officials.[18] For Disbrey, this is an example of "virtue ethics."[19] Several other interpreters follow this "pragmatic" line.[20]

---

13. Herzog, "Dissembling, a Weapon of the Weak."
14. See also Forman, *The Politics of Inheritance in Romans.*
15. Dunn, *Romans 9–16,* 773.
16. Ibid., 772.
17. Du Toit, "Die funksie en waarde van agtergrondstudie van die Nuwe Testament," 323. See also Keener, *Romans,* 153.
18. Gielen, "Der Römerbrief."
19. Disbrey, *Wrestling with Life's Tough Issues.*
20. For more examples, see Lategan, "Romans 13:1–7."

A Brief Update in View of Recent Readings

Does this typology of reading strategies still hold in view of more recent interpretations? When looking at readings from the last decade, it is clear that the passage continues to generate a variety of interpretations. Although there are some examples of affirmative readings,[21] the majority attempts to escape the apparent direct implications of the text.

The *interpolation move* occurs in various guises. Hoover bases his rejection of the passage on the observation that it does not reflect the inner logic of the gospel—it is the expression of a pious attempt to accommodate the powers that be and is clearly an interpolation.[22] Ho is more drastic: the Vulgate translation is to blame for the corruption of the spiritual meaning of the text, replacing it with this-worldly concerns.[23] Cassidy sees it rather as the expression of Paul's political naïveté, but with a similar result, namely, that impact of the passage is neutralized.[24]

Redefining the authorities continues with Jewett's insistence that Paul is not referring to the god(s) of the Roman civic cult, but to the God embodied in the crucified Christ. Whatever the Roman authorities themselves may think, their power really comes from the God of the Jewish and Christian faith. This is a "massive act of political co-option"[25] that is in essence subversive to the Roman Empire. Paul's advice of submission is not an expression of respect for the authorities, but an expression of respect for the God who stands behind them. Wright, in a similar way, refers to the Old Testament concept of the divine origin of power.[26] For Tardivel this implies that the appropriation of power by any individual or government is ruled out in principle, because it is based on a transcendent authority, namely, the will of God.[27] The ultimate aim of the passage is therefore not obedience to (civil) authorities, but to spread the gospel of love. Christians are obliged to be loyal citizens and do what is good, even in a society that is not expressly Christian;[28] Paul is not proclaiming a political doctrine, but urging

---

21. Holmes, "The Just War"; Lohse, "Humanitarian Ethics and Biblical Tradition in Modern Europe."

22. Hoover, "Identifying Interpolations in Paul's Letters."

23. Ho, "On the Challenges of Translating Culture."

24. Cassidy, "The Politization of Paul." See also Bernheim, "Interpolations in Romans."

25. Jewett, *Romans*, 790.

26. Wright, *Paul in Fresh Perspective*.

27. Tardivel, "Pouvoir et bien commun."

28. Lohse, "Humanitarian Ethics and Biblical Tradition in Modern Europe."

Christians to overcome their fear and extend their *agape* to all people;[29] Paul is not responding to a pragmatic situation but traces the origin of power to God in order to achieve the common good for all;[30] the Christian paradigm of love is the greater reality that encloses almost as a "by-product" good and generally approved behavior in the civic and political world.[31] This would be a "soft subversive reading"[32] by which Paul points out how the powerless can transform the world by love.

Since the rise of empire studies, the *reversal move*, which implies a critical attitude toward authority and the state, occurs frequently. An interesting example is the attitude of Dibelius (and with him, many members of the Evangelische Kirche in Germany). They rejected the notion that the DDR (Deutsche Demokratische Republik) could be seen as "authority" in the biblical sense and looked for ways to encourage individual Christians to live responsible lives.[33] See in this regard also White's discussion of the problems confronting the thesis of an "anti-imperial" Paul.[34]

An interesting form of *reading Romans under different presuppositions* is a collection of readings in modern Japan.[35] Here the attempt was to explore the way in which Japanese Christians understood the emperor-focused state from the time of the first Protestant missionaries in the nineteenth century to the demise of fascism during the Pacific war. The critique of the state and the quest for human rights, which was unthinkable in prewar Japan, found a sound basis in Romans 13 and became, according to Miyata, the greatest legacy of postwar democracy in Japan.

What does seem to be a new trend is to accept the ambiguity inherent in Rom 13:1–7 without trying to soften or shy away from its implications. Pao points out the textual ambiguities involved.[36] Singgih appreciates Jewett's attempt to read Romans 13 against the background of Paul's letters as a whole, but the impression remains that this text itself is ambiguous.[37] Iwasa is even more explicit: we are dealing with a "dual ethics" in the passage.[38] One should distinguish between the ethical standards for the state and for

---

29. Aletti, "La soumission des chrétiens aux autorités en Rm 13,1–7."
30. Krauter, "Auf dem Weg zu einer theologischen Würdigung von Röm 13,1–7."
31. Bertschmann, "The Good, the Bad and the State."
32. Pao, "The Ethical Relevance of New Testament Commentaries," 206.
33. Cf. Greschat, "Römer 13 und die DDR."
34. White, "Anti-imperial Subtexts in Paul."
35. Miyata, *Authority and Obedience*.
36. Pao, "The Ethical Relevance of New Testament Commentaries," 201–3.
37. Singgih, "Towards a Postcolonial Interpretation of Romans 13:1–7."
38. Iwasa, "Dual ethics in Romans 13."

the people. In this way, it becomes possible to protect conscientious people from moral blame when they obey (secular/civil) authority, but this makes it impossible to appeal to Romans 13 to justify tyranny. In a similar attempt to bridge the two opposing tenets inherent in the passage, Marshall proposes the concept of "hybridity,"[39] an idea originally developed by Bhabha. The simple binary oppositions (dominant/subaltern, collaboration/resistance, settler/native) are no longer adequate to deal with the intermingled nature of what is really going on. The reality of people living under colonial conditions is that they are compelled to use different and sometimes opposing strategies. Recognition of this condition of hybridity makes it possible to accommodate both affiliative and resistant readings of Romans 13. The concept of hybridity is further developed by Mukuka (with a play on the title of Bhabha's 1985 essay)[40] and applied specifically to an African context. For him, the reader is challenged to critique both oppressive and democratic forms of government, opening the way for a liberating rereading while acknowledging that the text is colonially inflected. For Bertschmann, both quietist and anti-imperial readings are on the wrong track.[41] Paul is not focused on the concrete political realities of his day, but uses political and imperial imagery as an analogy to point to the greater reality beyond these, namely, the paradigm of love. And Viviano concludes that it is not so easy to bring all of Paul's teaching on the state into a simple unity. We should not expect absolute consistency—it is rather "a dialectical zigzag that unfolds gradually the many facets of a jewel."[42]

Conclusion

Even from this very brief review of some of the latest readings of Romans 13:1–7, it becomes clear that the passage continues to challenge interpreters. New examples of old strategies make their appearance alongside innovative ways to deal with the text. What does seem to become more prominent is a fuller recognition of the complexity of the text and of the context in which it is read. The references to "hybridity" and a "dialectical zigzag" already point in this direction. This implies complexity in a double sense, for it relates to both the complexity of the text in its original setting in Rome and the complexity of the current context(s) in which it is read, more than twenty

---

39. Marshall, "Hybridity and Reading Romans 13."
40. Mukuka, "Reading/Hearing Romans 13:1–7 under an African Tree."
41. Bertschmann, *Bowing before Christ*.
42. Viviano, *Catholic Hermeneutics Today*, 149.

centuries later and in circumstances equally if not more remote from the original setting of the text.

The appreciation of this double complexity may, on the one hand, free the interpreter from the expectation to produce a single and only-possible reading, but on the other hand, it increases the responsibility—the *ethical* responsibility, as Pao reminds us[43]—of opening up the text in such a way that it speaks again and brings its own understanding in new and different contexts.

Bibliography

Aletti, J.-N. "La soumission des chrétiens aux autorités en Rm 13,1–7." *Biblica* 89 (2008) 457–76.

Bernheim, P.-A. "Interpolations in Romans: Loisy, O'Neill and Others Revisited." In *The Letter to the Romans*, edited by U. Schnelle, 827–38. Leuven: Peters, 2009.

Bertschmann, D. H. *Bowing before Christ—Nodding to the State? Reading Paul Politically with Oliver O'Donovan and John Howard Yoder.* Library of New Testament Studies 502. London: Bloomsbury, 2014.

———. "The Good, the Bad and the State—Rom 13.1–7 and the Dynamics of Love." *NTS* 60 (2014) 232–49.

Cassidy, R. "The Politization of Paul: Romans 13:1–7 in Recent Discussion." *Expository Times* 121 (2010) 383–89.

Collins, S. M. "Christian Faith and Military Service." May 6, 2012. http://www.Godward.org/archives/Special Articles/Christian_faith_and_military-ser.htm.

Disbrey, C. *Wrestling with Life's Tough Issues: What Should a Christian Do?* Peabody, MA: Hendrickson, 2008.

Dunn, J. D. G. *Romans 9–16*. WBC. Dallas: Nelson, 1988.

Du Toit, A. B. 1995. "Die funksie en waarde van agtergrondstudie van die Nuwe Testament." *Skrif en Kerk* 16 (1995) 310–33.

Forman, M. *The Politics of Inheritance in Romans*. SNTSMS 148. Cambridge: Cambridge University Press, 2011.

Gielen, M. "Der Römerbrief: Ein systematisch-theologisches Lehrschreiben ohne Situationsbezug?" *Bibel und Kirche* 65 (2010) 126–31.

Greschat, M. "Römer 13 und die DDR. Der Streit um das Verständnis der 'Obrigkeit' (1957–1961)." *Zeitschrift für Theologie und Kirche* 105 (2008) 63–93.

Groeben, N. *Rezeptionsforshung als empirische Literaturwissenschaft*. Kronberg: Athenaum, 1977.

Herzog. W. R. "Dissembling, a Weapon of the Weak: The Case of Christ and Caesar in Mark 12:13–17 and Romans 13:1–7." *Perspectives in Religious Studies* 21 (1994) 339–60.

Ho, O. N. K. "On the Challenges of Translating Culture: The Origins of Reading Rom 13:1–7 as 'The Doctrine of Unqualified Obedience' and Its Rectification for 'Modernity.'" *CGSTJournal* 52 (2012) 15–54.

Holmes, A. F. "The Just War." *Intervarsity News*, May 7, 2004.

---

43. Pao, "The Ethical Relevance of New Testament Commentaries," 212–13.

Hoover, R. W. "Identifying Interpolations in Paul's Letters: The Case of the Obligation to Obey Governmental Authorities (Romans 3:1–7)." *FourthR* 24 (2011) 9–10, 22.
Hurley, R. "Ironie dramatique dans la mise en intrigue de l'empire en Romains 13, 1–7." *Studies in Religion/Sciences Religieuses* 35 (2006) 39–63.
Iser, W. "The Reading Process: A Phenomenological Approach." *New Literary History* 3 (1972) 279–99.
Iwasa, N. "Dual ethics in Romans 13." *Journal of Dharma* 35, 159–69.
Jewett, R. *Romans: A Commentary*. Hermeneia. Minneapolis: Fortress, 2007.
Jüngel, E. "Jedermann sei untertan der Obrigkeit. Eine Bibelarbeit über Römer 13,1–7." In *Evangelische Christen in unserer Demokratie*, edited by E. Jüngel and H. Simon, 8–37. Gütersloh: Gütersloher Verlagshaus, 1986.
Keener, C. S. *Romans*. NCCS. Eugene, OR: Cascade, 2009.
Krauter, S. "Auf dem Weg zu einer theologischen Würdigung von Röm 13,1–7." *Zeitschrift für Theologie und Kirche* 109 (2012) 287–306.
Lategan, B. C. "Reading Romans 13 in a South African Context." In *The Reader and Beyond: Theory and Practice in South African Reception Studies*, edited by B. C. Lategan, 115–33. Pretoria: HSRC, 1992.
———. "Romans 13:1–7: A Review of Post-1989 Readings." *Scriptura* 110 (2012) 259–72.
Lategan, B. C., and J. Rousseau. "Lk. 12:35–48: An Empirical Study." *Neotestamentica* 22 (1988) 391–413.
Lohse, E. "Humanitarian Ethics and Biblical Tradition in Modern Europe: The Social Responsibility of Christians according to the New Testament." *Deltion Biblikon Meleton (Bulletin of Biblical Studies)* 26 (2008) 67–73.
Louw, J. P., and E. A. Nida, eds. *Greek-English Lexicon*. Vol. 2. New York: UBS, 1988.
Luttikhuizen, G., and H. Havelaar. "The Interpretation of Romans 13:1–7 in Four Political Parties." Paper presented at the SNTS Seminar on the Role of the Reader, Cambridge, 1988.
Marshall, J. W. "Hybridity and Reading Romans 13." *Journal for the Study of the New Testament* 31 (2008) 157–78.
Miyata, M. *Authority and Obedience: Romans 13:1–7 in Modern Japan*. Translated by G. Vanderbilt. New York: Lange, 2009.
Moo, D. *The Epistle to the Romans*. NICNT. Grand Rapids: Eerdmans, 1996.
Mukuka, T. "Reading/Hearing Romans 13:1–7 under an African Tree: Towards a *Lectio Postcolonica Contexta Africana*." *Neotestamentica* 46 (2012) 105–38.
Nürnberger, K. "Theses on Romans 13." *Scriptura* 22 (1987) 40–47.
Pao, W. D. "The Ethical Relevance of New Testament Commentaries: On the Reading of Romans 13:1–7." In *On the Writing of New Testament Commentaries: Festschrift for Grant R. Osborne*, edited by S. E. Porter et al., 193–213. Texts and Editions for New Testament Study 8. Leiden: Brill, 2013.
Schmidt, S. J. *Grundriss der empirichen Literaturwissenschaft II*. Brunswick: Vierweg, 1982.
Singgih, E. G. "Towards a Postcolonial Interpretation of Romans 13:1–7: Karl Barth, Robert Jewett and the Context of Reformation in Present-Day Indonesia." *Asian Journal of Theology* 23 (2009) 111–22.
Tardivel, É. "Pouvoir et bien commun: Une lecture non théologico-politique de Rm 13,1." *Transversalités* 131 (2014) 47–63.

Viviano, B. T. 2014. *Catholic Hermeneutics Today: Critical Essays*. Eugene, OR: Cascade Books.

Voelz, J. W. "A Response to Bernard Lategan: Reader Clues and Reader Uptake in Romans 13." Paper presented at the SNTS Seminar on the Role of the Reader, Cambridge, 1988.

White, J. "Anti-imperial Subtexts in Paul: An Attempt at Building a Firmer Foundation." *Biblica* 90 (2009) 305–33.

Wright, N. T. *Paul in Fresh Perspective*. Minneapolis: Fortress, 2005.

10

The Christian Life and the World Series

Does How We Live Matter?

—*Michael P. Middendorf*

The keen insights of Jim Voelz in the area of hermeneutics are well reflected in his textbook on the topic titled *What Does This Mean?* His *Fundamental Greek Grammar* and the regular items he authored in the Grammarian's Corner of the *Concordia Journal* aptly demonstrate his extraordinary acumen with the Greek language. His exegetical expertise and precision come across well in his recent Concordia Commentary on the first half of Mark's Gospel.[1] All these God-given skills were developed and put into practice throughout Jim's career as a classroom teacher. He has a well-deserved reputation for using any and every appropriate means to communicate a concept in order to make it stick with his students.

From this writer's perspective as Jim Voelz's first doctoral student, he has proven himself to be not merely a brilliant theologian but also an enthusiastic Renaissance man—no "ivory tower" theologian here! His use of physics to convey a theological framework provides but one example of his wide-ranging intellectual interests.[2] Furthermore, while many students in-

---

1. Voelz, *Mark 1:1—8:28*.

2. Raabe and Voelz, "Why Exhort a Good Tree?" 161, develop an analogy for understanding theological truths and the practicalities of everyday Christian experience by comparing two different approaches to physics, that of Newton and that of Einstein.

teracted with Jim as a classroom teacher, he engaged with numerous others on the various fields of athletics. He served as coach for seminary basketball, golf, and tennis teams, played soccer in adult leagues, and, as I learned by personal experience, became a vigorous opponent on the handball court. Perhaps his most striking integration of athletics and theology remains entrenched in my memory twenty-five years later. In the Theological Observer section of the January-April 1989 issue of the *Concordia Theological Quarterly*, he wrote a piece titled "Myth, Morality, and the World Wrestling Federation."

In striving to emulate my *Doktorvater*, I here propose another illustration from the world of sports as a framework for viewing the Christian life. The New Testament itself provides ample support for employing athletic metaphors, Paul being the most prominent example (e.g., 1 Cor 9:24–27; Gal 2:2; 5:7; Phil 3:12–14; 2 Tim 4:6–8; Heb 12:1–2). Rather than the World Wrestling Federation, however, I will utilize Major League Baseball's World Series. The main question the analogy addresses is, *"Does how God's people live matter?"*[3] Lutherans, well grounded in Eph 2:8–9, may answer in the negative. Those from Roman Catholic and Reformed churches might be more likely to reply in the affirmative. However, rather than a simplistic "yes" or "no" response, the World Series analogy describes how the better answer, as so often seems true in Lutheran theology, becomes both "no!" and "yes!"

The World Series

When you ask someone how many games there are in the World Series, the reply will often be "seven." But this is not exactly or even usually true. Actually it is a "best of seven" series. As a result, once one team wins four games, the other team has no hope, so everyone quits and goes home. The World Series actually lasts from four to seven games.

But what if, to keep the money made from advance ticket sales and television advertising revenue, all seven games were played no matter what? Imagine also that one team won the first four games of the World Series, and still had to play out games 5 through 7. Would how they played those

---

There is an everyday sort of experiential and phenomenological understanding of the universe (= Newton), and there is a deeper, more theoretical, and ontological understanding (= Einstein).

3. This may be only slightly different from the more traditional argument over whether we have to do good works or not (e.g., see Article IV of the Formula of Concord). But here the question will be posed more broadly, as articulated in the subtitle of this article.

games matter? *No, how they played would not ultimately matter.* Whether three additional victories, three forfeits, or anything in between followed, the worst they could do is win the World Series four games to three and be crowned champions. At the same time, the same championship trophy also represents the best that could be achieved. The obvious negative answer to the question explains why, in reality, those final three games are not played.

Yet this article ponders how a team with four victories already in hand would play out those last three games. Would they show up at all, or show up drunk, or lose by a score of 167–2? I doubt it. Instead, I think *they would strive to play well*, for the following reasons:

First, they would, in effect, already be the world champions. I think pride in their identity as such would lead them to reflect that on the playing field. To be sure, any and all efforts by the team already down four games to zero to capture the championship would be futile. Nevertheless, the opposing team might be motivated to settle a score or to make a better showing in the final three games. All the more reason for the actual champions to play like what they, in effect, already are.

Second, although baseball involves numerous individual confrontations (e.g., between pitcher and batter), it remains a team sport. Thus teammates depend upon each other. A runner who reaches base needs to be advanced and driven home; a pitcher relies on the defense behind him; and so forth. Even so-called bench players regularly play decisive roles as relief pitchers, pinch hitters, or late-inning defensive replacements. The supportive cohesion of any championship team is vital and, I contend, would still be evident on the field throughout those final three games.

Third, since the games were being played for the sake of revenue from ticket sales and television, I think a sizable number of people would still show up or watch on TV out of curiosity to see how things played out on the field. Striving to play well would be important to maintain the reputation of the world championship team, both among their own fans and with all the spectators watching.

Application to the Christian Life

Now apply this analogy to the Christian life. By (sinful) nature, we are like error-prone, inept athletes. In feeble attempts to play the game of life on our own, we regularly strike out. Before the contest even begins, we are in fact losers who are headed toward eternal defeat and the wrath of God. However, God sent Jesus into the world to, as it were, play the first four games of the series for us. By virtue of his incarnation, life, ministry, active and passive fulfillment of the law, suffering, death, and resurrection, he has won the first four games for us and for all people. It was, in fact, a complete trouncing and a clean sweep! There is no way, then, that Jesus' team can lose the series. As Dr. Luther sings of the ascending and reigning Son of God, "He holds the field victorious."[4]

Due to no talent or ability on our part, the Holy Spirit nevertheless drafts or gathers us onto Jesus' team. A minor league baseball team in my hometown goes by the name St. Paul Saints. As God's actual saints in Christ, we are now called up to "the Show" in order to play out the last three games of the series, games 5 through 7. So, *does how we live matter?*

On the one hand, as in the World Series analogy above, the answer is "No!" Paul assures us that "we are overwhelmingly victorious through him who loved us" (Rom 8:37; unless otherwise noted, translations are by the author).[5] In fact, the only way we can lose the series is by quitting the team. (Contrary to Calvin's theory of unconditional double predestination or notions of "once saved, always saved," we can renounce the faith and fall from it.) Yet, even while we hold onto the truth of the gospel and remain on the roster where Jesus places us, we still have struggles and may even suffer defeats. We might even lose a game or two, or even all three. After all, throughout the contest of this life we still have to fight our own sinful flesh (Gal 5:16–17) and battle against the unbelieving world (John 15:18–19). Furthermore, the devil continues to prowl around like a roaring lion looking for someone to defeat and devour (1 Pet 5:8–9; Rev 12:12).

But Jesus Christ has already won four games out of seven for us. So, despite the foes arrayed against Jesus' team, Dr. Luther provides this confident assurance: "They cannot win the day. The Kingdom's ours forever."[6] How powerfully and beautifully those words express the truth of the good news, the victory Jesus Christ has already given us. An eternal "triumphal procession" (2 Cor 2:14), which will make every World Series parade pale in comparison, surely awaits!

According to the ways of the world, as well as in baseball's World Series, you must "do" to "be" a winner. In other words, your works determine your status. But in the way of the gospel, who we "be" has been freely granted first and fully by our gracious God; he thereby establishes

---

4. Luther, "A Mighty Fortress," *Lutheran Service Book* (St. Louis: Concordia, 2006), no. 657, stanza 4.

5. The stative translation "overwhelmingly victorious" is to be preferred over the common "more than conquerors" (ESV, KJV, NKJV, NIV, RSV, NRSV) since the latter implies that we did the conquering. For an explanation of this translation, as well as other options, see Middendorf, *Romans 1–8*, 723.

6. Luther, "A Mighty Fortress," stanza 2.

our eternal identity. What we do then springs forth from who we already "be" in Christ.[7] Paul makes the distinction clear in Phil 3:4–11. Our works are neither necessary for salvation, nor do they contribute anything to it. So, does how we live matter? *In the arena of righteousness before God, the answer is a resounding "No!"*

On the other hand, and for different reasons, the answer is also "Yes!" How we live as Jesus' people does matter. It matters a great deal, for the following reasons:

First, as God's saints, we are to live like the champions that Jesus, the sole victor of games 1–4, has declared us also to be. Galatians 3 states, "For as many of you as were baptized into Christ, you clothed yourselves in Christ" (3:27).[8] Ever since our baptism into Jesus' name, we, as it were, wear his name on our jerseys; we belong to him; we play on his triumphant team with all the gracious gifts he freely bestows (e.g., righteousness, the fruit of the Spirit, spiritual gifts). Jesus says, "Make the tree good, and the fruit [will be] good.... The good man out of his good treasure brings forth good" (Matt 12:33, 35). Martin Scharlemann expresses the thought with this catchy phrase: "God has already declared you to be His saints; now show it."[9]

It is simply consistent with our new identity in Christ that we live and play like joyful champions because of who (and whose) we already are, and in response to what he has achieved and freely given to us. However, rather than living according to our true identity in Christ, our sinful nature tempts

---

7. Middendorf and Schuler, *Called by the Gospel*, 323, explain further as follows:

> Songs from the 1950s and 1960s often have background vocalists singing apparently nonsensical syllables and phrases. One example is, "Do-Be-Do-Be-Do." Those little words express the American work ethic all too well. First we do; then we become. Our work makes us who we are. To illustrate this, simply ask people, "Who are you?" Most will respond with their occupation. Christianity asserts just the opposite and this is a fundamental difference. Who we are in Christ is of first importance; that is our essence or "be-ing" (Ephesians 1–3). Who we are then determines what we do (Ephesians 4–6). So, "Be-Do" is a much more appropriate lyric for the believer.
>
> Some scholars make the same point about Paul's theology by speaking of the *indicative* and the *imperative*. First come indicatives—statements of fact—about what God has done for us in Christ; they "indicate" true reality and give us our identity. Paul then follows with imperatives. They exhort and urge believers toward particular godly behaviors in response to those indicatives.

8. For a complete exposition of the significance of this text, see Das, *Galatians*, 379–83.

9. Scharlemann, "Exodus Ethics," 169; note the connection with the minor league St. Paul Saints referenced above. Scharlemann rephrases the overall sentiment in *God's Word for Today*, 73, as "Be what you already are." It is also adopted by Deterding, *Colossians*, 138, in commenting on Col 3:1–4, citing also 1 Cor 5:7a; Eph 5:8.

us to play only for self and to make careless errors. But to lackadaisically succumb to the flesh is inconsistent with who we are as members of Jesus' team. Paul asserts, "Consequently then, brothers, we are debtors, not to the flesh to live in accord with the flesh" (Rom 8:12);[10] he therefore pleads, "Do not make provision for the desires of the flesh" (Rom 13:14). Furthermore, Scripture says this world in its present form is passing away (1 Cor 7:29-31). So why handle money, raise children, pursue selfish pleasures, and try to climb the ladder of so-called success as the unbelieving world does? That's like playing for the losing team! To give in to the devil's enticements seems as ridiculous as obeying signs given by the opposing manager. Failing to play well *for* Jesus and *against* the devil, the world, and our flesh also ignores the guidance of the Spirit of Christ, who dwells within us and urges us to walk in his ways (Rom 8:4, 9; Gal 5:22-25).

Second, we also have teammates, our fellow saints. Due to the work of the Holy Spirit, they are our brothers and sisters in Christ. Paul states, "For also in one Spirit we were all baptized into one body" (1 Cor 12:13). When incorporated into the body of Christ, we receive the fellow members of his church as our teammates. Do we squabble, divide into factions, bicker, whine, and complain against our own teammates? No! Instead, like teammates, we should reach out to, work together with, and root for one another. Yes, how we live matters a great deal to our fellow members in Christ's body, especially when they make errors or are in a slump and need someone to pick them up.

Third, for better or for worse, the manner in which the saints of God live stands on public display each day. The unbelievers in this world are like spectators watching Jesus' team play. How we perform out on the field can have a profound impact upon them. Jesus declares, "In this all people will know you are my disciples, if you have love for one another" (John 13:35). Paul makes a similar appeal in 1 Thessalonians 4, urging us to "walk properly before outsiders" (4:12; cf. Phil 2:14-16; 1 Tim 3:7). If unbelievers see us serving our Savior by serving each other, they observe divinely inspired teamwork. Perhaps they may even be enticed to join us. As Jesus says in the Sermon on the Mount: "In the same way, let your light shine before others, so that they may see your good works and give glory to your Father who is in heaven" (Matt 5:16 ESV).

Finally, we have a *fourth* motivation. Saint Paul expresses it concisely in these words: "But thanks [be] to God, the one who gives the victory to us through our Lord Jesus Christ" (1 Cor 15:57). The manner in which we live and play for Jesus daily expresses our worshipful gratitude to the God who

---

10. See Middendorf, *Romans 1-8*, 630-34.

has already made us champions in Christ (e.g., Rom 12:1–2; Col 3:16–17). Indeed, at the seventh-inning stretch of this article, it would be salutary to use the tune of "Take Me Out to the Ballgame"[11] in order to stand and sing these more appropriate lyrics:

> Praise we sing to the Father,
>
> Praise we sing to the Son,
>
> Praise to the Spirit who makes us one,
>
> Praises be sung to our God, Three-in-One!
>
> So we live to honor our Savior
>
> Let ev'ry tongue proclaim
>
> Tha-at "Jesus Christ is Lord,"
>
> Bless His Holy Name!

Let us rejoice in the victory that is ours because of Jesus Christ (Rom 8:37; 1 Cor 15:57; Phil 4:4). We have been given all the fruits of his four wins! As we play out games 5 through 7 in his name, we may suffer some defeats. But there is no way we can ultimately lose. On the way to our eternal celebration, let us live and work and practice and play together well as teammates, not because we have to, not to prove anything, not to earn anything, but just because that's who we are—God's chosen saints, those who are triumphant champions because of Jesus Christ!

Exegetical Corroboration

Does the framework of the World Series analogy fit well into the theology of the Christian life as taught in Scripture? In my own teaching, I have generally moved beyond the two categories of law and gospel, to use three, law, gospel, and response.[12] I like "response" better than the third use of the law since we still seem to be debating whether one even exists (cf. Article VI of the Formula of Concord). The term "response" also prompts us to continually ponder a more profound question, "Response to what?" The proper answer always brings us back to the good news of Jesus Christ! As the Augsburg Confession states,

> It is also taught that such faith should yield good fruit and good works and that a person must do such good works as God has

---

11. Original music and lyrics by Jack Norworth and Albert Von Tilzer; public domain.

12. See Middendorf and Schuler, *Called by the Gospel*, 155–56, 322–24.

commanded for God's sake but not place trust in them as if thereby to earn grace before God. For we receive forgiveness of sin and righteousness through faith in Christ, as Christ himself says [Luke 17:10]: "When you have done all [things] . . . , say, 'We are worthless slaves.'" The Fathers also teach the same thing. For Ambrose says: "It is determined by God that whoever believes in Christ shall be saved and have forgiveness of sins, not through works but through faith alone, without merit."[13]

The World Series analogy reflects all three parts. The second use of the law describes the inept losers we all were apart from Christ and points out the errors we continue to make, along with their negative consequences. The four victories Christ has won aligns with what God has accomplished for all people objectively through the gospel; subjective justification entails the work of the Holy Spirit, who calls and enlivens us through the gospel and gathers us into the body of Christ, his church.[14] The third category expresses how believers are called to live as God's people in response to the gospel. This involves exhortation and instruction in the ways God intends for Jesus' team to play out games 5 through 7 (see the discussion of Romans below).

1 Corinthians 6:9–12

A sequence of verses in the middle of 1 Corinthians 6 illustrates all three components and also provides a concise summary of Paul's theology.[15]

> [9]Or do you not know that the unrighteous will not inherit the kingdom of God? Do not be deceived: neither the sexually immoral, nor idolaters, nor adulterers, nor men who practice homosexuality, [10]nor thieves, nor the greedy, nor drunkards, nor revilers, nor swindlers will inherit the kingdom of God. [11]And such were some of you. But you were washed, you were sanctified, you were justified in the name of the Lord Jesus Christ and by the Spirit of our God. [12]"All things are lawful for me," but not all things are helpful. "All things are lawful for me," but I will not be enslaved by anything. (1 Cor 6:9–12 ESV)

---

13. Article VI of the Augsburg Confession, titled, "Concerning the New Obedience," in Kolb and Wingert, eds., *The Book of Concord*, 40.

14. For further explanation of the doctrinal categories, see Pieper, *Christian Dogmatics*, 2:347–51; Mueller, *Called to Believe, Teach, and Confess*, 233–35.

15. For a more complete explication, see Lockwood, *1 Corinthians*, 196–203, 214–15.

On the one hand, the law of verses 9–10 identifies the numerous strikes against us. As a result, no one deserves to be in the kingdom or on Jesus' victorious team; all people are "out." What made all the difference was not us getting into shape, demonstrating our own abilities, or even coming together as a team. Instead, in the way of the gospel, we were totally passive as God achieved the necessary victories for us and also changed our status before him. As verse 11 states, "You were washed, you were sanctified, you were justified in the name of the Lord Jesus Christ and by the Spirit of our God."

Then, *does how we live matter?* In verse 12, Paul answers "No" and "Yes." If the good news really means God does everything, then the answer is negative. Jesus fulfilled the law fully and completely for us and for our salvation (e.g., Matt 5:17; Rom 3:21–26; 8:2–4a; Nicene Creed). As a result, Paul can say it twice, "All things are lawful for me." This is no mere ploy or facetious slogan. Paul himself demonstrates this when he repeats the same double assertion in 1 Cor 10:23 at the conclusion of his lengthy discussion, thereby emphatically reaffirming it. Under the gospel, how we live does *not* ultimately matter.

In 1 Cor 6:12, however, Paul immediately adds two important "but's." Yes, "all things are lawful," but not everything is "helpful" for me or beneficial to those who live around me. Yes, "all things are lawful," but I will not become mastered or controlled by those things from which Christ has set me free (John 8:32, 36; Gal 5:1, 13). To succumb to their domination would be to change allegiances and join the opposing team.

For these reasons alone, believers should strive to live in accord with God's will for our own benefit, for the good of our believing teammates, and as a winsome witness to the unbelieving spectators watching us. Paul provides even more profound gospel motivations when he concludes chapter 6 with these words: "Or do you not know that your body is a temple of the Holy Spirit within you, whom you have from God? You are not your own, for you were bought with a price. So glorify God in your body" (1 Cor 6:19–20 ESV).

Romans

These same three parts, law, gospel, and response, appear regularly in that order in the overall structure of Paul's other letters. Walther identifies it in Romans 1–6 as follows:

> Let us pass on to the apostolic epistles, especially to that addressed to the Romans, which contains the Christian doctrine

entirely. What do we find in the first three chapters? The sharpest preaching of the Law. This is followed, towards the end of the third chapter and in chapters 4 and 5, by the doctrine of justification—nothing but that. Beginning at chapter 6, the apostle treats nothing else than sanctification. Here we have a true pattern of the correct sequence: first the Law, threatening men with the wrath of God; next the Gospel, announcing the comforting promises of God. This is followed by instruction regarding things we do after we have become new man.[16]

Once again, all are defeated under the law (Rom 1:18—3:20); but all are victorious in Christ (3:21—4:25). Throughout Romans 5–8 Paul then depicts *the life God gives* to those who have been joined together with our Lord Jesus Christ in baptism (e.g., 6:1–11).[17] Walther observes how Rom 6:12–23, in particular, implores believers to respond appropriately in daily living.[18]

When Paul turns to depict *the life a believer lives* more fully in Romans 12–16,[19] further instructions come to the fore. Once again, these summon us to play games 5 through 7 in specific ways. Raabe and Voelz summarize the force of Paul's exhortations in those chapters as follows:

> The first point that needs to be stressed is that Paul's exhortations are addressed to Christians, to those in Christ who want to and are able to live for God.
>
> Second, it is clear that, although the addressees are Christians, they cannot live for God by their own power and abilities. The power comes from the Spirit working through the Gospel. Therefore, Paul's exhortations are based on Gospel indicative statements.
>
> Third, Paul exhorts his hearers to live out their lives practically and experientially in a way that conforms with what they are already by virtue of Baptism. He calls for their new status to be actualized in their daily life.
>
> Fourth, Pauline paraenesis exhibits a twofold character of negative warning and positive encouraging. This is necessary because . . . sin remains an ever-present threat.
>
> Finally, Paul's intent in paraenesis is not to accuse the Romans as sinners. He does that in chapters 1–3, where the tone is notably different. Paraenesis uses the language of urging,

---

16. Walther, *Law and Gospel*, 93.

17. For an explanation of the dominant themes in Rom 5–8, see Middendorf, *Romans 1–8*, 377–80.

18. See Middendorf, *Romans 1–8*, 486–509 and especially 509–11.

19. This theme is adapted from Middendorf, *Romans 9–16*.

appealing, and beseeching rather than that of harsh demanding and condemning.[20]

Ephesians

The flow of Ephesians reflects a similar pattern. Ephesians 2 concisely and universally provides a classic expression of law and gospel. It depicts who we *were* apart from God's loving-kindness *in the past tense*—defeated, lifeless losers; dead in trespasses and sin; by nature children of wrath, as are all people (2:1-3). But God, who is rich in mercy and love, made us alive in Christ and saved us by grace through faith (2:4-10a). This explains how games 1 through 4 were won. The remainder of chapters 2 and 3 affirm the eternal victory that belongs to all who have been brought onto Jesus' team, the body of Christ.

Amidst regular reminders of God's love and kindness (e.g., 4:4-6, 32b; 5:1-2, 26-27), Ephesians 4-6 then calls forth a certain style of play in response (e.g., 4:1-2, 17-32a; 5:15—6:9).[21] Ephesians 5:8 summarizes the entire letter and all of Paul's theology well: "For you were formerly darkness; now [you are] light in the Lord; walk as children of light!" As in 1 Cor 6:9-12, we once again hear Paul broadcast all three parts—law in the past tense, gospel victory in the Lord (cf. games 1 through 4), and response with an active imperative (cf. games 5 through 7). The flow of Galatians, Colossians, and 1 Thessalonians reflects a similar pattern as well.

Conclusion: Three Analogous Illustrations

Admittedly, all analogies are imperfect. Yet the Scriptures themselves utilize numerous metaphors broadly and consistently in order to communicate God's message to us. In *Just Words*, J. A. O. Preus demonstrates this by identifying twenty-three different biblical expressions. He proposes that "each Gospel word, phrase, and idea is necessary to the fullness of the biblical doctrine of justification. Every Gospel word contributes something distinctive, something unique."[22] It is hoped that this article utilizes a contemporary

---

20. Raabe and Voelz, "Why Exhort a Good Tree?" 158-60.

21. Note, for example, that only *one* imperative appears in Eph 1-3, a call to "remember" in 2:11 (μνημονεύετε), whereas chapters 4-6 contain *forty imperative forms*. These tell believers how to respond properly to the gospel in their lives.

22. Preus, *Just Words*, 24; see also, Barclay, *The Mind of St. Paul*, 75-108; Middendorf, *Romans 1-8*, 340-44.

metaphor that also helps resolve the paradox involved in giving a biblically sound answer to the question, *"Does how God's people live matter?"*

One of the biblical metaphors Preus identifies is victory.[23] In this picture, the context could be either athletic or military. This article utilizes the former; however, the latter context functions comparably. Indeed, the World Series analogy aligns well with Voelz's military illustration of the *Christus Victor* motif. He contends that *"it is the essential orientation of the synoptic gospels and Acts, especially if one sees an analogy between the Christ event and D-Day in WWII."*[24]

> The enemy is, in principle, defeated and cannot win the war (cf. D-Day), but he continues to fight and does better or worse in his attacks until his weapons are finally taken away (cf. V-E Day). So also in the Christ-event, the decisive battle was fought and the gifts of the Age to Come were bestowed. Therefore, the final victory is assured. But the enemy does not disappear immediately; there are still battles to be fought. Yet it is only a matter of time until the final *coup de grace* (= the parousia/second coming).
>
> Indeed, the analogy to D-Day helps us to understand the fact that, after Christ's ascension, the kingdom and its presence has been significantly less "effective" and less apparent. Already in the ministry of the apostles, fewer people were healed, fewer dead were raised, the apostle James was killed (Acts 12:32 [cf. by contrast John 18:9]). And today, the kingdom is, in general, even less decisively seen to exert itself. We remember that after D-Day things were initially fine for the allies. But then problems developed—the enemy did better (cf. Battle of the Bulge). Yet even the Germans (cf. Rommel) believed that the outcome was assured.[25]

So, did how any individual allied soldier perform in the remaining months of the war matter? Perhaps the best answers would be, "No," in terms of the overall outcome, and, of course, also "Yes," in regard to his own well-being and the safety of his comrades.

Two further analogies give the same dual answer about the significance of our life in Christ. A BBC production entitled *Martin Luther: Heretic* contains this exchange between Dr. Luther, a professor at Wittenberg University, and his class:

---

23. Preus, *Just Words*, 201–6.
24. Voelz, *What Does This Mean?* 252, emphasis in original.
25. Voelz, *What Does This Mean?* 252–53.

> A student challenges Dr. Luther, "Man can do nothing about his sinfulness?" Luther answers, "Yes." The student responds, "God is to do everything?" Dr. Luther simply replies, "Yes." The student concludes, "Then I may do as I please. I can sin as much as I want. It makes no difference." Luther says, "Yes. You may do as you please. Now tell me what pleases you? ... Imagine it. No more laws. No more punishments. What do you do? Drink yourself senseless? Make faces at the Duke? Spend the rest of the week in a whorehouse? ... If you're a good man, you'll do good works, not to prove anything, not to gain anything, [but] just because that's how you are, how you are in your heart." The incredulous student asks, "Then what does it take to be a good man?" Luther answers with one word, "Faith."[26]

A final illustration also comes from the classroom, where both Dr. Luther and Dr. Voelz excelled. In so doing, they provide marvelous role models for many other teachers of the Christian faith and life who seek to follow in their train.

> Picture entering a university class in which there was a total of 700 possible points. In order to pass the class you had to earn all 700, a perfect score on everything, 100% all the time. What if, on the first day of class, the professor announced that everyone in the class was given 700 points. Unless you dropped the class, nothing could or would change your grade. How would you act the rest of the semester? Would you go to class or do the assignments or study for the exams? Perhaps not. This may be wishful thinking on the part of a professor, but maybe you would say something like this: "I am a '700 point, straight A' student because of this professor's gift. So, yes, I am free to do whatever I want. All the pressure is off. But out of my gratitude for that gift, I am going to act like a 'straight A' student the rest of the semester. 'Straight A' students attend class, do their homework and study hard for exams. That's what I am going to do, not to prove anything, not to earn anything, but just because that's who I am by grace, 'a 700 point, straight A' student."[27]

Such an already gifted student would then be richly blessed even further by the learning that ensues throughout the term.[28]

---

26. Screenplay by William Nicholson, *Martin Luther: Heretic*, directed by Norman Stone (London: British Broadcasting Corporation, 1993), segment 0:20:28–0:21:54.

27. See Middendorf and Schuler, *Called by the Gospel*, 133.

28. The context of the Beatitudes in Matt 5:1–12 is similar. Jesus speaks to his disciples (Matt 5:1), who already live in a blessed relationship with their heavenly Father

In conclusion, we give thanks to God for all we have learned from Jim Voelz. But, as all these metaphors have emphasized, we conclude, above all, with "thanks to God, the one who gives the victory to us through our Lord Jesus Christ" (1 Cor 15:57).

Bibliography

Barclay, William. *The Mind of St. Paul.* New York: Harper, 1957.
Das, Andrew. *Galatians.* Concordia Commentary. St. Louis: Concordia, 2014.
Deterding, Paul. *Colossians.* Concordia Commentary. St. Louis: Concordia, 2003.
Kolb, Robert, and Timothy Wingert, eds. *The Book of Concord.* Minneapolis: Fortress, 2000.
Lockwood, Gregory. *1 Corinthians.* Concordia Commentary. St. Louis: Concordia, 2000.
Middendorf, Michael. *Romans 1-8.* Concordia Commentary. St. Louis: Concordia, 2013.
———. *Romans 9-16.* Concordia Commentary. St. Louis: Concordia, 2016.
Middendorf, Michael, and Mark Schuler. *Called by the Gospel: An Introduction to the New Testament.* Eugene, OR: Wipf & Stock, 2007.
Mueller, Steve, ed. *Called to Believe, Teach, and Confess.* Eugene, OR: Wipf & Stock, 2005.
Pieper, Francis. *Christian Dogmatics.* 4 vols. St. Louis: Concordia, 1950-1957.
Preus, J. A. O. *Just Words: Understanding the Fullness of the Gospel.* St. Louis: Concordia, 2000.
Raabe, Paul, and James Voelz. "Why Exhort a Good Tree?" *Concordia Journal* 22 (1996).
Scharlemann, Martin. "Exodus Ethics." *Concordia Journal* (1976).
———. *God's Word for Today: 1 Peter, God's Chosen People.* St. Louis: Concordia, 1994.
Voelz, James. *Fundamental Greek Grammar.* 4th ed. St. Louis: Concordia, 2014.
———. *Mark 1:1—8:28.* Concordia Commentary. St. Louis: Concordia, 2013.
———. "Myth, Morality, and the World Wrestling Federation." *Concordia Theological Quarterly* 53 (1989) 89-92.
———. *What Does This Mean?* 2nd ed. St. Louis: Concordia, 1997.
Walther, C. F. W. *Law and Gospel.* St. Louis: Concordia, n.d.

(e.g., the phrase "your Father" occurs thirteen times in the Sermon on the Mount). Further blessings then flow from Jesus' own words of blessing to those who follow him.

11

Steps for the Definition of the Lexemes in the Greek-Spanish New Testament Dictionary

The Lexeme δῆμος

—*Jesús Peláez*

and

—*GASCO (Semantic Analysis Group, Grupo de Análisis Semántico. Cordoba) University of Cordoba (Spain)*

In this paper, in honor of our colleague and friend Prof. James Voelz, I'll try to present in a brief and concise way the semantic method we apply for the construction of the definition of the words or lexemes in our *Diccionario Griego-Español del Nuevo Testamento* (*Greek-Spanish New Testament Dictionary*).[1] To explain the methodology,[2] I have chosen the lexeme δῆμος,

1. The research group that is drafting the *Diccionario Griego-Español del Nuevo Testamento* is formed by the following members: Marta Merino, Pope Godoy, Israel Muñoz, Dámaris Romero, Lautaro Roig, Luis Domingo, Rufino Godoy, José I. Fernández, Juan Guillén, and Lourdes García, PSD or graduates in theology, biblical or classical philology. This project is directed by Jesús Peláez, retired professor of Greek philology, University of Cordoba.

2. The method and methodology applied in this article have been presented and

pertaining to the grammatical class of the noun and to the semantic class of the entity.

Statistics of Words and Concordances in the New Testament

The first step in writing the entries of the dictionary is always to consult Morgenthaler's[3] frequency statistics and Aland's New Testament concordances.[4] By doing so, we aim to determine the frequency of use of the lexeme under study and the different contexts in which it appears.

In addition, we use the Accordance software, which is specialized for processing biblical text, along with a module containing the latest Spanish version of the New Testament by Juan Mateos,[5] which has been chosen as the basic text for our dictionary. However, given that this version is a literary one, we modify it when necessary.

According to the concordances, δῆμος appears four times in the New Testament, all in the book of Acts:

- 12:22 ὁ δὲ δῆμος ἐπεφώνει· θεοῦ φωνὴ καὶ οὐκ ἀνθρώπου.
- 17:5 καὶ ἐπιστάντες τῇ οἰκίᾳ Ἰάσονος ἐζήτουν αὐτοὺς προαγαγεῖν εἰς τὸν δῆμον.
- 19:30 Παύλου δὲ βουλομένου εἰσελθεῖν εἰς τὸν δῆμον οὐκ εἴων αὐτὸν οἱ μαθηταί.
- 19:33 ὁ δὲ Ἀλέξανδρος κατασείσας τὴν χεῖρα ἤθελεν ἀπολογεῖσθαι τῷ δήμῳ.

Classical and Biblical Dictionaries

After checking the concordances, we consult the main Greek dictionaries, both classical and biblical, as our lexicographical study does not start from zero but takes into account data from Greek lexicography in general, and New Testament lexicography in particular.

---

developed in two books: Mateos, *Método de análisis semántico, aplicado al griego del Nuevo Testamento*, and Peláez, *Metodología del Diccionario Griego-Español del Nuevo Testamento*. These books have been translated into English by Andrew Bowden (University of Munich) and will be published in one volume under the title *New Testament Lexicography* by Walter de Gruyter, Berlin, January 2016.

3. Morgenthaler, *Statistik des Neutestamentlichen Wortschatzes*.
4. Aland, *Konkordanz zum Novum Testamentum Graece*.
5. Mateos, *Nuevo Testamento*.

Among the most important general Greek dictionaries is Lidell-Scott,[6] which we normally consult, along with the volumes published in the *Diccionario Griego-Español* (*Greek-Spanish Dictionary*), directed by Fco. Rodríguez Adrados;[7] for Greek etymologies we consult Chantraine's dictionary;[8] for New Testament Greek, Zorell's[9] and Bauer-Aland's[10] dictionaries, and also the ones that appear in the *Bible Works*[11] computerized program for text treatment of the Bible, which are the Friberg Greek lexicon, the United Bible Societies' Greek dictionary, the Louw-Nida lexicon,[12] the Bauer-Danker lexicon (BDAG),[13] and the Thayer Greek lexicon.[14] Other dictionaries with a theological orientation such as Kittel[15] or studies on lexemes published in specialized reviews are consulted for words referring to more specific concepts from Jewish or Christian theology.

After consulting the dictionaries, both classical and biblical, we get an idea about the word treatment. The dictionaries register four different translations of δῆμος:

1. In a local sense: *a country district, land*.

2. Like πλῆθος: *the people of a country, the commons*.

3. Like κῶμαι (Lat. *pagi*), in Attic and in plural, ancient divisions of the county, being (in the time of Herodotus) 100 in number: *townships* or *hundreds*.

4. Like ἐκκλησία: *the assembly of citizens*.

Thus, in writing an entry for the dictionary, the consultation of concordances and dictionaries is always the first step taken, before the construction of the term's definition. This is the way to get an idea of the frequency of the term, the contexts in which it appears, and the treatment afforded in lexicons, as well as its translation or translations and, in some dictionaries, such as Louw-Nida and BDAG, its definition.

6. Liddell et al., *A Greek-English Lexicon*.
7. Adrados, *Diccionario Griego-Español*.
8. Chantraine, *Dictionnaire étymologique de la Langue Grecque: Histoire des mots*.
9. Zorell, *Lexicon Graecum Novi Testamenti*.
10. Bauer, *Griechisch-Deutsches Wörterbuch zu den Schriften des Neuen Testament und der frühchristlichen Literatur*.
11. *Bible Works*⁷.
12. Louw and Nida, *Greek-English Lexicon of the New Testament Based on Semantic Domains*.
13. Bauer et al., *Greek-English Lexicon of the New Testament*.
14. Wilke-Grimm-Thayer, *A Greek-English Lexicon of the New Testament*.
15. Kittel, *Theologisches Wörterbuch zum Neuen*.

Therefore, after consulting the dictionaries, we can state a hypothesis about how the entry should be organized. This hypothesis will become thesis once the semantic analysis is completed.

The existing dictionaries of the New Testament, with the exception of the Louw-Nida and the BDAG dictionaries, do not usually make any distinction between meaning (= definition) and translation, except on rare occasions, the terms so named in Latin *de realia*. They are rather repertories of words in which for every Greek word a list of terms is given in the target language, not all of which correspond exactly to the lexical meaning of the word, but to different translations of the word in a particular context.

Bilingual dictionaries, which make no distinction between meaning and translation, although useful for translating, often confuse users who have no way of knowing how to choose one among the different translations for a given lexeme. It is quite a relief for users of bilingual dictionaries to find, among the examples provided, the word they are looking for with the corresponding context and proposed translation.

On the other hand, in NT dictionaries the structuring of the entries under different sections does not always correspond to different senses or meanings of the word. Divisions frequently obey grammatical and syntactic criteria rather than semantic ones.

Establishment of the Semantic Formula

Our next step to establish the semantic formula of δῆμος and to provide its definition will be to identify the semantic class or classes (if a lexeme has a simple structure with only one semantic class denoted or a complex structure, with two or more semantic classes denoted).

A sample of entity lexemes with simple structure denoting only one semantic class are λίθος, "rock," κύων, "dog," and ἄνθρωπος, "person":

Formula:

Ent

A sample of a lexeme with complex structure is ἄγγελος, "angel," which denotes three different semantic classes: an entity (Ent), a relation (R), and another entity (Ent').

Formula:

Ent + R + Ent'

ἄγγελος is an entity (Ent), belonging (R)
to the divine sphere (Ent').

There are, however, other entity lexemes with simple structure that not only *denote* a semantic class, but necessarily *connote* other class or classes, such as ἁλιεύς, "fisherman," whose semantic formula presents two semantic classes denoted (inside the box): entity (Ent) and event (Ev), and two connoted (outside the box): relation (R) and entity (Ent1):

$$\boxed{\text{Ent + Ev}} \longrightarrow R \longrightarrow \text{Ent1}$$

ἁλιεύς is someone (Ent) who catches (Ev) fish (R, Ent1).

As said before, the lexeme δῆμος belongs to the grammatical class of the noun, although from the semantic point of view it belongs to the semantic class of the entity.

Grammatical and Semantic Classes

Grammatical classes and semantic classes are two different concepts.

We understand by *grammatical classes* the so-called "parts of a sentence" that can be divided into main (noun and verb), adjunct (adjective and adverb), relative (prepositions and conjunctions), as well as auxiliary (article and pronoun).

By *semantic classes* we understand "a set of words which have the same dominant semantic class or features (seme)."

According to this definition, semantic classes classify terms according to their conceptual content. We acquire knowledge of the world that surrounds us, and to get our bearings and find our place in it, we express it from our own point of view; to do this, we classify and name *entities* (beings), we describe them by way of attributes (quality, dimension) or by stating *events* (states, actions, acts, or processes) that take place, considering the *relations* that are set up between them. We also use *determination* to update, identify, and situate them in time and place.

Thus, five semantic classes are established, each referred to by its initial letter or initial letters: entity (Ent), attributes (A), events (Ev), relations (R), and determination (D).

As we can see, the semantic classes do not correspond completely with the grammatical classes. The semantic class entity (Ent), for example, covers a narrower field than the grammatical class noun. In effect, there are nouns such as "beauty" or "height" that are from a semantic point of view *attributes* (A) denoting qualities; or *events* (Ev), as "stop, rest, walking, greeting, departure," if they denote *state, action, or process;* or *relations* (R) as "nearness, distance," which denote *localization*. Other nouns that are not abstract, such as "name" and "nickname," can be *determination* (D).

Given that our method is based on semantics, the next step in the preparation of the definition of the lexeme must be to describe the lexeme δῆμος according to its predominant semantic class. We have said that from the grammatical point of view δῆμος is a noun, but semantically it belongs to the semantic class entity.

Grammatical and Semantic Categories

At this stage, for example, you might wonder which class of entity is δῆμος. To answer this question, we apply to δῆμος the semantics categories of gender and number, characteristics of the nouns.

As said before, regarding the difference between grammatical and semantics classes, grammatical and semantics categories are two different concepts: the *grammatical categories* include gender and number (nominals and verbals), mode, tense, aspect and voice (verbals), and degree (of conjunctions, adjectives, and adverbs).

As with the grammatical and semantics classes, the *semantic categories* do not entirely correspond with the grammatical ones. Moreover, degree is not semantically a category but applies in the classes of relation and determination.

—Gender

The *grammatical gender* distinguishes between masculine, feminine, neuter, common, epicene, and ambiguous.

But *semantically* the following levels are highly important:

animate <---> inanimate
‖
personal <---> non-personal
‖
divine <---> human
‖
masculine <---> feminine

In some texts, such as the NT, "angelic" and "demonic" can be regarded as the opposite of "divine" and "human."

As a lexeme belonging to the semantic category of entities, we can say that δῆμος is an animate, personal, human (being).

—*Number*

From the *grammatical point of view*, number can be singular, plural, or dual; δῆμος is a singular noun. But from the *semantic point of view*, number is not based on the opposition *singular* versus *dual/plural*, but in that of *individual* versus *nonindividual* according to this scheme that also includes the collective:

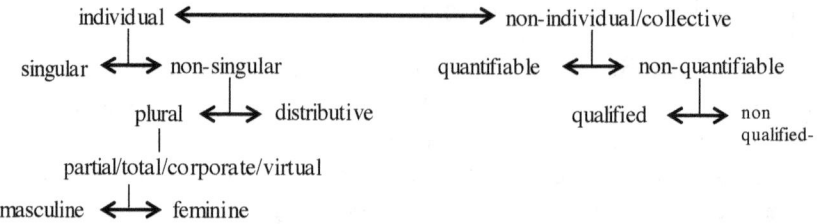

Taking both together, gender and number, we can say that δῆμος *grammatically* is a singular noun (number) but *semantically* is an entity, nonindividual-collective, nonquantifiable; if it is qualified or not will be determined by the contexts.

The nonquantifiable collective includes "groups of entities—animate or not," such as ὄχλος, "crowd," ἀγέλη, "herd" (animate), or "something's volume" (inanimate), for example, καρπός, "harvest." In contrast to the unqualified ὄχλος, the terms λαός (people [of God]) and ἔθνος (nation / pagan people) entail a distinctive mark that qualifies them.

The quantifiable collective is represented by σπεῖρα, "cohort" (John 18:3; Acts 27:1), because by the Roman cultural context we exactly know the number of soldiers forming a cohort, a hundred. This is the reason why we can say that it is a collective quantifiable entity.

But as a collective noun, δῆμος denotes also other semantic classes, as we can see by different contexts in which it appears specified as a numerous totality (determination) linked (relation) to a territory (Ent1).

In this way, the basic formula of the *lexical meaning* of δῆμος (that is, the first one that we consider from which we derive other contextual meanings) is composed by the following semantic categories:

Entity + determination + relation + Ent 1, and we represent it as follows:

[Ent + D] +R   → Ent1

So, the semantic formula of the lexeme includes in its box the denoted elements of the human collective (Ent) of all (D) the citizens (Ent) (not the inhabitants, since the slaves are excluded) and its connection (R) to a territory (Ent1), which is connoted and therefore located outside the box.

Semic Development of the Formula

Once we have established the semantic formula, we continue presenting the *semic development* of the semantic classes included in the formula, denoted or connoted as a previous step, to construct the definition of the lexeme.

The *semic development* is a list of the semes or semantic traits that correspond to each of the semantic classes of the formula, denoted and connoted, that we deduce from the consideration of the lexeme itself, enabling the constants or quasi constants to be determined.

The use of the semantic formula as an intermediate step—which is sandwiched between the lexeme and its semic development—is one of this study's unique features. This step offers two primary advantages.

Firstly, the formula provides guidance for breaking down the semes. Instead of haphazardly identifying the semes, which carries the risk of omitting many of them, the formula offers a clear pattern for the semic development. The procedure is simple: the elements that constitute the formula are identified by being categorized into denoted and connoted elements. The application of the semantic categories (gender and number in our case) to the elements of the formula serves as an easy starting point, which is completed by comparing related lexemes.

Secondly, the formula can serve as a paradigm. The semic polyvalence of the elements that constitute the formula allows the same formula to be used for various lexemes: domains or groups of lexemes are constructed that have the same structure, and formulas are adapted based on the addition or substitution of elements. In this way, we can say that δῆμος (crowd), φυλή (tribe), ἔθνος (nation), and πατριά (lineage, family) are related terms denoting other human collectives.

When possible, semes are referred to as abstract nouns. Given that it has to do with a metalanguage (that is, a technical language), it can be helpful to coin new terms if these are necessary to express the nature of the semes.

On the other hand, *semes* are often defined as elemental semantic units and are therefore indivisible. In reality, it is very doubtful that most of the semes used in the analysis are indivisible units that cannot be further broken down into smaller units. However, given that a method must be functional, the degree of abstraction used will have to remain proportionate to the purpose of the method. For example, the seme "humanity" can be clearly broken down into smaller semes ("entity," "corporeality," "vitality," "sensitivity," "rationality"), but to mention these semes each time "humanity" appears leads to endless, unintelligible lists of semic nuclei. Therefore, certain methods for simplifying the communication of the semes without compromising their exactitude are used.

To determine a lexeme's generic *nuclear semes,* the semantic categories are applied to each element of the formula. Nuclear semes are those that appear in the semic nucleus and are obtained by the development of the semantic formula.

In our case, if we apply to the entity δῆμος the categories of number and gender, we obtain the following list of semes:

Semantic Class Entity

–Generic semes

Ent Humanity (gender)

Collectivity (number)

–Specific seme

Citizenship

The specific nuclear semes are identified in the development of the generic semes by looking at the meaning of the lexeme in a given context. So the specific seme "citizenship" is obtained from the extratextual context or cultural context, because we know that δῆμος in the Hellenistic world does not refer to all the inhabitants of a city, because the slaves were excluded from citizenship.

The semic development is continued by determining the nuclear semes of the rest of the semantic categories included in the formula. In this way we get the list of generic nuclear semes that can be common to many other lexemes, enabling *semantic domains* to be formed.

We understand *semantic domain* as a group of lexemes that have common generic semes at different levels, giving the domain various degrees of breadth. Thus, for example, the generic seme "dynamism" includes the whole domain "activity." If the seme "mobility" is added (dynamism + mobility), this includes the entire domain "movement" in whatever direction. If the seme "horizontality" is also added (dynamism + mobility + horizontality), it only includes the domain "horizontal movement," etc.

If we continue specifying the rest of semes of the semantic classes of the formula, this is the result:

Semantic Class Determination

D Numerosity

Totality

Semantic Class Relation

R Connection

Semantic Class Ent1

Ent 1 Territoriality

Putting it all together, this is the semic development of the formula:

Ent	Collectivity
	Humanity
	Citizenship
D	Numerosity
	Totality
R	Connection
Ent1	Territoriality

Definition of the Lexical Meaning

According to the semic development, we are now able to state the definition of δῆμος as "a numerous group (D) of citizens (Ent) from (R) a territory (Ent1)": *the citizens, citizenship.*

This definition can be considered as a lexical meaning of δῆμος. But δῆμος does not appear with this meaning in the New Testament texts, because in the four cases in which it appears, the δῆμος is presented as *gathered* (a contextual factor that excludes the seme of totality). Examining all the contexts in which δῆμος appears, we can still distinguish two different meanings. In the first one (Acts 12:22), the δῆμος, composed of citizens from Tyre and Sidon, comprises a multitude that hails King Herod. In the second (Acts 17:5; 19:30–33), δῆμος has the role of a protagonist as an institutional assembly that must make a decision.

Sememes or Contextual Meanings

Two sememes can thus be constructed from the lexeme by adding some semes to or omitting them from the formula.

Sememe I. In this sememe δῆμος means a crowd of citizens gathered in a meeting place. In the semantic formula of sememe I, the contextual element of common location (R') is added:

$$[Ent + D] + R + R' \longrightarrow Ent_1$$

Two new features appear in the formula's semic development: the changed content of the determination (D, "partialness" instead of "totality") and the semes corresponding to the common location (R'):

Semic development

Ent	Collectivity
	Humanity
	Citizenship
D	Numerosity
	Partialness
R	Connection
R'	*Simultaneousness*
Ent1	Territoriality

The definition of this sememe can be as follows: "A numerous group (D) of citizens (Ent) of a territory (Ent1) gathered (R')": *crowd / multitude of citizens.*

With this meaning, we read in Acts 12:22: ὁ δὲ δῆμος ἐπεφώνει, *the crowd was calling out.*

Sememe II. In the rest of the texts of Acts, δῆμος also means a crowd gathered in a meeting place, but the group has the specific purpose of deliberating about measures that must be adopted concerning certain people. Therefore, the formula adds to the elements denoted in sememe I the event of deliberation with official character. It also acquires a new connotation, which is the subjects (Ent2) about whom (R') the others must deliberate and make a decision:

$$\longrightarrow Ent_1$$
$$[Ent + D] + R + R' + Ev$$
$$\longrightarrow R_1 \longrightarrow Ent_2$$

The semic development therefore presents the semes of R' (gathering, like in sememe I) and also those of the activity (Ev) and of the individuals (Ent2) that are affected (R1).

Ent	Collectivity
	Humanity
	Citizenship
D	Numerosity
	Partialness
R	Connection
R'	*Simultaneousness*
Ent 1	Territoriality
Ev	Activity
	Officialness
	Deliberation
	Decision
R1	Affecting
Ent2	Individuality/Plurality
	Humanity

The definition of this sememe can be the following: "A numerous group (D) of citizens (Ent) from (R) a territory (Ent1), gathered (R') to deliberate and officially decide (Ev) about (R1) other people (Ent2)": *assembly (of citizens)*:

- Acts 17:5: ἐζήτουν αὐτοὺς προαγαγεῖν εἰς τὸν δῆμον, *they intended to bring them before the assembly.*

- Acts 19:30: Παύλου δὲ βουλομένου εἰσελθεῖν εἰς τὸν δῆμον οὐκ εἴων αὐτὸν οἱ μαθηταί. *Wishing Paul to go into the assembly* (= ἐκκλησία; cf. 19:32), *the disciples would not let him.*

- Acts 19:33: ἤθελεν ἀπολογεῖσθαι τῷ δήμῳ, *he wanted to make his defense before the assembly.*

Entry of the Dictionary

Having identified the different sememes or meanings of the lexeme δῆμος, we are now able to write the entry for the dictionary. It could be as follows:

δῆμος ου, ὁ (4)

"A numerous group of citizens from a territory": *citizenship, people*:

In the four NT texts, the δῆμος appears gathered and the trait of totality is excluded:

I. Occasionally gathered before Herod: "A numerous group of citizens from a territory gathered": *crowd/multitude* (of citizens): ὁ δὲ δῆμος ἐπεφώνει· θεοῦ φωνὴ καὶ οὐκ ἀνθρώπου, *the crowd kept shouting, "The voice of a god, and not of a mortal!"* (Acts 12:22).

II. Institutionally gathered to deliberate: "A numerous group of citizens from a territory, gathered to deliberate and officially decide about other people": *assembly* (of citizens): ἐζήτουν αὐτοὺς προαγαγεῖν εἰς τὸν δῆμον, *they were intending to lead them to the assembly* (Acts 17:5); Παύλου δὲ βουλομένου εἰσελθεῖν εἰς τὸν δῆμον οὐκ εἴων αὐτὸν οἱ μαθηταί, *Wishing Paul to go into the assembly* (= ἐκκλησία, cf. 19:32), *the disciples would not let him* (Acts 19:30); ἤθελεν ἀπολογεῖσθαι τῷ δήμῳ, *he was intending to present his defense before the assembly* (Acts 19:33).

As can be seen, in the entry of the dictionary we have omitted all the technical terms relative to the semantic analysis. We gave only the definition of the lexical meaning and sememes, and the corresponding citation together with its translation, because the dictionary is aimed not only at specialists in semantics but also at a wider public.

δῆμος: Lexical Meaning, Sememes, Definition, and Translation

Lexical Meaning	Sememe I	Sememe II
Semantic Formula	*Semantic Formula*	*Semantic Formula*
		—➤ Ent 1
[(Ent + D) + R]—➤ Ent1	[(Ent + D) + R + **R'**] —➤ Ent1	[(Ent + D) + R +R' + **Ev**] —➤ **R1** —➤ **Ent2**
Semic development	*Semic development*	*Semic development*
Ent Collectivity	Ent Collectivity	Ent Collectivity
Humanity	Humanity	Humanity
Citizenship	Citizenship	Citizenship
D Numerosity	D Numerosity	D Numerosity
Totality	**Partialness**	**Partialness**
R Connection	R Connection	R Connection
	R' **Simultaneousness**	R' **Simultaneousness**
Ent1 Territoriality	Ent1 Territoriality	Ent1 Territoriality
		Ev **Activity**
		Officialness
		Deliberation
		Decision
		R1 **Affecting**
		Ent2 **Individuality**
		Plurality
		Humanity
Definition	*Definition*	*Definition*
"A numerous group (D) of citizens (Ent) from (R) a territory Ent1)."	"A numerous group (D) of citizens (Ent) from (R) a territory (Ent1), **gathered (R')**."	"A numerous group (D) of citizens (Ent) from (R) a territory (Ent1), **gathered (R') to deliberate and officially decide (Ev) about (R1) other people (Ent2)**."
Translation: the citizens, citizenship.	*Translation:* crowd, multitude of citizens.	*Translation:* assembly of citizens.

Bibliography

Adrados, Fco. Rodríguez. *Diccionario Griego-Español.* Fasc. I (1980), II (1986), III (1991), IV (1994), V (1997), and VI (2002). Madrid: CSIC, Instituto Antonio de Nebrija, 1980–2002.

Aland, K. *Konkordanz zum Novum Testamentum Graece.* Von Nestle-Aland, 26 Auflage und zum *Greek New Testament.* 3rd ed. Institut für Neutestamentliche Textforschung, und vom Rechenzentrum der Universität Münster. Berlin and New York: de Gruyter, 1987.

Bauer, W. *Griechisch-Deutsches Wörterbuch zu den Schriften des Neuen Testament und der frühchristlichen Literatur.* Edited by K. Aland and B. Aland. 6th ed. Berlin and New York: de Gruyter, 1998.

Bauer, Walter, et al. *Greek-English Lexicon of the New Testament and Other Early Christian Literature.* 3rd ed. Chicago: University of Chicago Press, 2000.

Bible Works^7. Software for Biblical Exegesis and Research. 7th ed. Norfolk, VA: Bible Works LLC, 2002.

Chantraine, P. *Dictionnaire étymologique de la Langue Grecque: Histoire des mots.* New ed. Paris: Klinchsieck, 1999.

Liddell, Henry George, et al. *A Greek-English Lexicon.* 9th ed. Oxford: Clarendon, 1996.

Louw, J. P., and E. A. Nida, eds. *Greek-English Lexicon of the New Testament Based on Semantic Domains.* 2 vols. New York: United Bible Societies, 1988.

Mateos, Juan. *Método de análisis semántico, aplicado al griego del Nuevo Testamento.* Córdoba: El Almendro, 1989.

———. *Nuevo Testamento.* Córdoba and Madrid: El Almendro-Edibesa, 2012.

Morgenthaler, R. *Statistik des Neutestamentlichen Wortschatzes.* Frankfurt: Gotthelf-Verlag Zürich, 1958.

Peláez, Jesús. *Metodología del Diccionario Griego-Español del Nuevo Testamento.* Córdoba: El Almendro, 1995.

Wilke-Grimm-Thayer. *A Greek-English Lexicon of the New Testament: Being Grimm's and Wilke's Clavis Novi Testamenti.* Translated, revised, and enlarged by Joseph Henry Thayer. 4th ed. Edinburgh: T. and T. Clark, 1898; reprint, 1999.

Zorell, F., SJ. *Lexicon Graecum Novi Testamenti.* 4th ed. Paris, 1990; original 1930.

12

Eye for an I

An Intertextual Reading of Matthew 5:38 and the Artwork of Samuel Bak

—*Gary A. Phillips*

What's at stake in reading biblical texts that are implicated in violence toward others, in particular the unspeakable violence of the Holocaust? How are we to engage Matthew's Gospel, whose legacy of vehemence directed against Jews, especially Jewish children, stands in stark tension to its lofty vision of justice? How do we press back against texts that press readers forward into anti-Jewish and anti-Semitic vitriol and hatred? An intertextual reading provides a way of engaging Matthew's composition and complicity in violence toward others and, as I will suggest, a means as well for its interruption. This essay explores these issues in an intertextual reading of the *lex talionis* citation in Matthew 5:38 and the artwork of Holocaust survivor Samuel Bak. Bak's stunning visual representations of the biblical *lex talionis* and Lady Justice press us to see and to confront Matthew's text and its effects in a disruptive light. We begin by setting the wider context for this post-Holocaust reading and the ethical and interpretive concerns that motivate it.[1]

---

1. I offer this essay in deep admiration for Jim Voelz, passionate reader and teacher of biblical texts, whose unflinching moral and critical integrity models for students and colleagues alike responsible biblical interpretation. He presses his students with the press of the biblical text.

The Abyss

After Auschwitz, interruption of Matthew's Gospel and Christian readings of it is demanded for historical and ethical reasons. According to Emil Fackenheim, an abyss of historic proportions has opened up between the biblical text written there and then and the reader interpreting here and now.[2] The event of the Holocaust, emblemized in the deaths of 1.5 million children, has permanently ruptured Jews and Christians from their respective scriptures, the interpretive practices, and one another. Situated now on this side of the abyss, after Auschwitz, we can no longer read the biblical text seamlessly cushioned by theological commentary and spiritualize interpretations as if the historical events of 1933–1945 had never transpired. Rachel's children who are no more (Jer 31:15, cited in Matt 2:18) are not symbolic but real children. Auschwitz has created a seismic shock that reverberates through readings of Matthew's Gospel and the wider Bible brought about "not by theologizing about the Holocaust but by the event itself,"[3] by the million and a half flesh-and-blood children who were murdered. Matthew's readers are confronted then by a *novum* in history, namely, the reality that Jewish *"existence itself is a crime, punishable by humiliation, torture, and death."*[4] Rachel's children were born to die.

Matthew's Gospel and its reception have fueled Christian contempt for Jews by enflaming anti-Jewish hatred and violence toward the innocent.[5] The deicide charge and blood libel in 27:25 and Herod's slaughter of the innocents in 2:16–18 are two Matthean texts of terror that have inspired carnage over the centuries.[6] While many Matthean scholars acknowledge the vitriol that pervades the Gospel from its negative portrayal of Jewish teaching and piety to its apocalyptic vision of perpetual violence and suffering,[7] biblical scholarship has largely failed to come to grips with the textual violence and its afterlife among Christian readers. For example, recognizing Matthew 27:25 to be "one of those phrases which have been responsible for oceans of

---

2. Fackenheim, *Jewish Bible after the Holocaust*, vi–viii.

3. Ibid., 20.

4. Fackenheim, "The Holocaust and Philosophy," 509, emphasis in original. For the wider issues facing a post-Holocaust reading of the Bible, see Doukhan, "Reading the Bible after Auschwitz," 683–86.

5. See Crossan, *Who Killed Jesus?*, 31–38, 154–57. On historical Christian anti-Semitism see Parkes, *The Conflict of the Church*, 33–45.

6. See Phillips, "Killing Fields," 233–35; Langmuir, *Toward a Definition of Antisemitism*, 266–71.

7. Of importance are Carter, "Construction of Violence," 81–108, and Destro and Pesce, "The Cultural Structure of the Infancy Narrative," 94–115.

human blood and a ceaseless stream of misery and desolation," Raymond Brown can still praise Matthew as "the most effective theater among the Synoptics, outclassed in that respect only by the Johannine masterpiece."[8] We witness a disconnect between story and history, aesthetics and ethics, reading and responsibility. Such seamless reading fails to do justice to the real innocents—particular women and children—who have been targeted by the Gospel text and its readers.

Scholars can and must do better.[9] In the ethical terms of Emmanuel Levinas, Matthew's text and its readings must be interrupted by the faces of the real innocents whose defenseless eyes disrupt any and all theological projects and seamless interpretations. The suffering of others imposes upon me the ethical burden of interrupting Gospel-portrayed and Gospel-inspired violence.[10] Matthew underscores this responsibility—ironically perhaps—in Jesus' Sermon on the Mount discourse where the ethical demand for justice and peace anchored in the *lex talionis* is voiced: "An eye for an eye, a tooth for a tooth" (ὀφθαλμὸν ἀντὶ ὀφθαλμοῦ καὶ ὀδόντα ἀντὶ ὀδόντος, 5:38). But for all its ethical power, Matthew's call for a surpassing, excessive justice still comes at the expense of Jews (περισσεύσῃ ὑμῶν ἡ δικαιοσύνη πλεῖον τῶν γραμματέων καὶ Φαρισαίων, 5:20). Despite Matthew's contradictory call for justice, readers can and must do better. When reading Matthew's description of Jews and justice in light of the Holocaust, we must hold the Gospel text and its readers to the exceedingly high standard voiced by Irving Greenberg: "No statement, theological or otherwise, should be made that would not be credible in the presence of the burning children."[11] The historical abyss has forever altered the conditions and character of Christian reading of the Gospel and elevated ethical accountability for the innocent. Matthew must be held accountable to the gospel's vision of justice expressed in the *lex talionis*, and that can happen only when the violence is interrupted by reading Matthew against itself.

Intertextuality as Interruption

Julia Kristeva's notion of intertextuality aids a post-Holocaust interruptive reading of Matthew in two important ways. First, the concept of intertextuality points to the dynamic process of disruption and interruption that is a condition of all textuality and reading. "[E]very text is constructed as

---

8. Brown, *Death of the Messiah*, 831n22. See Crossan's pointed critique (ix).
9. Crossan, *Who Killed Jesus?*, x.
10. Levinas, *Totality and Infinity*, 199.
11. Greenberg, "Cloud of Smoke," 23.

a mosaic of citations; every text is the absorption and transformation of another";[12] every text is a permutation of one text by another. From this perspective texts are sites of multiple, contesting voices. "[I]n the space of a text utterances from multiple texts *intersect and neutralize* one another."[13] Texts are by their very nature marked by internal and external tensions. Intentionally disruptive readings of Matthew participate in the agonistic contest between and transformation of text and reader by other texts and readers.

Second, in historical terms Kristeva's poststructural theory of intertextuality is a response to the Holocaust. Along with other poststructural theoretical efforts, intertextuality was a response to the tumultuous crisis of humanism that swept post-WWII French society, in particular the specter of European anti-Semitism and the unresolved issues of French complicity in the Final Solution.[14] Intertextual theory seeks to redefine the relationship of literature to society by contesting the privileged place afforded the author and elevating the ethical role and responsibility of the reader.[15] The disruptive and ethical dynamics of intertextual theory are frequently ignored by biblical scholars intent on applying Kristeva's concepts in support of traditional source, comparative, and influence criticism.[16] The downplaying of the socially disruptive role reflects the powerful hold of an aesthetic ideology that sustains seamless theological readings of the biblical text. Against the historical backdrop of dehumanization and violence associated with Matthew's narrative and its history of reception, an intertextual reading of the *lex talionis* in Matthew's Sermon on the Mount discourse, in conversation with Samuel Bak's destabilizing representations of justice, accentuates the ethical demand for an exceeding justice expressed by Matthew's very own citation of the *lex talionis*.[17] Intertextual reading offers a way to respond then to the contested character of textuality and to the ethical challenge presented by the post-Holocaust abyss.

---

12. Kristeva, *Desire in Language*, 146.

13. Ibid., 113, emphasis mine.

14. Carton, "The Holocaust," 18: French poststructuralism was a complex response that "at once confronted, commemorated, deflected, and veiled the Holocaust." On the social setting of the crisis, see B. Brown, *Protest in Paris*.

15. As Kristeva, *Desire in Language*, ix, remarks: "The theoretical stance ... is the only guarantee of ethics."

16. Hatina, "Intertextuality and Historical Criticism," 32–33, points out the irony that intertextuality has been "adopted by the very group it was intended to dislodge." Also see Van Wolde, "Trendy Intertextuality," 43.

17. Also see Phillips, "Textual Instability and Responsible Reading."

The Lex Talionis Citation and the Matthean Narrative

Let's situate Matthew's citation ("eye for an eye, tooth for a tooth" [ὀφθαλμὸν ἀντὶ ὀφθαλμοῦ καὶ ὀδόντα ἀντὶ ὀδόντος, 5:38]) within its wider textual and historical networks. The *lex talionis* citation stands as Jesus' opening words in a tightly woven discursive unit (5:38–43) that functions as the fifth of six thematically linked antithetical sayings (5:21–48) embedded within the larger Sermon on the Mount discourse.[18] The antitheses are preceded by a preamble (5:17–20), also in Jesus' voice, that, by contrast, lacks thematic and formal unity and is racked with nearly insoluble compositional, redactional, and interpretive problems.[19] Traditional scholars underscore the tension between Jesus' saying about the quantitative fulfillment of the Law in the antitheses emblemized by the love command (5:44) and his demand for obedience to the individual commandments of the law expressed in 5:17–19.[20] They often seek to resolve these tensions by diminishing the core demand for justice in the *lex talionis*: the Mosaic law is qualitatively differentiated from Jesus' call to resist evil, thereby reinforcing the superiority of the new covenant over the old, Jesus' heightened justice over the diminished righteousness of the scribes and Pharisees. But such binary, supercessionist constructions ignore the citational dynamic and continuity that exist between the *lex talionis* and Jesus' call for higher justice within Matthew's Gospel. Luz is on the right track in saying that the tensions between fulfillment of the law and excessive justice are a matter of quantity and particularity, not quality and universal difference between past and present, the *lex talionis* and Jesus' excessive ethical demands. Continuity and tension mark the citational relationship. In intertextual terms, the *lex talionis* citation is dynamically absorbed and transformed within Matthew's text and remains in tension with the thematics of excessive violence that mark the Gospel. The *lex talionis* serves as a dynamic anchor *of* Jesus' excessive peace in chapter 5 and a contesting voice *for* justice in the wider Matthew world of

---

18. See Luz, *Matthew 1–7*, 274–78; Davies and Allison, *The Gospel according to Saint Matthew*, 533–40.

19. Luz, *Matthew 1–7*, 256. The preamble "poses a decisive problem for interpretation." "Hopelessly unclear," "very difficult," "dilemma" "difficulties" "a problem" are terms Luz employs (257–73).

20. Ibid., 270. "The history of interpretation of [v. 17] shows how difficult it is to find a *precise* meaning for Matt 5:15 and how much the context of the Antithesis, the total witness of the Bible, and one's own situation played a role from the beginning in the interpretation" (264). Novakovic, "Turning the Other Cheek," 17, argues that the tensions in the Matthean redaction of the *lex talionis* support the creation of an alternative way to establish justice, namely, one based not on proportional justice but rather on the restoration of human dignity of both victim and perpetrator (17).

divinely legitimated eschatological violence that plays out in later chapters.[21] In this respect the *lex talionis* citation helps neutralize other voices in the Gospel—for example, the blood libel directed against Jewish children in 27:25—by interrupting and destabilizing the textual violence.

The *lex talionis* has deep roots and wide dissemination in antique Near Eastern societies and texts. The *talion* is cited, for example, in the Code of Hammurabi and Middle Assyrian Laws, as well as in Greek, Roman, and Jewish scriptural and rabbinic formulations. One or another version of the *lex talionis* may well have circulated as an extrabiblical compendium of laws incorporated intact in the Torah, albeit in different forms and contexts.[22] Although its origin is lost to us, the ubiquitous citational presence of the *lex talionis* has led scholars to conclude the near-universal demand for public and private justice across cultural and textual systems.[23] Its core meaning is pecuniary: a person who injures will receive back in payment/punishment the same injury inflicted on a victim, thereby paving the way for a financial restitution of balance, the making whole of that which is thrown out of whack, a return of peace or shalom שָׁלוֹם.[24] As Frymer-Kensky and Daube argue, the *lex talionis* returns parties to a type of status quo; its aim is to maintain symmetry and to preserve the balance of forces weighed out on the scales of justice.[25] To mete out justice is thus to measure and rebalance, to restore imbalances and rectify injustices.[26] The intimate link between themes of measurement and dispensing of justice reverberates in Matthew's alliterative and assonant pronouncement in 7:22: "For with the judgment (κρίματι) you judge (κρίνετε) you will be judged (κριθήσεσθε), and the measure (μέτρῳ) you measure (μετρεῖτε) will be the measure (μετρηθήσεται) you get." Beyond the euphony of this phrase, perhaps modeled upon the rhetoric of the *lex talionis* itself (ὀφθαλμὸν ἀντὶ ὀφθαλμοῦ καὶ ὀδόντα ἀντὶ ὀδόντος), exactly what balance and restoration is to be envisioned in Matthew's world and beyond? Is it more than phraseological and rhetorical? In Matthew's case, what are we to make of the relationship of excessive justice (5:20) and

---

21. Destro and Pesce, "The Cultural Structure of the Infancy Narrative," 113–15, are right that tensions are not resolved in the Gospel.

22. Sarna, *Exodus*, 126.

23. Miller, *Eye for an Eye*, 206.

24. The conventional argument is that the *lex talionis* articulates an upper bound to violence. See Tigay, *Deuteronomy*, 185. Miller, *Eye for an Eye*, 21, points out it may set a lower limit as well, thus not completely eliminating violence. Few scholars hold that the *talion* held literal sway. Daube, "Lex Talionis," 130–32.

25. Frymer-Kensky, "Tit for Tat," 230–34; Daube, "*Lex Talionis*," 133–40. Levinas argues that the ethical relationship is radically dissymmetrical.

26. Miller, *Eye for an Eye*, xii.

the *lex talionis* envisioned in a narrative world marked by wholesale eschatological violence?

The variety of citational forms of the *lex talionis* and their intertextual relationships to one another have been the source of interpretive problems for traditional biblical scholars. As in Matthew's case, all three Pentateuchal instances appear to be interpolations in their neighboring narrative contexts attesting to the *talion*'s citational character and circulation.²⁷ In both Exodus (21:24–25) and Leviticus (24:20) the surrounding context concerns assault and battery; in Deuteronomy, false witness (19:21). The Exodus citation, "life for life, eye for eye, tooth for tooth, hand for hand, foot for foot, burn for burn, wound for wound, stripe for stripe," is in order descending from head to foot. Leviticus adds breach for breach to the eyes and teeth but omits the others. Deuteronomy keeps Exodus's lives, eyes, teeth, hands, and feet but jettisons burns, wounds, and stripes.²⁸ The elements common to all three versions—and Matthew's—are the eyes and teeth.²⁹ This leads Daube to speculate that a minimal "eye and teeth" wisdom saying must have circulated and was likely available to Jesus, and eventually Matthew.³⁰ Not only were eyes and teeth a manageable mouthful, teeth and eyes had the material advantage over hands and feet of being discrete body parts easier to quantify and manipulate as units of measure for restoring balance on the scales of justice. In opting for the shortened eyes and teeth version, Matthew reflects a preference for the organ of sight with an eye-popping seventeen references to the eye (ὀφθαλμός) distributed throughout the narrative. In Matthew's narrative imagination the eye's meaning oscillates: as a healthy lamp of the body, the eye renders the body full of light (φωτεινὸν ἔσται, Matt 6:22), while in the blink of an eye (ἐν ῥιπῇ ὀφθαλμοῦ; cf. 1 Cor 15:52) the unhealthy eye can produce darkness (σκοτεινὸν ἔσται, Matt 6:23) or outright evil (πονηρός, 20:15), causing one to stumble (σκανδαλίζει σε, 18:9) and leading to sin and the fires of hell (τὴν γέενναν τοῦ πυρός, 18:9). The ultimate recourse for Matthew, it appears, is for the eye to be plucked out and tossed away (ἔξελε αὐτὸν καὶ βάλε ἀπὸ σοῦ, 5:29).³¹ This intersection of violence and vision,

---

27. Sarna, *Exodus*, 125, argues that the formula citations are inapplicable to the legal contexts in Leviticus and Deuteronomy where they are imbedded.

28. Sarna, *Exodus*, 126. Daube, "*Lex Talionis*," 112–13, suggests the burning, wounding, and stripe of *talion* in Exod 21:23–25 are late introductions.

29. Miller, *Eye for an Eye*, 28.

30. Daube insists, however, that the saying was not literally applied ("Matthew v.38 f.," 178). The financial meaning of the talion is well attested in the rabbinic literature in Daube, "*Lex Talionis*," 108.

31. Matthew tops the Synoptics with seventy-four references to mutilated or mentioned body parts.

and the relationship to the *lex talionis*, contributes to a Matthean universe of meaning that sustains the text's visionary and violent history of reception. It is an invitation as well to read Matthew intertextually using Samuel Bak's post-Holocaust visual representations of the *lex talionis* and Lady Justice. In this way Matthew's text becomes a site for contested readings.

The World of Matthean Violence

Before turning to Bak's images, what are we to make of Matthean violence and the role the *lex talionis* plays in the broader ecology of Gospel violence? Matthean violence is confounding to Gospel interpreters. Warren Carter's assessment of elites and empire proposes a historical context and interpretive approach that explain the narrative world. Carter argues that the violent social forces at play in Matthew's first-century Gospel community are narratively encoded in the various overlapping and intertwined identities of the Gospel characters—the elites, Jesus' followers, his nonfollowers, the Jews, Gentiles, the crowd, and more. (To this list we could also add the implied author and reader.) Violence is amplified by the Gospel's frequent citations of Hebrew Scriptures and fulfillment formulas that function metonymically to evoke narratives of imperial aggression by elites in quest of power, territory, and human and nonhuman resources (Carter has in mind Egypt, Assyria, and Babylon aggression).[32] Radically different societal visions and experiences of justice collide in the Matthean Jesus' life and death. The clash creates destabilizing tensions between Jesus' call for justice here and now as expressed in an "eye for an eye, tooth for a tooth" and God's anticipated eschatological justice there and then where not only eyes and teeth but also hands, ears, and other body parts cut off (ἔκκοψον, 5:30; 18:8) and plucked out (ἔξελε, 5:29; 18:9) serve as fungible commodities in restoring end-time balance. Eschatological justice means justice taken out of lopped-off human hands and vested in God's.

Traditional commentators disagree over which Pentateuch version of the *lex talionis* citation influenced the Matthean author.[33] Traditional views of intertextuality taken as influence typically reduce the intertextual

32. Carter, "Construction of Violence," 95. In a similar way Destro and Pesce's social conflict analysis argues that Matthew constructs a religious system of opposed cultural frames ("The Cultural Structure of the Infancy Narrative," 112–15). The absolute certainty of the advent of the kingdom of heaven entails a "fatal hostility and fight to the death" in which the adversary to the kingdom is annihilated. Eschatological violence is thus both "cathartic and renewing."

33. For example, Weaver, "Transforming Nonresistance," 37, puts her money on Deuteronomy. Horsley, "Ethics and Exegesis," 3–4, bets instead on Leviticus.

relationship to a single point of contact between two texts governed by authorial intent. They miss the mosaic quality of the text and the systems that intersect and permeate each other. Kristeva's model of transformational intertextuality invites us instead to see the Matthean text as a surface where a vortex of sign systems dynamically intersect and neutralize, absorb and transpose one another. So viewed, the *lex talionis* evokes the larger Pentateuchal *justice systems* of payment and repayment that contest the Matthean *religious system* in which love of the enemy and annihilation of the enemy vie with one another for dominance.[34] Against the backdrop of Matthew's irreconcilable antinomies, the Pentateuchal prohibition against vicarious punishment ("Fathers shall not be put to death for *their* sons, nor shall sons be put to death for *their* fathers; everyone shall be put to death for his own sin," Deut 24:16) explicitly contests Matthean eschatological violence whereby children become liable for the blood libel (Matt 27:25). Tensions persist. The *lex talionis* functions as a voice for justice, for rebalancing, that extends beyond the explicit confines of Jesus' antithetical units in the Sermon on the Mount discourse (whether about false court witnesses or localized economic hardship) outward to Matthew's broader religious system characterized by present and future violence. Jesus' voicing of the *lex talionis* serves as a potential disruption from within, a counter to the narrative's vicarious blood libel, and a challenge to unjust imbalances that enflame bloodletting readings.[35]

The tension between justice measured as peace and justice as pieces permeates the narrative air. Justice teeters in the balance between past and present, between present and future, and between an excessive shalom (Matt 5:38–42) and an excessive violence (18:8–9). All is in tension with Matthew's affirmation of Jesus' mission as fulfilling the promise and potential for justice (πληρῶσαι πᾶσαν δικαιοσύνην, 3:15).[36] We see this internal tension bubble up in the Gospel's tenuous ending when Jesus, atop yet a different mountain, assures wavering disciples that he remains with them until the close of the age (28:20). Readers, like narrative characters, are rightly confused and torn by the Gospel message. They are seemingly presented with the binary choice of resisting Matthean violence or reproducing it. On Carter's reading, Matthean readers really have no choice: "In resisting and

34. Destro and Pesce, "The Cultural Structure of the Infancy Narrative," 109–12, focus on the fight and flight dynamic in Matthew first two chapters.

35. Langmuir, *Toward a Definition of Antisemitism*, 266. See Dundes, *The Blood Libel Legend*, 273–303, for his discussion of children. On Jesus' use, see Daube, "Matthew v.38 f.," 179–82.

36. On the Matthean theme of justice, see Senior, *The Passion of Jesus*, 26–30. The precise meaning of δικαιοσύνην is hotly debated (27).

redeeming the violence of the imperial status quo the gospel also affirms that some violence, namely the violence of God, the supreme ruler who is 'Lord of heaven and earth' (11:25), and of God's agent Jesus, is legitimate and necessary."[37] Entrapped within a world of systemic violence that implicates God, Jesus, and reader, "Matthew's gospel," Carter concludes, "finally, but ironically, capitulates to and imitates the imperial violence from which it seeks to save."[38] Like Matthew, it seems the reader is destined not to escape the impossible tensions of a narrative world where violence against the innocent becomes a script enacted in the real world.

But can and should Matthew's reader do otherwise? Must readers, as Carter says, "capitulate to and [imitate] the imperial violence" that perfuses the Gospel text? Is a different choice possible, one that resists, and does not reinforce, the violence (5:39)? Carter observes that structural violence "is attested ... by the gospel's intertextuality or frequent citations of the Hebrew Scriptures." Interestingly, he does not comment directly on the *lex talionis* and its challenge to Matthew's systemic violence. His use of intertextuality is allusional and metonymic rather than interruptive and contesting. But might we see the recitation of the *lex talionis*, evoking the Pentateuchal citations, as in fact disruptive from within Matthew's destabilized narrative world of God-handled and God-inspired eschatological violence and helping possibly to interrupt seamless readings that legitimate and inspire real-world violence? Might the desire for excessive peace associated with a surpassing righteousness that Matthew envisions (5:20) affirm an excessive shalom that, despite the internal tensions and contradictions of Matthew's religious system, tips the scales back in favor of human restoration and restitution where it now belongs? After Auschwitz, peacemaking and justice making rest in the reader's, not God's, hands. Samuel Bak's representations of the *lex talionis* invite us to wrestle with this possibility and responsibility, to imagine it, to do it, to do justice. Bak's unblinking look at the Holocaust's aftermath challenges Matthew's readers to engage in the disruptive prophetic and practical work of justice. This means contesting tilted and dishonest scales (Amos 8:6) and removing scales from the eyes of seamless readers for the sake of others. Bak's post-Holocaust graphic renderings of the *lex talionis* visualize the interruption of Matthean violence. The aim is to disturb the visual violence, textual space, and reading patterns by placing the demand of justice squarely before our eyes, in our mouths, on our backs, and ultimately in our hands.

---

37. Carter, "Construction of Violence," 102.
38. Ibid.

Matthean Justice and Bak's *Just Is*

In a collection of fifty-five paintings and drawings entitled *Just Is*, Holocaust survivor and artist Samuel Bak[39] takes up the theme of the *lex talionis* and its complicated connection to justice. Across his many canvases iconic Lady Justice appears and disappears, guised and disguised in ways that invite readers to explore the nature of justice and responsibility in light of the Holocaust. What form does Lady Justice take? Do we even recognize her? Does she us? What connections still exist between the iconic biblical demand for justice and the associations of peace and shalom in the shadows cast by crematoria chimneys? With peace in tatters, are pieces all that remain of a world shattered by unspeakable violence and riven by injustice on a scale heretofore unimagined, a world were Jewish existence is by definition a crime, where Jewish life is codefined as death? The implications of a post-Holocaust reading of Matthew's Gospel and its reception history could not be graver.

In his *Just Is* series, Bak appropriates the icon of Lady Justice along with biblical and legal icons of covenant, community, rainbow, tablets of the law, and scales of justice in an unnerving, intertextual clash that disrupts the syntax of our visual and ethical senses. In Western iconography justice is traditionally figured as a young, strong woman crowned with plant sprigs, often laurel or grain stalk, draped in flowing robes.[40] Often suspended from her left hand is a balance scale; in her right a sword frequently points downward. Since the sixteenth century Lady Justice has been portrayed blindfolded, an addition that introduces its own instability into the image. Bak plays upon both blinded and bared eyes, often leaving his viewer to decide which is which, what is seen and what not, and what purpose is served by sight in any case. Blindfolded eyes signify impartiality and fairness, but we are reminded that blindfolds can also block us from seeing whether the scales of justice are in balance and how the sword is being wielded. Before the connection with justice in the early modern period, the blindfold connoted stupidity or lack of righteousness.[41] But by the late fifteenth century, blindness had lost this negative association and was transformed into a virtue. Blind justice is meted out objectively and fairly, without fear or favor,

---

39. See the full *Just Is* catalogue at http://www.puckergallery.com/artists/Bak_justis/bak_justis_all.html

40. Miller, *Eye for an Eye*, 1–3.

41. So the sentiment of the Exodus writer: "And you shall take no bribes, for a bribe blinds the officials and subverts the cause of those are in the right" (23:8).

regardless of identity, money, power, or weakness: blind justice and blind impartiality now go hand in hand.[42]

Genealogically Lady Justice is not a simple icon (or visual text) but a site where contested images and ideas collect and collide.[43] Her origin is ancient and uncertain. The Egyptian goddess Ma'at, the daughter of the sun god Ra, carried a sword but not a scale of justice. Themis, the Greek goddess of divine order, law, and custom, and her daughter Dike, goddess of human justice who maintains social and political order, are depicted as blindfolded, carrying scales and sword. The Roman goddess Justitia, who adorns modern Western courthouses and courtrooms, is also represented with balance scales and sword, although she is not consistently blindfolded, an amalgam of blindfolded Roman Fortuna (fate), Hellenistic Greek Tyche (luck), and sword-carrying Nemesis (retribution).[44] In the medieval period the classical goddesses of justice joined the quartet of Christian cardinal virtues alongside Prudence, Temperance, and Fortitude to become one of seven theological virtues teamed up with faith, hope, and charity.[45] Other eye-catching images of justice compete with traditional Lady Justice. Images of judges with hands or arms severed or undergoing gruesome punishment Matthean-style remind us that justice in the hands of certain persons can be perverted, as the Hebrew prophets knew all too well.[46] Parodies of Lady Justice with sagging blindfold and eyes barely discernible through the blindfold material amplify the icon's inherent ambiguity. Trading upon these images and themes, Bak's paintings invite us to consider how sight, insight, and lack of sight work together for and against justice.

The scales Lady Justice holds in her hand also have rich, contested Near Eastern, Greco-Roman, and biblical intertextual connections. The earliest documented use of scales is to be found in the ancient Egyptian depiction of the judgment of the dead (*psychostasia*) in the *Book of the Dead*.[47] Anubis judges the fate of the dead person whose heart or soul lies in one pan with an ostrich feather of the goddess Ma'at in the other. In the *Iliad* Zeus, weary of the conflict between Achilles and Hector, weighs the twin Keres, the female spirits of violent and cruel death, on a pair of scales (*kerostasia*). In popular medieval Christian iconography, Saint Michael weighs believers'

42. Resnic and Curtis, "Images of Justice," 1729–30.

43. Ibid.

44. Ibid., 1741–42.

45. Ibid., 1744.

46. See Mundy, "A Preparatory Sketch," n. 25, 122–23, cited in Resnic and Curtis, "Images of Justice," 1734.

47. Miller, *Eye for an Eye*, 3; "Weighing of souls." https://en.wikipedia.org/wiki/Weighing_of_souls.

souls at the last judgment. The tipping of the scales or their equipoise can have life-or-death consequences. In ancient Egypt hearts heavier or lighter than the feather of Ma'at meant immediate demise at the hands of Ammit, the devourer of souls. In second millennium BCE Babylon, a merchant's scales had to be in balance or the business transaction could not be concluded.[48] In first millennium BCE Israel, a tipped or equipoise position of the scales was less a concern than whether the weights were rigged against justice: "A false balance is an abomination to the Lord, but a just weight is his delight" (Prov 11:1). "A just balance and scales belong to the Lord" (Prov 16:11). The prophet Hosea reserved special condemnation for the merchant whose false balances oppressed the poor (Hos 12:7), and the swallowing up of the needy with false balances Amos ominously promised Yahweh would not soon forget (Amos 8:5). What balance or imbalance means rests finally upon the culture and context along with what and who is being measured. After Auschwitz, when the *lex talionis*, the covenantal promises of justice, the tablets of the law, and eyes all hang in the balance, what are the prospects of justice or peace in a world of unspeakable violence? How does one pick up the pieces and restore balance?

In *By Hook* (see p 193) Bak gives us Lady Justice in pieces.[49] Expecting to find her posed regally atop a grand courthouse dome or at an entry portal as a sentinel to justice, we instead confront her in fragments, a diminished version of her former iconic self. Her upper torso is perched on a shelf precariously balanced on broken stone slabs with no lower body in view, her arms severed from her body Matthean-style. We wonder, what disaster has transpired? Who is responsible? And with justice in pieces, who is responsible for gathering the parts and provisionally reassembling them before our eyes? Is this done to assure us that justice, even if not whole in appearance, prevails by any means necessary? Does justice persist despite circumstances, despite history? Her left arm sustains the balance handle upright, even though scales are akimbo and ropes hang slack. A pan holds an eye hewn from stone awaiting suspension and balanced by a second eye. Behind it a different eye peeks out from a blue box half lidded. A third eye sketched on paper is tacked to a wall that overlooks this piecemeal scene. Many eyes but nothing in focus or balance. We are reminded that Matthew's text is replete with eyes as well as a multitude of amputated hands and feet, a promised consequence of the Matthean God's eschatological justice. But is this real justice by any measure? The second pan is nowhere in sight. How

---

48. Miller, *Eye for an Eye*, 5–6.

49. For a full color image see http://www.puckergallery.com/artists/Bak_justis/bk1939_justis_images.html

are we to rebalance one eye with another, one eye for another, how are we to reestablish the peaceful balance affirmed by the *lex talionis* if the very instrument of justice lies in shambles and the parts no longer rest in human hands? Bak's post-Holocaust justice feels provisional, precarious, makeshift, at best, but not altogether lacking a measured determination. Reading Matthew's text intertextually in light of Bak's eye-conic constructions of justice creates a parallax perspective. Perspectives clash by the near intersection. After Auschwitz, will we interrupt Matthew's religious system and narrative world with a makeshift construction and different angle of vision that restores justice for the innocent? Will we see Matthew's savaging of innocent children differently? Bak's Lady Justice stares at us with one unblinded eye, and the question mark atop the scales' handle presses us for an answer to the question, What will we do?

Samuel Bak, *By Hook,* 2015. Image courtesy of Pucker Gallery, Boston.

Samuel Bak, *By Law*, 2015. Image courtesy of Pucker Gallery, Boston.

In *By Law*[50] Bak juxtaposes multiple iconic images, layering them onto the surface of his canvas in a disruptive mosaic of color and shape. Lady Justice, the tablets of the law, the Noahic ark and rainbow, and the doomed *St. Louis* with smokestack/crematoria–like chimneys compete for our eye. Lady Justice stands erect with both hands extended in traditional pose. In her raised right hand she holds the Hebrew letter tsade, a serious play upon the Yiddish *tsaddik*, the righteous one. Hebrew letters stand for words, numbers, and laws, and they too must be measured for meaning. In her left hand she grasps a rainbow-colored arch from which hangs suspended the scales of justice, incomplete, and fractured tablets of the law. The covenantal laws are literally and figuratively suspended. They invite troubling questions about the relationship between Jews and YHWH, justice and covenant. From the arch droops a blindfolding cloth through which Lady Justice may or may not be sneaking a peek. We cannot be certain. Her sheathed wooden sword protrudes downward through a pan that holds one of two Mosaic tablets engraved with four Hebrew letters (dalet, he, zayin, and chet). The broken tablets of the law are pieced together by a sixth letter, vav, signifying the prohibition against murder, riveted through the wooden sword handle. The scene is deeply ironic, given that mass murder and justice ought to share nothing in common, yet here they clash. The matching pan holds up a second tablet inscribed with the oversized letters aleph and bet, the prohibition against icon making, also ironic given the extensive imaging Bak does and invites us his viewers to do. We recall the Bible's explicit prohibition against imaging God. How is the ancient covenant with its implicit demand for justice by law now to be imagined, measured, and enacted? Is that too prohibited?

Behind Lady Justice our eye catches sight of two unblemished tablets blindfolded by a cloth-draped broken rainbow. The tablets mimically peek over her shoulders as she looks over the suspended stone tables before her. The contrast between broken and unbroken tablets perhaps underscores the reality that in Bak's abysmal world the ideal of justice is far removed from its practice. Perched upon a distant mountain peak we vaguely make out the shape of a ship, the SS *St. Louis* perhaps, that modern Jewish ark that failed to deliver to safety its cargo of 908 Jewish children and adults seeking to escape the Nazi catastrophe. The double smokestacks are a sobering symbolic reminder that Sobibór and Auschwitz, not Havana and Miami, were the final ports of call for two hundred of the *St. Louis*'s innocents. By international law, the refusal of port may have been legally justified; but

---

50. For a full color image see http://www.puckergallery.com/artists/Bak_justis/bk1930_justis_images.html

by what moral law was it just? The covenants of the law were intended to uphold and sustain justice, but in light of the events of 1939–1945, both ancient covenant and modern law are now to be measured against a far different standard of justice. The covenant and the narrative texts that relate it are now to be read, weighed, measured, and scaled for justice by Greenberg's excessive standard. When applied to Matthew's text and readers, are we to think of the innocent children of 2:15 and 27:25 as collateral or vicarious damage? Who are Rachel's children there and then who are no more here and now? Are we blinded to the difference between narrative and flesh-and-blood children?[51] What can the First Gospel's call for excessive justice mean for real children here and now, and how are we to measure it if not by concrete saving actions that bring today's ships filled with Syrian, Iraqi, and Afghani refugees safely to port?

Where do Bak's *Just Is* images lead us if not directly to interrupt Matthew's text and its contradictory call for apocalyptic violence and the shalom of *lex talionis*? Bak's iconic images call for readers of Matthew's Gospel to confront its violent excesses and to hold it and themselves accountable to the *lex talionis* it cites and the imperative of balance and peace it commands. Like Bak's broken tablets of the law, Matthew's fissured text and world and the disturbing readings it propagates are to be disturbed by the very texts and voices Matthew cites and the standards it would impose upon others: "For with the judgment you judge you will be judged, and the measure you give will be the measure you get" (7:2). Reading Bak against Matthew, citing Matthew against itself, is an explicit intertextual action intended to unsettle and transform text and image, reader and icon in the name of a justice that seeks to remove the scales from eyes of readers who may then perceive the difference between narrative and real children, violence and shalom, aesthetics and ethics, injustice and justice.

The citation of the *lex talionis* in both word and image means nothing less than a settling of accounts, a return to balance, a zeroing out of imbalances, a rebalancing of the scales. In short, an act of justice. An intertextual reading of Matthew's text that employs Bak's visual icons contributes to that settling up by unsettling a text that narratively encodes violent social forces as Carter describes and scales up that violence for readers who enact the worst. And the worst we have witnessed. Through Bak's canvases we visually confront Matthew's texts of terror, we hear the voice of the *lex talionis* contest the flawed justice of seamless readings with paint and pen and real justice for flesh-and-blood innocents.[52] Like Bak's canvases, Matthew's text

---

51. Fackenheim, *The Jewish Bible after the Holocaust*, 80–83.

52. For Levinas, restitution for suffering is not possible. "Yes, eye for eye. Neither

is a mosaic of citations, a surface onto which are inscribed voices and faces that call for recognition and reaction. Human eyes, the organ of sight, favored among body parts by Matthew, and featured excessively in Bak's *Just Is* paintings, are the site not only of human vulnerability and suffering but also, we must remember, of a commanding call to excessive responsibility and justice toward others expressed in the *lex talionis*. The sight and sound of contested justice must disrupt seamless reading. Despite Matthew's conflictual efforts, the Gospel text and its readers may not narratively sequester or silence the call of shalom that Bak visually reinforces. Readers may not easily supersede the call for justice and shalom with a messianic apocalyptic appeal to some yonder world. Justice is a here and now, this-worldly reality. Critical intertextual reading after Auschwitz challenges readers, in particular Christian readers, to face up to the burden of responsibility for a damaging text and for justice denied to so many real innocents. Bak sharpens our eye for Matthew, for the icon, and for images of all the other I's who await from us a measure of justice delayed.

Bibliography

Brown, Bernard. *Protest in Paris: Anatomy of a Revolt*. Morristown, NJ: General Learning Press, 1974.

Brown, Raymond. *Death of the Messiah: From Gethsemane to the Grave*. Vol. 1, *A Commentary on the Passion Narrative in the Four Gospels*. Anchor Yale Bible Reference Commentary. New Haven: Yale University Press, 1998.

Carter, Warren. "Construction of Violence and Identities in Matthew's Gospel." In *Violence in the New Testament*, edited by Shelly Matthews and E. Leigh Gibson, 81–108. New York: T. & T. Clark, 2005.

Carton, Evan. "The Holocaust, French Poststructuralism, the American Literary Academy, and Jewish Identity Poetics." In *Historicizing Theory*, edited by Peter Herman, 17–47. Albany: SUNY Press, 2004.

Crossan, John Dominic. *Who Killed Jesus? Exposing the Roots of Anti-Semitism in the Gospel Story of the Death of Jesus*. New York: Harper, 1996.

Daube, David. "Eye for Eye." In *New Testament Judaism: Collected Works of David Daube*, edited by Calum Carmichael, 177–86. Vol. 2. Berkeley: University of California Press, 2000.

———. "Lex Talionis." In *Studies in Biblical Law*, 102–53. Cambridge: Cambridge University Press, 1947.

———. "Matthew v.38 f." *Journal of Theological Studies* 45 (1944) 177–87.

Davies, W. D., and Dale Allison. *The Gospel according to Saint Matthew*. International Critical Commentary, vol. 1. London: T. & T. Clark, 1988.

---

all eternity nor all the money in the world, can heal the outrage done to man. It is a disfigurement or wound that bleeds for all time" ("Eye for an Eye," 148).

Destro, Adriana, and Mauro Pesce. "The Cultural Structure of the Infancy Narrative in the Gospel of Matthew." In *Infancy Gospels: Stories and Identities*, edited by C. Clivaz et al., 94–115. WUNT281. Tübingen: Mohr Siebeck, 2011.
Doukhan, Jacques. "Reading the Bible after Auschwitz." In *Remembering for the Future: The Holocaust in an Age of Genocide*, edited by John Roth and Elisabeth Maxwell, 2:683–99. New York: Palgrave, 2001.
Dundes, Alan, ed. *The Blood Libel Legend: A Casebook in Anti-Semitic Folklore*. Madison: University of Wisconsin Press, 1991.
Fackenheim, Emil. "The Holocaust and Philosophy." *Journal of Philosophy* 82 (1985) 505–14.
———. *The Jewish Bible after the Holocaust: A Re-reading*. Bloomington: Indiana University Press, 1990.
Frymer-Kensky, Tikva. "Tit for Tat." *Biblical Archaeologist* 43 (1980) 230–34.
Greenberg, Irving. "Cloud of Smoke, Pillar of Fire: Judaism, Christianity, and Modernity after the Holocaust." In *Auschwitz: Beginning of a New Era? Reflections on the Holocaust*, edited by Eva Fleischner, 7–57. New York: Ktav, 1977.
Hatina, Thomas R. "Intertextuality and Historical Criticism in New Testament Studies: Is There a Relationship?" *Biblical Interpretation* 7 (1999) 28–43.
Horsley, Richard. "Ethics and Exegesis: 'Love Your Enemies' and the Doctrine of Nonviolence." *Journal of the American Academy of Religion* 54, no. 1 (Spring 1986) 3–31.
Kristeva, Julia. *Desire in Language: A Semiotic Approach to Language and Art*. Edited by Leon S. Roudiez. Translated by Thomas Gora, Alice Jardine, and Leon S. Roudiez. New York: Columbia University Press, 1980.
Langmuir, Gavin. *Toward a Definition of Antisemitism*. Berkeley: University of California Press, 1990.
Levinas, Emmanuel. "Eye for an Eye." In *Difficult Freedom: Essays in Judaism*, 146–48. Translated by Séan Hand. Baltimore: Johns Hopkins University Press, 1990.
———. *Totality and Infinity: An Essay on Exteriority*. Translated by Alphonso Lingis. Pittsburgh: Duquesne University Press, 1969.
———. "Useless Suffering." Translated by Richard Cohen. In *The Provocation of Levinas*, edited by Robert Bernasconi and David Wood, 156–67. London: Routledge and Kegan Paul, 1988.
Luz, Ulrich. *Matthew 1–7: A Commentary*. Translated by Wilhelm Lins. Continental Commentaries. Minneapolis: Augsburg, 1989.
Miller, William Ian. *Eye for an Eye*. Cambridge: Cambridge University Press, 2006.
Mundy, E. James. "A Preparatory Sketch for Gerard David's Justice of Cambyses Panels in Bruges." *Burlington Magazine* 122 (February 1980) 122–25.
Novakovic, Lidija. "Turning the Other Cheek to a Perpetrator: Denunciation or Upholding of Justice?" 2006 Annual SBL Meeting Matthew Section: Reading Matthew in a Time of War. https://www.sbl-site.org/assets/pdfs/Novakovic_Cheek.pdf.
Parkes, James. *The Conflict of the Church and the Synagogue: A Study in the Origins of Antisemitism*. New York: Atheneum, 1981.
Phillips, Gary. "The Killing Fields of Matthew's Gospel." In *A Shadow of Glory: Reading the New Testament after the Holocaust*, edited by Tod Linafelt, 232–47. New York: Routledge, 2002.

———. "Textual Instability and Responsible Reading: A Post-Structural Approach to Matthean Intertextuality." In *Exploring Intertextuality: Diverse Strategies for the New Testament Use of Texts*, edited by B. J. Oropeza and Steve Moyise. Eugene, OR: Cascade, 2016.

Resnic, Judith, and Dennis Curtis. "Images of Justice." *Faculty Scholarship Series*. Paper 917, 1727–72, 1987. http://digitalcommons.law.yale.edu/fss_papers/917.

Sarna, Nahum. *Exodus*. JPS Torah Commentary. Philadelphia: Jewish Publication Society, 1991.

Senior, Donald. *The Passion of Jesus in the Gospel of Matthew*. Collegeville, MN: Liturgical, 1990.

Tigay, Jeffrey. *Deuteronomy*. JPS Torah Commentary. Philadelphia: Jewish Publication Society, 1996.

Turner, David L. *Israel's Last Prophet: Jesus and the Jewish Leaders in Matthew 23*. Minneapolis: Fortress, 2015. *Project MUSE*. https://muse.jhu.edu/.

Van Wolde, Ellen. "Trendy Intertextuality." In *Intertextuality in Biblical Writings: Essays in Honour of Bas van Iersel*, edited by Sipke Draisma, 43–50. Kampen: Kok, 1989.

Weaver, Dorothy Jean. "Transforming Nonresistance: From *Lex Talionis* to 'Do Not Resist the Evil One.'" In *The Love of Enemy and Nonretaliation in the New Testament*, edited by Willard Swartley, 32–71. Louisville: Westminster John Knox, 1992.

13

Isaiah's Philistia Oracle and Hermeneutics

Isaiah 14:28–32

—Paul R. Raabe

While there is much literature on biblical hermeneutics in general, more scholarly discussion is needed on the specific hermeneutical considerations that pertain to reading prophetic literature. How does one read a poetic, prophetic text? What are the tasks to keep in mind, and in what order should they be followed? While it is possible to discuss these questions in the abstract, it is more helpful—at least in my opinion—to consider them while working on a specific text. To that end this article will suggest some hermeneutical procedures while treating Isaiah's Philistia oracle, recorded in Isa 14:28-32.

I am delighted to dedicate this article to James W. Voelz, my valued colleague and longtime friend. Over the years his excellent work in hermeneutics along with Greek and Mark's Gospel has proven invaluable.

Philological Approach

What are the specific procedures for interpreting a prophetic text, and in what order should they be followed? I suggest that the first task is to work through the text in a philological way informed by lexical semantics and grammar. For now, the reader should avoid considerations of overall meaning or historical setting. Those concerns are important but should enter the reading process at a later stage. For now, the reader should simply focus on translating the Hebrew text, avoiding idiosyncratic definitions and instead attributing to each phrase, expression, and construction its usual, normal, and expected use. While it is possible for an author to use an expression in a unique way, at the start the reader should assume typical *usus*. Here space permits only a limited discussion on the philological level.

Verse 28. *In the year of the death of the king Ahaz, this Burden came.*[1] The demonstrative pronoun "this" refers to the following block of material, the cataphoric use.[2] The verb הָיָה frequently appears in the related formula "the word of Yahweh came to so-and-so," where it means something like "to come into existence, occur, happen, be present" to the prophet. The noun מַשָּׂא derives from the verb נשא, "to lift up, carry," and denotes something to be carried and endured, "load, imposed burden." Here it functions as a genre label to designate a certain type of discourse, a prophetic message that refers to a coming hard time or "burden" to be endured.

Verse 29. *Stop rejoicing, O Philistia, all of you.* The construction with the negative particle אַל + second person jussive indicates a prohibition, sometimes called a vetitive. It means "do not do so-and-so," either as "do not begin doing it" or, as is the case here, "stop doing it." The Philistines have been rejoicing for some time, but now they ought to and will have to desist. The vocative addressee is the place-name Philistia, which refers to the collection of Philistine city-states. The addition of "all of you" emphasizes the inclusion of all the Philistine city-states together with their inhabitants. The same words, "Philistia, all of you," recur in verse 31.

Verse 29. *that the scepter which smote you has been broken.* The discourse continues to address Philistia. Verse 29 has two כִּי-clauses. The first introduces an object clause (indirect discourse with the verb "rejoice"), and the second the explanatory cause for the prohibition. Philistia is presently rejoicing *that* (כִּי) the scepter has been broken. The term "scepter" (שֵׁבֶט), by virtue of metonymy, refers to a king as wielder of power. It symbolizes a king's authority. The scepter is qualified with the hiphil participle of נכה, "to smite, strike." Often in Isaiah the subject of this verb is God, but here a human authority is meant, one who has oppressed Philistia.[3] The verb "to break" is appropriate for the noun "scepter."

Verse 29. *For from the root of the snake will go forth a poisonous snake.* This כִּי-clause explains why Philistia should stop rejoicing, *because* she

---

1. All translations are by the author.
2. Joüon, *A Grammar of Biblical Hebrew*, §143b.
3. See Isa 10:20, 24; 14:5–6.

must experience two more tyrants. The imagery shifts to a mixed metaphor, "from the root of the snake." The deceased king designated as a "scepter" in the previous clause is now seen both as a tree that has been chopped down and as a snake. The cutting down of the tree is not the end of the tree. From its "root" will go forth another oppressor, seen as "a poisonous snake" that descends from a predecessor "snake."

The noun "snake" (נָחָשׁ) is a general, nonspecific term for any snake or serpent (thirty-one times). The second term (צֶפַע) is a more specific term that denotes a poisonous snake, such as viper, cobra, or adder.[4] The idea is that the offspring of the previous figure will be even deadlier for Philistia.

Verse 29. and his fruit will be a flying seraph. The phrase "flying seraph" is of interest.[5] The root שׂרף denotes "to burn"; hence, "seraph" is often translated "fiery serpent." The burning probably refers to the inflammation resulting from the bite. The same expression occurs again in Isaiah 30:6, part of the "Burden" concerning the beasts of the Negev: "In a land of distress and oppression, from which are the lioness and lion, the *poisonous snake* and the *flying seraph*, they carry their wealth on the backs of donkeys." Note how the expression is paired with "poisonous snake" (אֶפְעֶה). It is clear from Isa 14:29 and 30:6 that "flying seraph" refers to some kind of venomous snake.[6] In light of the above texts, one might interpret the modifier "flying" as simply a reference to the quick darting movement of the snake (cf. NIV). However, one reads of flying seraphs also in Isaiah 6, and there they fly with wings. Perhaps we should identify it with a winged cobra, depicted on eighth-century B.C. Judean seals.[7]

Verse 30. And the firstborn of the poor will graze, and the needy in safety will lie down. The sequence begun with an imperfect verb in verse 29b continues in verse 30 with the initial *waw*-consecutive perfect verb. Because the first was considered the best, the noun "firstborn" gained a superlative force, as it has here, "the poorest of the poor."[8] The term "firstborn" continues the thought of offspring along with the previous reference to "his fruit."

The verb רעה is used intransitively in the sense "to graze, pasture," with "the firstborn of the poor" as the subject and no direct object.[9] Both this

---

4. The noun צֶפַא occurs only here, and צִפְעוֹנִי occurs four times: Isa 11:8; 59:5; Jer 8:17; Prov 23:32.

5. See Weinfeld, *Deuteronomy 1–11*, 395.

6. Note also the story of the Israelites bitten by snakes in Num 21. There the word "seraph" is used as an adjective, but the term can also be used nominally by itself as a substitute for "snake," as is the case in Isa 14:29 (cf. Num 21:8).

7. See Roberts, "The Rod that Smote Philistia: Isaiah 14:28-32," 392-393.

8. Tsevat, בְּכוֹר, 2:126.

9. See Isa 5:17; 11:7.

verb and the next one, "will lie down" (רבץ), are used metaphorically. The poor and needy are depicted as sheep and cattle pasturing in peace.[10] The adverb "in safety" (לָבֶטַח) emphasizes their security from external enemies.[11] They need not fear the forthcoming enemy "snakes."

Verse 30. *But I will put to death by famine your root, and your remnant he will slay.* The addressee is still Philistia. The discord between the two verbs in the MT, one a first person and the other a third person, raises the textual critical question. Some of the ancient witnesses read both verbs as either first person (1QIsa-a, Vulgate) or third person (LXX, Targum). 4QIsa-o reads the first verb as first person in agreement with 1QIsa-a and the MT but has a lacuna for the second verb. The witnesses that present both verbs as either first person or third person probably reflect attempts at harmonization; the discord is to be preferred.[12]

The subject of the first verb is Yahweh, the speaker. The subject of the second clause could be the "famine" personified ("it will slay"), but seeing a sequence here, I take it as the person represented by the "flying seraph" (see below).

Verse 31. *Wail, O gate! Cry out, O city! Melt away, O Philistia, all of you!* The first verb means "to wail, howl" and is onomatopoeic for the actual sound of wailing (a hiphil of ילל). The noun "gate" (שַׁעַר) is masculine everywhere else in the Hebrew Bible, but here it takes a feminine verb (הֵילִילִי), perhaps because the "gate," like the other vocatives, is being personified as a woman.[13] Isaiah frequently personifies cities and nations, and such is the case here. The second verb זעק denotes "to cry out in distress."

The third verb, נָמוֹג, is an infinitive absolute (niphal). "The inf. abs. in itself expresses the simple idea of verbal action; the intonation or the circumstances indicate that the listener must do this action."[14] Here the preceding imperatives indicate its use as the equivalent of an imperative. It has the sense of "melt, dissolve" and can be applied to the panic of the heart experienced by those facing a military attack, thus "to melt away in fear."[15]

---

10. See Isa 17:2; 27:10; 30:23; Ezek 34:14.

11. See Lev 26:5–6; 1 Kgs 5:5[4:25]; Ezek 28:26; 34:28; Hos 2:20[2:18].

12. See Barthélemy, *Critique textuelle de l'Ancien Testament*, 109–10.

13. Albrecht, "Das Geschlecht der hebräischen Hauptwörter," 41–121, note p. 86. This is cited as an explanation by Brown, Driver, and Briggs, *A Hebrew and English Lexicon of the Old Testament*, 1044.

14. Joüon, *A Grammar of Biblical Hebrew*, §123u.

15. See Exod 15:15–16; Josh 2:9, 24; Ezek 21:20; McCarthy, "Some Holy War Vocabulary in Joshua 2," 228–30.

There seems to be no noticeable semantic difference between the niphal and the qal of מוּג.[16]

Verse 31. For from the north smoke is coming. The causal clause with כִּי provides the basis for the preceding imperatives. Philistia should panic *because* it is about to suffer a military attack. What is coming Isaiah calls "smoke" (עָשָׁן). The term specifically refers to the dust and clouds kicked up by a marching army (cf. Song 3:6-8). Here it is a metonym for the army itself.

Verse 31. and there is no one isolated in its ranks. The antecedent of the pronoun "its" is "smoke," used as a metonym for an army. The participle בּוֹדֵד denotes one who is separate, isolated. It could refer to a straggler or a deserter.[17] What is coming is a well-disciplined army where everyone acts in concert as a cohesive unit. For the prepositional phrase בְּמוֹעָדָיו, although the form of the noun מוֹעָד is unique, it is probably to be taken as similar in sense to מוֹעֵד, "in its appointed places, in its ranks."[18]

Verse 32. But what should one answer the messengers of a nation? With verse 32 there is an abrupt change of scene. The prophet no longer addresses Philistia but now turns to the palace in Jerusalem. Verse 32 begins with an interrogative: "What" (מָה) is the response to be given to the messengers of another nation? According to the MT, the direct object is the indefinite expression "messengers of a nation" (מַלְאֲכֵי גוֹי). While Isaiah probably had in mind specific messengers and possibly even messengers of Philistia itself, he employed nonspecific wording. In effect, Isaiah formulated a general policy statement for the palace. This is to be the standard response to delegates from any foreign nation seeking Israel's cooperation.

Verse 32. that Yahweh has founded Zion. The connector כִּי introduces the answer to the previous question. The answer focuses on Zion, both its foundation and its function. Yahweh has founded Zion. Zion is the only secure place, because Yahweh himself has founded it. Here we have the piel and not the qal of the verb יסד, "to establish, found, fix into place." While this root has a fairly even distribution between the qal/niphal (21x) and the piel/pual (17x), the latter are preferred when the discourse concerns the founding of a temple, palace, or city. Of the fifteen places that speak of the founding of a temple, palace, or city, twelve use the piel/pual. Perhaps the piel and pual are preferred because of the many individual actions necessary for laying the foundations of a building or city.

Verse 32. and in her the afflicted of his people will find shelter. The fronting of the prepositional phrase "in her" places it in focus. Not any

---

16. Waltke and O'Connor, *An Introduction to Biblical Hebrew Syntax*, §23.6.1c.

17. See Hos 8:9; Ps 102:8.

18. So Brown, Driver, and Briggs, *A Hebrew and English Lexicon of the Old Testament*, 418.

international coalition but Zion, the place established by Yahweh, is to be their security and protection. The contrast is illustrated by Isaiah 30:2–3, which condemns those who "find shelter in the shade of Egypt." The verb חסה denotes "to take refuge, find shelter" and takes the preposition "in" (ב) for its object. Usually the object is Yahweh himself, as in 1QIsa-a (בו—"in him"). But in MT 14:32 the object is Zion, the place established by Yahweh where he dwells among and for his people.

Translation

On the basis of the philological work, here is a translation, admittedly rather wooden. I use indentation to show the poetic parallelism. Apart from the heading in verse 28, I count sixteen lines.[19]

> V. 28. In the year of the death of the king Ahaz this Burden came.
> V. 29. Stop rejoicing, O Philistia, all of you,
>> that the scepter which smote you has been broken.
>> For from the root of the snake will go forth a poisonous snake,
>> and his fruit will be a flying seraph.
>
> V. 30. And the firstborn of the poor will graze,
>> and the needy in safety will lie down.
>> But I will put to death by famine your root,
>> and your remnant he will slay.
>
> V. 31. Wail, O gate!
>> Cry out, O city!
>> Melt away, O Philistia, all of you!
>> For from the north smoke is coming,
>> and there is no one isolated in its ranks.
>
> V. 32. But what should one answer the messengers of a nation?
>> That Yahweh has founded Zion,
>> and in her the afflicted of his people will find shelter.

---

19. I use the term "line" to denote what is also called "colon." See Couey, *Reading the Poetry of First Isaiah*, 29–30.

Filling in the Gaps

That was the first trip around the track, so to speak, a philological approach that tries to assign to every expression its normal, typical sense. I propose that the second trip around the track tries to fill in the gaps.

Clearly these five verses belong together as a textual unit. Verse 28 gives a heading that provides a genre label for the following material, and Isaiah 15:1 begins a new unit with its own genre label as heading. Given that these five verses form a distinctive unit, the reader assumes they cohere and should be read and understood in a holistic way. Hebrew poetry juxtaposes lines. Line is contiguous with line, verse with verse. Now the key question becomes how to fill in the gaps. What is the relationship between the lines and verses? How does the whole unit flow?

I propose three key rules: (1) fill in the gaps by respecting the parallelism; (2) fill in the gaps with conventional and expected sequences, based on standard biblical Hebrew usage; (3) fill in the gaps with the immediate context.

Verse 28. The heading dates the oracle to the year when King Ahaz died (see below). It labels the material as a "Burden," some misfortune to be endured. We expect bad news for Philistia.

Verse 29. The speaker commands Philistia to stop rejoicing. The speaker is not yet identified, but we learn from the first-person discourse in verse 30 that the speaker is Yahweh, presumably speaking through his prophet Isaiah. The verse further states why Philistia is now rejoicing, because "the scepter" that used to smite them "has been broken." The "scepter" is a metonym for a king's power and authority. The expression "a scepter has been broken" suggests the death of a king (cf. Isa 14:4–5, 25).

Verse 29 then explains why Philistia should stop its partying. This line and the next employ a mixed metaphor by combining the image of trees ("root" // "fruit") with that of snakes ("snake" // "poisonous snake" // "seraph"). With the phrase "from the root of the snake," verse 29 portrays the deceased king as both a tree and a snake. In terms of a tree, the successor comes from the king's "root," implying that the tree has been cut down, that is, the king has died.[20] Yet the tree (= dynasty) still has a future. In terms of a snake, his successor will be "a poisonous snake."

For the next line, what is the antecedent of the pronoun "his" in "his fruit"? If one takes the two lines as completely synonymous, the antecedent could be the "snake." Thus the expression "from the root of the snake will go forth" would be summarized as "his fruit," and the "poisonous snake" would

---

20. For the imagery of "root" as implying that the predecessor died, see Isa 11:1. It speaks of another figure coming from "the stump of Jesse" and from the "roots" of Jesse.

designate the same figure as "flying seraph." According to this reading, the two lines would predict only one figure.[21]

However, it is more natural to take the antecedent of the pronoun "his" ("his fruit") as "the poisonous snake," since צֶפַע is the immediately preceding noun. The "fruit" produced by this successor, this second snake-tree, is yet a third snake, "a flying seraph." In this way the couplet presents a movement of succession and intensification.

Verse 30. In contrast to the Philistines, who have to fear the rise of two more deadly snakes/kings, others will exist peacefully and safely. These others are identified as "the firstborn of the poor" and "the needy." The terms "poor" (דַּלִּים) and "needy" (אֶבְיוֹנִים) form a standard word pair. The term "needy" expands the group beyond the poorest of the poor.

Is the reference to the "poor" and "needy" an alien intrusion into this context? In the words of James W. Voelz, "If the hat does not fit the box, don't trim the hat. The text might surprise us."[22] The mention of the "poor" and "needy" fits this context, because they are the ones who will have a future in contrast to Philistia's remnant. The identity of this group receives further clarification from verse 32 as the afflicted of Yahweh's people who take refuge in Zion and Zion's God.

The agricultural imagery continues into the next couplet. Unlike the one group that safely "grazes," the other group, the Philistines, will die by "famine." Yahweh is the speaker, and he announces in first person that he will put Philistia's root to death by using famine as his weapon.

The subject of the first verb ("I") is Yahweh as the speaker. But what is the subject of the second verb, "he will slay"? One could see the shift to third person as simply a stylistic variation so that Yahweh remains the subject of the second colon. Or the subject could be personified "famine" ("it will slay"). While both interpretations are possible, if we see a sequence here as in verse 29, then we should find a subject that fits into the sequence. Such an actor is readily available at the end of verse 29, the "flying seraph." Accordingly, the couplet pictures Yahweh with his weapon of famine and a third enemy king working jointly to annihilate Philistia.

Verse 30 speaks of Philistia's "root" being put to death by Yahweh. It continues the tree imagery used in verse 29. In contrast to the future generations appointed for the oppressive "scepter," Philistia will have no future at all.[23] Nothing will come from Philistia's "root." Paired with Philistia's "root"

---

21. This interpretation is suggested by Becker, "Wurzel und Wurzelspross," esp. 28; Oswalt, *The Book of Isaiah*, 332.

22. In his teaching Voelz often emphasizes this point.

23. Unlike a felled tree that might still have hope (cf. Job 14:7–9), nothing will grow from Philistia's "root."

is Philistia's "remnant": "I will put to death your root // he will slay your remnant." The couplet provides an example of pseudosorites. Philistia's root is put to death. But even if the root should produce another tree with fruit (a "remnant"), they will be killed as well.[24]

Verse 31. The divine speech continues to address Philistia. The opening three short clauses create a powerful effect in sound and meaning, conveying the sense of impending doom. The vocatives follow a sequence from part to whole: "gate—city—Philistia—all of you." The language fits Philistia as a collection of fortified cities. Philistia should and will wail, cry out, and melt away in heart because a foreign army is coming, an army that is well disciplined and cohesive.

Verse 32. Now the discourse changes. The speaker is probably the prophet, since "Yahweh" occurs in third person. Apparently the prophet now speaks to the palace in Jerusalem and asks the court a question: "But what should one answer the messengers of a nation?" Isaiah then provides a twofold response to be given by the palace to foreign ambassadors. They must not join any multinational coalition. Instead, the afflicted of Yahweh's people will take refuge in Zion, which was founded by Yahweh himself.

Structure

The oracle consists of two parts: verses 29–31 addressed to Philistia and verse 32 addressed to the palace in Jerusalem. For the first part, verses 29–31 present the material in a symmetrical way. The sequence of an initial command plus its supporting reason appearing in verse 29 repeats itself in verse 31:

> "Stop rejoicing, O Philistia, all of you. . . . For from the root of the snake . . ."

> "Wail, O gate! Cry out, O city! Melt away, O Philistia, all of you! For from the north . . ."

The initial verbs create a negative-positive correspondence, "stop rejoicing and instead start wailing." In each case the reason is introduced with the כִּי-clause, "For." The middle couplet—"And the firstborn of the poor will graze, and the needy in safety will lie down"—receives more clarification at

---

24. A parallel text occurs in Hos 9:16, a pseudosorites with the same motif and similar vocabulary: "Ephraim has been smitten; their root is dried up; they will produce no fruit. Even if they should give birth, I will put to death the precious ones of their womb." On pseudosorites as a device, see the discussions in Andersen and Freedman, *Hosea*, 393–94, 496–99, 538; and in O'Connor, "The Pseudosorites," 161–72.

the end of verse 32: "and in her [= Zion] the afflicted of his people will find shelter."

Fit within the Surrounding Material

I propose that only after the philological work and filling in the gaps is one ready to ask about the bigger picture. How does the unit fit in with the surrounding material? The reader assumes the role of implied reader and approaches the text in a synchronic way.[25] Isaiah 14:28 calls the oracle "Burden," a genre label that refers to a coming hard time and "burden" to be endured by a certain group of people. In Isa 13–23 this genre label occurs ten times.[26] Thus our unit constitutes the second "Burden" in a series of ten.

The book of Isaiah mentions the Philistines three other times. In Isaiah 2:6 the prophet condemns Israel for filling their land with "diviners like the Philistines." Isaiah 9:11 [English 9:12] speaks of the Philistines "devouring Israel" as an action of Yahweh's punishment against arrogant Israel. Isaiah 11:14 promises that during the messianic age a reunited Israel will victoriously rule over the Philistines. Each passage depicts the Philistines as non-Yahwistic enemies of God's covenant people. Our text announcing judgment against Philistia fits into the same picture.

According to Isaiah 14:30, Philistia will have no remnant and posterity. In this respect Philistia will experience the same future as predicted of Babylon, when God "will cut off regarding Babylon name and remnant and progeny and posterity" (14:22). It sets forth one example of the generalization given in Isaiah 14:20, "The offspring of evildoers will never be named." The coming judgment will eliminate false objects of refuge and trust (14:32; 17:10–11; 20:3–6). It will demonstrate the folly of human attempts at establishing security (19:3–4, 11–15; 22:8–14).

As for the promise given in Isa 14:32, a close parallel appears in 28:16, "Behold, I am the one who has founded (piel) a stone in Zion." The book of Isaiah repeatedly advocates refuge in Zion (e.g., 8:9–10; 10:24–27; 16:4–5; 17:14; 25:1–10a; 28:16; 29:5–8; 30:19; 31:4–9; 33:5–6, 20–22).[27]

Those who can enjoy protection in Zion are called "the afflicted of his people" (3:15; 10:2; 49:13). This is another designation for the group mentioned in verse 30a—the poor and needy. The three terms belong together:

---

25. For an introduction to "implied reader," see Voelz, *What Does This Mean?* 218–19.

26. Isaiah 13:1; 14:28; 15:1; 17:1; 19:1; 21:1; 21:11; 21:13; 22:1; 23:1.

27. On Zion theology, see Roberts, "Solomon's Jerusalem and the Zion Tradition," 163–70.

"poor" and "afflicted";[28] "needy" and "afflicted."[29] These terms refer to the poor and lowly who were unjustly oppressed by the rich and powerful.[30] They are the ones who look to Yahweh, in contrast to the ruthless, the scoffers, and those bent on injustice (29:19-21). They are protected by Yahweh (25:4), and one day will be exalted and satisfied when the tables are turned (26:6; 41:17). They will receive vindication in the messianic age to come (11:4).

Historical Setting

I propose that only after studying a prophetic text semantically in a holistic way is the reader ready to ask historical questions. We should ask questions that are answerable to some degree.

1. *When did "this Burden" come to the prophet?* Verse 28 dates the oracle to the year of King Ahaz's death. Unfortunately there is considerable uncertainty regarding the year of Ahaz's death. The issues are quite complex and cannot receive a thorough treatment here. Basically there are two dates under debate, an early date in 728-727 BC or a late date in 715 BC.[31]

2. *Which army is coming "from the north" against Philistia (v. 31)?* Typically Mesopotamian powers, both Assyria and Babylonia, would travel by way of the Fertile Crescent and approach the southern Levant from the north. Verse 31 speaks of "smoke" coming from the north.[32] Earlier Isaiah 5:28 uses a similar image to describe a nation coming from afar, with bows and arrows ready, horses' hoofs like flint and chariot wheels "like the storm-wind." Isaiah 14:25 identifies this nation as Assyria. Assyria is coming against both Israel and Philistia. Their respective fates, however, are different. According to verse 25, Assyria will be thwarted in the land of Israel, but according to verses 29-31, it will succeed in its effort to destroy Philistia.

3. *Who was the "smiting scepter" (= king), which had been "broken" (v. 29)?* Readers are offered three possibilities.

---

28. Isaiah 10:2; 11:4; 26:6.
29. Isaiah 29:19; 32:7; 41:17.
30. Isaiah 3:14-15; 10:1-4.
31. For the early date, see Cogan and Tadmor, *II Kings*—727 BC; Hayes and Hooker, *A New Chronology for the Kings of Israel and Judah*—728 BC; Barnes, *Studies in the Chronology of the Divided Monarchy of Israel*—727 BC. For the late date, see Albright, "The Chronology of the Divided Monarchy of Israel"—715 BC; Thiele, *The Mysterious Numbers of the Hebrew Kings*—715 BC; Na'aman, "Historical and Chronological Notes"—715 BC.
32. The motif of "enemy from the north" became especially popular with Jeremiah.

a. They can identify the breaking of the "scepter" with the death of Ahaz in verse 28. This "scepter" is thus considered to belong to the Davidic dynasty (cf. Isa 11:4). The threat against Philistia in verse 29 is connected with Isa 11:14, which speaks of Ephraim and Judah conquering Philistia in the future messianic age. However, three considerations speak against this interpretation. First, according to the superscription, what is coterminous with Ahaz's death is the oracle, not necessarily the breaking of the "scepter." Second, the structure of the oracle pairs the oppressors of Philistia in verse 29 with "the smoke from the north" in verse 31. "The smoke from the north" is not the Davidic dynasty or Israel. Third, if Ahaz is the first snake, then who are the next two snakes? Maybe Hezekiah would be the next one, but then who?

b. They can identify the scepter with a king of Babylon. The king of Babylon is called "the scepter of rulers" to be "broken" by Yahweh (14:3-6). Verse 29 could provide the fulfillment of the promise announced earlier in chapter 14. What speaks against this possibility is the date given for the oracle in verse 28. History does not inform us of any king of Babylon who oppressed Philistia and died during the time of Ahaz.

c. They can identify the scepter with a king of Assyria. Earlier in chapters 9–10 the term "scepter" designated the authority of the Assyrian king who "smites with the scepter."[33] This identification would establish a correspondence with "the smoke from the north," a reference to the Assyrian army (14:31).

Option c makes the most sense and has produced general agreement from the commentators. But which king of Assyria died in verse 29? Most likely, Tiglath-pileser III (d. 728-727 BC) is to be identified with the broken "scepter." In terms of ancient Near Eastern history, we know that in 734-731 BC Tiglath-pileser suppressed an anti-Assyrian coalition that included Ashkelon and Gaza.

4. *Who were the two kings of Assyria who followed the one "broken" in verse 29?* The book of Isaiah mentions both Sargon II and Sennacherib in or near Philistia. Chapter 20 speaks of the time when Sargon II attacked the Philistine city of Ashdod in 712 BC. At Ashdod archaeologists found a fragment of a stela commemorating Sargon's victory over Ashdod. From Isaiah 36:2, which mentions that Sennacherib was at Lachish (near Philistine Gath) in 701 BC, the reader may infer from the book of Isaiah alone

---

33. Isaiah 9:3[4]; 10:5, 15, 24.

that Sennacherib went against Philistia. We know from other sources that Sennacherib in fact campaigned in Philistine territories.[34]

The materials concerning Philistia in the book of Isaiah seem to be arranged in a pattern of prophecy and fulfillment. Isaiah 14:29 announces against Philistia that subsequent to the death of one oppressive Assyrian king (Tiglath-pileser III), there will follow not peace and freedom but two more oppressive Assyrian kings. Chapter 20 presents the first stage of the fulfillment with Sargon II, and chapter 36 the second stage with Sennacherib.[35]

Rhetorical Force

We are now ready to ask about the rhetorical aims of the prophet. What purposes did the speech serve? When it comes to this issue, the area of "speech acts" is helpful.[36] A speech-act approach tries to identify the illocutionary force and the perlocutionary force of a given utterance. The illocutionary force answers the question: What was the prophet doing by saying these words? By a given text, for example, was the prophet exhorting, warning, promising, accusing, or condemning? The perlocutionary force answers the question: With a given utterance, what response did the prophet desire from his original hearers? Did the prophet desire the hearers to respond by being comforted, terrified, contrite, believing, or having hope?

Illocutionary Force

What was the illocutionary force when Isaiah announced coming judgment against Philistia? The answer is both simple and profound. Isaiah was sentencing Philistia to death.[37] Philistia received the death sentence from Yahweh, the God of Israel and the almighty Creator. This death sentence also served to warn Israel against joining with Philistia in any anti-Assyrian alliance. Moreover, Isaiah was promising that the poor and afflicted of Israel would have a future with their God in Zion.

---

34. Kuan, "Sennacherib," 1183.

35. Tiglath-pileser III, Sargon II, and Sennacherib are the three kings known to have had dealings with Philistia. This entails skipping over Tiglath-pileser's immediate successor, Shalmaneser V (d. 722 BC).

36. See Austin, *How to Do Things with Words*. Also see Voelz on pragmatics in *What Does This Mean?* and Mitchell on "speech acts" in *The Meaning of* BRK *"To Bless" in the Old Testament*.

37. See Houston, "What Did the Prophets Think They Were Doing?" 167–88.

Perlocutionary Force

To address the question of perlocutionary force, we must first identify the original hearers. The original hearers certainly included the people of Jerusalem and especially the king with his advisers. Yet we should also inquire whether or not the foreign nations themselves heard Isaiah's words.

One possible scenario is to envision Isaiah, much like Elijah and Jonah, traveling around to different nations and proclaiming. However, that scenario seems rather unlikely. At least, there is no evidence in the book of Isaiah or the Old Testament that Isaiah himself traveled to other countries.

A more likely scenario is that the other nations sent their ambassadors or envoys to Jerusalem. One instance is recorded in Isaiah 39 (= 2 Kgs 20:12–19), when the envoys from the king of Babylon came to King Hezekiah.[38] Jerusalem was no insignificant, isolated town but a cosmopolitan city with merchants from other countries. It was also a very strategic city in the area and much involved in negotiations for international coalitions. It is reasonable to suppose that the prophet in Jerusalem would have had occasion to address these visiting envoys or merchants with a prophetic message. Isaiah 14:32 presupposes such occasions by explicitly stating how one should respond to the messengers of a foreign nation. Therefore we will consider both Jerusalem and Philistines as the original audience.

What were the perlocutionary forces desired by Isaiah? First, the *Philistine* hearers should respond to the judgment oracle by lamenting and wailing (vv. 29, 31). In fact, Isaiah exhorts all inhabitants of the earth to "wail" because the day of the Lord is coming as destruction (Isa 13:6). We should take these imperatives seriously. This is the proper response to coming judgment.[39] A response of lamentation would give evidence that the hearers believed the message, namely, that Yahweh, the Holy One of Israel, was indeed about to bring disaster and that the nation's efforts to establish its own security were futile.

Second, the *Israelite* hearers were to take the message against Philistia as a warning not to seek shelter in any multinational coalition. The schemes of the nations will not work. Isaiah 14:32 explicitly states this response.[40] It locates the prophet in the palace in Jerusalem. With reference to the pres-

---

38. Isaiah 21:11 speaks of an Edomite seeking a prophetic word from Isaiah. During the Assyrian crisis the Rabshakeh of Assyria came from Lachish and spoke to Jerusalem (Isa 36–37 = 2 Kgs 18–19). Another instance of a prophet addressing visiting envoys is recorded in Jer 27.

39. See also Isa 21:3–4; 22:4, 12–13; 23:1–14; Hillers, "A Convention in Hebrew Literature," 86–90.

40. This is also the meaning of Isaiah's action prophecy expressed in Isa 20:6.

ence of foreign ambassadors, the prophet gives advice to the royal court. They should refuse to join any anti-Assyrian coalition and instead seek refuge in Zion and in the God who dwells in Zion.[41]

Theological Reflections

After doing the necessary philological work and reading the text contextually, historically, and rhetorically, we are now prepared to reflect on the text theologically in light of the entire biblical canon. Here are some reflections.

The God of Israel is the Lord over all nations. At the time of Isaiah he used Assyria as his weapon to execute his just wrath against the wicked. Divine judgment begins with God's own covenant people, but it also extends to the foreign nations (cf. 1 Pet 4:17–18). After the opening section in Isaiah 13:1—14:27, Philistia is the first specific nation so targeted. The judgment announced against Philistia particularizes the judgment in store for the entire world (Isa 14:26–27).[42]

The proper response to the announcement of coming judgment executed by the God of Israel is to wail and lament. Its contrast is carnal security, thinking that our country or well-being is made ultimately secure by our own efforts or thinking that the prophet's announcement consists of idle threats from a weak deity. Why should Philistia fear the deity worshiped by Israel? In opposition to such carnal security, Yahweh, through his prophetic mouthpiece, announces that destruction is coming soon to Philistia. They should stop rejoicing and instead start wailing.

Announcing coming judgment against sinners constitutes an important part of the ancient prophet's job description. The same announcement needs to be heard today as well. Through his word God calls on the carnally secure to prepare to meet their Maker and Judge. Their efforts at self-security are futile. The day is coming, and coming soon, when Jesus, God in the flesh, will come to judge the living and the dead. This is not an idle threat. Sinners should not misunderstand God's patience. God is being patient, "not wishing that any should perish, but that all should reach repentance" (2 Pet 3:9). But the day of judgment will most certainly come. The proper response on the part of all sinners is wailing.

---

41. Zephaniah 3:12–13 provides an intertextual commentary on Isa 14:30a and 32: "I will leave as a remnant in your [= Zion's] midst a people humble and poor, and they will take refuge in the name of Yahweh. As for the remnant of Israel, they will not do wickedness and will not speak a lie. A tongue of deceit will not be found in their mouth. For they will graze and lie down and none will terrify."

42. See Raabe, "The Particularizing of Universal Judgment in Prophetic Discourse," 652–74.

All human efforts at self-security are futile, but there is one place of certain refuge from the coming storm. Yahweh, the true God himself, has established this place. It is located in Zion, in the place where he is graciously present for people. At the time of Isaiah this place was found in the temple in Jerusalem. After the return from exile, it was found in the rebuilt temple in Jerusalem. Then came the fulfillment in a new and greater way. Jesus the Messiah is the antitype, the new and greater temple, God-with-us. And he established his church to be the new Zion, the heavenly Jerusalem on earth (e.g., Heb 12:22). In Jesus Christ and in his church, trusting in his promises proclaimed by the gospel and administered by the sacraments, sinners find refuge and safety from the coming day of judgment. The gates of hell shall not prevail against Christ's church (Matt 16:18). The promise of Isaiah 14:32 reaches its ultimate consummation with the second coming of Christ and the heavenly Jerusalem coming down to earth (Rev 21). In short, the promise of refuge in Zion should be traced through the different stages of fulfillment: BC temple > incarnation and work of Immanuel > the church gathered around and by his gospel and sacraments where he is present > the eschatological Jerusalem. BC Zion was a type of the AD Zion.

There is only one place of secure refuge, eternally secure refuge. One is reminded of the well-known hymn "My Hope Is Built on Nothing Less" (verse 3):

> His oath, His covenant and blood
> Support me in the raging flood;
> When ev'ry earthly prop gives way,
> He then is all my hope and stay.
> On Christ, the solid rock, I stand;
> All other ground is sinking sand.[43]

Bibliography

Albrecht, Karl. "Das Geschlecht der hebräischen Hauptwörter." *Zeitschrift für die alttestamentliche Wissenschaft* 16 (1896) 41–121.

Albright, William F. "The Chronology of the Divided Monarchy of Israel." *Bulletin of the American Schools of Oriental Research* 100 (1945) 16–22.

Andersen, Francis I., and David Noel Freedman. *Hosea*. Anchor Bible 24. Garden City, NY: Doubleday, 1980.

Austin, John L. *How to Do Things with Words*. Edited by J. O. Urmson and M. Sbisa. 2nd ed. Oxford: Clarendon, 1975.

---

43. *Lutheran Service Book* (St. Louis: Concordia, 2006), hymn 575.

Barnes, William Hamilton. *Studies in the Chronology of the Divided Monarchy of Israel.* Harvard Semitic Monographs 48. Atlanta: Scholars Press, 1991.
Barthélemy, Dominique. *Critique textuelle de l'Ancien Testament: 2. Isaïe, Jérémie, Lamentations.* Orbis Biblicus et Orientalis 50/2. Göttingen: Vandenhoeck & Ruprecht, 1986.
Becker, Joachim. "Wurzel und Wurzelspross: Ein Beitrag zur hebräischen Lexikographie." *Biblische Zeitschrift* 20 (1976) 22–44.
Berlin, Adele. *The Dynamics of Biblical Parallelism.* Bloomington: Indiana University Press, 1985.
Brown, Francis, S. R. Driver, and Charles A. Briggs. *A Hebrew and English Lexicon of the Old Testament.* Oxford: Clarendon, 1951.
Cogan, Mordechai, and Hayim Tadmor. *II Kings.* Anchor Bible 11. Garden City, NY: Doubleday, 1988.
Couey, J. Blake. *Reading the Poetry of First Isaiah: The Most Perfect Model of the Prophetic Poetry.* Oxford: Oxford University Press, 2015.
Hayes, John H., and Paul K. Hooker. *A New Chronology for the Kings of Israel and Judah and Its Implications for Biblical History and Literature.* Atlanta: John Knox, 1988.
Hillers, Delbert R. "A Convention in Hebrew Literature: The Reaction to Bad News." *Zeitschrift für die alttestamentliche Wissenschaft* 77 (1965) 86–90.
Houston, Walter. "What Did the Prophets Think They Were Doing? Speech Acts and Prophetic Discourse in the Old Testament." *Biblical Interpretation* 1 (1992) 167–88.
Joüon, Paul. *A Grammar of Biblical Hebrew.* Translated and revised by T. Muraoka. Subsidia Biblica 14. Rome: Biblical Institute, 1991.
Kuan, Jeffrey K. "Sennacherib." In *Eerdmans Dictionary of the Bible*, edited by David Noel Freedman, 1183. Grand Rapids: Eerdmans, 2000.
McCarthy, Dennis J. "Some Holy War Vocabulary in Joshua 2." *CBQ* 33 (1971) 228–30.
Mitchell, Christopher W. *The Meaning of BRK "To Bless" in the Old Testament.* Society of Biblical Literature Dissertation Series 95. Atlanta: Scholars, 1987.
Na'aman, Nadav. "Historical and Chronological Notes on the Kingdoms of Israel and Judah in the Eighth Century B.C." *VT* 36 (1986) 71–92.
O'Connor, M. "The Pseudosorites: A Type of Paradox in Hebrew Verse." In *Directions in Biblical Hebrew Poetry*, edited by Elaine R. Follis, 161–72. JSOTSup 40. Sheffield: Sheffield Academic, 1987.
Oswalt, John N. *The Book of Isaiah: Chapters 1–39.* NICOT. Grand Rapids: Eerdmans, 1986.
Raabe, Paul R. "The Particularizing of Universal Judgment in Prophetic Discourse." *CBQ* 64 (2002) 652–74.
Roberts, J. J. M. "Solomon's Jerusalem and the Zion Tradition." In *Jerusalem in Bible and Archaeology: The First Temple Period*, edited by Andrew G. Vaughn and Ann E. Killebrew, 163–70. Society of Biblical Literature Symposium Series 18. Atlanta: Society of Biblical Literature, 2003.
Roberts, J. J. M. "The Rod that Smote Philistia: Isaiah 14:28–32." In *Literature as Politics, Politics as Literature: Essays on the Ancient Near East in Honor of Peter Machinist*, edited by David S. Vanderhooft and Abraham Winitzer, 381–95. Winona Lake, IN: Eisenbrauns, 2013.
Thiele, Edwin R. *The Mysterious Numbers of the Hebrew Kings.* 3rd ed. Grand Rapids: Zondervan, 1983.

Tsevat, M. בָּכוֹר. In *Theological Dictionary of the Old Testament*, edited by G. Johannes Botterweck and Helmer Ringgren, translated by Geoffrey W. Bromiley et al., 14 vols., 2:121–27. Grand Rapids: Eerdmans, 1974–2004.

Voelz, James W. *What Does This Mean? Principles of Biblical Interpretation in the Post-Modern World.* St. Louis: Concordia, 1997.

Waltke, Bruce K., and M. O'Connor. *An Introduction to Biblical Hebrew Syntax.* Winona Lake, IN: Eisenbrauns, 1990.

Weinfeld, Moshe. *Deuteronomy 1–11.* Anchor Bible 5. New York: Doubleday, 1991.

14

From Learners to Apostles—Will We Ever Learn?

The Parable of the Sower in Mark's Narrative World

—*Dieter Reinstorf*

As a young pastor who had just enrolled in a master's program at the University of Pretoria, South Africa, I met James Voelz for the first time. He was part of a delegation from the Lutheran Church–Missouri Synod (LCMS), engaged in talks with the Free Evangelical Lutheran Synod in South Africa (FELSISA) on establishing church fellowship. What struck me then was his intimate interest in me as both a pastor of a church and a young scholar on a path of intense scientific research, not at a church seminary but at a public university. Then already I sensed something of the tension that exists between strict scientific research and the role of the pastor who is called to proclaim the gospel of Christ, the arriving kingdom of God, to his present-day listeners. It is a role that characterizes my life today more than ever, being a research fellow at the University of Pretoria and both a pastor of a congregation and the bishop of a small Lutheran church. For me, being involved in the academy and the church, the two worlds can hardly be separated. Scientific research of the biblical canon inevitably leads to the act of theologizing, which in turn impacts on my life and challenges me to be different. In the effort to combine these two worlds, the boundaries between sound scientific research and proclamation often get fused. This applies also to this essay, where I will interpret the parable of the sower in the narrative world of *Mark's* Gospel, then move to the Acts of the Apostles, written by Luke,[1] and also seek to address the church of today, not least of all my own.

The choice of exploring the parable of the sower in *Mark's* Gospel is based purely on James Voelz's interest in the Evangelist Mark, culminating in his momentous commentary of 2013, *Mark 1:1—8:26*. The choice of moving to Luke and the Acts of the Apostles and also reflecting on a painting is made on the basis of application, where the interpreter is not a detached scholar but a disciple of Christ who is being directly addressed, hence the question in the title, "Will *we* ever learn?"

Methodological Approach

The interpretation of Jesus' parables has been on a roller-coaster ride. In the early church and throughout the medieval period, they were seen to be detailed *allegories*. Every item or entity in the parable was seen to have a referent outside of the parable, providing it with its spiritual meaning (*sensus spiritualis*). The parable of the sower, with an explanation given by Jesus to the select few to whom "the secret of the kingdom of God" (Mark 4:11) is revealed, served as the primary impetus of the allegorical approach in interpreting Jesus' parables. Although this approach dominated parable interpretation from the early church through the medieval period, its weaknesses eventually became apparent: (1) Two expositors rarely agreed on what the individual elements in the parable referred to. (2) Some of the meanings attributed to details of the parable were clear anachronisms.[2] (3) It seemed highly improbable that Jesus would tell his parables with the intention that they should not be understood by the listeners. This led to the provocative statement by Adolf Jülicher, doubtlessly the most renowned parable interpreter of the late seventeenth and early eighteenth century: "Trotz der Autorität so viele Jahrhunderte, trotz der grösseren Autorität der Evangelisten, kann ich die Parabeln Jesu für Allegorien nicht halten. Es spricht nämlich nicht weniger als alles dagegen."[3]

---

1. A scientific misdemeanor within the historical-critical paradigm.

2. Augustine's interpretation of the parable of the good Samaritan in Luke 10:30–37 provides the classical example: the man is Adam; Jerusalem is the heavenly city; Jericho is the moon, which stands for our mortality; the robbers are the devil and his angels; the priest and the Levite represent the Old Testament Law, which can save no one; the good Samaritan who binds the man's wounds is Christ, who forgives sin; the inn is the church; and the innkeeper is the apostle Paul (a shortened summary from *Quaestiones Evangeliorum* 2.19; cf. Longenecker, "From Allegorizing to Allegorizing," 4).

3. Jülicher, *Die Gleichnisreden Jesu*, 61. Translation by the author: "Despite the authority of so many centuries, despite the even greater authority of the evangelists, I

The main premise for Jülicher's argument was that parables do not disguise meaning, but by their simple and vivid pictures they render the meaning evident to all of Jesus' listeners. Jülicher judged that the explanations of the parables in the Gospels were inventions of the Evangelists and could not be traced back to the historical Jesus. Jülicher's rejection gained support with the discovery of the *Gospel of Thomas*, where various parables that appear in the Synoptic Gospels with explicit allegorical interpretation, including the parable of the sower, occur without explanations.[4]

Strongly opposing the idea that Jesus' parables serve to conceal mysteries, Jülicher proposed that they serve to *illustrate* a certain point in Jesus' teaching. The illustration is served by a comparison (*similitude*) between *Sache* (the reality being presented) and *Bild* (the figure representing that reality). These two parts are to be bridged by the *tertium comparationis*, the third item of comparison, revealing the point of the parable. Since Jülicher, parable interpreters have searched for that *single* point of comparison, which, once discovered, rendered the rest of the story superfluous.

A new approach to interpreting the parables of Jesus is traced back to the rise of the New Hermeneutics in the twentieth century, with its shift from the meaning of a single word to the *impact* a *story* has on its listeners.[5] Decisive for its first proponents, Ernst Fuchs and Gerhard Ebeling, was the theory of *speech acts* as developed by the British philosopher John L. Austin. In his lectures *How to Do Things with Words*, Austin distinguishes between performative and constative utterances.[6] A constative utterance refers to a state of affairs that has already been constituted. It manifests and discloses what already is. A performative utterance, in contrast, does something, and it creates something that wasn't there before. As a key example Austin cites promises. A promise like "I will be faithful to you until death parts us" is not a description, but an *act*. It brings about what previously did not exist. This is true for most stories. They evoke emotions and feelings, and have the potential to impact and to change a listener's life.[7]

Within parable research, this led to the understanding of Jesus' parables as *metaphors*, in particular as *diaphors*. Peter Wheelright made the distinction between an *epiphor* (an illustrative metaphor) and a *diaphor*

---

cannot accept the parables of Jesus as allegories. Not less that everything speaks against it."

4. Cf. Scott, *Hear Then the Parable*, 44.

5. Cf. Perrin, *Jesus and the Language of the Kingdom*, 110–26.

6. Austin, *How to Do Things with Words*. For a discussion on Austin's theory, see Bayer, *Theology the Lutheran Way*, 126–28.

7. Voelz, *Mark 1:1—8:26*, 300, refers to this as the "pragmatic dimension" of parables.

(a tensive metaphor).⁸ In the *diaphor* the metaphorical movement is not "upon" (*epi*) but through (*dia*). Two entities are juxtaposed that simply do not fit. In fact, at first glance there may be no similarities at all, but the interaction caused by the juxtaposition of paradoxical entities *creates* a reality that wasn't there before.

The question therefore is not in the first place, what *are* Jesus' parables but how do they *function*? This question is in turn closely linked to our understanding of *who* Jesus was. Was he a teacher of conventional wisdom, reaffirming the known through vivid illustrations, or was he a teacher of alternative wisdom, questioning and challenging his hearers to see reality differently?⁹ The role that Jesus performed and the way a particular parable functions are of course largely determined by the listeners. If Jesus is addressing his opponents, which may include his own disciples, a *diaphoric* approach seems the most plausible. This, however, does not exclude the functioning of a parable as an *epiphor*, where a known truth may be reaffirmed through illustrative teaching. The latter is the exception rather than the norm.

In contrast to Jülicher's understanding, a metaphorical reading of Jesus' parables does not reject the notion of allegory per se. In the parable of the sower there is little doubt, even without the interpretation given, that the seed refers to the word of God. Voelz is in agreement.¹⁰ He resists the trap into which some scholars in the post-Jülicher era have fallen, of presenting metaphors and allegories as two totally exclusive entities, or simply attributing an allegorical interpretation to the Evangelist or the early church. Rejected is the notion of *allegorizing*, a distinction first made by Hans-Josef Klauck.¹¹ He defines "allegory" as a rhetorical device that gives a symbolic dimension to text. "Allegorizing," in turn, refers to the process of ascribing hidden (often anachronistic) meaning to the text never intended by the author, based on an ideology manifested later.¹²

---

8. Wheelwright, *Metaphor and Reality*, 72.

9. On Jesus as a teacher of alternative wisdom, see Borg, *Meeting Jesus Again for the First Time*, 69–95.

10. Voelz, *Mark 1:1—8:26*, 297.

11. Klauck, *Allegorie and Allegorese in synoptischcen Gleichnissen*, 91.

12. In a recent essay, Ernest van Eck argues that *all* parables recorded in Scripture have been allegorized by the Gospel writers, giving them a theocentric understanding never intended by the historical Jesus. He argues for a *realistic* reading of the parables that function as symbols for social transformation. See Eck, "Die gelykenisse van Jesus" (this paper has been accepted for publication in *HTS Teologiese Studies/Theological Studies*). For Voelz, however, decoding the parables to determine the real referents of a parable forms an essential part of understanding Jesus' parables, with Jesus often using "standard imagery," well understood by his first listeners. See Voelz, *Mark 1:1—8:26*,

My own parable research has led to a number of theses that guide and inform me as I interpret Jesus' parables.[13] Central is the thesis that Jesus' parables are figurative stories, depicting everyday life, that *function* as metaphors, in particular as *diaphors*. As I read Jesus' parables, I therefore invariably look for the juxtaposition of *dissimilarities*, resulting in the unexpected twist in the story, something that will shock the listener. This is not confined to a reading of the parables attributed to the historical Jesus; it also applies to the parables of Jesus as they feature in the Synoptic Gospels, retold by the Evangelists and placed in a particular literary context.[14]

Notably, however, *metaphor* is not to be understood as a genre, but as a *model* of interpretation.[15] A model is not a complete picture, but a simulation of reality from a certain point of view. It functions as a lens that focuses on a specific area or enlarges one area of an otherwise complex system. The primary area on which I am focusing the lens in this particular paper is the narrative world of Mark's Gospel. But first I will look at the parable itself, after which I will look at the allegorical interpretation and the impact it has on the listener/reader within Mark's narrative world.

The Contrasts in the Parable of Jesus

At first glance the parable of the sower seems to illustrate the obvious. There is no unexpected twist, no shocking moment that challenges the reader to view reality differently. However, the contrast(s), the so called *diaphor(s)*, in the parable could be overlooked, as the parable is seldom read in isolation. Invariably the focus of the interpreter falls on the allegorical interpretation provided by Jesus in Mark 4:14–20. If, however, in a first step, the parable is read in isolation, the reader may indeed by surprised by the action of the

---

300–302.

13. Reinstorf, "The Parable of the Shrewd Manager (Lk 16:1–7)," 2.

14. See the dissertation of Reinstorf, "Metaphorical Stories in Luke's Narrative World." This dissertation is a case study in interpreting the parables peculiar to Luke as *methaphors/diaphors*.

15. Bruce J. Malina defines a model as "an abstract simplified representation of some real world object, event or interaction constructed for the purpose of understanding, control, or prediction." See Malina, *New Testament World*, 231. The use of models is not dispensable. Thomas Carney notes: "we do not have a choice of whether we will use models or not. Our choice, rather, lies in deciding whether to use them consciously or unconsciously." See Carney, *The Shape of the Past*, 5.

sower, who, in a limited good society,[16] scatters valuable seeds (in limited supply) rather carelessly.[17]

This becomes all the more apparent when contemporary sowing methods are observed in an age of large-scale production. In preparing for the act of sowing, great care is taken in what today is a highly mechanized world. Sowing machines are calibrated in such a way that the exact quantity of seeds (not too few and not too many) is put in the soil at exactly the right depth. It is in fact the task of a responsible sower to ensure that, if possible, no seeds are lost or fail to produce a crop.

In a limited good society, a responsible sower would have been hardly less careful. In the light of this, the debate whether seeds were first sown on the field and then plowed, or vice versa, is largely irrelevant. The fact is, a responsible sower, even in using his one hand to sow the seeds, would do so carefully to ensure that as few seeds as possible were lost. An original listener to Jesus' parable might have been *surprised* or even *shocked* by the irresponsible manner in which this sower sowed the seeds. The question may rightly be asked, How could this sower be so careless that only "some" seeds fell on good soil (Mark 4:8)?

It is only when the natural process of sowing in its original farming logic is interpreted that a kingdom world emerges that characterizes the very life of Jesus.[18] In bringing the message of God's dawning kingdom, Jesus scattered the seed generously without due care for which soil it fell on. From an agricultural perspective, Jesus' actions are irresponsible, even wasteful and doubtlessly uneconomical. But Jesus is not driven by economics but by relationship. His focus is not on the gains he might achieve with a limited number of seeds. Instead he scatters the seeds generously, hoping and trusting on a positive response leading to new and healed relationship with God.

If the focus is solely on the abundant crop, and not on the generous act of scattering the seed, then the frustration in sowing seeds that do not yield a crop (or in the implied sense, people that do not understand the message of the kingdom) will always abound. It is a frustration that clearly

16. On the perception of limited good, see, *inter alia*, Malina, *New Testament World*, 90–116.

17. Cf. Leicht, "Göttinger Predigtmeditationen," 139–45.

18. Voelz advocates that the parables of Jesus in the Gospels fall into two large categories: (1) those dealing with the kingdom/reign of God, and (2) those dealing with everyman. See Voelz, *Mark 1:1—8:26*, 301. Although not explicitly stated, the parable of the sower is inherently about the kingdom of God, that is, the new realm that is dawning on the listeners as Jesus speaks. As Jesus himself embodies the dawning kingdom of God (cf. Luke 17:20–21), the kingdom parables invariably mirror (in certain aspects) the very life of Jesus.

characterized the ministry of Jesus and the early Christian community, as it does the church today, all the more so in the light of a kingdom message that conveys not a glorious but a suffering Christ, so central in Mark's Gospel.

In the light of such frustration and disappointment, this parable serves as a word of *encouragement* to sow freely and generously and that, despite failures, the proclamation of the kingdom will in due course yield an abundant harvest.[19] That is the reality of God's kingdom. The word is always *active*, a truth well captured in Isa 55:10-11, which may have served, as Arland J. Hultgren suggests,[20] as a backdrop to this parable:

> As the rain and the snow come down from heaven,
>   and do not return to it without watering the earth
> and making it bud and flourish,
>   so that it yields seed for the sower and bread for the eater,
> so is my word that goes out from my mouth:
>   It will not return to me empty,
> but will accomplish what I desire
>   and achieve the purpose for which I sent it.[21]

Trusting God as his *abba* whose words never return without achieving their purpose, Jesus unwaveringly proclaimed the kingdom message and encouraged his disciples to do the same, and to do so freely and abundantly. The intended listener/reader of Mark's Gospel is to identify with the *sower*, and in spite of how ineffectual the word[22] at times may seem, it does produce an abundant crop.

Undaunted, therefore, the sower scatters his seeds. He knows some seed will fall along the path, on rock places and between thorns, and will bear no crop. But these failures are not his focus. Important for the sower is alone the knowledge that some seeds will fall on good soil and bear a crop, multiplying thirty, sixty, or even a hundred times.[23] Critical is that the word of God is proclaimed.

---

19. Cf. Hultgren, *The Parables of Jesus*, 188.
20. Cf. Braudler, *Jesus in Spiegel seiner Gleichnisse*, 51-52.
21. All English translations are cited from the NIV.
22. That the seed refers to the word of the reign and rule of God by preaching is, according to Voelz, one of the "stock metaphors" commonly used and generally known by all listeners in Jesus' time. See Voelz, *Mark 1:1—8:26*, 301.
23. The debate whether the abundant yield is hyperbole or represents a realistic crop in favorable conditions is not critical for the story line.

The Parable and Its Allegorical Interpretation in Mark's Narrative World

The allegorical interpretation of the parable is not unproblematic. In the parable the focus is on the sower who scatters the seed and on the outcome of the seed, that is, the yield that the seed produces. In the allegorical interpretation, however, there is a shift in focus, a change in object. The focus is no longer on the sower and the seed that he scatters, but on the terrain, the *people* that *hear* the word of God's kingdom. There is a definite discrepancy in what the seeds represent: Do they refer to the word of God, or do they symbolize the people who hear the word of God?

Furthermore, the parable itself provides comfort and promotes joy. Where seeds are sown, despite some losses, an abundant crop can be expected. In the crescendo of a multiplying yield of thirty, sixty, or even a hundred times, the comfort and joy find a climax. The allegorical interpretation, in contrast, is more of an exhortation to those who fail to *listen* and don't *understand*. It is only the last group that yields a crop. The allegorical interpretation reflects a high level of *frustration* by the storyteller, captured in the way Jesus addresses his disciples, "Don't you understand this parable?" (Mark 4:13). This already characterizes a feature unique to Mark's narrative world.

Parables, as all stories, feature differently in different contexts. Our focus falls on the parable of the sower not in isolation of, but *together* with, its allegorical interpretation and the role it plays in the macronarrative of Mark.

A distinctive Markan feature is the aspect of Jesus *teaching* his disciples and exhorting them to listen (Mark 4:1–3).[24] Three times in the first two verses, words with the root *didas* (teach) are employed. This raises the question: Did the disciples of Jesus indeed *learn* what Jesus taught them? And did they become true disciples of Jesus who followed his example?

The centrality of the disciples in Mark's Gospel is well documented.[25] Apart from Jesus himself, the disciples are the most prominent characters within the narrative. At the beginning of his ministry, Jesus calls Simon, Andrew, James, John, and the other disciples to follow him (1:16–20). From that point on the disciples are Jesus' constant companions, until they abandon him at the moment of his arrest (14:50). They are mentioned only once more, after Jesus' resurrection. The young man in the empty tomb

---

24. Cf. Stolle, *Das Markusevangelium*, 105–10.
25. See, *inter alia*, Matera, *What Are They Saying about Mark*, 38–55.

commands the women: "Go tell his disciples and Peter that he is going before you to Galilee, there you will see him as he told you" (16:7).

The role of Jesus' disciples in Mark's Gospel is not without ambiguity. Although they leave everything behind and follow him, several passages highlight their failure to grasp Jesus' message and the meaning of discipleship.[26] The parable of the sower with its allegorical interpretation *foreshadows* the development of Mark's story. Its placement so early in the Gospel, with no apparent link to the preceding pericope, disrupts the Gospel's narrative flow but importantly prepares the listener/reader for what is to follow: disciples of Jesus listening but not hearing, being taught but not understanding.

The allegorical interpretation serves as an *epiphor*, an *illustration* of the parable. Each item in the parable finds a counterpart in the interpretation. However, in the narrative world of Mark, the interpretation acts as a shocking *diaphor*.

When Jesus calls his disciples, the purpose of his call is stated clearly: they are designated *apostles*, that they may be with him and that he might *send them out to preach* (3:14). In Mark 6 the first step of this calling is realized: two by two, Jesus sends his disciples out to *preach* repentance, that is, to scatter seeds. When they return after a successful journey (the word proving to be active), they are for the first time officially called apostles: "The *apostles* gathered around Jesus and reported to him all they had done and taught" (6:30). Immediately afterward they are called upon to hand out bread (the product of grain that has been harvested) to their own people (6:30-44), and then again to "another" crowd (possibly non-Israelites) (8:1-10). However, in both cases they fail miserably. There is a lack of trust in God's word and what it can achieve. They do not become agents of Jesus, sowing seed that multiplies thirty, sixty, and a hundred times. Their lack of action expresses this thought: no man can do what Jesus expects from him. They fail to be *apostles*, sent out to proclaim the kingdom of God. They don't understand. Especially after the feeding of the four thousand, Jesus voices his frustration repeatedly: "Do you still not see or understand? Are your hearts hardened? Do you have eyes but fail to see and ears but fail to hear? . . . Do you still not understand?" (8:17-21).

Strikingly, the word "apostle" does not feature in Mark's Gospel again. The designated apostles remain disciples (learners). They fail to become sowers who freely scatter the seed and experience the joy of an abundant crop. The allegorical interpretation prepares the listener/reader for the shocking sequence of events that follows:[27]

---

26. Voelz notes that "Mark's depiction of the disciples, especially the Twelve, is disturbing." They are portrayed in extreme, negative terms. See Voelz, *Mark 1:1—8:26*, 42.

27. See Scott, *Hear Then the Parable*, 345-46.

a. Directly following Peter's groundbreaking confession that Jesus is the Christ (8:29b), Jesus again *teaches* his disciples that the Son of Man must suffer many things. On hearing this, Peter rebukes Jesus for his teaching, who in turn accuses him of being on the side of Satan: "Get behind me, Satan!" (8:33). In the interpretation of the parable, the birds are decoded as Satan, who snatches up the seed fallen on the path. Peter, a central figure among Jesus' disciples (the "bishop"), is likened to Satan. What a terrible *diaphor!*

b. In 10:17–21 the story is told of a man who questions Jesus concerning eternal life. He is a law-abiding person, but fails to respond to Jesus' call to follow him. He has too many possessions. Selling everything he has would make him vulnerable and dependent on God, whom he needs to trust more than his possessions. In the interpretation, the thorns where some seed has fallen are decoded as "the worries of *this life*, the deceitfulness of *wealth* and the desire for *other things*" that choke the word (4:19) (emphasis mine). Again the disciples of Jesus don't understand and fail to identify with the sower, who sows trusting God that some seed will fall on good soil, leading to an abundant harvest. "Who then can be saved?" they ask, perplexed (10:26).

c. The Gospel concludes with Jesus' passion, preceded in Mark 13 by a lesson on the signs of the end of the age. Jesus is addressed as a "teacher" who sits on the Mount of Olives teaching his disciples (14:1–3). He prepares them for hardships that lie ahead; this is followed in Mark 14 by Jesus' own passion, his arrest and trial. In the parable interpretation, the seeds that fall on rocky places resemble people who experience afflictions and persecutions and are immediately offended by the word.[28] This depicts the very behavior of Jesus' disciples. Jesus' arrest in the Garden of Gethsemane concludes with the narrator's remark that the disciples (everyone) deserted Jesus and fled (14:50). Later that same night Peter denied knowing Jesus (14:66–72).

Like a good storyteller, Mark initially intimates to his listeners/readers that Jesus' disciples, who "at once left their nets and followed him" (1:18), would—in an *epiphoric* sense—be sowers *like* Jesus, that is, apostles who preach the message of the kingdom of God to all. However, in Mark's narrative world the designated apostles fail miserably and—in a *diaphoric* sense—do not sow but hamper growth and oppose the spreading of God's kingdom.

---

28. In Mark 4:17 the word *skandaliso* is used, the same word stem used by Paul in 1 Cor 1:23 in describing the proclamation of Christ crucified as a stumbling block (*skandalon*) to the Jews.

That some seed nevertheless fell on good soil is portrayed *diaphorically* by two very unexpected characters at the beginning and end of the Mark's passion narrative: the woman who anoints Jesus' body for his burial (14:1–9) and the Roman centurion under the cross who exclaims: "Surely, this man was the Son of God!" (15:39). A sinful woman and a heathen centurion portray the faith that accepts the message of a *suffering* Christ, emphatically rejected by Peter and the rest of Jesus' disciples.

In summary, in Mark's Gospel the disciples of Jesus serve as a *negative/shocking* example to the intended readers. They are encouraged to follow the example of the sower, who sows (the word of a suffering Christ) generously, unperturbed by the soil on which the seeds fall. The reality of God's kingdom is: Some seeds fall on good soil and produce an abundant crop. It is all a matter of trusting and obeying God's word and command. His word never returns empty.

The Parable of the Sower in the Acts of the Apostles

The parable of the sower is, of course, *not* recorded in the book of Acts, but the *acts* of the apostles are a living testimony of what Jesus wished to teach his designated apostles. The word "apostle(s)" features more than thirty times in Acts, and the word "proclaim" more than twenty times. What according to Mark the disciples of Jesus failed to do, they accomplish in and through the power of the Holy Spirit after Jesus' resurrection and ascension. Like Jesus, they are sowers of the message of the kingdom of God. Persecutions and sufferings are no longer obstacles, but propel the sowing of the seed.

The scope is not given to expose the book of Acts in detail.[29] Instead attention is drawn to a painting by Hans Georg Anniès (1930–2006) depicting

---

29. The book of Acts presents the dynamic story of the gospel's journey from Jerusalem to Rome based on the promise of the risen Christ to his apostles in Acts 1:8. The word "apostle" features as early as Acts 1:2. They receive the Holy Spirit, and in Christlike manner proclaim the gospel without fear. Notably, however, the apostles do not take center stage. The main protagonist is God himself, the Holy Spirit. Furthermore, the book of Acts does not only recall the acts of the apostles, such as healings or missionary journeys, but the acts are crystallized into several extended speeches (e.g., 1:15–22; 2:14–40; 3:12–26; 4:8–12) stressing that the words of Jesus' eyewitnesses, implicitly identified with the "word of God" (cf. 4:31; 6:2, 7; 8:14; 12:24), provide the essence of what the apostles did, sowing the seed. The term "disciple(s)" also features several times, but no longer refers to the Twelve, who have now indeed become apostles, but to the followers of Jesus in a general sense. Acts concludes on the positive note that the Gentiles will *listen* (28:28) and that the apostle Paul continued to *proclaim* the kingdom of God boldly and without hindrance (28:31), thereby commissioning and encouraging the church of Christ to continue its work as sowers, that is, being apostles, who spread the word of God generously, trusting an abundant harvest.

Traditional studies on the book of Acts since the Enlightenment have largely shared a common methodology that can broadly be labeled historical-critical. It stresses the

Jesus' parable of the sower. It is a painting that aptly portrays how learners (in Mark's Gospel) have graduated to apostles (in the book of Acts):[30]

Hans Georg Anniès (1930–2006), Courtesy of Uta Welcker-Anniès

Peter Mahlke[31] gives an insightful interpretation of this painting, on which my own interpretation is largely based:

---

importance of reading Acts as an extension of Luke's Gospel. More recently, however, scholarly interpretation of Acts has reflected a number of innovating reading strategies clustering around three interests: (1) literary-narratological, (2) social-historical, and (3) canonical-theological. It is the latter approach that provides the impetus to read the book of Acts as an extension not only of Luke, but also of the entire fourfold Gospel corpus, including Mark. The canonical approach hardly presents a new exegetical strategy, but focuses on the text's final literary and canonical functions. See Wall, "Reading the New Testament in Canonical Context," 370–93. For an extensive bibliography on Acts, see Spencer, *Journeying through Acts*. Spencer largely combines the above-mentioned three reading strategies.

30. The image is taken from Mahlke, *Bibel*, 100, public domain.
31. Mahlke, *Bibel*, 100–102.

Looking at the painting, your eyes are drawn to the center, where another painting is seen. This smaller painting depicts the parable of the sower as told by Jesus. A farmer scatters seeds on his field. Some of the seeds fall along the path and the birds feed on them (top left corner). Other seeds fall on shallow soil with underlying rock (top right corner). Other seeds fall among thorns, which choke the tender plants (bottom right corner). Still other seeds fall on good soil and produce an abundant crop (bottom left corner).

Then your eyes move from the inside to the outside, from the picture in the picture to the man holding the picture. This man is Jesus, who tells the parable. His face resembles the face in the smaller picture. He is the Sower who scatters the seed, the word of God, the message of the kingdom. His eyes look toward you intently, as if he wishes to address you personally. While he scatters the seed, his right hand is invitingly open toward you.

The scattering of the seed leads to an action. Small concentric waves move outward. They extend even beyond the frame of the painting, depicting an ever-continuing scattering of the seed.

This action has an effect. Depicted are not four different results, as in the smaller painting, but only the last result, the seed falling on good soil, spreading to all four corners of the world.

There it is received by people who *listen* to the word of God, depicted by the hand behind the ear, and *do* what he commands—the open right hand that sows the seed. Eyes and feet are all directed toward you. Their facial expression is friendly, inviting, like that of Jesus. In every aspect they resemble the sower. They *hear* the word and become sowers, *apostles*, who generously scatter the seed, irrespective of the land on which it may fall.

Above them the heaven is open, conveying God's blessing and continued presence as they fulfill Christ's commission.

As a contrast to the main picture of those "who hear the word, accept it, and produce a crop—thirty, sixty, or even a hundred times what was sown" (Mark 4:20), people are depicted at the bottom of the painting who "do not hear" the word of God "nor do" what it commands. They are alone, withdrawn, locked up in a cave or a room. With both their hands they keep their ears shut. Others rest their hands on their laps; they are those who have no intent to act. They sit motionless, without feet that can walk. Their faces are sad, possibly characterized by anxiety. No waves ripple outward.

The bottom frame depicts the frustration of Jesus with his own disciples, as depicted in Mark's narrative world. Jesus' own disciples fail to listen. Despite Jesus' repeated teaching, they do not understand the message of the kingdom of God, of a *suffering* Christ, and in a *diaphoric* sense become Jesus' own enemies. They do not scatter the seed. The main picture, however, depicts the Acts of the Apostles. Unperturbed by the seed that may not fall on good soil, and despite frustrations and personal hardships, the apostles, likened to Jesus himself, scatter the seed of God's word generously and unabatedly, and experience the reality of a harvest that yields an abundant crop.

Will We Ever Learn?

The Free Evangelical Lutheran Synod in South Africa (FELSISA) is a very small, largely German-speaking confessional Lutheran church in South Africa, founded in 1892. Its membership numbers peaked around three thousand about three decades ago, but the denomination has since shown a marginal yet steady decrease in membership. For at least half a century it served an almost exclusive German-speaking community, an ever-decreasing minority group in South Africa. Since then divine services in both English and Afrikaans have been introduced, motivated primarily by intermarriages. Presently it is facing the challenging and often daunting task of being a Lutheran church for all South Africans, where not only everyone is welcomed, but concerted effort is made to cross divides of the past and to reach out to all communities, trusting the promises of God. The task is that of being a sower who freely and generously scatters the word of God, unperturbed by the soil on which the seeds may fall, joyfully awaiting the promised harvest.

Needless to say, frustrations abound, not only by seeds that fall on the path or in rocky areas, but especially by the seeds that fall among the thorns. Anxieties about an uncertain future, personal loss of income in an ever-shrinking economy, and a greater reliance on personal security through the accumulation of wealth not only curtail the sowing (further confining it to those areas already repeatedly harvested) but also obstruct the hearing, in particular, the hearing of a kingdom message of a suffering yet victorious Christ that is to be proclaimed to the ends of the world. For decades pastors and church conferences have mirrored the same theological questions from different perspectives, mostly focused on the right and pure understanding and application of God's word, which in turn is to shape, among others, our church services and ecclesiastical lives. Important topics indeed. But do we really *listen*, and do we trust the promises of God? And do we become sowers who scatter the word freely, unperturbed by the soil on which the seeds fall and the challenges of everyday life, as some seed *will* fall on good soil and *will* lead to an abundant harvest?

A recent visit to a remote area in the heartland of Mozambique, called Vila de Sena, has deeply touched my heart. The occasion was the ordination of the first eight pastors to serve the newly established Concordia Lutheran Church in Mozambique. Although the education was basic and the pastors had as yet not been ordained, those involved in the past years and present for the ordination service witnessed *apostles* of Christ in action. In but a few years, more than eight congregations had already been established, with over 1,200 members baptized by visiting missionaries. In Mozambique are Christlike sowers, apostles, who scatter the word of God freely amid an uncertain future with hardly any personal income. They are not the protagonists. God whose promises can be trusted is. But their story presents a *diaphoric* challenge to many established churches, not least of all my own, and to me personally.

Bibliography

Austin, John L. *How to Do Things with Words: The William James Lectures Delivered at Harvard University in 1955.* Oxford: Clarendon, 1962.

Bayer, Oswald. *Theology the Lutheran Way.* Edited and translated by Jeffrey G. Silcock and Mark C. Mattes. Grand Rapids: Eerdmans, 2007.

Borg, Marcus J. *Meeting Jesus Again for the First Time: The Historical Jesus and the Heart of Contemporary Faith.* San Francisco: Harper, 1994.

Braudler, Georg. *Jesus in Spiegel seiner Gleichnisse.* Stuttgart: Calver, 1986.

Carney, Thomas. *The Shape of the Past: Models and Antiquity.* Lawrence, KS: Coronado, 1975.

Eck, Ernest van. "Die gelykenisse van Jesus: Allegorieë of simbole van sosiale transformasie." Paper presented at the conference on Matthew's Gospel in honor of Prof. Dr. Wim J. C. Weren, January 27 and 28, 2015.

Hultgren, Arland J. *The Parables of Jesus: A Commentary.* Grand Rapids: Eerdmans, 2000.

Jülicher, Adolf. *Die Gleichnisreden Jesu. Zwei Teile in einem Band.* Darmstadt: Wissenschaftliche Buchgesellschaft, 1976.

Klauck, Hans-Josef. *Allegorie and Allegorese in synoptischcen Gleichnissen.* Münster: Aschendorf, 1978.

Leicht, Robert. "Göttinger Predigtmeditationen." 57. *Jahrgang* (2002/2003) 139–45.

Longenecker, Richard N. "From Allegorizing to Allegorizing: A History of the Interpretation of the Parables of Jesus." In *The Challenge of Jesus' Parables,* edited by Richard N. Longenecker. Grand Rapids: Eerdmans, 2000.

Mahlke, Peter. *Bibel: Unterrichtsmodell für den Konfirmandenunterricht.* Vorbereitungshilfen und Unterrichtsblätter. Gross Oesingen: Lutherische Buchandlung Heinrich Harms, 2003.

Malina, Bruce J. *The New Testament World: Insight from Cultural Anthropology.* 2nd ed. Louisville: Westminster John Knox, 1993.

Matera, Frank J. *What Are They Saying about Mark?* New York: Paulist, 1987.

Perrin, Norman. *Jesus and the Language of the Kingdom: Symbol and Metaphor in New Testament Interpretation*. Philadelphia: Fortress, 1976.

Reinstorf, Dieter H. "Metaphorical Stories in Luke's Narrative World: A Challenge to a Conventional Worldview." University of Pretoria, 2002.

———. "The Parable of the Shrewd Manager (Lk 16:1–7): A Biography of Jesus and a Lesson on Mercy." HTS *Teologiese Studies/Theological Studies* 69.1 (2015).

Scott, Bernard Brandon. *Hear Then the Parable: A Commentary on the Parables of Jesus*. Minneapolis: Fortress, 1990.

Spencer, F. Scott. *Journeying through Acts: A Literary-Cultural Reading*. Peabody, MA: Hendrickson, 2004.

Stolle, Volker. *Das Markusevangelium: Übersetzung und Kommentierung (unter besonderer Berücksichtigung der Erzähltechnik)*. Oberurseler Hefte Ergänzungsband 17. Göttingen: Vandenhoeck & Ruprecht, 2015.

Voelz, James W. *Mark 1:1—8:26*. Concordia Commentary. St. Louis: Concordia, 2013.

Wall, R. W. "Reading the New Testament in Canonical Context." In *Hearing the New Testament: Strategies for Interpretation*, edited by Joel B. Green. Grand Rapids: Eerdmans, 1995.

Wheelwright, Philip. *Metaphor & Reality*. Bloomington: Indiana University Press, 1962.

15

Communication Models, Relevance Theory, Bible Translation, and Exegesis

—*Vilson Scholz*

Almost everybody is familiar with the traditional communications model in terms of sender, message, and receiver. This model was originally developed by Claude Shannon in 1949 as a tool for measuring the electronic transmission capacity of telephone circuits.[1] It may be called the transportation model, inasmuch as communication is viewed as the transportation of a message from one source to another through a medium or agent. Some call it the "code model paradigm,"[2] because it assumes that communication is basically a process of encoding and decoding. Here, the sender somehow controls the message and becomes the yardstick against which the transported message is measured. The receiver gives some sort of feedback, and if the message differs, this must be due to "noise" in the channel.

The code model is useful up to a point. It has its appeal because it is so simple. It was popularized in the mid-1970s, and its popularity may have something to do with the fact that it can be applied to face-to-face communication, communication in writing, as well as electronic communication.

---

1. This model was set forth in what was called the mathematical theory of communication. Soukup, "Communication Models, Translation, and Fidelity," 220.

2. Gutt, "Translation, Metarepresentation and Claims of Interpretive Resemblance," 96.

Eugene Nida made use of this model in his translation theory. In 1981 he wrote, "In every verbal communication there are always three elements—a source, a message, and one or more receptors. In reality, however, in every such verbal communication there are always at least two messages being communicated. In oral language, for example, there are not only the words, but also the tone of voice."[3] Nida talks about two messages being communicated, which points to the fact that not everything can be encoded in words.

My dear mentor and friend James Voelz uses a similar model, only that, in reference to written communication, he has a preference for author—text—reader. However, he quickly adds that this process also works in the reverse direction: reader—text—author.[4] This is a clear indication that the reader or receptor is as active as the author or sender. In his hermeneutics textbook, Voelz presents a more elaborate model.[5] A glance at the page immediately reveals that things are much more complex than just sending signals through a channel. Voelz is aware of this. He points to a "complex of characteristics evoked from the memory world," which is placed above the traditional communications model. This has a lot to do with relevance theory, to which I will now turn.

Relevance Theory

Relevance theory was developed by Dan Sperber and Deirdre Wilson, in *Relevance: Communication and Cognition*.[6] This book was originally published in 1986, and a second edition came out in 1995. Since then the theory has been applied to translation studies,[7] and it is also being incorporated into modern hermeneutics textbooks.[8] As presented by Sperber and Wilson, the theory is not easy to follow, at least not for beginners, due to the use of complex technical language. The reader runs into terms and expressions like "cognitive environment," "contextual effect," "implicature," "explicature," "ostensive-inferential communication," "processing effort," and so on.

---

3. Nida, "Bible Translation for the Eighties," 138.
4. Voelz, *Mark 1:1—8:26*, 69–70.
5. Voelz, *What Does This Mean?* 212.
6. Sperber and Wilson, *Relevance: Communication and Cognition*. The work was translated into Portuguese in 2001.
7. Hill, *The Bible at Cultural Crossroads*; Hill et al., *Bible Translation Basics*.
8. Jeannine K. Brown has a section on relevance theory in *Scripture as Communication*, 35–38.

Relevance theory is not so much a communication theory as it is a theory of cognition that aims to explain how human beings make sense out of what is being communicated. Cognition is not simply a matter of decoding what has been encoded, although that is part of the process. In other words, the traditional code model or transportation model explains a lot, but it does not explain everything. This is confirmed by the realization that an utterance that sounds pretty straightforward from a semantic point of view may be understood in different ways, in a process that has nothing to do with the so-called noise in the channel. A classic example is the following dialogue: Question: "Do you want some coffee?" Answer: "Coffee would keep me awake."[9] Is this reply a "yes" or a "no"? The answer does not depend on decoding correctly, but on context. If the addressee needs to stay awake, the reply would mean "yes." But if the addressee is about to go to bed, the reply means "no, thank you." Similar to this is Jesus' reply to Pilate's question, "Are you the king of the Jews?" Jesus answered, "You have said so," but not everybody is convinced that the answer means "yes."

Granted that not everything can be crammed or encoded into a sentence, and to the extent that so much depends on context, relevance theory stresses that human communication tends to be shorthand. As Stephen Pattemore explains, "we rarely say exactly what we wish to communicate. We usually say less than we intend, and choose our words for their ability to point efficiently to our meaning."[10] We don't need to say everything at length all the time. In some situations we communicate by *also* resorting to words. For deaf people then, words are usually not part of the process. Yet for hearers, the use of words results in a quicker and much more precise communication process.

Communication works essentially by inference. As Harriet Hill explains, "relevance theory posits that communication is inferential. Communicators guess the background information their audience possesses, and design their utterance (or non-verbal stimulus) to say just enough to stimulate in the audience certain assumptions they have, so that between what is said and what they know, the audience can infer the intended meaning."[11]

This inferential process is based on what is called cognitive environment. An individual's total cognitive environment is the set of all the facts that he or she can perceive or infer; all the facts that are manifest to him or her. As Sperber and Wilson have it, "it consists of not only all the facts that

---

9. Sperber and Wilson, *Relevance*, 34. This illustration comes up time and again in Sperber and Wilson.

10. Pattemore, "On the Relevance of Translation Theory," 266.

11. Hill, *The Bible at Cultural Crossroads*, 14.

he [sic] is aware of, but also all the facts that he is capable of becoming aware of, in his physical environment."[12] Cognitive environment is the pool of presuppositions, information, and memories we have in our mind and that we can access upon receiving a verbal input.[13] The historical and geographical environment, people's personal experience, and someone's relationship with the person who is communicating are all part and parcel of the cognitive environment. When someone hears or reads words, phrases, and texts, those function like icons that give access to data that is stored up in one's mind and makes cognition possible.

Two or more people can share a cognitive environment, which amounts to a mutual cognitive environment, that is, the set of facts that are mutually manifest.[14] This does not imply that the audience and the speaker *make* the same assumptions, but that they *can* do so.[15] If the speaker and the hearer do not make the same assumptions, there will be a breakdown in communication. In other words, it is not so much a matter of encoding or decoding incorrectly, but of "a mismatch between the context envisaged by the speaker and the one actually used by the hearer."[16]

And what is context? According to relevance theory, context is not what comes before or after an utterance, but is that part of the cognitive environment that is being accessed whenever we process or interpret a verbal (or nonverbal) input. It is a subset of one's cognitive environment, "a psychological construct, a subset of the hearer's assumptions about the world."[17] The speaker evokes a context, and by doing so guides the listener toward a specific interpretation. Quickly we put the utterance we hear or read into a psychological context and understand it in a way that makes sense to us. At that point we stop processing. If we realize that we have formed the wrong context or if the speaker signals that we have misunderstood him or her, we immediately rearrange the context, in search for relevance.

The ideas derived inferentially from an input or from a communication are called contextual effects, which may be explicatures or implicatures. "Explicatures are assumptions derived from the text itself, including the results of assigning reference to pronouns, general terms. . . . Implicatures, by

---

12. Sperber and Wilson, *Relevance*, 39.

13. This comes close to James Voelz's "second text," which is a "text" the hearer or reader already has in his or her mind and which has the potential to overwrite the text that is being heard or read.

14. Sperber and Wilson, *Relevance*, 42.

15. Pattemore, *Souls under the Altar*, 18.

16. Sperber and Wilson, *Relevance*, 16.

17. Ibid., 15.

contrast, can only be derived by processing the text *in a particular context*. They result from the *interaction* of text and context."[18]

What, then, is relevance, according to relevance theory? Relevant is not what is pertinent or what has practical value or applicability, as the common dictionary definition says, but what results in greater contextual effects. If we hear something we have never heard before, and which we cannot in any way connect to our cognitive environment, the result is no contextual effect whatsoever. If we hear something new, but which we can connect to our cognitive environment, that will result in greater contextual effects. Thus relevance is always a matter of degree, which means that an input can be more or less relevant. There are three types of contextual effects: reinforcement of our presuppositions, negation of our presuppositions, and extension or deepening of what we already know.

Yet another factor is involved in relevance, namely, the processing effort that is required, which means that "human cognition takes place in a balancing act between processing effort and contextual effect."[19] This means that, other things being equal, the greater the positive cognitive effects achieved, the greater the relevance of the input. However, the processing of the input involves some effort of perception, memory, and inference. Other things being equal, the smaller the processing effort required, the greater the relevance of the input. Or as Sperber and Wilson put it, "an assumption is relevant in a context to the extent that its contextual effects in this context are large; and an assumption is relevant in a context to the extent that the effort required to process it in this context is small."[20]

Relevance theory takes into account the tendency toward efficiency in communication, which means that it is essentially optimistic.[21] Human communication is a wonderful thing. We assume that the speaker or writer is truthful and has something meaningful and coherent to say. And our default is to put the best construction on what we hear or read.

In summary fashion, one may say that relevance theory suggests that when we hear or read an act of deliberate (ostensive) communication, we assume that the communicator not only intended us to understand the communication but also shaped it to be optimally relevant. We interpret it within the context of ideas already present in our minds that, when we add the new information, will yield a flow of good results for acceptably low

---

18. Pattemore, "On the Relevance of Translation Theory," 267.

19. Ibid., 268.

20. Sperber and Wilson, *Relevance*, 125.

21. This should come as no surprise, inasmuch as relevance theory is an offshoot of Paul Grice's theory of conversation, in particular his so-called *cooperative principle*. See ibid., 33–34.

processing effort. Central to this is the understanding that the context that shapes our understanding of a communication is a context in our minds, a cognitive construction. Our physical and social environment, the history and geography of the world, our life history, and the history of our relationship with the communicator all affect the way we understand a communication, but they do so by affecting our minds.[22]

Implications for Translation Projects, Preachers, and Missionaries

In the light of relevance theory, Bible translation agencies are nowadays reevaluating their approach to translation projects, particularly in oral cultures. There is no doubt that the launching of a translation of the New Testament or of the whole Bible is always a big event in a given community. And yet the question is: Will it be relevant? For people that are not used to reading, how relevant will the whole New Testament or the whole Bible be? Therefore some Bible translation agencies are changing their approach, publishing small portions of the Bible, maybe a few Bible stories, preferably in audio format, for this will be much easier to process. At the same time, relevance theory questions the assumption that everything can be communicated to everyone or to every audience, irrespective of background knowledge. This means that, besides making the message as accessible as possible and easy to process, in simple language and in small pieces, there is still a need to form the audience. Thus background materials like study Bibles will always be helpful.

Mindful of the principles outlined in relevance theory, preachers should know that it will be impossible to transport a message into the brains of the audience. All one can do is send verbal and nonverbal signals that the audience will hopefully put into the right context. One cannot put it all in words, but one has to send the right signals. It is important to send signals that people can recognize. What we say has to be sharp or pointed. Words have to make an impact. What is said in a straightforward way is much more relevant than long musings and boring reflections.

At the same time, the preacher must take into consideration the mutual cognitive environment. If one cannot assume that theological shorthand such as "Word and sacrament" will be understood, it will be of little use to the audience. If it requires too much processing effort, as is the case with definitions, which tend to be abstract, it will not be relevant. Depending on the location (a seminary campus, for instance), a Greek or Hebrew word

22. Pattemore, *Souls under the Altar*, 24.

may be useful. In most cases it will turn the audience off, because it is too demanding.

In terms of cross-cultural communication, a story told by Eugene A. Nida illustrates the importance of cognitive environment and the right amount of information.[23] Writing about evangelization, Nida takes issue with the suggestion that one should always hand out a complete New Testament. He points out that in some circumstances this can lead to serious misunderstanding. This is exactly what happened in Thailand, where a missionary gave a New Testament to a Thai Buddhist. When the missionary later saw the man and asked, "How did you like the book?" the Buddhist replied as follows: "Oh, that is a wonderful book, and such a remarkable man! Why, he was born and he died, he was born and he died, born and died, born and died. In four reincarnations he made it to Nirvana." For this man the four Gospels represented four separate lives, and what surprised this man more than anything else became evident in his further statement, "Why, this man Jesus made it to Nirvana in four reincarnations, while Buddha required 1,000."

Implications for Exegesis and Translation

Relevance theory also helps us to reflect on the complexities of exegesis and translation. A few examples will suffice, two from each Testament.

The first text is Isaiah 5:10, which reads as follows in the ESV:

> "For ten acres of vineyard shall yield but one bath,
> and a homer of seed shall yield but an ephah."

This certainly was formulated by Isaiah in a way that was meaningful, easy to understand and therefore relevant to the original audience. Isaiah did not need to say more than what he said. It probably did not require much processing effort by his listeners (and readers). They were able to form the right context, given the mutually shared cognitive environment. Baths, homers, and ephahs were part of their daily life. However, this is very demanding for a modern reader (and listener), especially if he or she was born and raised in a place like Chicago or Manhattan. Just how much is an acre of vineyard? And one bath, a homer of seed, and a yield of an ephah? And is this good news or bad news?

The ESV translation has been formulated in a way that signals to the reader that this is bad news: "*but* one bath ... *but* an ephah," even though

---

23. Nida, "Bible Translation for the Eighties," 133.

the "but" is not part of the original text. Context (v. 9) helps, indicating that this is the right interpretation:

> The LORD of hosts has sworn in my hearing:
> "Surely many houses shall be desolate,
> large and beautiful houses, without inhabitant."

One gets the impression that one bath is not much for ten acres of vineyard, and that one ephah is a small yield for a homer of seed, but just how much or how little is it? Isaiah's audience must have been able to figure this out easily. The modern reader must apply a lot of processing effort. What complicates matters is that those liquid measures and dry measures are debated, which means that nobody knows for sure the exact size or capacity.

Modern translations try to make things easier for the reader. The Good News Translation (GNT) says: "The grapevines growing on five acres of land will yield only five gallons of wine. Ten bushels of seed will produce only one bushel of grain." Leaving aside the fact that people living in South America will have a hard time processing the information about acres and gallons, even a reader raised in an urban area in the United States may have difficulty with bushels. However, the main point seems to be clear: ten bushels produce one bushel, which is definitely not a good outcome.

For someone living in Brazil and familiar with hectares and liters, the Contemporary English Version (CEV) is much more relevant, inasmuch as it requires less processing effort: "Four hectares of grapevines will produce only 27 liters of juice, and 180 liters of seed will produce merely 18 liters of grain." However, "four hectares" is more relevant (for it is less demanding) if you were raised on a farm, which is my case, than if you were raised in an urban area.

The other text from the Old Testament is Isaiah 7:20, which reads: "In that day the Lord will shave with a razor that is hired beyond the River—with the king of Assyria—the head and the hair of the feet, and it will sweep away the beard also" (ESV). Leaving aside the fact that in our time razors or barbers (GNT) are no longer hired and that we don't know at first blush to which king of Assyria the prophet is referring, this text sounds pretty straightforward, no matter which translation one is reading. And yet what is not clear is if this is good news or bad news. In our world, that might sound like good news: a thorough job of haircutting and depilation by an international barber! However, in the biblical context the implicature (a point made by relevance theory) is just the opposite. It is hard to communicate this in the text of the translation. In some cases the translator helps the reader in a footnote, as is done in the CEV: "This would have been a terrible insult."

A good example from the New Testament is Acts 18:1-2: "After this Paul left Athens and went to Corinth. And he found a Jew named Aquila, a native of Pontus, recently come from Italy with his wife Priscilla, because Claudius had commanded all the Jews to leave Rome. And he went to see them" (ESV). For his audience, Luke only needed to say what he said. He could assume (implicatures!) that Athens and Corinth were well-known cities, and that people knew what "Jew" meant, that Pontus was a province and not a town, and that Claudius was an emperor and not just a commander. To put this information in the right context, the modern reader needs a lot of historical and geographical data that has to be available in his or her cognitive environment. This will be much easier and more relevant for people living in Europe than for a tribesman in the Amazon jungle! Modern translations try to help readers by inserting classifiers like "city," "emperor," and so forth. The GNT and the CEV bring out the implicature that Claudius was an emperor. The CEV has a footnote, indicating that the Jews had to leave Rome probably in AD 49 or maybe in AD 41. This information does not help the reader to understand the text. In a sense, it makes things worse, inasmuch as it brings additional information that the reader has to process. The Portuguese common language translation is more explicit, adding that Corinth was a city and that Pontus was a province. Yet how far is it from Pontus to Rome and from Rome to Corinth? A map may be helpful, but this information will be much more relevant for someone who lives in that area, and even more relevant for a person that has actually traveled from place to place.

Another quick example from the New Testament is Rom 16:22: "I Tertius, who wrote this letter, greet you in the Lord" (ESV). Letter writing and the sending of greetings are activities that most people are familiar with even today. And Tertius is no doubt the name of a man. And yet the reader may be intrigued by the information that Tertius wrote the letter that is well known as Paul's epistle to the Romans. There was no need to say anything to the original audience, because they could form and visualize the right context in the light of their shared cognitive environment. However, to put this in the right context, the modern reader has to be informed that in those days people used to dictate letters to a secretary, as a note in the CEV explains. The Brazilian common language translation puts this information in the text: "I, Tertius, who wrote this letter that Paul dictated to me, send you greetings."

Conclusion

Relevance Theory is not a translation theory or, for that matter, a communication theory; it deals with human cognition. It helps us realize how human beings are able to understand each other. Relevance Theory emphasizes that not everything can be squeezed into a text and that a lot of what is communicated is so to speak "in the air". This means that Biblical writers could and did write shorthand. It also means that listeners and readers are as active as the person that communicates or sends the message.

This also means that translators and preachers are allowed to spell out explicatures and implicatures. Translators though, need to stay within the confines of the Biblical world; they are not allowed to modernize the Biblical text. Preachers in turn, must take an extra step, translating and speaking the Word of God to their modern audiences in a language that is striking and which is not too demanding in terms of processing effort. In all of this, the amazing thing is that communication works!

Bibliography

Brown, Jeannine K. *Scripture as Communication: Introducing Biblical Hermeneutics.* Grand Rapids: Baker Academic, 2007.
Buttrick, David. "The Language of Jesus." *Theology Today* 64 (2008) 423–44.
Green, Gene L. "Relevance Theory and Theological Interpretation: Thoughts on Metarepresentation." *Journal of Theological Interpretation* 4 (2010) 75–90.
Gutt, Ernst-August. "Translation, Metarepresentation and Claims of Interpretive Resemblance." In *Similarity and Difference in Translation*, edited by Stefano Arduini and Robert Hodgson Jr., 93–101. Rome: Storia e Letteratura, 2007.
Jobes, Karen H. "Relevance Theory and the Translation of Scripture." *JETS* 50 (2007) 773–97.
Hill, Harriet S. *The Bible at Cultural Crossroads: From Translation to Communication.* Manchester, UK: St. Jerome, 2006.
———. "Relevant Study Bibles." *Bible Translator* 61 (2010) 191–207.
Hill, Harriet, et al. *Bible Translation Basics: Communicating Scripture in a Relevant Way.* Dallas: SIL International, 2011.
Nida, Eugene A. "Bible Translation for the Eighties." *International Review of Mission* 70 (1981) 130–39.
Pattemore, Stephen. "On the Relevance of Translation Theory." *Review and Expositor* 108 (2011) 263–77.
———. *Souls under the Altar: Relevance Theory and the Discourse Structure of Revelation.* New York: United Bible Societies, 2003.
Soukup, Paul A. "Communication Models, Translation, and Fidelity." In *Fidelity and Translation*, edited by Paul A. Soukup and Robert Hodgson. New York: American Bible Society, 1999.
Sperber, Dan, and Deirdre Wilson. *Relevance: Communication and Cognition.* 2nd ed. Cambridge, MA: Blackwell, 1995.
Voelz, James W. *Mark 1:1—8:26.* Concordia Commentary. St. Louis: Concordia, 2013.
———. *What Does This Mean? Principles of Biblical Interpretation in the Post-Modern World.* St. Louis: Concordia, 1997.

16

Effective Justification and Its Hermeneutical Implications

—Mark A. Seifrid

For Jim Voelz, dear friend and colleague

Paul

It is a distinctive and remarkable feature of the Corinthian correspondence that within it Paul consistently speaks of justification in terms of an *event* in *Christ* in which the fallen human being is made right with God and given a new *being*. This description of God's justifying work is clearly a response to the situation in Corinth: with it the apostle repeatedly addresses the Corinthian misjudgment of themselves and the world with "the word of the cross" (1 Cor 1:18).

1 Corinthians 1:30–31

At the opening of First Corinthians, Paul introduces the language of justification in terms of a new reality that is "located" in Christ: "By (God's doing) you are in Christ Jesus, who became for us wisdom from God, and righteousness, and sanctification, and redemption, in order that, just as it is written, 'Let the one who boasts, boast in the Lord'" (1 Cor 1:30–31).

Paul's understanding of justification here remains irreducibly forensic: that the Corinthians have their wisdom and righteousness in the crucified and risen Christ is an expression of God's judgment on the world, for which the word of the cross remains foolishness. Yet Paul does not speak of justification here as the imputation of Christ's righteousness to the believer. He speaks instead of God's *placing* the foolish, weak, and lowly Corinthians "into" Christ. The new "location" brings with it a new relation and a new reality. In this new relation, the justification of the Corinthians has taken place. One cannot adequately summarize Paul's word to the Corinthians here by saying that they have now received acquittal for their transgressions or have Christ's righteousness credited to their account. This way of describing justification retains its validity in that it asserts the extrinsic nature of the event of salvation. But this formulation is far from capturing the whole of what Paul is saying. It is not the case that the Corinthians now have their own "righteousness, sanctification, and redemption," not even as a status imputed to them. Their righteousness is found *in their relation* to "Christ Jesus" in whom they have been "placed" by God. God has so worked, Paul announces, in order that the word of Jeremiah 9:22–23 might be fulfilled: "Let the one who boasts, boast *in the Lord*." As is clear from the monitory nature of Paul's argument, he is calling the Corinthians to "grasp" that which has been given them, to live in the saving relationship with the crucified Christ into which they have been placed by God. At the same time, Paul's word is a re-presentation of what God has done for the Corinthians. By God's doing, they are "in Christ." The apostolic "reminder" is again to function as an effective word, performing in the Corinthians what God did in them at the start.

Paul describes the new reality in which the Corinthians have been placed in a threefold manner. As the "wisdom" of the Corinthians, "Christ Jesus" has become for them "righteousness, sanctification, and redemption." Paul does not speak of the *work* of Christ that might be broken down into distinct elements in an *ordo salutis*, but of the indivisible *person* of the crucified and risen Christ. The benefits that Paul names are differing aspects of the one new reality that is present in Christ. For this reason, he is able to summarize them in the single statement that Christ has become "wisdom" for the Corinthians.

This summary term already signals the hermeneutical implication of God's justifying work that Paul presses upon the Corinthians. The "Christ" in whom the Corinthians have been placed is the crucified Christ, whom Paul proclaims (1 Cor 1:23; cf. 1:18). In him, God has made the self-seeking "wisdom of the world" foolishness (1:19-20). In Christ, God hides true wisdom in that which is foolish and his power and glory in weakness and shame. God saves us by saving us from ourselves. The Corinthians, upward-striving though they are, primarily are members of the lower social strata. By God's doing, Christ has become for them "the wisdom of God." The terms of what is "good" therewith have been changed for them radically. Now "righteousness, holiness, and redemption" replace any earthly good that they might seek in the wisdom of the world. The Corinthians have been *given* faith in the crucified and risen Christ (cf. 2:5). This faith entails their seeing themselves, God, and the world for what they are, and thus seeing the crucified Christ as the wisdom and power of God. Paul confronts the Corinthians in their upward aspirations with the truth of the gospel that God alone can bring home to the rebellious human heart. Beyond and before all true understanding stands God's work in Christ. This work of creating understanding in the heart has been performed by the Spirit of God, first in the apostle and then in his hearers, as Paul makes clear in his following argument to the Corinthians (2:6–16). Paul thus presents the Corinthians with a *material* hermeneutic, the apostolic proclamation of the crucified Christ. In bringing the *gospel* home to the human heart, the Spirit creates the basis of true understanding. For Paul as well as for the psalmist, "the fear of the Lord is the beginning of wisdom" (Ps 111:10; Prov 1:7). And that "fear" is itself a work of God. Justification by faith, particularly when seen in its effective dimension, entails this material hermeneutic.

1 Corinthians 6:11

Paul's understanding of "justification" as a new reality in Christ takes on another dimension in 1 Cor 6:11, where Paul again describes "justification" in a threefold series of terms. Here he obviously recalls his opening description of God's work in Christ, and now reverses its order: "And such were some of you, but you were washed, you were sanctified, but you were justified, by the name of the Lord Jesus Christ, and by the Spirit of our God" (1 Cor 6:11).

Paul replaces the nouns of 1 Cor 1:30 with verbs, as he emphatically reminds the Corinthians that something has taken place for them. "Justification" appears here explicitly as an *action* of God, alongside "sanctification" and "washing." The Corinthians have been *made* new. Together with the reference to "washing," the closing reference to the name of Christ and the Spirit of God suggests that Paul has in view the baptism of the Corinthians. Furthermore, the emphatic, final member of the series, "you have been *justified,*" corresponds to his warning in verse 9, "Do you not know that the *unjust* shall not inherit the kingdom of God?" Even though some of the Corinthians formerly had lived in open unrighteousness that Paul describes in verses 9–10, they have been made new. He speaks here of the "washing" of the Corinthians, rather than their "redemption" from sin and evil, as he did earlier in 1:30. The picture of deliverance from slavery has changed to that of cleansing. Paul now focuses his attention on the change *of the Corinthians* that has been effected in Christ. As we have noted, he describes that change as an event, almost certainly alluding to the baptism of the Corinthians. The singularity of that event, "by the name of the Lord Jesus, and by the Spirit of our God," again reinforces the impression that Paul is not presenting a series of independent benefits, but describing different dimensions of a single, saving action as it has been communicated and given to the Corinthians. Indeed, his reference to "the name of the Lord Jesus and the Spirit of our God," with its baptismal overtones, binds the benefits Paul names to the one person of the crucified and risen Lord, whose name has been pronounced over the Corinthians. Just as is the case in 1 Cor 1:30, his threefold description of "justification" appears as a *forensic act* of God that is present in the crucified and risen Christ. The promises of God have their fulfillment in him: because God's word is an effective word, forensic justification is effective justification, and vice versa. The fundamental figure that Paul employs in both instances is "location"; in this case that location is fixed "in Jesus' name." Once again in this text, Paul calls the Corinthians back to that which has been given to them once and for all in Christ.

2 Corinthians 5:21

A third, highly significant reference to justification appears in Paul's summary of his apostolic message in 2 Cor 5:21: "The one who did not know sin, God made to be sin on our behalf, in order that we might become the righteousness of God in him."

Once again here, much as in 1 Cor 1:30, Paul interprets the cross and resurrection in terms of Christ's person. Yet Paul here also speaks of God's action—now as God's deed with respect to Christ—so that the *justifying action* that we find in 1 Cor 6:11 reappears here, in new terms. In a dynamic exchange in Christ, God has *effected a new creation*. This exchange is irreducibly ontological: just as God made Christ *to be* sin, we *become* the righteousness of God in him. While Paul's statement certainly implies Christ's *work*, it cannot be reduced to a mere work of Christ. In the first place, properly speaking, the exchange here is God's work, not Christ's work. Moreover, this work has to do with the *person* of Christ, who "was made sin" for us. Here, as he does elsewhere, Paul speaks of "sin" not merely as an act, but as the power of evil that has taken up residence in the human being. In God's making Christ to "be sin," Christ was put in our place. He did not take our place in the sense of becoming just one sinner among other sinners. Indeed, Paul is emphatic: "*the one who knew no sin*, God made to be sin on our behalf." As Michael Cameron has put it, Christ became for us "the sinless sinner." Christ's place-taking is thus simultaneously inclusive and exclusive, at once substitutionary and corporate.

This defining description of Christ as "the one who knew no sin" again makes evident the *personal* and ontological orientation of the apostle's thought here. It is not merely Christ's work that God offered in our place, but the person of Christ, in whom a dramatic exchange has taken place: "God made him to be sin, in order that we might become the righteousness of God *in him*." Paul's description of Christ as the "one who knew no sin" makes clear his conception of the full depth of the reality of sin. It is not confined to mere deeds, but has taken possession of the entire human being—and thus, in exchange, Christ himself. Embodied evil is overcome only by an *effective* judgment that brings death. Righteousness likewise is communicated as an effective reality, a participation in the righteousness of God as it has been manifest in the crucified and risen Christ.

Paul's description of salvation as a "becoming the righteousness of God" recalls the reality of the new creation, present in Christ, that he already has announced in 5:17. The obvious connection between "the new creation" and "the righteousness of God" again underscores the ontological nature of the event. In now speaking of "the righteousness of God," Paul recalls his description of the new covenant of the Spirit that brings righteousness, in contrast to the condemnation effected by "the letter" (3:9). He likewise echoes the scriptural references to "God's righteousness," especially the passages in the Psalms and in the book of Isaiah that celebrate this "righteousness" as the Lord's act of deliverance and of revelation awaited by God's people, and indeed, by all creation. This "righteousness" is an act of judgment and deliverance, in which God reveals *what* is right, and in so doing *reveals* that he is *right*. The Lord is the one Ruler and Creator, who fulfills his promises for his people and for the world, overcoming evil, disobedience, idolatry. Paul's shift in terminology thus brings to light another dimension of the "new creation." It presupposes an act of judgment and revelation that establishes *saving communication* between God and humanity. In 2 Cor 5:21, that communication appears in ultimate form: in Christ, fallen human beings *become* the righteousness of God. They are made new in such a way that their very being is an announcement of God as the one, true, saving Creator and Lord. Once again in this text, Paul locates this communicative relation "in Christ." The Corinthians do not have God's righteousness in themselves. Indeed, Paul calls them afresh to be reconciled to God (2 Cor 5:18–20; 6:2).

They have been made to be God's righteousness outside themselves, "in Christ," in whom this exchange of life and death has taken place.

Excursus: Luther on Justification

The understanding of justification as an event located in the crucified and risen Christ in which the fallen human being is made new is not entirely alien to our ears. Indeed, Paul's categories are at some points so remarkably close to those of Luther, or, more properly stated, Luther's are so close to those of Paul, that it is natural to recall the Reformer when reading the Pauline texts. One thinks, for example, of *The Freedom of a Christian*, where Luther discusses the power of faith to "unite the soul" to Christ in a true marriage, so that the two become one flesh. As a result, there is a "wondrous exchange" between the two, so that our "sins, death, and damnation" belong to Christ, and his "grace, life, and salvation" become ours. That is so, Luther explains, because of the "blessed struggle" that takes place in Christ, the human being who is God. As a human being, he took upon himself all that is ours. Yet he remains God, whose righteousness, life, and salvation are unconquerable, eternal, and omnipotent. In union and exchange with him, our sin is swallowed up in his righteousness. We are thus endowed with an eternal righteousness. Luther speaks in similar ways elsewhere, especially in the 1535 Galatians commentary, perhaps most dramatically in his discussion of Gal 3:13 ("Christ redeemed us from the curse of the Law, having become a curse for us"). Here again, he describes "the doctrine of righteousness" in terms of a battle, or duel, in which sin and righteousness both come to be "located" in the one person of Christ. Because Christ is "the divine Power, Righteousness, Blessing, Grace, and Life," he conquers and destroys the "monsters" of "sin, death, and the curse." These "monsters" attack him, because in taking on our sins, Christ "became" the maximal sinner, the greatest thief, adulterer, murderer. It is not that he was such a person in himself, but he put on our clothing and mask: he took upon himself our sinful person, in order to give us his innocent and victorious person. Furthermore, and wonderfully, just as in the risen Christ there is no more "mask of a sinner or vestige of death," so these things are no longer in our person, because he took upon himself that which was ours. Thus, Luther says, we confess in the Apostles' Creed, "I believe in the holy church," even though our reason and our eyes tell us otherwise. Paul could well affirm this truth with respect to the Corinthians! Here Luther's understanding of justification as an effective event in Christ is evident. More than once in his discussion of Gal 3:13, Luther appeals to 2 Cor 5:21, in order to reinforce his point that Christ not only bore the curse of the Law, but became a curse.

Luther also speaks of God not imputing sin to us, and imputing righteousness to us for the sake of Christ or for the sake of faith. The personal dimension of justification comes to expression here, just as it does with Paul. The language of imputation describes God's extralegal act of forgiving our sins, and therewith God's personal recognition and acceptance of us, unacceptable though we are. Luther also describes Christ's atoning *work* in itself. Yet, for Luther, God grants us Christ's benefits because Christ, who is grasped by faith, is present in the heart, in the way that a ring clasps a gem. Here, as earlier, Luther speaks of Christ as our righteousness. Luther did not reject the alternative, more narrowly forensic understanding of justification that Melanchthon offered, but his understanding went well beyond it.

The difference between Luther and Melanchthon appears quite clearly in a letter written by Melanchthon to Johannes Brenz on May 12, 1531, to which Luther adds a note of his own. Brenz had adopted at this point a basically Augustinian understanding of justification, which had been the topic of correspondence between him and Melanchthon. Now Melanchthon and Luther offer advice and correction, each in his own way. A brief section of Melanchthon's response suffices to show his thought: "Thus we are righteous by faith alone, not because faith is the root (sc. of renewal), as you write, but because it grasps Christ, for whose sake we are accepted."

In a concluding note, Luther adds his own thought, which we may cite at greater length:

> I, too, in order to grasp this matter better, picture for myself that there is nothing in my heart of this quality, which might be called faith or love, but rather in its place, I set Christ himself, and say: this is my righteousness, he himself is the quality and my formal righteousness (as they say), in order that I free myself from looking upon the Law and works, and even from looking at the object itself, Christ, insofar as he is understood as a teacher or giver of gifts. But I want him to be to me the gift and teaching in himself, in order that I might have all things in him. Thus he says, "I am the way, the truth, and the life." He does not say, "I give you the way, the truth, and the life," as if it were at work within me from without. It is necessary for him to be, to live, and to speak, not through me, but in me (εἰς ἐμέ) 2 Cor 6[5]: in order that we might become righteousness in him, not in love or in the gifts that follow (sc. faith).

Here we again find with Luther the same structure of thought concerning justification that appears in *The Freedom of a Christian* and the Galatians commentary. While he certainly does not stand at odds with Melanchthon, the distance between them is apparent.

The basic outlines of Luther's understanding of justification become apparent in the brief examples that we have considered, even if his thought on the topic is broader and more complex. Justification for Luther is an event, indeed, a battle and struggle. This battle has taken place in the person of Christ, who as true God and true human has taken our place, and, in the communication of these attributes with one another, has overcome sin and death for us. It is faith that unites us with the crucified and risen Christ, so that in a relationship of communication, our sin and death are his, and his righteousness is made ours. As is the case with Paul, the event of the cross and resurrection becomes an event in us and for us in faith. There thus comes to be an abiding relationship of communication between the sinner and Christ, by which our sin is overcome. Our justification involves our being relocated outside ourselves, and placed in Christ. In him, for Luther as well as for Paul, there is a new creation, in which we are not only declared righteous, but made righteous by being made entirely new. This "eccentricity" of our righteousness, and indeed, of our entire life, is especially apparent in Luther's response to Brenz, in which he distinguishes his understanding from both that of Augustine and that of the scholastic theologians. We may well speak of Luther's conception of justification as an "effective justification," just as we may with Paul. To be sure, there are differences between Paul and Luther, which we cannot explore here. Luther's thought is quite understandably much more developed christologically than that of Paul. He speaks explicitly of a communication between the divine and human nature of Christ in the drama of salvation. Nevertheless, while Paul does not employ the categories of Chalcedon, the basic idea that we find with Luther is present in Paul's presentation of Christ in the Corinthian correspondence.

Justification as a Hermeneutical Event

There are significant ways in which Luther's appropriation of Paul's understanding of justification as an effective (and, to be sure, forensic) act of God in Christ speaks to two basic questions that have plagued the usual Protestant understanding of justification: the question of why faith is not a work, and similarly, the question of what connection exists between an extrinsic justification and the good works of a Christian. A basis for an answer to these questions has emerged already from the three texts from the

Corinthian correspondence that we have considered: Paul "locates" our justification in Christ and God's saving work in him. The one who has Christ has the whole of salvation, including the gift of faith itself. If Christ in his saving work is not ours, we have nothing at all.

Yet we also have touched upon another dimension of Paul's descriptions of justification that has relevance not only to how we understand justification, but also to how we understand ourselves, God, and the world. Paul's descriptions of justification as God's effective work in Christ in the Corinthian context are irreducibly hermeneutical statements. Indeed, it is arguable that their very form as statements of an effective act of God is due to their hermeneutical function in Paul's argument.

We may recall that Paul's opening statement on justification in 1 Cor 1:30 appears within a hermeneutically charged context. Paul's point in this verse is that Christ is God's counterwisdom to the rebellious and self-seeking wisdom of the world, and that it was God himself who "placed" the Corinthians in Christ, who thus became their wisdom in ways they could not have imagined, namely, "righteousness, holiness, and redemption." The Spirit who disclosed the "mystery" of God found in the crucified Jesus to the apostle did so through him as well to the Corinthians (1 Cor 2:1–5). The Corinthians had been "interpreted" by God in Christ, together with the "world" from which they had been removed. Their wisdom had been shown to be folly in the crucified Jesus.

The same hermeneutical dynamic is at work in 2 Cor 5:21. Only in this verse in Second Corinthians does Paul speak of Christ in his saving work and of "sin" in a theological sense. His epigrammatic description of God's saving work in Christ serves to fill in the "christological deficit" of his presentation of the nature of apostolic ministry in 2 Cor 3:1–18, where he begins his answer to the question of what constitutes the marks of an apostle. Are they to be found in the rhetoric, charisma, and power that Paul's opponents display? Or are they to be found in the apostle of the crucified Christ, who himself is thrust into distress and trial again and again? Paul's appeal to the story of Moses' ministry of the Law is not intended to combat advocates of Judaizing (who nowhere appear in the Corinthian correspondence), but to expose what is at stake in Corinth in the figures found in Scripture. The thrust of the argument is distinctly hermeneutical in nature. Paul does not speak of "Christ" and "the Law" but of "the letter" and "the Spirit." The fallen state of the "sons of Israel" is manifest in their inability to look upon the glory of Moses' face. Moses' act of judgment in placing a veil over his face then prevented them from doing so: "their minds were hardened." Only "in Christ" is the old covenant that brought this condemnation done away (2 Cor 3:14). Just as Moses removed the veil over his face only when he "turned to the Lord" in the tent of meeting, there is freedom only where the Spirit is present, namely, in the apostolic proclamation of the crucified and risen Christ (3:16–17). In the face of the doubts of the Corinthians, Paul asserts the glory of the apostolic ministry that is seen only through the ears. Like the first word of the Creator, the gospel performs a hermeneutical function, opening the mind and heart of the fallen human being to see the glory of God in the person of Christ (4:6).

The same hermeneutical concern appears within the larger context of 2 Cor 5:21, in which Paul describes himself as an "agent of reconciliation with God" (5:11–21). He wants the Corinthians to see beyond those who boast in appearance (5:12). As one captured by the love of Christ, he no longer judges anyone "according to the flesh." Indeed, even if he once judged Christ in this way, he does so no longer (5:17). In Christ there is a new creation, in which he has been reconciled to God—a reconciliation that entails the overcoming of his blindness and rebellion. As the apostle of Christ, he now urges the Corinthians to be reconciled to God—to have their blindness overcome in Christ (5:20). His concise and powerful description of God's justifying work in Christ in 5:21 is to serve a hermeneutical function in God's hand, opening the eyes of the Corinthians to see the truth about God and themselves as it is manifest in the crucified and risen Christ.

The hermeneutical function of God's justifying work that appears so clearly in the Corinthian correspondence should provoke us to further reflection on Paul's description of justification elsewhere. That is especially so in Romans, where he twice announces the "revelation" of God's righteousness (Rom 1:16–17; 3:21–26). It is also the case in Galatians, where Paul insists on the "truth of the gospel" (Gal 2:5, 14) and associates the knowledge of God with the message of faith (3:5; 4:9). It is not clear that we have fathomed the hermeneutical implications of Paul's teaching on justification, nor that they have been widely appreciated. The material basis of this hermeneutic in the cross and resurrection of Christ implies not only our need for our blindness to be overcome, but also the limit to our reasoning with respect to God and God's work. It also points us to the true subject matter of theology, namely, "the human being guilty of sin and condemned *and* God the justifier and Savior of the sinner."

17

Doubting "Doubting Thomas"

—William C. Weinrich

That James Voelz merits the public appreciation of friends and peers such as this volume intends is clear to all who know him. As it happened, my own personal sojourn as a theological student and as one who teaches theological students has paralleled and coincided with that of Jim. We have been friends and colleagues for a long time, and no one has my respect for intellectual vigor and theological integrity more than does James Voelz. May then what follows prove worthy both of his merits and of my high regard.

The climactic scenes of the Gospel of John are those of the appearance of the resurrected Jesus first to the disciples with Thomas absent (20:19–23) and then again to the disciples with Thomas present (20:24–29). In the first scene Jesus appears to the disciples, who are behind closed doors "out of fear for the Jews." Assuming a position in their midst, Jesus, in succession, greets them with the declaration "Peace be unto you"[1] (εἰρήνη ὑμῖν), shows them his hands and side, repeats the greeting "Peace be unto you," commissions the disciples, breathes upon them the Holy Spirit, and grants to them the authority to loose and retain sins (20:19–23). We then learn that Thomas was absent at the time of that first appearance. Upon hearing the testimony of the disciples, "We have seen the Lord!" Thomas declares, "Unless I see in his hands the mark (τύπον) of the nails and place my finger into the place (τόπον) of the nails and place my hand into his side, I will in no wise believe" (20:25).[2]

---

1. Unless otherwise noted, all biblical translations are cited from the RSV.
2. Against the reading of some manuscripts (and Nestle-Aland, 27th ed.) that read

The strong conditional introduction to the words of Thomas (ἐὰν μὴ ἴδω) and the equally strong negation (οὐ μὴ πιστεύσω) give to Thomas's reply the character of vigorous and insistent determination. They have also given to Thomas the common, traditional, and popular reputation of being "doubting" Thomas. As such, Thomas has found himself to be the prime example of weak faith, false faith, and even no faith in homily, hymn, and commentary. A few illustrations will suffice. Proclus of Constantinople (c. 450) rhetorically depicts the unbelief of Thomas as occasion for the firm belief of the Christian: "O Thomas, continue, do continue with your beautiful disbelief.... Be an unbeliever, be an unbeliever even more, in order that I may firmly believe."[3] Thomas as doubter appears also in the well-known hymn "O Sons and Daughters of the King":

> That night the apostles met in fear;
> Among them came their master dear
> And said, "My peace be with you here."
>
> When Thomas first the tidings heard
> That they had seen the risen Lord,
> He doubted the disciples' word.[4]

Commentary has hardly been more charitable to Thomas. Lagrange claims that Thomas responded to the disciples' witness "with a frigid denial." Morris writes of Thomas as a "hard-headed disciple," a "skeptic," and of his "blank incredulity." Moloney writes in more measured terms. Thomas possesses a "conditioned faith" that Jesus will command him to transcend.[5]

τύπον twice, we favor those witnesses that have both τύπον and τόπον (A Q 078 0250 pc lat sys.h). Cf. Brown, *Gospel according to John (xiii–xxi)*, 1025.

3. Proclus of Constantinople, Homily 33, in *Homilies on the Life of Christ*, 185.

4. See *Lutheran Service Book* (St. Louis: Concordia, 2006), hymn 470, stanzas 4 and 5. Even more poetically critical of Thomas is the hymn "These Things Did Thomas Count as Real" (*Lutheran Service Book*, hymn 472):

> The vision of his skeptic mind,
> Was keen enough to make him blind,
> To any unexpected act,
> Too large for his small world of fact.
> His reasoned certainties denied,
> That one could live when one had died,
> Until his fingers read like Braille,
> The markings of the spear and nail.

In his novel *The Haunted Hotel*, the nineteenth-century novelist Wilkie Collins refers to Thomas as the "celebrated saint and doubter."

5. Lagrange, *Évangile selon Saint Jean*, 517: "par une froide denegation"; Morris,

Why did the words of Thomas receive this common opprobrium? Certainly a principle cause is indicated by Barrett: "Doubting the resurrection is . . . a feature of all the gospels." He cites Matt 28:17; Mark 16:14; Luke 24:11, 25, 37, 41.[6] Thus, the demonstration of the wounds of Jesus is simply situated in the Gospel tradition for a distinctly apologetic, antidocetic purpose, and Thomas's initial refusal to accept the testimony of his fellows must be interpreted accordingly. Thomas, for whatever reason, does not believe the reality of the resurrection of Jesus. Most commonly the resurrection appearances in John's Gospel are compared with those in Luke, and, to be sure, in Luke the appearance of Jesus to the disciples is explicitly associated with their startled fear that they were seeing a "spirit" (ἐδόκουν πνεῦμα θεωρεῖν). Jesus' response to this is to show his hands and feet to the disciples and exhort them to touch him and see "that a spirit has not flesh and bones as you see that I have" (Luke 24:36-40).[7] The apologetic intent is evident: the Jesus who appears to the disciples is identical with him who was crucified. He who was crucified is risen from the dead! Given what seems to be similar scenes (the same scene?) in Luke and in John, it is not surprising that already in the second century the Lukan and Johannine resurrection narratives were conflated. In a distinctly antidocetic context, the *Epistula Apostolorum* (c. 140) reports:

> And he came and found us inside, veiled. And we doubted and did not believe. He came before us like a ghost and we did not believe that it was he. But it was he. And thus he said to us, "Come, and do not be afraid. I am your teacher whom you, Peter, denied three times; and now do you deny again?" And we went to him, thinking and doubting whether it was he. And he said to us, "Why do you doubt and why are you not believing? I am he who spoke to you concerning my flesh, my death, and my resurrection. And that you may know that it is I, lay your hand, Peter, (and your finger) in the nailprint of my hands; and you,

---

Gospel according to John, 751-52; Moloney, *The Gospel of John*, 537. Cf. also *Concordia Self-Study Bible*, 1647: "Hardheaded skepticism can scarcely go further than this."

6. Barrett, *Gospel according to St. John*, 571. As Barrett notes, the observation was made earlier by Dodd, *Tradition in the Fourth Gospel*, 145: the Thomas episode is "a dramatization (in our author's manner) of the traditional motive of the incredulity of some or all of the disciples."

7. Common to the resurrection appearances in both Luke and John are the following: Jesus stands in their midst, Jesus gives the greeting of "Peace be unto you," Jesus shows the marks of his passion (hand and feet in Luke, hands and side in John), Jesus asks the disciples to touch him (all the disciples in Luke, Thomas only in John), the disciples respond to the sight of Jesus with joy (although in Luke this joy is the cause of the disciples' ongoing disbelief).

Thomas, in my side; and also you, Andrew, see whether my foot steps on the ground and leaves a footprint. For it is written in the prophet, 'But a ghost, a demon, leaves no print on the ground.'" But now we felt him, that he had truly risen in the flesh.[8]

However, is it legitimate to interpret John's report concerning Thomas by way of the narrative of Luke? Even if the scenes of Luke and of John are of the same tradition, it hardly follows that John's thematic appropriation of the appearance of Jesus is merely that of Luke.[9] More convincing would be an interpretation that allows the Gospel of John itself to establish the thematic basis for understanding Thomas's demand. As the epithet of "doubting" Thomas and other such characterizations indicate, the Thomas scene is frequently interpreted according to what we might call a faith profile. Literary approaches to the Gospel seem to be especially tempted in this direction. An example is the recent study by William Bonney, who subtitles his treatment of Thomas's statement "Thomas' Statement in Light of the Manner in Which John Portrays Him."[10] Thomas appears twice earlier in the Gospel (John 11:16; 14:5). In the first Thomas expresses his willingness to die with Jesus; in the second Thomas admits that he does not understand Jesus' word about his "way." From these small entries Bonney depicts Thomas as a "realist" who is "worldly-wise" and expresses himself with sarcasm and an "acerbic tongue." Thus Thomas's response to the disciples' report that they had seen the Lord is "in keeping with his character." "He ridicules their claim with an exaggerated realism." It is easier to see Thomas's demand to see the wounds of Jesus as "befitting a personality that tends towards sarcasm than it is to see it as a genuine request to probe Jesus' wounds."[11]

---

8. *Epistula Apostolorum* 11-12, in *New Testament Apocrypha*, vol. 1, *Gospels and Related Writings*, 255-56. See also Ignatius of Antioch, *To the Smyrnaeans* 3:1: "For I know and believe that even after the resurrection he was in the flesh. Indeed, when he came to those around Peter, he said to them, 'Take hold and touch me, and see that I am not a disembodied spirit'" (δαιμόνιον ἀσώματον).

9. It is a commonplace that John knew and wrote in response to or in interaction with the Synoptic tradition. A vigorous example of this view is Thyen, *Das Johannesevangelium*. In his introduction he expresses his opinion that John engages in an "intertextual play" with the Old Testament and with the Synoptic Gospels in their traditional redacted forms, that is, with Mark as well as with Matthew and Luke as we have them (p. 4). My own opinion is that the Evangelist John either did not know the Synoptic Gospels or did not use them. His Gospel in form, content, and characters is so different as to make the assumption, let alone the certainty, of Synoptic influence highly dubious.

10. Bonney, *Caused to Believe*, 158.

11. Ibid., 158-59. Also: "Thomas' words in 20:25 are more likely a sarcastic expression of unbelief than a request for proof" (159-60).

If Thomas's demand to see the wounds of Jesus is a piece of sarcasm expressed out of a "realistic" worldview, then, of course, the appearance of Jesus functions to overcome and transform Thomas's character defect. What effect this change are Jesus' words (μὴ γίνου ἄπιστος ἀλλὰ πιστός), which Bonney translates "Stop being unbelieving; become believing."

> Thomas' response (20:28) makes it clear to the reader that he has undergone such a personal change.... Radically changed, Thomas can only utter, "My Lord and my God" (20:28).... John demonstrates that, in order for Thomas to gain his vision, his earth-bound mode of being had to be transcended by the only one who has access to heavenly realities, God's Son. John presents faith not as something that can be generated from within the potential believer, as an act of human will. It can only come through the will of God, in an act of grace. The reader here sees Jesus revealed as the agent of Thomas' change.[12]

However correct these comments might be in themselves, one may well doubt that they express the narrative intent of John. It is not the intention of the Gospel of John to "present faith" or to depict the stages of faith.[13] As the prologue affirms, the Gospel of John intends to present the eternal Word of God in the flesh (1:14–18). As elementary as it seems, the enfleshed Word is and remains throughout John's Gospel the unique and only focus of the evangelical presentation: "Not the consistency of a figure, rather the consistency of the material content and intent of the Gospel remains in the foreground, when Jesus is depicted in his meetings with individual persons."[14] If the demand of Thomas to see the nail prints in the hands of Jesus and to place his hand into Jesus' side has its legitimacy in fundamental thematic claims of the Gospel as a whole, then far from being a doubter, Thomas insists on experiencing precisely what the Gospel proclamation promotes and promises.

Hengel noted that in John's Gospel a concentration of statements concerning the fulfillment of Scripture occurs in reference to the death of

---

12. Ibid., 166–68.

13. Cf. Moloney, *The Gospel of John*, 537. Commenting on Thomas's confession (John 20:28), he writes: "Parallel with the faith journeys of the Beloved Disciple and Mary Magdalene (cf. vv. 8, 18), this final statement of faith in Jesus concludes Thomas' journey of faith."

14. Kohler, *Kreuz und Menschwerdung*, 173 (my translation). "The consistency of the material content and intent of the Gospel" is my attempt to render the meaning of Kohler's more simple "die Konsistenz der Sache." Kohler is rightly rejecting attempts to give a "Charakterbild des Thomas" that depict him as a "Prototyp des Glaubensschwachen."

Jesus or within the passion narrative itself. Moreover, a change of terminology marks this density. While earlier in the Gospel the Scriptures were introduced by the rather commonplace formula "it is written" (γεγραμμένον ἐστίν: 2:17; 6:31, 45; 10:34; 12:14, 16) or by the usual term for the fulfilling of Scripture (πληρόω: 12:38; 13:18; 15:25; 17:12; 19:24, 36), in the scene of Jesus' death itself the Evangelist employs the terminology of completion (19:28–30: τελέω; τελειόω).[15] Only here does the Gospel speak of the Scriptures coming to their completion or to their end (19:28: ἵνα τελειωθῇ). In contrast to the more formulaic "to fulfill" (πληρόω), this is an intensification of the terminology and presents the death of Jesus as the concluding fulfillment of all christological prophecies and pronouncements of the Scripture.[16] Moreover, this reference to the completion of the Scriptures is placed between the twofold "it is completed" (τετέλεσται) by which Jesus expresses his victorious claim that the purpose of his sending has been faithfully brought to its end and that his identity as the Son has been manifested and vindicated: "My food is that I do the will of him who sent me and bring his work to completion" (τελειώσω; 4:34). In the perfect enactment of the Father's will, the unity of Jesus' will with that of the Father is manifested, that is, Jesus as the true Son of the Father is manifested.

The twofold τετέλεσται of Jesus brings the initial claims of the prologue to their conclusion. The ἐν ἀρχῇ of John 1:1 indicates from the outset that the story of Jesus would be the account of a new creation and that his story would be the revelation of the Truth that consummates the various shadows and figures of the Old Testament (cf. 1:17; 5:39, 45–47). With his cry of "it is completed," Jesus proclaims that what was "in the beginning" has been revealed in the reality of its final purpose (ἐν ἀρχῇ—τετέλεσται).[17] The purpose and goal of Jesus' coming has been accomplished, and that precisely in his death (cf. 12:27). Secondly, Jesus knew that "all things were now completed" (ἤδη πάντα τετέλεσται: 19:28). The πάντα echoes 1:3: "All things

---

15. The employment of πληρόω to speak of the fulfillment of the Scriptures is already wholly in view of the passion of Jesus. It appears in John 12:38 as the first explicit mention of the fulfillment of the Scriptures, namely, when Jesus has entered Jerusalem and reference to his death has taken center stage (12:32).

16. See Hengel, "Schriftauslegung," 278–79; also Frey, "Die 'theologia crucifixi,'" 222–23.

17. As is often noted, the ἐν ἀρχῇ of John 1:1 echoes the ἐν ἀρχῇ of Gen 1:1 (LXX). While, however, the beginning of Gen 1:1 appears to be temporal ("at the beginning"), the beginning of John 1:1 has no temporal sense. It refers to the preexistent, eternal reality of God "in which" the Word "was." The narrative of Jesus, therefore, does not express a will that, so to speak, is contingent to God's being. The story of Jesus reveals the will of God to redeem the world, a will that lies intrinsic to the Word and so a will that reveals God *as he is* (see 1 John 4:7–10).

happened through him" (πάντα δι' αὐτοῦ ἐγένετο), where "all things" refers not to the universal, first creation, but to the narrative content of the Old Testament.[18] In this way as well, Jesus' cry of "it is completed" announces that *in his death* the story of God's work of redemption for the life of the world has reached its end. Finally, Jesus' cry proclaims the fact that *in his death* the flesh, that is, man, has united his will with that of God. "The Word became flesh" (1:14) thematically announces that the flesh of the Word will be not only the instrument but also the instantiation of the divine glory. In the death of Jesus man participates in the will of God to give eternal life to the world.[19] "It is completed"—man has become, in Jesus the crucified, the manifestation of the divine glory.[20]

The "it is completed" of Jesus makes evident that in this Gospel the crucifixion requires no addition. In it lies revealed the full reality of the manifestation of God, the Truth of the Old Testament and of the consummation of God's will to save. This is also demonstrated in one other unique characteristic of John's Gospel, his depiction of Jesus' crucifixion as his "exaltation."[21] One point must be emphasized at the outset. In the language

---

18. The terminology of ἐγένετο clearly derives from Genesis (LXX Gen 1:3, 5, 6, 8, 9, 11). However, elsewhere in the prologue ἐγένετο has historical referents (John 1:6, 14). Moreover, the following present perfect refers to the event of Jesus' mission that is the subject matter of the Gospel (John 1:3c–4a: ὃ γέγονεν ἐν αὐτῷ ζωὴ ἦν). That requires that the previous two occurences ἐγένετο have historical, not cosmological, referents as well. See Pollard, "Cosmology and the Prologue of the Fourth Gospel," 147–53.

19. See John 3:14–15. As whoever looked upon the bronze serpent received healing, so whoever believes may *in the Crucified* has eternal life. The "lifted up" Jesus is the *locus* of eternal life. Not surprisingly, therefore, in the postresurrection appearance of Jesus to his disciples, the demonstration of the marks of his crucifixion leads straightway to Jesus' sending his disciples as the Father sent him (John 20:20–21).

20. Hengel ("Schriftauslegung," 279) speaks of Jesus' twofold τετέλεσται as the expression of his "knowledge of the end and his death cry" (*Todesschrei*). But Jesus' "it is completed" is not a death cry, at least not in the Gospel of John. In no way does this Evangelist depict the crucifixion of Jesus as a humiliation. It is the manifestation of God's will to redeem, of the true filial obedience of the Son, and so the manifestation of the divine glory. "The manifestation of the Son is knowledge of the Father" (Irenaeus, *Adversus haereses* 4.6.3). Thus, Jesus' cry is the shout of victory (cf. John 16:33).

21. The terminology comes from Isa 52:13. The servant of God "shall be exalted and glorified exceedingly" (LXX: ὑψωθήσεται καὶ δοξασθήσεται σφόδρα). As this passage suggests, the language of glorification in John's Gospel also focuses on the crucifixion of Jesus. See John 12:28: πάτερ, δόξασόν σου τὸ ὄνομα. The context assumes the Gethsemane scene, and Jesus' consent to the will of his Father. Here "glorify" means "crucify your Name and *thereby and therein* reveal his glory, that is, your glory as well." In this article we will discuss only the "exaltation" passages, which suffice for our purpose.

of "exaltation" the Evangelist refers only and exclusively to the crucifixion of Jesus.[22] A brief review of the three exaltation passages will make this clear.

The terminology of "exaltation" for the crucifixion of Jesus appears three times in John's Gospel (3:14; 8:28; 12:32). In the first, the "lifting up" of Jesus is presented as corresponding to the lifting up of the bronze serpent on the pole (Num 21:4-9). However, the Evangelist does not present only a typological correspondence; as Frey has rightly argued, the "theological depiction" gives a broad set of correspondences. In addition to the lifting up of the serpent and of Jesus, the looking at the serpent finds its correspondent in faith (Num 21:8; John 3:15), and the remaining alive finds its correspondent in the eternal life that the one who believes has in the Crucified (LXX Num 21:8: ζήσεται; John 3:15: ἐν αὐτῷ ἔχῃ ζωὴν αἰώνιον).[23] As the typology of the lifted-up serpent makes evident, the "lifting up" (ὑψωθῆναι) of the Son of Man in John 3:14 can refer only to the crucifixion of Jesus.

In the second occurrence of ὑψοῦν, the Jews are the subject of the verb: "When you have lifted up the Son of Man, then you will [have] knowledge that I AM" (John 8:28). Obviously, here any reference to the resurrection or ascension of Jesus is excluded. To be noted, however, is the association between the crucifixion of Jesus and the knowledge of God. Given the context of the Feast of Tabernacles in which the passage occurs (cf. 7:2), the background of this association is very likely prophecies such as those of Isaiah and Ezekiel that promise a new exodus from bondage and the reconstitution of a new and obedient Israel (see Isa 43:16-19; 60:1-22; Ezek 37:12-14). If indeed such texts are in view, the prophecy of Ezekiel 37:12-14 is especially noteworthy: "And I will bring you into the land of Israel. And you shall know that I am the LORD when I open your graves and raise you from your graves, O my people. And I will put my Spirit within you, and you shall live, and I will place you in your own land." In John's Gospel the new exodus and the reconstitution of new Israel take place in the "exaltation" of the Son of Man. Here again, as in John 3:14-15, the "exaltation" of Jesus and the giving of life are connected.

---

22. Not infrequently, commentators efface the theology of the cross of John's Gospel by claiming that the language of "exaltation" includes the resurrection and ascension of Jesus. For example, Raymond Brown comments: "The phrase 'to be lifted up' refers to Jesus' death on the cross.... However, the verb *hypsoun*, 'to be lifted up,' is used in Acts (ii 33, v 31) for references to the ascension of Jesus.... Thus, in John 'being lifted up' refers to one continuous action of ascent: Jesus begins his return to his Father as he approaches death (xiii 1) and completes it only with his ascension (xx 17)" (*Gospel according to John I-XII*, 145-46). This is a good example of foisting the structure of Luke upon John. See rather Frey, who writes of the *Staurozentrik* of the language of "exaltation" ("Die 'theologia crucifixi,'" 228-31). Also Knöppler, *Die theologie crucis*, 154-65.

23. Frey, "Die 'theologia crucifixi,'" 228.

In the third occurrence of ὑψοῦν, reference to the cross and to the attendant ideas briefly elaborated above becomes thematically more explicit. In a highly charged eschatological context,[24] Jesus says, "And I, when I am lifted up from the earth, I will draw all to myself" (John 12:32). The Evangelist himself makes the singular reference to the cross evident when he explains, "This he said, indicating by what death he was going to die" (12:33). The point is reinforced when, at the moment the Jews hand Jesus over to the Romans to be crucified, the Evangelist reminds the reader of the words of Jesus: "[This happened] in order that the word of Jesus which he spoke indicating by what death he was going to die might be fulfilled" (18:32).

The term "exaltation" suggests an eschatological finality beyond which there is no further revelation. It is wholly probable that the Evangelist knew of the employment of exaltation language to refer to the ascension of Jesus. As the exalted One, Jesus is Lord and the mission of the church begins.[25] In John 12:32 Jesus associates his crucifixion with the promise that he will draw all people to himself. In doing so, Jesus gives to his crucifixion universal salvific significance and effectiveness that extend beyond the resurrection and encompass the mission of the church. The phraseology of Jesus requires some comment. Jesus says, "And I, when I am lifted up *from the earth*" (ἐὰν ὑψωθῶ ἐκ τῆς γῆς). The phrase "from the earth" is apparently inspired by Genesis 2:6–7 (LXX), which speaks of the creation of Adam.[26] Be that as it may, the phrase corresponds to the earlier parable of Jesus concerning "the seed of wheat" (ὁ κόκκος τοῦ σίτου) that, unless it "falling into the earth should die" (πεσὼν εἰς τὴν γῆν ἀποθάνῃ), remains alone. But should it die, it bears much fruit (John 12:24). The seed of wheat is Jesus himself, and the language of falling "into the earth" and dying refers to his death. His death is then immediately associated with the bearing of much fruit, that is, with the mission of the church through which Jesus acquires many disciples (see 12:25–26). The resurrection and ascension/mission lie

---

24. Note the terms "hour" (John 12:27) and the repeated "now" (νῦν) marking the time of the judgment of the world (κρίσις) and the casting out of "the ruler of this world" (12:31). The association of these markers with the "exaltation" of Jesus reinforces the point that the cross bears full eschatological significance.

25. This is the exact sequence of Luke-Acts (Luke 24:44–49; Acts 1:8–11) and of Matthew (Matt 28:18–20).

26. Frey suggests Isa 53:8b (LXX) as background: "In his humiliation the judgment is taken away; who will declare his generation? For his life is taken away from the earth (ἀπὸ τῆς γῆς)" ("Die 'theologia crucifixi,'" 229). If our suggestion that Old Testament texts such as Ezek 37:12–14 are background has merit, we might also suggest that "from the earth" is similar to the language of resurrection in Ezek 37:12, 13 (LXX): ἐκ τῶν μνημάτων, ἐκ τῶν τάφων.

within the death of Jesus and come forth from it. Precisely this is suggested by Jesus' words, "When I am lifted up from the earth." In view of the "into the earth" of 12:24, the "from the earth" of 12:32 suggests Jesus' resurrection from the dead and his ascension to the Father. Jesus' further words, "I will draw all to myself," refer quite openly to the ongoing universal salvific efficacy of the Crucified One ("to myself") after Easter, that is, to the mission of the church as the ongoing mission of the Crucified. Yet as Frey notes, "The Fourth Evangelist, exactly in the context of Jn 12:32-34, holds fast to the fact that he intends by the term ὑψοῦσθαι to refer quite concretely to the event of the crucifixion of Jesus which precisely through the employment of this term and in the view of the post-resurrection understanding comes to expression *as salvific event (als Heilsgeschehen)*."[27] The crucifixion of Jesus is the place and the form of the Lordship of Jesus. According to the Gospel of John, the crucifixion of Jesus is not overcome by the resurrection and ascension, nor is it placed, as it were, in the past. Rather, the eschatological moment in all its aspects lies within the crucifixion of Jesus itself.

The crucifixion of Jesus expressed through the terminology of "completion" and "exaltation" gives necessary information for the interpretation of the Thomas episode.[28] On the evening of the day of resurrection, Jesus appears to the disciples, who, out of fear of the Jews,[29] have closed their doors. The focus and interest in the scene specific to John may be clarified by comparing it with the parallel scene in Luke.[30] Jesus appears and stands in their midst and greets them with "Peace be unto you." In Luke's account this appearance causes the disciples to be startled and frightened because

---

27. Frey, "Die 'theologia crucifixi,'" 229.

28. One could also consider those passages that speak of the eschatological "hour" of Jesus (John 2:4; 7:30; 8:20; 12:23, 27; 13:1). See Knöppler, *Die theologie crucis*, 102-15. Most helpful in the interpretation of the Thomas episode are Kohler, *Kreuz und Menschwerdung*, 163-91; Frey, "Die 'theologia crucifixi,'" 231-36; and Knöppler, 266-68.

29. It is possible that this aspect of the scene corresponds to John 12:42, which is part of the concluding section of the first major part of the Gospel. Many from the "leaders" believed on Jesus, but because of the Pharisees "they did not confess," lest they be expelled from the synagogue. This "critique" may be important for the interpretation of Jesus' exhortation to Thomas to become πιστός (John 20:27).

30. Compare Luke 24:36-43 with John 20:19-23. Commentators often note the similarities and claim that John probably adopted the Lukan tradition and recast it for his purposes (e.g., Frey, "Die 'theologia crucifixi,'" 232). That both Gospels have the same event in view seems probable. Yet, why the certitude that John adopted Luke? I would claim the opposite. John wishes to emphasize the *identity* of the Resurrected as the Crucified (as we shall argue). That claim is an essential aspect arising from his *scriptural* argument against the Jews. Luke emphasizes the *physical reality* of the Resurrected, clearly against docetic counterclaims. This suggests a different, and later, polemic context.

they "thought that they were seeing a spirit" (Luke 24:37). Jesus' greeting of εἰρήνη ὑμῖν (if original) has no positive effect. Rather, the appearance of Jesus elicits in them fear and confusion because they thought Jesus was a "spirit" (πνεῦμα).³¹ John reports nothing like this. In John Jesus' greeting, εἰρήνη ὑμῖν, is immediately followed by his showing them his hands and his side. While in Luke the demonstration of Jesus' hands and feet intends to alleviate the disciple's fearful misunderstanding, in John Jesus takes the initiative in "showing" them his hands and side. The fact that Jesus continues to bear the signs of his crucifixion is central and significant. Several further factors, in contrast with Luke, serve to substantiate this fact. Firstly, it is quite evident that in the Lukan account the hands and feet, as the marks of Jesus' passion, are in themselves of no special importance. For, when Jesus entreats his disciples to touch and see that he is no "spirit," he mentions not his hands and feet but his flesh and bones. The antidocetic intent is determinative. In John, however, the marks of Jesus' passion, as such, remain central and the focus of attention (cf. John 20:25, 27: τύπος, τόπος). Secondly, in Luke, even after Jesus' demonstration of his flesh and bones, the joy of the disciples is deeply qualified: "And while they yet disbelieved from joy and wondered" (Luke 24:41).³² In John, on the other hand, Jesus' showing of his hands and side is the *cause* for bringing the disciples to joy: "Therefore, the disciples rejoiced (ἐχάρησαν οὖν), seeing the Lord" (John 20:20). Finally, straightway after this scene Jesus gives his greeting a second time, "Peace be unto you" (John 20:21). Thus, the twofold greeting, and the book-ending showing by Jesus of his wounds and the joy of the disciples, function to highlight the resurrected Jesus *as he who still bears the signs of his crucifixion*, as he who brings and is the reality of the eschatological peace. The identity of the resurrected Jesus is that of the crucified Jesus. Or, otherwise stated, the resurrected Jesus comes as the Crucified: "His identity lives entirely from the signa crucifixi. These point to the historical reality of the crucified man, Jesus of Nazareth. This Crucified One is resurrected into the *life* of the Crucified. That the Resurrected One bears the *signa crucifixi*, signifies moreover that he has not left his death *behind* him, rather has taken

---

31. Codex Beza (D) reads φάντασμα ("phantasm," "ghost"). Tertullian reports that this term stood in Marcion's text. There is doubt about the originality of καὶ λέγει αὐτοῖς· εἰρήνη ὑμῖν in Luke 24:36. While it has strong support ($\mathfrak{P}^{75}$ *rell*), it is missing in D and the Old Latin tradition. I am inclined to believe that copyists added the greeting in John to the Lukan account.

32. Two observations further indicate how qualified the disciples' joy is. Their joy is mentioned in a prepositional phrase that explains their continuing disbelief. Furthermore, their joy is mentioned in a genitive absolute construction; that is, their joy is circumstantial and does not receive the emphasis of a declarative statement.

it up *into* himself and now bears it about *on* himself."³³ The marks of the Crucified characterize the resurrected Jesus and, therefore, reveal how and in what manner the life of the resurrection appears and is lived.³⁴

Upon the second greeting Jesus sends his disciples *as the Father has sent me* (καθὼς ἀπέσταλκέν με ὁ πατήρ) and breathes upon them the Holy Spirit (John 20:21-22). The sending of Jesus was for the salvation of the world, that is, unto the "hour" of his cross (3:14-17; 4:34; 12:27). As the present perfect suggests (ἀπέσταλκεν), the sending of Jesus continues in the sending of his apostolic messengers (cf. 17:20-23). This does not mean that Jesus' sending is extended beyond itself, or that a sending of others, as it were, adds to the sending of Jesus. Rather, all apostolic mission lies within the cross of Jesus so that precisely in those whom Jesus sends is Jesus the crucified himself confronted.³⁵ In coming as the Crucified, Jesus comes as the Exalted (3:14; 8:28; 12:32). Therefore, it is thematically coherent with the rest of the Gospel that in the context of his appearance bearing the wounds of his passion, Jesus gives the Holy Spirit (see 1:29-34; 7:37-39; 19:30).

Thomas was absent from the first coming of Christ. We are not told why. However, when the disciples report to him, "We have seen the Lord," Thomas does not accept the sufficiency of their witness. He responds by demanding to see what the disciples have seen. But what did they see? Their report to Thomas was a simple claim, "We have seen the Lord." But what in fact they saw were the hands and side of Jesus, which Jesus himself had showed to them. Thus, the demand of Thomas is to behold and to experience the concrete form and manner of the Resurrected such as the disciples themselves beheld and experienced it. The simple report of the disciples was devoid precisely of this necessary qualification.³⁶

---

33. Kohler, *Kreuz und Menschwerdung*, 166 (my translation; italics Kohler's). The words "bears it about *on* himself" translate "*an* sich herumträgt."

34. From this perspective we can understand why Paul articulates his apostolicity in terms of his sufferings (see 2 Cor 4:7-12; 11:22-33; Gal 6:17), and why the martyr, precisely in his/her death, was a "witness."

35. In contrast to the Lukan account, Frey makes the essential point: "Yet more central than the proof of the physical-real nature of the body of the Resurrected One, here the question of the identity of the Resurrected One with that of the Crucified seems to be the question. This can in no other way be recognized than in the marks of the crucifixion. And this recognition brings the disciples to faith, so that they can now be sent out for preaching and the continuation of the work of Jesus" ("Die 'theologia crucifixi,'" 232, my translation).

36. Note the parallel between John 20:20 (ἰδόντες τὸν κύριον) and John 20:25 (ἑωράκαμεν τὸν κύριον). However, from John 20:20 the reader knows that "the Lord" is he who showed them his hands and feet. Thomas's demand is, so to speak, the demand that John 20:20 be also his experience.

The narrative, therefore, does not concern the person of Thomas. He is not a representative figure of weak faith; nor is he presented as a figure of one who demands sight over belief in the word. Nor does the demand of Thomas arise from a doubt that the one crucified has in truth arisen. Doubt about the fact of the resurrection is not the point. The figure of Thomas provides the occasion for the Evangelist to bring his christological narrative to its proper conclusion. The demand of Thomas that belief is to be given only to that one who was crucified for the life of the world arises out of the fabric of the Gospel of John as a whole. Belief in the Resurrected, therefore, is to be granted only if the Resurrected One comes *as* the one who was crucified: "The Easter stories of Jn 20:19–29, therefore, do not have the intent to show the Crucified to be the Resurrected One. Rather, the matter is the other way around. The intent is to make the Resurrected One recognizable as the Crucified. From such a recognition arises the Easter faith in Jesus Christ who in his personal identity as the Resurrected and Exalted One remains precisely the Crucified."[37]

Jesus' word to Thomas that he place his finger and hand into the marks of his wounds is in no way a word of rebuke. Nor is it an accommodation to "doubting" Thomas. Rather, Jesus in fact comes as he came previously to the disciples and grants to Thomas, not a proof of his resurrection, but an appearance of the Resurrected in the marks of the Crucified. Here again, as in John 20:19–20, the greeting of "Peace be unto you" is followed immediately by the demonstration of Jesus' wounds. The Evangelist does not report whether Thomas did in fact touch the wounds of Jesus. Apparently that does not matter. What does matter is that the appearance of the Resurrected as the Crucified is the constitutive fact of faith in the reality of that God who gives life to the world. And so, Thomas confesses: "My Lord and my God!" (20:28). Thomas's confession is, to be sure, the highest confession given in John's Gospel. However, it is not simply "the most remarkable confession of Jesus' divinity in the gospel."[38] Rather, the confession of Thomas is the doxological recognition of faith that the God of love and life comes and proffers himself and all that is his in and through the Crucified (cf. 1:1, 14–18; 3:14–16; 8:28; 12:45; 14:7).

The final words of Jesus in the Gospel of John are given in 20:29: "Because you have seen me, you have believed. Blessed are they who,

---

37. Frey, "Die 'theologia crucifixi,'" 235 (my translation). Frey speaks also of the Resurrected as the Crucified as the *Urdatum*, which constitutes the preaching of Easter (233). See also, Kohler, *Kreuz und Menschwerdung*, 174–79. Cf. Paul's statement in 1 Cor 1:23: "We preach Christ the crucified . . . , to those who are called, Jews as well as Greeks, Christ the power of God and the wisdom of God."

38. Bonney, *Caused to Believe*, 161.

although not having seen, yet have become believing."³⁹ These words of Jesus also are not a rebuke to the stance of Thomas, as though Jesus were saying, "You, Thomas, demanded sight in order to believe. Blessed are they who do not demand sight." Rather, Jesus' words are best taken with the following purpose statement of the Gospel. To the mind of the Evangelist, future generations are at no disadvantage because, unlike Thomas, they are not able to see or to touch the risen Crucified. It is the very purpose of "this book" to present the signs that Jesus did, so that "you might believe." The seeing of faith is possible through the witness of the Paraclete-Spirit, who gives witness through the Gospel of John itself (14:25-29; 16:13-22; 19:35; 20:30-31; 21:24). The meaning, then, is this: "Blessed are they who, although not having seen, yet have become believing. These things are written in order that you might believe."⁴⁰

One final reflection may be helpful. Upon exhorting Thomas to feel his hands and side, Jesus adds: "And do not show yourself to be one who is unfaithful but one who is faithful" (John 20:27: καὶ μὴ γίνου ἄπιστος ἀλλὰ πιστός). The terms ἄπιστος and πιστός are in John unique to this context and so demand some scrutiny. It is probable that the language of ἄπιστος/πιστός is related to Thomas's assertion that he will not believe unless he sees the wounds of Jesus (20:25: οὐ μὴ πιστεύσω). Thus, the terms are frequently translated "unbelieving/believing." Brown renders, "And do not persist in your disbelief, but become a believer."⁴¹ But Brown is of the opinion that Thomas doubts the reality of Jesus' resurrection.⁴² Our arguments above, however, suggest that this perspective leads to a thorough misunderstanding of John's intention. Another possibility concerning ἄπιστος and πιστός commends itself.

---

39. Of course, Jesus also speaks in the epilogue of John 21. Yet, even if John 21 is original, the Thomas episode and the following purpose statement (20:30-31) form a narrative climax to which concluding statements are added.

40. In my judgment, the Gospel of John is a thoroughly sacramental text. Therefore, the "not having seen" of future believers is not to say that they have nothing to see. They cannot see as Thomas and the other disciples saw. What they do see is the coming of the Crucified in baptism (3:3-16) and in the Eucharistic Bread from heaven (6:30-58).

41. Brown, *Gospel according to John (XIII-XXI)*, 1026.

42. Brown avers that the Johannine narrative assumes the Lukan account, in which doubt in the physical reality is up front. That John has no reference to doubt, in Brown's opinion, makes Jesus' showing of his wounds in John 20:20 "illogical." Originally, he suggests, an expression of doubt existed, but "the evangelist has transferred this doubt to a separate episode and personified it in Thomas." "The doubt now expressed by Thomas is used by the evangelist as an apologetic means of emphasizing the tangible character of Jesus' body, just as Luke xxiv 41-43 has Jesus answer the continuing doubt of the disciples by eating" (ibid., 1032). Luke again trumps John!

Long ago, in discussing the second-century grave marker of Aberkios of Hierapolis, Franz Joseph Dölger noted that terms such as "friends" (φίλοι: cf. John 15:9–17) and "faithful" (πιστοί) were terms of associates or comrades who shared common commitments and expressed those common commitments in the context of communal feasting. Friends or the faithful were those who participated together in the meal that defined their common allegiance: "Only the baptized or those who have accepted the Faith and at baptism ceremoniously have confessed, namely, those who for that reason were called πιστοί and *fideles*, were allowed to partake of the Eucharistic celebration, for that was the *mysterium fidei*."[43] Although he uses ἄπιστοι rather than πιστοί, Melito of Sardis clearly has such associations in mind. Referring to the Egyptians on the night of Passover, he writes: "Then came the angel to strike Egypt, the uninitiated (τὴν ἀμύητον) in the mystery, the non-participating (τὴν ἄμοιρον) in the Pascha, the unmarked (τὴν ἀσφράγιστον) with the blood, the unguarded (τὴν ἀφρούρητον) by the Spirit, the hostile (τὴν ἐχθράν), the faithless (τὴν ἄπιστον)."[44] The language employed uniquely in John 20:27, in the context of what appears to be a liturgical gathering (τῇ μιᾷ σαββάτων), suits well such ideas. If this background applies to our Gospel, the confession of Thomas may be the doxological confession of the faithful gathered together as the risen Crucified comes into their midst. Jesus' word to Thomas to show himself "faithful," then, is the word of the risen Lord that he confess and participate in the common liturgical *collegium* of the church, the paschal community of the new Israel.[45] The pervasive paschal allusions of John's Gospel support the probability that this is the case.[46]

---

43. Dölger, *Eucharistie*, 42–63, quote 60. Concerning *fivloi*: "The holy supper of the Fish is by the Faith set before 'the friends.' In antiquity the purpose of the common meal was to give expression to the friendship. The common eating and drinking was to be accompanied by love; for that reason the betrayal of Judas was so hateful" (58). Dölger is commenting on these lines from the grave marker of Aberkios: καὶ τοῦτον ἐπέδωκε φίλοις ἔσθειν διὰ παντὸς οἶνον χρηστὸν ἔχουσα κέρασμα διδοῦσα μετ' ἄρτου (Greek: *Eucharistie*, 14).

44. Melito of Sardis, *On the Pascha* 16, Oxford Early Christian Texts 8.

45. Does this give us some explanation for the previous absence of Thomas? Unlike the Jews who believe but do not openly confess the Crucified lest they be excluded from the synagogue, Thomas is to believe and show himself to be such by confession and participation in the new synagogue of Jesus (John 12:42).

46. See Ignatius of Antioch, *To the Magnesians* 5.2. "There two kinds of coins, one of God and the other of the world. Each bears its own image (χαρακτῆρα) stamped upon it, the faithless (οἱ ἄπιστοι) of the world, the faithful (οἱ πιστοί) in love that of God the Father through Jesus Christ." See also, Ignatius of Antioch, *To the Smyrnaeans* 2.2.

Bibliography

Barrett, C. K. *The Gospel according to St. John: An Introduction with Commentary and Notes on the Greek Text*. 2nd ed. Philadelphia: Westminster, 1978.
Bonney, William. *Caused to Believe: The Doubting Thomas Story at the Climax of John's Christological Narrative*. Biblical Interpretation Series 62. Leiden: Brill, 2002.
Brown, Raymond. *The Gospel according to John (I–XII)*. Anchor Bible 29. New York: Doubleday, 1966.
———. *The Gospel according to John (xiii–xxi)*. Anchor Bible 29A. New York: Doubleday, 1970.
Concordia Self-Study Bible. Edited by Robert G. Hoerber. St. Louis: Concordia, 1986.
Dodd, C. H. *Tradition in the Fourth Gospel*. Cambridge: Cambridge University Press, 1965.
Dölger, Franz Joseph. *Die Eucharistie nach Inschriften frühchristlicher Zeit*. Münster: Aschendorff, 1922.
Frey, Jörg. "Die 'theologia crucifixi' des Johannesevangeliums." In *Kreuzestheologie im Neuen Testament*, edited by Andreas Dettwiler and Jean Zumstein. Wissenschaftliche Untersuching zum Neuen Testament 151. Tübingen: Mohr/Siebeck, 2002.
Hengel, Martin. "Die Schriftauslegung des 4. Evangeliums auf dem Hintergrund der urchristlichen Exegese." In *Jahrbuch für Biblische Theologie* 4. Neukirchen-Vluyn: Neukirchener, 1989.
Homilies on the Life of Christ. Translated by Jan Harm Barkhuizen. Early Christian Studies 1. Brisbane: Australian Catholic University, 2001.
Knöppler, Thomas. *Die theologie crucis des Johannesevangeliums: Das Verständnis des Todes Jesu im Rahmen der johanneischen Inkarnations- und Erhöhungschristologie*. Wissenschaftliche Monographien zum Alten und Neuen Testament 69. Neukirchen-Vluyn: Neukirchener, 1994.
Kohler, Herbert. *Kreuz und Menschwerdung im Johannesevangelium: Ein exegetisch-hermeneutischer Versuch zur johanneischen Kreuzestheologie*. Abhandlungen zur Theologie des Alten und Neuen Testaments 72. Zürich: Theologischer Verlag, 1987.
Lagrange, M.-J. *Évangile selon Saint Jean*. Études Bibliques. Paris: Gabalda, 1947.
Moloney, Francis J. *The Gospel of John*. Sacra Pagina 4. Collegeville, MN: Liturgical, 1998.
Morris, Leon. *The Gospel according to John*. Rev. ed. NICNT. Grand Rapids: Eerdmans, 1995.
New Testament Apocrypha. Vol. 1, *Gospels and Related Writings*. Edited by Wilhelm Schneemelcher. Translated by R. McL. Wilson. Rev. ed. Louisville: Westminster John Knox, 1991.
Pollard, T. Evan. "Cosmology and the Prologue of the Fourth Gospel." *Vigiliae Christianae* 12 (1958) 147–53.
Thyen, Hartwig. *Das Johannesevangelium*. Handbuch zum Neuen Testament 6. Tübingen: Mohr/Siebeck, 2005.

18

Beyond Exegesis

The Summons of Contemporary Context

—*Gerald West*

From January 25 to 30, 2015, a significant workshop was held in Bogotá, Colombia, entitled "Networking 'Contextual Bible Reading' Project: Structures of Violence." Among those hosting the workshop were CEBI (Centro de Estudos Bíblicos) (Brazil) and the Ujamaa Centre for Community Development and Research (South Africa). These organizations have a long history, with CEBI having been established in 1979, and the Ujamaa Centre in 1989.

The Ujamaa Centre, the base from which I do much of my biblical studies work,[1] and CEBI have related to each other since the early 1980s. Gunther Wittenberg, a South African biblical scholar standing within the liberation theology tradition,[2] visited CEBI in 1988, and I visited CEBI for the first time in 1990, and there have been many other visits since that time. Indeed, among the factors in the formation of the Ujamaa Centre was the model that CEBI provided.[3]

The purpose of the workshop in Colombia was, as the title suggests, to network with those who were doing forms of "contextual Bible reading."

---

1. I offer this essay in honor of James W. Voelz, a regular dialogue partner for my work as we have wrestled with the relationship between exegesis and contemporary contextual appropriation. See especially Voelz, *What Does This Mean?*
2. Wittenberg, *Resistance Theology in the Old Testament*.
3. West, "Locating Contextual Bible Study within Praxis."

The diversity of participants required regular clarification of the forms of "contextual Bible reading" being experienced through this workshop. But as this was a "process"-driven workshop, theoretical and methodological clarification was not done immediately. The workshop was structured within a see-judge-act process (see below). Each of the three components was itself embedded in a sharing of our local spiritualities and in corporate spiritual formation. The "see" component began with a recognition and sharing of our different realities. So the first day and a half was devoted to a series of liturgical and group-process exercises, enabling participants to get to know each other and to share their contextual realities. The second, third, and fourth days were dedicated to particular experiences of contextual Bible reading, as part of the process of the "judge" moment within the see-judge-act process. The workshop offered four in-depth experiences with four different, yet related, forms of contextual Bible reading. The first was the intercultural form of contextual Bible reading that had been practiced in Colombia,[4] which included a number of local Colombian participants in the project. The second was a visit to a number of the Casitas Bíblicas projects located on the outskirts of Bogotá. The third was the contextual Bible study form of contextual Bible reading of the Ujamaa Centre from South Africa,[5] and the fourth was da Leitura Popular da Bíblia form of contextual Bible reading practiced by CEBI.[6]

In each case workshop participants were given the opportunity to participate in and so experience each of these forms of contextual Bible reading before being offered analysis of the theoretical and methodological scaffolding of each of these forms. The experience of these different forms of contextual Bible reading generated a host of questions among participants, and so the morning of the final day, as the workshop was moving into the "act" moment, was given over to theoretical and methodological reflection.

In preparation for this conceptual "clearing" and clarification, CEBI and the Ujamaa Centre met to draft a joint presentation, recognizing as we have for more than twenty-five years that our theoretical and methodological "commitments" were very similar. The next section of this essay draws on our presentation, focusing in particular on the work of the Ujamaa Centre.

---

4. Schipani, Brinkman, and Snoek, *New Perspectives on Intercultural Reading of the Bible*.

5. See, for example, West, "Newsprint Theology."

6. See, for example, Mesters, "The Use of the Bible in Christian Communities"; Mesters, *Defenseless Flower*; Dreher, *The Walk to Emmaus*; and Schinelo, *The Bible and Popular Education*.

The Core Values

We agreed that it was important to clarify our "political" (to use CEBI's term) or "ideological" (to use Ujamaa's term) values. To put it crudely, we shared certain core values or commitments that we felt were "nonnegotiable." To do contextual Bible reading within our conceptualization of this practice required a commitment to these core values.

As we discussed our core values together, we drew on the long conceptual conversation that characterized our work. Within the literature of CEBI there were five core values, one for each finger of a hand. Within the literature of Ujamaa there were four or five core commitments.[7] This workshop gave us an opportunity, as was intended, both to learn from each other and to consolidate our reflections on our practices. As we talked together we discerned that our various core value categories could be consolidated in the form of five *C*'s (for pedagogical purposes): Community, Criticality, Collaboration, Change, and Context. We also agreed, among those present, that there was a sixth *C*. This sixth *C* had already been discerned from our work within the Ujamaa Centre,[8] but remained a point of conversation among CEBI practitioners. We decided to include this sixth *C* in our presentation: Contestation. In what follows I offer an overview of the Ujamaa Centre's contextual Bible study practice, indicating how we embody these values.

Collaborative Work and Interpretation

Liberation theologies have forged a range of collaborative reading processes, but the focus here is on a form that has developed in South Africa since the mid-1980s. Contextual Bible study, as it has come to be called, inhabits a collaborative nexus, captured by the six core values, between the epistemology of the poor and marginalized and the critical capacities of socially engaged biblical scholarship.

For those socially engaged biblical scholars and theologians who hold to strong notions of hegemony, arguing that the poor and marginalized have been "colonized" by the dominant ideology and are trapped in "a culture of silence,"[9] the critical capacities of biblical scholarship are pivotal, providing "the theologian who wants to carry out a de-ideologizing task with valuable

---

7. West, *Contextual Bible Study*; Nadar, "Beyond the 'Ordinary Reader' and the 'Invisible Intellectual'"; Nadar, "Hermeneutics of Transformation?"

8. West, "Tracing the 'Kairos' Trajectory."

9. Frostin, *Liberation Theology in Tanzania and South Africa*, 10, alluding to Freire, *The Politics of Education*, 72.

cognitive tools."[10] However, for others of us who hold to weak notions of ideological hegemony, the apparent silence of the poor and marginalized is not the silence of a consent to hegemony, but the silence of an embodied and lived but yet to be articulated "local" ideology.[11]

Those of us socially engaged biblical scholars who work with a strong sense of the epistemological privilege of the poor and a weak sense of social hegemony recognize that the critical resources of biblical scholarship are brought alongside the array of critical capacities that has already been forged in the sequestered sites of organized communities of the poor and marginalized. These additional critical resources, the tools of the biblical studies discipline, derive their usefulness in part from their capacity to render the Bible "other." They slow down the interpretive process,[12] facilitating rereading, retranslation, reinterpretation. Within the contours of contextual Bible study, alterity enables reappropriation for social transformation.

There are various ways of describing the contextual Bible study praxis, but here I will focus on a series of interconnected "movements" that shape the collaborative reading process. While a little abstract at this point in the essay, these movements will take on a fuller form in the final section.

The overarching movement is that of "see-judge-act," a process formed in the worker-priest movement in Europe in the 1930s–1940s.[13] This movement begins within the organized formations of the poor and marginalized as they analyze ("see") their context, "from below." This analysis of "reality" is then brought into dialogue with the "prophetic" voices of the Bible, enabling "the God of life" to address ("judge") the social reality. Through this dialogue with the Bible, "the shape of the gospel"[14] is used to plan a series of actions ("act") that will bring about transformation of the social reality, so that all may have life, and have it abundantly.

Within this overarching movement there is another movement, from community consciousness to critical consciousness to community consciousness. The "see" moment of social analysis generates a particular contextual concern that becomes the "theme" for the Bible study. The engagement with the Bible (the "judge" component) begins with a community's thematic appropriation of the biblical text being used (community

---

10. Segundo, "The Shift within Latin American Theology," 28; Nadar, "Beyond the 'Ordinary Reader' and the 'Invisible Intellectual'"; Nadar, "Hermeneutics of Transformation?"

11. Scott, *Domination and the Arts of Resistance*.

12. Riches et al., *What Is Contextual Bible Study?* 41.

13. Cochrane, "Questioning Contextual Theology," 76–77; West, *Biblical Hermeneutics of Liberation*, 188–93.

14. Nolan, *God in South Africa*.

consciousness), allowing every participant to share his or her particular understanding of the text. This moment not only makes it clear to the participants that the Bible study belongs to them, it also offers a reception history of that text's presence in a particular community. The Bible study then moves into a series of rereadings of the text, slowing down the process of interpretation, using the resources of socially engaged biblical scholarship (critical consciousness). The particular sets of "critical" tools that constitute the trade of biblical scholarship are offered to the participants as additional resources with which to engage the biblical text. After a series of critical-consciousness questions, the Bible study moves back into community consciousness, as the participants appropriate (en-act) the biblical text for the particular social project identified in the "see" moment.

With respect to the particular biblical "criticisms," there is another layer of movement. The movement begins within the "see" moment with an initial thematic "in-front-of-the-text" engagement with the text (community consciousness), bringing the generative contextual theme of the community workshop into dialogue with a particular biblical text. The interpretive process then slows down, entering the critical-consciousness moment via a literary engagement with the text. The choice to focus critical engagement "on the text" offers an egalitarian entry point to critical consciousness, enabling all participants to engage with the detail of the text. In most cases, literary engagement leads "behind the text" to a sociohistorical engagement with the text, as participants probe the world that produced the text, seeking for lines of connection between both the literary dimensions and the sociohistorical dimensions of the text and their contextual realities, seeking lines of connection between contemporary communities of faith and struggle and "biblical" communities of faith and struggle. While these dimensions of the biblical *text* are the focus of these second and third moments, the process moves in the fourth moment back "in front of the text" (into community consciousness), as the participants now appropriate this critically reconstituted text for their particular project of social transformation ("act"). Together, as the example that follows in the next section illustrates, these concentric and intersecting movements constitute the contextual Bible study process.

Processes of facilitation (the term used by the Ujamaa Centre) and animation (the term used by CEBI) are vital to the contextual Bible study, enabling both "group process"—the active participation of each participant—and the contextual Bible study process—the slow but steady procession through the three movements of that process.[15] Part of the "con-

---

15. Hope and Timmel, *Training for Transformation*.

version" of the socially engaged biblical scholar is becoming reschooled as a facilitator, collaborating with other community-based facilitators to enable participatory transformation.

So contextual Bible study begins and ends under the control of a particular local community, which uses the resources of contextual Bible study, along with a range of other resources, to plan for and implement community-based action. The socially engaged biblical scholar is already involved in the struggles of and work with particular communities for survival, liberation, and life, so that the invitation (and motivation) to do contextual Bible study together comes from within this larger praxis. More than half a century of liberation hermeneutics has demonstrated the usefulness of the critical capacities of biblical scholarship to particular liberation struggles. More than twenty-five years of contextual Bible study have demonstrated the usefulness of this particular form of liberation hermeneutics to a range of struggles (both in South Africa and beyond), and it is from these that the example in the final section of this essay is drawn.

Reading "with" Local Communities

Focusing on the economic dimensions of text and context remains a distinctive feature of biblical liberation hermeneutics, even while other, intersecting marginalizations have been incorporated into this primary focus. I use this example not only to signal this economic emphasis but also to indicate a refusal to make an ideologically distinctive translation and interpretation. What is foregrounded is the potential for contestation in both biblical text and social context.

The casualization of work has become a feature of the contemporary neoliberal capitalist global world order. South African reality is characterized by casual workers sitting on street corners of every city and town waiting for work. The haunting line in one of the parables of Jesus (Matt 20:1–15) summoned us to reread this text with these workers: "Why are you standing here idle all day?" (v. 6).[16] The history of reception of this text within biblical liberation hermeneutics, particularly within the Young Christian Workers tradition, has been to read this text as envisioning a "socialist" world economic order, characterized by a reality in which the following saying, popularized by Karl Marx, would be true: "From each according to his ability, to each according to his needs."[17]

16. West and Zwane, "Why Are You Sitting There?"
17. Marx, *Critique of the Gotha Program*.

However, in our work with the working-class sector, many of whom are casual workers, we had become disturbed by certain textual details.

> "⁸When evening came, the owner of the vineyard said to his manager, 'Call the laborers and give them their pay, beginning with the last and then going to the first.' ⁹When those hired about five o'clock came, each of them received the usual daily wage. ¹⁰Now when the first came, they thought they would receive more; but each of them also received the usual daily wage. ¹¹And when they received it, they grumbled against the landowner, ¹²saying, 'These last worked only one hour, and you have made them equal to us who have borne the burden of the day and the scorching heat.' ¹³But he replied to one of them, 'Friend, I am doing you no wrong; did you not agree with me for the usual daily wage? ¹⁴Take what belongs to you and go; I choose to give to this last the same as I give to you. ¹⁵Am I not allowed to do what I choose with what belongs to me? Or are you envious because I am generous?'" (Matt 20:8–15 NRSV)

Casual workers were disturbed that "the owner," having hired the workers, now sends his "manager" to pay them. Why this change? they asked. They were particularly distressed by the strategy of the manager, isolating the representative of the workers (v. 13), singling him out, refusing to engage with the concerns he brought to the manager on behalf of the other workers who had been working the whole day, and then dismissing him. This "divide and rule" strategy was familiar to casual workers; it occurred whenever they raised concerns with those who hired them. But what was most troubling to them was the assertion of the manager that he could act in an arbitrary manner because he had the power to do so (v. 15a).

Such concerns required that we socially engaged biblical scholars reread this text from this reality. When we did, we found sociohistorical resources that resonated with what workers had discerned in the literary detail. Among the vast array of New Testament scholarship on this text, we were drawn in particular to William Herzog's reading of this parable, identifying with his notion of Jesus as "pedagogue of the oppressed," and his location of this parable within the realities of the conflictual interface between peasant subsistence farmers and the exploitative and extractive economies of city-based elites.[18] When it is read from such a perspective, the contours of the parable are clearer. The owner of the vineyard is likely an absentee landowner, a member of the economic urban elite, employing a manager to handle the daily affairs of the vineyard, and engaged in a form

---

18. Herzog, *Parables as Subversive Speech*.

of agriculture that produced "a crop that can be converted into a luxury item (wine), monetized, and exported."[19]

Unable to calculate how many laborers he will need—such is the extent of his land holdings—the owner must make a number of trips to the agora to hire workers. Regular assessment of the number of workers he needs also enables the landowner to keep his workers to the minimum necessary to harvest the crop within the designated time period. Furthermore, by hiring small numbers of laborers during the day, the landowner exercises his "unilateral power," negotiating only with those hired at the beginning of the day for the minimum daily wage,[20] but leaving the wage for those hired later in the day indeterminate (vv. 4, 7).[21] For in a context of chronic systemic unemployment and underemployment, the day laborer is in no position to insist on a just wage and must accept "a malnutrition wage."[22] "Far from being generous," as he claims, "the householder is taking advantage of an unemployed work force to meet his harvesting needs by offering them work without a wage agreement."[23]

By telling a story in which the landowner is actively involved in the economic process, Jesus foregrounds the socioeconomic contestation of his time, making the usually invisible absentee landlord visible and so setting up a direct encounter between "the elites and the expendables."[24] The arbitrary economic power of the landowner is evident in the payment process. His power is signaled in the delegation of his manager to make the payments, but is fully manifest in his deliberate flaunting of protocol by refusing to pay the first-hired laborers first; by making the first-hired wait until last, he flaunts his power and shames them. The dignity of those who have worked all day demands a response, and so they risk a protest (vv. 11-12), speaking back to power, invoking the principle of equal pay for equal work.[25] Singling out their spokesperson (v. 13a), the landowner condescendingly reminds the resisting workers of their contractual agreement, knowing full well that the day laborers were never in a position to negotiate anything other than the minimum wage, and then goes on to dismiss their complaints, reiterating his right to do what he pleases with his power (v. 14), and concluding by blasphemously asserting that the land, which has been systemically coerced

19. Ibid., 85.
20. Ibid., 89–90.
21. Ibid., 6.
22. Ibid., 2.
23. Ibid., 86.
24. Ibid., 87.
25. Ibid., 91–92.

from the very peasant farmers who are now day laborers, belongs to him (v. 15).[26] On this reading, the systemic economic violence behind this text is palpable.[27]

Given this analysis, we have been tempted to offer an ideologically loaded translation of *oikodespotes* as "a landowning elite" or even "a white landowner," and *epitropos* as "labor-broker"; these designations would resonate immediately with South Africa's casual workers. Such translations would remove any ambiguity as to whether this text was advocating a form of socialism or critiquing a form of capitalism. Instead, we have chosen to go with the more "neutral" translations of most versions, translations like "landowner" and "manager," respectively. We have then offered two options for reading this parable. The Bible study begins (in this version) with a series of common questions and then divides into two separate sets of questions, before concluding with a return to common questions.

1. A poster picture of workers sitting at a street corner is used as an introductory exercise. Participants are asked: *What do you see in this picture?*

2. Matthew 20:1–15 is then read aloud. Participants are asked: *What is the text about?*

After general discussion of these two questions, participants are divided into small groups for the remaining questions.

3. *Who are the characters in this text, and what is their relationship to each other?*

After each small group has given its report to question 3, the facilitator says the following:

> In the time of Jesus many peasant farmers had been forced off their land by becoming indebted to wealthy city-based elites from whom they had taken loans in times of economic hardship. Those who lost their land became day laborers. So there are two very different ways of reading this text:
>
> A. This text can be read as presenting the egalitarian "socialist" vision of Jesus and the early Jesus movement (Acts 4:32–35), where there is work for all and decent wages for all. As Karl Marx said, "From each according to his ability, to each according to

---

26. Ibid., 92–94.
27. Ibid., 94.

his needs." From this perspective, we might read the parable as a utopian vision of a "socialist" society.

B. This text can also be read as a critique by Jesus of the arbitrary and discriminating practices of "capitalist" landowners, who hire when they like and pay what they like. From this perspective, the workers do not receive a just wage; they receive the exploitative minimum daily rate, and no more.

The small groups are then divided into two sets, set A and set B. Each set takes up its respective questions:

A: A "Socialist" Interpretation

4. *If the landowner represents the egalitarian communal vision of Jesus and the kingdom of God, what is the relationship between the landowner and the workers in this text?* Focus on the detail of the text.

5. *What aspects of this parable are relevant to the current context of unemployment?*

B: A "Capitalist" Interpretation

4. *If the landowner represents the exploitative ruling economic elite in the first century, what is the relationship between the landowner and the workers in this text?* Focus on the detail of the text.

5. *What aspects of this parable are relevant to the current context of unemployment?*

After each set of small groups has reported on these questions, the participants work together on the following questions:

6. Which of these interpretations do you think is Matthew's? Do you think Matthew represents what Jesus might have been saying by telling this parable?

7. What does each of these two readings say to our context?

8. What actions will we take in response to these readings?

Resisting a particular ideological option in this case creates the opportunity for a different kind of pedagogical experience, within which participants grapple with the notion that Scripture does not have one voice. Contending voices can be discerned, whether using literary or sociohistorical (redactional) resources. Question 6 deals directly with different redactional perspectives, but may deflect some groups from moving into community consciousness in questions 7 and 8. The recognition that the Bible is itself a site of struggle has become increasingly important in the work of the Ujamaa Centre. Because our work destabilizes dominant readings of the Bible, we have to guard against giving the impression that the Bible is unambiguously about liberation.

Conclusion

Contextual Bible study constructs a safe, sequestered site in which communities of the poor and marginalized can be both translators and interpreters, both of their contexts and of their Bibles. Contextual Bible study also offers access to the detail of the biblical text. This alterity enables liberatory appropriation in African contexts, for "other" detail unsettles the singular and certain "message" of the Bible. Claims to a contextually transcendent message serve Africa's ruling elites, forestalling the contending voices that cry out for structural change.[28]

Contextual Bible study as a particular form of liberation hermeneutics occupies a tensive interpretive space in which we risk a decisive ideo-theological framing that enables a collaborative discerning of critical textual detail that is both "true" to the text's otherness and potentially "useful" for particular local contextual struggles. Contextual Bible study occupies a collaborative nexus between the epistemology of the poor and marginalized and the critical capacities of socially engaged biblical scholarship. The socially engaged biblical scholar who inhabits this collaborative nexus is both accountable to the particular communities of this collaborative praxis and responsible to the disciplinary detail of biblical scholarship.

This nexus then is characterized by a dialectical relationship between alterity and appropriation, with appropriation seeking "exegesis" and "exegesis" seeking appropriation. The alterity that the detail of biblical scholarship offers to organized poor and marginalized "readers" of the Bible is, this essay argues, a significant resource in appropriations of the Bible for social transformation within a liberation paradigm. And the appropriations of poor and marginalized "readers" generate their own forms of alterity, summoning the socially engaged biblical scholar to return to the discipline of biblical scholarship in order to discern other detail that might be potentially useful. Biblical liberation hermeneutics as it is construed within the processes of contextual Bible study recognizes that the distinctive detail of a biblical text (its alterity) and a particular community's appropriation of that text are always partial, in both senses of the term: they are ideo-theologically constituted and incomplete.

As this brief example has indicated, contextual Bible study is not just technique, it is embedded and embodied in a set of core values. Its value derives from these hermeneutical values.

---

28. West, "Unstructural Analysis of the Bible."

Bibliography

Cochrane, James R. "Questioning Contextual Theology." In *Towards an Agenda for Contextual Theology: Essays in Honour of Albert Nolan*, edited by McGlory T. Speckman and Larry T. Kaufmann, 67–86. Pietermaritzburg: Cluster, 2001.
Dreher, Carlos A. *The Walk to Emmaus*. São Leopoldo: Centro de Estudos Bíblicos, 2004.
Freire, Paulo. *The Politics of Education: Culture, Power, and Liberation*. Westport, CT: Greenwood, 1985.
Frostin, Per. *Liberation Theology in Tanzania and South Africa: A First World Interpretation*. Lund: Lund University Press, 1988.
Herzog, William R., II. *Parables as Subversive Speech: Jesus as Pedagogue of the Oppressed*. Louisville: Westminster John Knox, 1994.
Hope, Anne, and Sally Timmel. *Training for Transformation: A Handbook for Community Workers*. 4 vols. Book 1. Gweru, Zimbabwe: Mambo Press, 1984.
Marx, Karl. *Critique of the Gotha Program*. Marx & Engels Internet Archive, 1875. http://marxistsfr.org/archive/marx/works/1875/gotha/index.htm.
Mesters, Carlos. *Defenseless Flower: A New Reading of the Bible*. Translated by Francis McDonagh. Maryknoll, NY: Orbis, 1989.
———. *God's Project*. Cape Town: Theology Exchange Programme, n.d.
———. "The Use of the Bible in Christian Communities of the Common People." In *The Bible and Liberation: Political and Social Hermeneutics*, edited by Norman K. Gottwald and Richard A. Horsley, 3–16. Maryknoll, NY: Orbis, 1984.
Nadar, Sarojini. "Beyond the 'Ordinary Reader' and the 'Invisible Intellectual': Shifting Contextual Bible Study from Liberation Discourse to Liberation Pedagogy." *Old Testament Essays* 22.2 (2009) 384–403.
———. "'Hermeneutics of Transformation?' A Critical Exploration of the Model of Social Engagement between Biblical Scholars and Faith Communities." In *Postcolonial Perspectives in African Biblical Interpretations*, edited by Musa W. Dube, Andrew M. Mbuvi, and Dora Mbuwayesango, 389–406. Atlanta: Society of Biblical Literature, 2012.
Nolan, Albert. *God in South Africa: The Challenge of the Gospel*. Cape Town: Philip, 1988.
Riches, John, et al. *What Is Contextual Bible Study? A Practical Guide with Group Studies for Advent and Lent*. London: SPCK, 2010.
Schinelo, Edmilson, ed. *The Bible and Popular Education: Encounters of Solidarity and Dialogue*. São Leopoldo: CEBI, 2009.
Schipani, Daniel S., Martien Brinkman, and Hans Snoek, eds. *New Perspectives on Intercultural Reading of the Bible: Hermeneutical Explorations in Honor of Hans De Wit*. Elkhart, IN: Institute of Mennonite Studies, 2015.
Scott, James C. *Domination and the Arts of Resistance: Hidden Transcripts*. New Haven: Yale University Press, 1990.
Segundo, Juan Luis. "The Shift within Latin American Theology." *Journal of Theology for Southern Africa* 52 (1985) 17–29.
Voelz, James W. *What Does This Mean? Principles of Biblical Interpretation in the Post-Modern World*. 2nd ed. St. Louis: CPH, 1997.
West, Gerald O. *Biblical Hermeneutics of Liberation: Modes of Reading the Bible in the South African Context*. 2nd ed. Maryknoll, NY: Orbis, 1995.

———. *Contextual Bible Study*. Pietermaritzburg: Cluster, 1993.

———. "Locating Contextual Bible Study within Praxis." *Diaconia* 4 (2013) 43–48.

———. "Newsprint Theology: Bible in the Context of HIV and AIDS." In *Out of Place: Doing Theology on the Crosscultural Brink*, edited by Jione Havea and Clive Pearson, 161–86. London: Equinox, 2011.

———. "Tracing the 'Kairos' Trajectory from South Africa (1985) to Palestine (2009): Discerning Continuities and Differences." *Journal of Theology for Southern Africa* 143 (2012) 4–22.

———. "Unstructural Analysis of the Bible Reinforcing Unstructural Analysis of African Contexts in (South) Africa." *Old Testament Essays* 23.3 (2010) 861–88.

West, Gerald O., and Sithembiso Zwane. "'Why Are You Sitting There?' Reading Matthew 20:1–16 in the Context of Casual Workers in Pietermaritzburg, South Africa." In *Matthew*, edited by Nicole Duran Wilkinson and James P. Grimshaw, 175–88. Texts@Contexts. Minneapolis: Fortress, 2013.

Wittenberg, Gunther. *Resistance Theology in the Old Testament: Collected Essays*. Pietermaritzburg: Cluster, 2007.

19

"Saved through Child-bearing"?
Theology and Hermeneutics in
Reading 1 Timothy 2:15

—*Thomas M. Winger*

Although I have no memory of it, I probably bumped into Jim Voelz when I was a child and he was a young doctoral candidate in Cambridge, living at Westfield House. He had followed his teacher Martin Franzmann (whom I *do* remember), called as Westfield tutor in 1969. Three decades later, when I was the Westfield tutor, the stories I heard from his old housemates mostly recalled Jim as a card shark, playing bridge at all hours. But though I spent no small number of hours playing soccer (not cards!) with Jim in St. Louis, what had drawn me to Concordia Seminary for graduate studies in 1990 was his fastidious devotion to the details of the text, which he wielded without the antidogmatic and atheological vacuity of so much modern exegesis. It is in honor of that spirit that I devote to him this brief examination of a fiendishly difficult Pauline text[1] where theology and hermeneutics collide.

σωθήσεται δὲ διὰ τῆς τεκνογονίας, ἐὰν μείνωσιν ἐν πίστει καὶ ἀγάπῃ καὶ ἁγιασμῷ μετὰ σωφροσύνης. (1 Tim 2:15)

---

1. Köstenberger, "Ascertaining Women's God-Ordained Roles," 108, suggests this may have been the text Peter had in mind when he referred to Pauline passages that were misunderstood and twisted (2 Pet 3:15–16)!

The Revised Standard Version that was the companion of my youth not only provides a baseline translation but also stirs the interpretative waters with its probing footnotes:

> Yet woman will be saved through bearing children,[c] if she continues[d] in faith and love and holiness, with modesty. (RSV)
>
> RSV footnotes: c Or *by the birth of the child*; d Greek *they continue*

The RSV thus lays out a matrix of interpretative possibilities, firstly, by asking whether "bearing children" refers to *any* maternal act or specifically to "*the* Child" (the promised Messiah), and, secondly, by flagging the grammatical non sequitur involved in the switch from singular to plural verb form. The RSV could also have noted that "woman" and "she" are absent from the Greek text—raising the difficult question of who is the verbal subject in both cases. Indeed, the number of semantic and grammatical questions multiplies far beyond the RSV's simple 2 x 2 matrix.

But as every modern reader will quickly acknowledge, the real reason this text is "fiendishly difficult" is not linguistic, but theological and philosophical. On the one hand (μέν), the text is bound up in the contentious debate about whether women may be ordained to the office of the holy ministry. Is (and in what way is) this verse presenting to women a vocational alternative to the pastoral office (as a conclusion to the chapter)? The more immediate theological challenge is whether the proposal that one can be saved by "child-bearing" is compatible with the fundamental Pauline teaching on justification. Those who reject the Pauline authorship of the Pastorals pounce on this verse. There is perhaps no more prototypical example of the hermeneutical use of the *articulus stantis et cadentis ecclesiae*, the gospel as the rule of faith; so long as the gospel stands, any interpretation of this verse that would posit works as a means of salvation must fall.

On the other hand (δέ), this text also appears to violate the most sacred egalitarian principles of our modern Western society. Objections range from a simple bristling at the "old-fashioned" notion that a woman's vocation is defined by child-bearing to the offense taken at an apparently demeaning view of woman's character and abilities, as this chapter seems to teach that her prohibition from the pastoral office is rooted in a deficient nature—witness her predictable susceptibility to the devil's wiles in Eden (1 Tim 2:14)![2] Readers inclined to such a view are persuaded that the author

---

2. Hanson, *The Pastoral Epistles*, 74: "The natural interpretation is that woman, a weak, gullible creature, should find her natural vocation in a life of domesticity in subordination to her husband."

of 1 Timothy has failed to cast off the misogynistic moorings shared with Jewish contemporaries like Philo, who offers a deceptively similar interpretation of Genesis 3:

> Why did the serpent accost the woman, and not the man [Gen 3:2]? The serpent, having formed his estimate of virtue, devised a treacherous stratagem against them, for the sake of bringing mortality on them. But the woman was more accustomed to be deceived than the man. For his counsels as well as his body are of a masculine sort, and competent to disentangle the notions of seduction; but the mind of the woman is more effeminate, so that through her softness she easily yields and is easily caught by the persuasions of falsehood, which imitate the resemblance of truth.[3]

On this view, 1 Tim 2:15 is little more than an admonishment to womankind to stay barefoot and pregnant in the kitchen.

The ever-expanding matrix of interpretative possibilities—while grounded in linguistic uncertainties—therefore seems chiefly to reflect the diversity of readers seeking an interpretation they can live with. In an important summative article, Stanley Porter puts his finger on this embarrassment at the outset: "What the text seems to be saying to many of its interpreters is apparently formulated more on the basis of ideology than critical exegesis."[4] But beware the interpreter who claims that everyone else (but not he!) is driven by ideology, as Porter continues: "This ideological criticism has been of two kinds. The first simply dismisses or marginalizes the verse, and the second tends to over-theologize various elements of its interpretation."[5] Does not the claim that some interpreters "over-theologize" the text itself express an ideological prejudice against any exegesis that goes beyond his own kind of Protestant minimalism? The question is not whether a particular interpretation is "overly theological" but whether it is consistent with the context of the text and Pauline theology in general. In other words, it remains to be seen whether a messianic reading of "child-bearing" is "over-theological" or faithful to the text.

Thus, while the semantic and grammatical problems of the text have been explored to the point of exhaustion[6]—though such studies are not

---

3. Philo, *Questions and Answers on Genesis* 1.33. http://www.earlyjewishwritings.com/text/philo/book41.html.

4. Porter, "What Does It Mean to Be 'Saved by Childbirth'?" 87.

5. Ibid., 87–88.

6. Köstenberger, "Ascertaining Women's God-Ordained Roles," and Porter, "What Does It Mean to Be 'Saved by Childbirth'?" cover the field exhaustively. Among the

without their flaws—it seems to the present writer that the theological and hermeneutical aspects have been treated only quite superficially. This essay is a brief approach to these problems from a decidedly Lutheran exegetical perspective.

A Question of Meaning?

The linguistic questions are by no means unimportant, and are certainly fundamental to the subsequent theological investigation. Porter summarizes (and evaluates) them as well as anyone: "The major lexical and grammatical questions raised in this single verse include [1] determining the subject of the verb σωθήσεται with respect to 'the woman' of v. 14, [2] the sense of the verb σώζω, [3] the denotation of the term τεκνογονία, [4] the function of the preposition διά with the genitive case, [5] the shift in number of the verbs from singular to plural, and [6] the use of the third-class conditional construction."[7] The significance of these six questions will soon become apparent. But—at the risk of tipping one's hand before the game is played out—it is worth asking whether the questions have been posed precisely. Question 1 assumes (correctly?) that the subject of σωθήσεται, "X will be saved," is "the woman" of the preceding verse—but the more difficult question is, "whom does she represent?"

Question 2 addresses "the sense of the verb σώζω" (Porter later writes of the verb's "meaning"). Köstenberger poses the question in similar terms: "The preceding survey of interpretations of 1 Tim 2:15 has indicated that determining the intended meaning of σωθήσεται may well be the key to a correct interpretation of the passage. Should the term be taken to connote physical preservation (fourth view), spiritual salvation (fifth view), eschatological salvation (sixth view), or spiritual preservation from Satan (or the curse) (seventh view)?"[8] Surely, though, the *meaning* of the verb is the same in all four interpretations; the real question is its *external entailments* or their *referents*.[9] In other words, while σώζω means something like "to rescue/save/

---

commentaries, Knight is most helpful: Knight, *The Pastoral Epistles*. See also the debate between Moo and Payne: Moo, "1 Timothy 2:11–15," 62–83; Payne, "Libertarian Women in Ephesus," 169–97; and Moo, "The Interpretation of 1 Timothy 2:11–15," 198–222.

7. Porter, "What Does It Mean to Be 'Saved by Childbirth'?" 88; bracketed enumeration added.

8. Köstenberger, "Ascertaining Women's God-Ordained Roles," 122.

9. On "external entailments," see Voelz, *What Does This Mean?* 188–90. Voelz has often remarked that the enumerated sections of an entry in standard lexicons (like BDAG) do not usually represent distinct *meanings* of the word, but group its uses and connotations on the basis of its referents and external entailments.

preserve from harm or danger," whether that rescue is from physical illness ("healing"), danger in the present life ("deliverance"), or eternal damnation ("salvation") depends on how one completes the thought: rescue *of what* (body, mind, or soul) *from what* (pain, illness, or death). When the external entailments are absent (as in the present verse), the interpreter must fill in the gaps to answer those questions.[10] The result depends on how one reads both the immediate context (of 1 Tim 2) and the broader context (of Paul's theology). Thus, in 1 Tim 2:15 the verb σωθήσεται is modified by a phrase that gives the *means* of deliverance (διὰ τῆς τεκνογονίας, "through [the] child-bearing"—itself ambiguous), but the crucial accompaniment explaining "from what?" is unexpressed. When σῴζω is used absolutely, does one automatically fill the gap with a theological phrase like "from sin, eternal death, God's wrath, and/or the devil"? Or does a reticence to connect such "salvation" with the "work" of child-bearing incline one toward "from the dangers of childbirth" or "from the devil's attempt to lead woman into a role not meant for her"?

The distinction between "meaning" and "external entailments" is critical in order to avoid two dangers. First is the common exegetical technique of surveying Paul's use of σῴζω and concluding that it normally *means* "spiritual salvation" for Paul, and so must mean that in the present verse. Second is the interrelated theological error evident in the quotation from Köstenberger (above): sharply distinguishing "physical" from "spiritual" saving (as "meanings" of σῴζω). Lutherans are particularly sensitive to this Platonic/Gnostic (choose your label) tendency that they observe in interpreters of a Calvinist bent. "Healing" ought not to be distinguished from "salvation" as *physical* versus *spiritual*;[11] for, firstly, "salvation" in Paul is most often an eschatological event culminating in the resurrection of the *body* on the last day (e.g., Rom 13:11), and, secondly, any temporal healing the Lord chooses to grant people is rarely disconnected (in biblical examples) from faith. This is precisely why it can be so difficult to know whether the appropriate English rendering of the verb is "heal" or "save" (e.g., Luke 7:50)! The presence of the phrase ἐν πίστει, "in faith," in the latter half of our verse (1 Tim 2:15b) is both part of the dilemma and part of the solution.

Porter's third linguistic question, "the denotation of the term τεκνογονία," again expresses the issue wrongly. The fact that τεκνογονία is an exceedingly rare noun[12] presents no real difficulty, for the noun's *meaning* is

10. See Voelz, *What Does This Mean?* 185, who cites 1 Tim 2:15 as a case where the author omits signifiers that are necessary to understand the complete thought.

11. For a typical example of this false dichotomy, see Knight, *The Pastoral Epistles*, 144–45.

12. τεκνογονία is used only here (1 Tim 2:15) in the entire Greek Bible. The cognate

beyond dispute: "the bearing of children,"[13] though one might quibble over the plural in this definition, as the noun can certainly denote one nonrepeated act of "child-bearing."[14] This quibble is significant, as it relates to the real question in our text: the noun's *referent*. To *which* act of "child-bearing" does Paul refer? Is he referring to the natural vocation of womankind as the bearer of children, generation after generation, or more specifically to *"the* Child-bearing" par excellence, the birth of the Messiah (as an allusion to Gen 3:15)? Or to both? This observation is again significant in the face of attempts to determine its "meaning" on the basis of Paul's use of the related verb τεκνογονέω, "to bear children," in 1 Tim 5:14, which indisputably refers to normal human procreation by remarried young widows. This parallel text, significant as it is for elucidating the *meaning* of the noun, does not determine its *referent* in 1 Tim 2:15. So long as the birth of Jesus the Messiah is understood as "natural" in the broad sense (confessing his true flesh born of the Virgin Mary), there is no inherent incompatibility between a messianic reading of "child-bearing" in 1 Tim 2:15 and the later application of the cognate verb to ordinary family life (1 Tim 5:14). Even the patristic interpretation of τεκνογονία in our verse in the sense of "child-*rearing*" does not establish a different denotation of the noun, but is an example of synecdoche, "child-bearing" as part for whole—indeed, almost all modern interpreters of the verse take "child-bearing" as synecdoche for something, whether (negatively) the demeaning subordination of women or (positively) the God-ordained role to which she ought willingly and faithfully to submit.

Porter's three remaining grammatical questions will pop up as we examine the multitude of possible translations of the verse, and the above critique is in no way meant to denigrate his thorough investigation. But suffice it to say that the exegetical puzzle of 1 Tim 2:15 is incorrectly conceived if it is primarily framed as a lexical problem. Establishing the meaning of σῴζω and τεκνογονία, even their most common usage in Paul or the New Testament, cannot determine their referents and external entailments in this verse. In fact, in addition to the important question of its present-day relevance, the most significant exegetical issue is probably the nature and degree of correspondence to Genesis 3, to which Paul undoubtedly refers in the immediately preceding context. Thus, it is really about how the Old Testament relates to the New. And it will not do to claim either that an allusion

---

verb τεκνογονέω is used only in 1 Tim 5:14. Though rare in classical literature, there are enough clear references to establish the meaning beyond doubt. See also "child-bearing" as a positive Christian vocation in *Diognetus* 5.6.

13. BDAG, s.v. τεκνογονία.

14. The definition given in LSJ, s.v. τεκνογονία.

to Gen 3:15 in the current verse is too obscure to be possible[15] or that Paul presents a flawed exegesis of the OT account![16]

The Options

Multiplying the linguistic options by the various referents results in (at least) the following possible translations/interpretations of the text:

1. *"But she [woman] will be brought safely [temporally] through child-bearing, if they [women] remain in faith, etc."* This interpretation assumes a reference to Genesis 3:16, the curse of pain in childbirth, and has Paul countering the deception of Eve with the promise that God will preserve faithful Christian women through this ordeal. Though once popular (Moffatt, Phillips), it is rarely championed today, as most argue that Paul does not use σῴζω this way. However, in light of the parallel use of σωθήσεται and διά in 1 Cor 3:15, "preserved through fire," it should not be completely discounted.

2. *"But she [Eve/woman] will be saved [eternally] from [the pain of] child-bearing, if they [women] remain in faith, etc."* Retaining the allusion to Genesis 3:16, this interpretation takes "child-bearing" as synecdoche for its pain and danger, which itself is synecdoche for "the consequences of original sin." This compound figure of speech is not only unlikely for its complexity, but also requires a tortured gloss of διά as "from." Furthermore, it requires an implied reference to the curse of sin that has not been part of the Genesis reference thus far.

3. *"But she [woman] will be saved [eternally] through bearing children, if they [women] remain in faith, etc."* Probably the most common reading of the text, this interpretation is also the most problematic. Certainly, no one would contend that "bearing children" itself is a work that merits eternal salvation; all proponents take it as some sort of synecdoche. Protestant interpreters from Reformation times to today are quick to distance themselves from the possibility that child-bearing represents good works as a means of salvation. This is universally regarded as incompatible with

---

15. Guthrie, *The Pastoral Epistles*, 78, famously called the messianic interpretation of "child-bearing" an "improbable suggestion," contending "if that were the writer's intention he could hardly have chosen a more obscure or ambiguous way of saying it."

16. E.g., Johnson, *First and Second Letters to Timothy*, 208: "But the logic is flawed. . . . Such corrections of Paul's exegesis of Genesis are beside the point, except to make clear that Paul was not in this case engaging in sober exegesis of Genesis, but supporting his culturally conservative position on the basis of texts that in his eyes demonstrate the greater dignity and intelligence of men and, therefore, the need for women to be silent and subordinate to men."

Pauline theology. Hence, most modern Protestant interpreters run a slightly different kind of synecdoche: "bearing children" is shorthand for submitting to one's God-given vocation. Thus, whereas Eve led the world into sin by casting off Adam's headship and submitting to the devil's deception, faithful Christian women can reverse the curse by submitting to their proper place in God's order. This popular interpretation has been central in the conservative opposition to women's ordination. It makes good exegetical sense in the context of 1 Timothy as an anti-Gnostic assertion (cf. 4:1–5). But despite its usefulness, this solution still founders on the central article: even proper submission to one's God-given vocation cannot be a means to eternal salvation (even if it is "in faith"). Some modern interpreters try to avoid this danger by drawing a distinction between "getting saved" and "staying saved"—but this sort of "covenantal nomism" is scarcely less synergistic.

4. *"But she [woman] will be saved [eternally] through bearing children, if they [the children] remain in faith, etc."* While this interpretation posits a different subject for the plural verb μείνωσιν, "they remain," it really offers little more than a variant on the previous: "child-bearing" is now synecdoche for the entire domestic vocation of a faithful Christian woman as evidenced by the results in her children. It is famously associated with Chrysostom, who saw "child-*rearing*" as an opportunity for womankind to reverse the curse of their forebear Eve.[17] Today this view is usually cited only in order to reject it—except, perhaps, among feminist critics of the text. While it is unclear whether Chrysostom meant to offer a synergistic reading, that would be a fair critique. It is ironic that Pelagius offered a distinctively monergistic variant: "When Paul speaks of the salvation that comes through childbearing, he refers to the baptism and rebirth to which their children are led by the believing mother."[18] It is unfortunate that this ingenious solution founders on the question of who is then the referent of σωθήσεται (surely not "the children will be saved").

5. *"But she [Eve/woman] will be saved [eternally] through the Childbearing, if they [women] remain in faith, etc."* This would seem to be the interpretation that Porter considers to be "over-theologizing." Other Protestant interpreters object that it seems to give too high a role to Mary,[19] and Porter

---

17. Chrysostom, *Homilies on Timothy*, NPNF[1] 13:436. According to Johnson, *First and Second Letters to Timothy*, 28, Theodoret of Cyr offers a similar interpretation.

18. Pelagius, *Commentary on the First Letter to Timothy*, in Gorday, *Colossians, 1–2 Thessalonians, 1–2 Timothy, Titus, Philemon*, 167. Ambrosiaster expresses a similar thought: "The salvation that comes to women through childbearing applies only to the children who are reborn in Christ" (*Commentary on the First Letter to Timothy*, in ACCS 9:167).

19. E.g., Moo, "The Interpretation of 1 Timothy 2:11–15," 205.

contends that the shift from Eve to Mary is not prepared for in the text.[20] Some interpreters contend either that τεκνογονία must "mean" ordinary child-bearing or that the article τῆς can scarcely bear the weight required.[21] But these objections are overdrawn. Firstly, seeing a reference to the birth of the Messiah is not "theologizing" the text but identifying an extension of the previous references to Genesis 3. Secondly, this interpretation requires no more than one single change of referent in comparison to the popular third interpretation (above): the birth of *which* child? That child promised to Eve (Gen 3:15). Thus, there is no need to posit any explicit reference to Mary, since the promise of a child was made to Eve. More anon. But before proceeding to a further investigation of this possibility, a brief digression.

Luther and the Lutheran Confessions

Porter is certainly correct in pointing to the role of the interpreter's context in reading this text. The Lutheran Reformers seem to have framed their exposition in reaction to an established use by their Roman opponents to support either salvation by works[22] or clerical celibacy. Martin Chemnitz points to Jerome's interpretation of the passage, by which children who remain virgins atone for their mothers' loss of the same, thus interpreting "if *they* remain ... in chastity" as a reference to the children.[23] In response, Chemnitz expounds on the sanctity of the divine institution of marriage and child-bearing, turning our text against his opponents.[24] Against this background we may read Luther's lectures on Timothy: "It is a very great comfort that a woman can be saved by bearing children, etc. That is, she has an honorable and salutary status in life if she keeps busy having children. We ought to recommend this passage to them, etc. She is described as 'saved'

---

20. Porter, "What Does It Mean to Be 'Saved by Childbirth'?" 92.

21. If τεκογονία refers to any child-bearing, then the article is generic, like τοὺς ἄνδρας, "[the] men in every place" (1 Tim 2:7). In the messianic reading it is either demonstrative (the Child referred to in Gen 3, just as ἡ γυνὴ, "the woman," in 1 Tim 2:14, refers back to Eve), par excellence (the Child above all children), or "well-known" (*that* Child).

22. For the allegorical reading of "child-bearing" as "producing good works," see Gregory of Nyssa, *De Virginitate* 4, NPNF² 5:350; ACCS 9:167; and Augustine, *De Trinitate* 12, NPNF¹ 3:159.

23. Chemnitz, *Examination*, 3:29, citing Jerome, *Against Jovinianus* 1.27, NPNF² 6:366–67; see also Jerome, *Letter 107*, NPNF² 6:192.

24. See Chemnitz, *Examination*, 2:722; 3:31, 50, 52, 56, 57, 60, 76. See also, Chemnitz, *Ministry, Word, and Sacraments*, 147–49.

not for freedom, for license, but for bearing and rearing children."[25] Luther's coy gloss of διά, shifting from "through" to "for [child-bearing]," is justified by his reading of "in faith" in the second half of the verse: "[Paul] does not merely say that bearing children saves; he adds: if the bearing takes place in faith and love.... Paul had to add this, lest women think that they are good in the fact that they bear children. Simple childbearing does nothing, since the heathen also do this. But for Christian women their whole responsibility is salutary."[26] Thus, in notable contrast to modern Protestant interpreters, Luther does not attribute to a woman's vocation the ability either to save her or preserve her in salvation. Rather, he attributes her salvation to faith alone and sees child-bearing as a glorious, God-pleasing work that flows from it—although, somewhat inconsistently, he adds: "hardship and all things [in married life] are salutary, for through them they [married people] are moved forward toward salvation and against adultery."[27] Melanchthon's use of the passage against clerical celibacy in the Apology to the Augsburg Confession follows Luther closely, concluding: "So a woman's duties please God because of faith, and a believing woman is saved if she serves faithfully in these duties of her calling."[28]

Exploring the Messianic Reading

That these three sixteenth-century "Lutherans" ignore the messianic interpretation of the text may be owing to their polemical context; but it is also likely that they were simply unaware of it. This certainly calls into question Porter's claim that "this is perhaps the most popular view in the light of church history"[29]—and, indeed, it is difficult to find any early church father who explicitly refers "the child-bearing" in this verse to Christ.[30] An exhaustive study that would uncover the earliest such exegesis would be welcome. It appears in Ellicott (1856), who may have influenced the Revised Version (1881–1885) that popularized this view, followed by Lock's influential

25. Martin Luther, *Lectures on Timothy* (1527–1528), AE 28:279.
26. Ibid., 28:279.
27. Ibid., 28:279. See also his *Scholia* on Rom 10:19, AE 25:420; *Lectures on Genesis*, Gen 24:4, AE 4:242; and *Table Talk*, no. 3528, AE 54:223.
28. Melanchthon, Apology to the Augsburg Confession, 23:32.
29. Porter, "What Does It Mean to Be 'Saved by Childbirth'?" 90n8. Payne, "Libertarian Women in Ephesus," 177, makes the same indefensible claim.
30. According to Quinn and Wacker, *First and Second Letters to Timothy*, 232, the eleventh-century Bulgarian archbishop Theophylact was aware of some exegetes who read the text messianically (PG 125:40).

endorsement of the same (1924).³¹ Lock cites an anonymous Greek father, but without an attribution it is impossible to evaluate the significance of this gloss: "through her giving birth, according to the flesh, to Christ [διὰ τοῦ ἐξ αὐτῆς κατὰ σάρκα τικτομένου Χριστοῦ]."³²

The Patristic Evidence

The absence of early patristic evidence in favor of this interpretation must be weighed against Johnson's admission that he could find only one explicit reference to 1 Tim 2:11–15 in the first four centuries.³³ In other words, there is little evidence for *any* particular interpretation. Four early patristic sources (prior to Jerome) are commonly cited. But none of the four explicitly refers to this verse, and it is quite possible that exegetes repeated them from earlier sources without bothering to look them up! We shall not repeat this error, though full citations of all the texts will not be possible.³⁴ What these four texts *do* establish is that the typology of Adam-Christ was understood to be paralleled by Eve-Mary, such that it would not have been impossible for early exegetes to have seen a fulfillment of Genesis 3:15 in "the childbirth."

1. Ignatius includes Jesus' birth from Mary among the mysteries of our salvation: "And the virginity of Mary, and her giving birth [ἡ παρθενία Μαρίας καὶ ὁ τοκετὸς αὐτῆς] were hidden from the Prince of this world, as was also the death of the Lord. Three mysteries of a cry which were wrought in the stillness of God."³⁵ It is the explicit emphasis on "her giving birth," using vocabulary at least cognate to τεκνογονία, that opens the possibility that Ignatius had our verse in mind.

2. Justin Martyr wields Genesis 3 against his Jewish opponent Trypho, and appears to parallel Paul's exegesis of the same in a messianic manner:

> For we know ... that He became man by the Virgin, in order that the disobedience which proceeded from the serpent might receive its destruction in the same manner in which it derived its origin. For Eve, who was a virgin and undefiled, having

---

31. Ellicott, *A Critical and Grammatical Commentary*, 37; Lock, *A Critical and Exegetical Commentary*, 33. Ellicott, 37, indicates that earlier exegetes had considered and mostly rejected this view, except for Hammond (with no clear reference).

32. Cramer, *Catene in Sancti Pauli*, 7, 22; cited from Dibelius and Conzelmann, *The Pastoral Epistles*, 48n26. Cramer introduces the citation simply with "Ἄλλος φησί [another says]."

33. Johnson, *First and Second Letters to Timothy*, 23.

34. See Köstenberger, "Ascertaining Women's God-Ordained Roles," 109–13.

35. Ignatius, *To the Ephesians* 19.1.

conceived the word of the serpent, brought forth disobedience and death. But the Virgin Mary received faith and joy, when the angel Gabriel announced the good tidings to her... And by her has He been born, to whom we have proved so many Scriptures refer, and by whom God destroys both the serpent and those angels and men who are like him; but works deliverance from death to those who repent of their wickedness and believe upon Him.[36]

Key here is his belief that the faith-full work of Mary overturned the disobedience of Eve.

3. Irenaeus on various occasions works the same typological connection, often subsuming it under his characteristic theology of recapitulation. The following is representative: "Mary the Virgin is found obedient, saying, 'Behold the handmaid of the Lord; be it unto me according to thy word.' But Eve was disobedient; for she did not obey when as yet she was a virgin. And even as she, ... having become disobedient, was made the cause of death, both to herself and to the entire human race; so also did Mary, having a man betrothed [to her], and being nevertheless a virgin, by yielding obedience, become the cause of salvation, both to herself and the whole human race."[37] Note Irenaeus's attribution of "salvation" to the faith-full submission of Mary.

4. Tertullian likewise attributes "salvation" to the birth of the Messiah through the Virgin Mary:

> But the whole of this new birth was prefigured, as was the case in all other instances, in ancient type, the Lord being born as man by a dispensation in which a virgin was the medium.... For it was while Eve was yet a virgin, that the ensnaring word had crept into her ear which was to build the edifice of death. Into a virgin's soul, in like manner, must be introduced that Word of God which was to raise the fabric of life; so that what had been reduced to ruin by this sex, might by the selfsame sex be recovered to salvation.... Indeed she gave birth to a fratricidal devil; whilst Mary, on the contrary, bare one who was one day to secure salvation to Israel.[38]

Although it is demonstrable that none of the above explicitly cites 1 Timothy 2, when read in their full context these brief citations are at least

---

36. Justin, *Dialogue with Trypho* 100; *ANF* 1:249.

37. Irenaeus, *Against Heresies* 3.22.4; *ANF* 1:455. See also *Against Heresies* 5.19.1; *ANF* 1:54; and *Demonstration of the Apostolic Preaching* 33.

38. Tertullian, *On the Flesh of Christ* 17; *ANF* 3:536.

compatible with a messianic reading of our text. But one can and should say more. It is clear that these four fathers are reading Genesis 3 the same way that Paul reads it in 1 Timothy 2, so that one could justifiably draw the conclusion that they were indeed drawing on our verse to establish the Eve-Mary typology. Thus, it is possible that, prior to the hijacking of the verse by proponents of celibacy in the fifth century, the dominant reading of the text was christological.

Points of Contact with Genesis

If it is to be asserted that Paul had the *Protevangelium* (Gen 3:15) in mind when he wrote of "the child-bearing," one should be able to find clues that he was interpreting Genesis 3.[39] While no sane exegete could deny Paul's reference to the same in 1 Tim 2:13-14 (Adam and Eve), exegetes frequently declare any subsequent allusion (in 2:15) to be obscure and indefensible. But there are clear connections between these verses and the (Septuagintal) text of Genesis 3:

1. Paul names Adam and Eve using Greek transliterations of their Hebrew names in Genesis 3: Ἀδάμ and Εὕα. Intriguingly, however, in the relevant verses (Gen 3:1-19), while the man is consistently referred to as הָאָדָם (LXX ὁ Ἀδάμ), "the man" or "Adam," Eve is always הָאִשָּׁה (LXX ἡ γυνή), "the woman." Her proper name, "Eve," is not introduced until Genesis 3:20. Thus, when Paul uses "Adam" and "the woman" in 1 Tim 2:11-15, he is simply following the vocabulary of the OT source.

2. The verb ἐπλάσθη, "was formed" (1 Tim 2:13), is the aorist passive of πλάσσω, the same verb used in the LXX to distinguish the "molding" of man and animals out of the ground (Gen 2:7, 8, 15, 19; cf. Rom 9:20) from the *creatio ex nihilo* of the earth and heavens (ברא/ποιέω in Gen 1).

3. While the vocabulary of πρῶτος, "first," and εἶτα, "then" (1 Tim 2:13), does not appear in Genesis, the order of Adam and Eve's formation certainly reflects the creation account (Gen 1:27; 2:7, 22-23).

4. Paul's verbs in 1 Tim 2:14, "Adam was not deceived [ἠπατήθη], but the woman having been deceived [ἐξαπατηθεῖσα]," reflect the LXX of Genesis 3:13, "the serpent deceived [ἠπάτησέν] me [Eve] and I ate." Paul uses the compound form ἐξηπάτησεν when describing the same

---

39. Genesis 3 may be the νόμος "Law" to which he refers in 1 Cor 14:34.

deception in 2 Cor 11:3. Neither Genesis nor Paul uses this verb of Adam.

5. While the unusual noun τεκνογονία, "child-bearing" (1 Tim 2:15), does not appear in the Genesis account, the LXX uses cognates in Genesis 3:16: "you shall bear children [τέξῃ τέκνα]."

Interpreters commonly see an allusion to Genesis 3:16 in our verse, suggesting that salvation overturns the curse symbolized by Eve's pain in childbirth, but are often skeptical of an allusion to Genesis 3:15. But if one, why not the other? This lengthy sequence of references to the Genesis account leaves entirely plausible (indeed likely) the view that Paul also had the *Protevangelium* in mind.

1 Timothy 2 in Pauline Context

One way of framing the interpretative question is to ask whether Paul draws upon Genesis 3 merely for its narrative of Eve's deception, or whether he also has the messianic promise in mind. That Paul might have seen Genesis 3 only as an illustration of Eve's role in bringing sin into the world has been proposed on the basis of 2 Cor 11:1-3, 14. There Paul speaks of the Corinthian church as a virgin bride whom he has betrothed to Christ, but who, like Eve, has succumbed to the deceptions of false teachers. Paul does not match that stinging proclamation of law with any gospel comfort on the basis of Genesis 3, suggesting to some exegetes that he was not inclined to such a reading. Certainly it is also true that Paul's use of the "order of creation" in 1 Corinthians 11 and 14, as well as in his *Haustafel* in Ephesians 5, focuses on the headship of man over woman without any reference to her salvific role in bearing the Messiah. This reality is only slightly tempered by observation that in Ephesians 5 he moves quickly toward a gospel interpretation of marriage as an image of Christ's sacrificial love for the church.

But, *mutatis mutandis*, Rom 5:12-21 offers a direct and compelling parallel to the messianic interpretation of 1 Tim 2:15. In that crucial chapter Paul runs a lengthy allegorical/typological parallel between the sin of Adam and salvation through Christ. He sets it up with an initial statement on the cosmic significance of Adam's sin: "Therefore, just as through one man sin entered into the world and through sin death, and so also death came through to all men" (Rom 5:12).[40] He then makes explicit the "typological" connection between Adam and Christ: "But death reigned from Adam until Moses, even over those who did not sin in the likeness of the transgression

---

40. Intriguingly, Sir 25:24 makes a similar statement about women.

of Adam, who is a type [τύπος] of the coming one" (Rom 5:14). The next seven verses then run the antithetical parallel between Adam and Christ from every conceivable angle, with rhythmic drive announcing that the sin, death, and condemnation worked by Adam are overturned by the grace, life, and righteousness of Christ (Rom 5:15–21).

While this Adam-Christ typology scarcely raises an eyebrow, the thought of a parallel Eve-Mary typology in 1 Tim 2:11–15 is often met with fierce opposition. Douglas Moo objects to "the excessive stress upon Mary which his [Payne's messianic] interpretation suggests" and asks, "is Mary's role in the birth of Christ therefore the means . . . of salvation?"[41] This instinctively negative Protestant reaction is open to criticism at a number of levels. First is the suspicion that a certain Gnostic/Calvinist disparagement of the role of ordinary means in the way of salvation is at work. Consider a crucial parallel in Peter: "God's patience waited in the days of Noah while the ark was being prepared, in which a few, that is, eight souls, were saved through water [διεσώθησαν δι' ὕδατος]; baptism, by way of an antitype to this, now saves [σῴζει] you" (1 Pet 3:19–20). Mary's role in the way of salvation stands in direct linguistic and theological parallelism to the water of baptism as a means of grace. Secondly, therefore, it is surely clear that Mary's role is merely as the vessel by which God incarnate was delivered into the world; the emphasis in "the Child-bearing" is on the *Child*, not the bearing. Thirdly, it is not entirely clear that it is *Mary's* child-bearing that Paul has in mind. He may be thinking chiefly of *Eve's* child-bearing as a counterpart to her sin, an activity standing at the head of a multigenerational child-bearing through the history of Israel that culminated in the birth of the Messiah, who would crush the serpent's head (Gen 3:15).

Conclusions

The classical Lutheran law/gospel hermeneutic can be misunderstood as an either-or. If 1 Timothy 2 is read as law, it entails a criticism of woman for her role in bringing sin into the world, excludes her from holding the pastoral office, and commends to her the God-pleasing role of mother. Perhaps the rejection of the messianic reading by conservative Protestants is rooted in a fear that a gospel reading might supplant or overturn this important word of law.[42] But just as Paul in Ephesians 5 proclaims the gospel through marriage

---

41. Moo, "The Interpretation of 1 Timothy 2:11–15," 205.

42. Payne, "Libertarian Women in Ephesus," e.g., promotes the messianic (gospel) reading in a study advocating the ordination of women.

without overturning the ordered relationship between man and woman,[43] so also the messianic reading of 1 Tim 2:15 need not entail a denial of the earlier law message. Indeed, by any reading of the text, this final verse offers some form of consolation (gospel in at least a broad sense) to the women Paul has previously addressed. The crucial question is what kind of "salvific" consolation it offers: the comfort of knowing that one's child-bearing vocation is God-pleasing, or the promise that the way of salvation is found through faith in the Child born of Mary? (Or both?!)

If 1 Timothy 2 is received as a faithful interpretation of Genesis 3, then the *Protevangelium* must surely function as a significant part of its message. It is, firstly, important to note that Paul does not argue (as does Philo) that Eve was bound to be deceived because women are weaker than men. He simply points to the *fact* of Eve's deception. But even this is the second point. Paul first points to the (literal) order of God's creation, first Adam, then Eve. Her sin involved a denial of this order. So also, under the terms of the New Testament, the restriction of the pastoral office to men, insofar as Paul explains it in this text, has nothing to do with woman's purported inferiority in character or ability but simply derives from her God-given place in creation. This place was subsequently confirmed by her failure to resist Satan's attack in Eden. It is significant, then, that Paul does not conclude the line of argumentation by simply consigning her to the role of mother (as noble as that is). Rather, he introduces the language of salvation, faith, love, and holiness.

There is a rhythm to Paul's rhetoric as he appeals, in 1 Timothy 2, to the story of Genesis 3:

> 2:13For *Adam* first was formed, then *Eve*.

> 14And *Adam* was not deceived, but the *woman* having been deceived came to be in transgression.

> 15But [*3rd sing. pronoun*] shall be saved through the Child-bearing, if *they* remain in faith and love and holiness with sobriety.

> 3:1aFaithful is the saying.

First, a word on the ending: it is a famous exegetical conundrum whether Paul's well-known slogan πιστὸς ὁ λόγος, "faithful is the saying," refers to what precedes or what follows. The Nestle-Aland editors have (rightly in our opinion) attached it to 1 Tim 2:15, rather than to Paul's statement about aspiration to the episcopal office (3:1b). The most appealing explanation is that Paul uses this succinct slogan to call attention to profound statements

---

43. See Winger, *Ephesians*, 633–53.

of creedal, catechetical, or liturgical import.[44] This strongly encourages us to read 1 Timothy 2:15 as a proclamation of the gospel of Christ.

But who is the subject of the verb σωθήσεται, "X shall be saved"? On the one hand, it is theologically and pastorally satisfying to translate, "*she shall be saved*," understanding the referent of "she" initially as Eve herself, whose role in the Fall is counterweighted by her salvific role in bearing the Messiah (Gen 3:15). Eve then stands in for every woman in the messianic line, culminating in Mary. In a way, they represent all women, who are saved through this Childbirth, so long as they believe the gospel ("remain in faith," etc.; cf. Col 1:23!). But what if one were to continue the rhythm of the preceding two verses? The natural referent of the verb's implied subject would then not be the closest noun ("woman") but the noun at the beginning of the preceding verse: "Adam"![45] If so, Paul would be holding up before women a far more profound vocation than simply bearing children. Whereas Eve played a role in bringing sin to all men, she herself would become the very instrument of mankind's salvation by bearing the Messiah: "But *he* will be saved by *her* Child-bearing."

This possibility remains speculative, and the messianic interpretation of "Child-bearing" in no way depends on it. It has the great advantage of offering a satisfactory explanation of the shift from singular to plural verbal subject: "if *they* remain" does not then refer to "all women," but draws together the two parties in the preceding exegesis: "Adam and Eve," "man and woman" (cf. 1 Pet 3:7). Thus, woman's role in bearing the Messiah brings salvation not only to womankind, but to all people. Whether or not this speculation suits one's fancy, the messianic interpretation of "Child-bearing" offers a particularly satisfying conclusion to this difficult chapter. While in his church Christ gives the office of proclaiming the gospel to men alone, it is through *women* that the Messiah, and thus salvation itself, came into the world. What could be more glorious than that?

---

44. This is borne out by an examination of 1 Tim 1:15; 4:9; 2 Tim 2:11; and Titus 3:8. Luther translates it, "Das ist je gewißlich wahr," and places the statement at the end of his explanation of each article of the creed in the *Small Catechism*: "This is most certainly true."

45. This possibility was suggested orally by Jim Voelz. Clement of Alexandria is one ancient writer to assume the male referent: "In fact, he [Paul] expresses approval of the man who is husband of a single wife, whether elder, deacon, or layman, if he gives no ground for criticism in his conduct of his marriage. He 'will be preserved by the generation of children'" (*Stromateis* 3.12.89–90).

Bibliography

Chemnitz, Martin. *Examination of the Council of Trent*. Translated by Fred Kramer. St. Louis: Concordia, 1971–1986.

———. *Ministry, Word, and Sacraments: An Enchiridion*. Translated by Luther Poellot. St. Louis: Concordia, 1981.

Cramer, John A. *Catene in Sancti Pauli: Epistulas ad Timotheum, Titum, Philemona et ad Hebraeos*. Catenae Graecorum Patrum in Novum Testamentum 7. Oxford: Clarendon, 1843.

Dibelius, Martin, and Hans Conzelmann. *The Pastoral Epistles: A Commentary on the Pastoral Epistles*. Translated by Philip Buttolph and Adela Yarbro. Hermeneia. Philadelphia: Augsburg Fortress, 1972.

Ellicott, Charles John. *A Critical and Grammatical Commentary on the Pastoral Epistles*. London: John W. Parker and Son, 1856.

Gorday, Peter. *Colossians, 1–2 Thessalonians, 1–2 Timothy, Titus, Philemon*. ACCS 9. Downers Grove, IL: InterVarsity, 2000.

Guthrie, Donald. *The Pastoral Epistles*. Tyndale New Testament Commentaries. Leicester, UK: Inter-Varsity, 1957.

Hanson, A. T. *The Pastoral Epistles*. New Century Bible Commentary. Grand Rapids: Eerdmans, 1982.

Johnson, Luke Timothy. *The First and Second Letters to Timothy*. Anchor Bible 35A. New York: Doubleday, 2001.

Knight, George W., III. *The Pastoral Epistles: A Commentary on the Greek Text*. NICNT. Grand Rapids: Eerdmans, 1992.

Köstenberger, Andreas J. "Ascertaining Women's God-Ordained Roles: An Interpretation of 1 Timothy 2:15." *Bulletin for Biblical Research* 7 (1997) 107–44.

Lock, Walter. *A Critical and Exegetical Commentary on the Pastoral Epistles (I & II Timothy and Titus)*. ICC. Edinburgh: T. & T. Clark, 1924.

Moo, Douglas J. "1 Timothy 2:11–15: Meaning and Significance." *Trinity Journal* n.s. 1 (1980) 62–83.

———. "The Interpretation of 1 Timothy 2:11–15: A Rejoinder." *Trinity Journal*, n.s. 2 (1981) 198–222.

Payne, Philip B. "Libertarian Women in Ephesus: A Response to Douglas J. Moo's Article, '1 Timothy 2:11–15: Meaning and Significance.'" *Trinity Journal*, n.s., 2 (1981) 169–97.

Porter, Stanley E. "What Does It Mean to Be 'Saved by Childbirth' (1 Timothy 2:15)?" *Journal for the Study of the New Testament* 49 (1993) 87–102.

Quinn, Jerome D., and William C. Wacker. *The First and Second Letters to Timothy: A New Translation with Notes and Commentary*. Eerdmans Critical Commentary. Grand Rapids: Eerdmans, 2000.

Voelz, James. *What Does This Mean? Principles of Biblical Interpretation in the Post-Modern World*. 2nd ed. St. Louis: Concordia, 1997.

Winger, Thomas M. *Ephesians*. Concordia Commentary. St. Louis: Concordia, 2015.

The Reverend Professor James W. Voelz

Dr. Jack Dean Kingsbury
Professor of New Testament Theology,
Concordia Seminary, St. Louis, MO

The life and career of James Voelz has spanned the globe and engaged scholarship at a world-class level, but his roots remain anchored in the everyday life of everyday people, grounded in the good earth of Wisconsin, specifically the south side of Milwaukee. His pedigree includes St. Martini Lutheran School, one of the few remaining parishes that had a vintage bowling alley in its church hall, and Pulaski Sr. High School, from which he graduated in 1963. His sainted parents were down-to-earth, solid Lutheran Christians, with a strong faith and sense of service to the Lord. Jim's mother received Concordia Seminary's Christus Vivit award for her work with many Lutheran organizations, and Jim inherited a lot of energy, integrity, and a forthright outspokenness from her especially. Like his mother, he will speak his mind but always has something to say well worth hearing. Jim's own strong faith and commitment to service, his overall work ethic, an insatiable curiosity, and the ability to communicate across the spectrum of socio-economic and educational backgrounds remain a hallmark of that grounding, including summer jobs in the old Pabst brewery and a relentless loyalty and optimism about the Green Bay Packers.

Jim left a legacy back at the "Old Milwaukee" campus of Concordia College, then a pre-seminary junior college, from academic achievement to sports excellence, particularly on the tennis team. The tandem of scholarship and sports followed him to the now closed Concordia Senior College, Ft. Wayne, IN, a grand experiment in liberal arts pre-seminary education that existed from 1957-1977. He graduated at the apex of that era in 1967, "With Highest Distinction" and as valedictorian of his class, with a B.A. major in classics.

His seminary experience included a vicarage (internship) at the campus ministry of University Lutheran Chapel at the University of Illinois, Champaign, where his deep appreciation for learning and Christian faith served him well, as he served well in that academic community. From seminary his academic journey took him to Westfield House in Cambridge, where he sat at the feet of Martin Franzmann, sainted New Testament scholar, theologian, and poet. Jim also quickly took in both the larger academic life of Cambridge and the sports life of England, laying the foundation for teaching Greek and New Testament and for coaching soccer.

His extended stay in Cambridge led to doctoral studies, which included the highly prized participation in the graduate seminar and in the informal evening group with C.F.D. Moule, with whom Jim continued a fond friendship throughout the remaining years of "Charlie's" life. Most significant to his lifelong prowess in the Greek language was his dissertation on "The Use of the Present and Aorist Imperatives and Prohibitions in the New Testament" under Prof. G. W. H. Lampe, conferred in 1978.

Meanwhile, back nearer to his roots, doctorandus Voelz was called to the faculty of Concordia Theological Seminary, where he began his teaching career in 1975, and to his vocation as husband and father, marrying Judy Hayes in 1977. Son Jonathan arrived in 1984, and he would help his father hone his golf skills to round out yet a third sport in which the would-be Concordia Seminary Sportsman of the Year for 1997 excelled. In 2003, his junior college alma mater, now Concordia University Wisconsin, inducted him into their Sports Hall of Fame.

As a seminary professor, Dr. Voelz became well known and well-loved for his care for students, from nascent seminarians in elementary Greek to the rigors of supervising doctoral candidates. He held to the highest academic standards at the same time that he engaged a teaching style that made even the trials of Greek paradigms compelling, complete with the notorious weasel and other novelties from his bag of tricks. He embodied in future pastors, and modeled for all, the key balance between academics and pastoral care, theory and practice, global level scholarship and the care for persons within local communities, all seasoned with good humor and a sense that while we take God's Word very seriously we don't need to take ourselves quite so.

His own professional career was enhanced by fellowship-supported study and sabbatical research at the University of Basil in 1982-83 and the University of Oxford in 1983. In 1989 he became one of the few professors in his church body to serve on the faculty of both seminaries of The Lutheran Church-Missouri Synod when he was called to serve at his alma mater, Concordia Seminary, St. Louis. As a loved and respected teacher and colleague, he has been a champion of the importance of reading, marking, learning, and taking to heart the words of God in sacred scripture incarnated in the very languages of Moses and the prophets, of Paul and the evangelists. He has written and lectured on scholarly topics in national and international venues, on the political and social issues of church and world over lunch and in newspaper editorials, and on the pros and cons of "Cover 2" defenses while watching Packer games. And he has taught us all to appreciate fine wine.

He has provided distinguished service in scholarly societies, most notably as the chair and ongoing member of the Steering Committee of the Gospel of Mark Group of the Society of Biblical Literature, and in various leadership positions in the *Studiorum Novi Testamenti Societas* (SNTS), with his special interests in hermeneutics and Greek language studies. His ability to work with scholars and interact with challenging ideas even far beyond the mainstream of Lutheran theology has been a model of intellectual stimulation without losing one's own bearings, indeed of testing and strengthening one's own commitments, all done with the highest standard of respect for others along with personal and theological integrity.

He has served Concordia Seminary as Dean of the Graduate School from 1998-2002, during which tenure he revitalized the curriculum, transformed the dated Th.D. program into a more research-focused Ph.D., established a graduate student lounge, and advocated for advanced study throughout the church that would engage also the scholarly world outside one's own denominational part of the church.

In that same vein, he was instrumental in establishing the seminary's annual Theological Symposium program. He fostered publication of theological scholarship and played a major role in encouraging the Concordia Commentary series. Building on his own original translational work of the Gospel of Mark, he has initiated and continues to participate in an oral presentation of this Gospel, bringing extraordinary, fresh insights to audiences around the church.

Professor Voelz' leadership within his faculty collegium led to his role as Dean of the Faculty from 2006-10, and he then served as Chairman of the Exegetical Department from 2013-2015. In 2015 he was named Graduate

Professor and the inaugural holder of the Dr. Jack Dean Kingsbury Professor of New Testament Theology.

He has also served the church at large in various ways, including service on the Commission of Theology and Church Relations from 1992-2000 and a variety of committees and task forces. He represented his church in dialog with the *Freie Evangelische Lutherische Synode in Süd-Afrika* (FELSI-SA) at Piet Retief, Republic of South Africa, 1994, and with the Evangelical Lutheran Church in America in 1999-2000. Locally, he provided leadership in the faculty dialogs between Concordia Seminary and Kenrick-Glennon Seminary of the Roman Catholic Archdiocese of St. Louis, where he also served as adjunct faculty from 2009-2014.

The bibliography that follows reflects only his major works. Not documented are the almost countless Theological Observers in the *Concordia Journal*, the practical observations on the importance of reading the New Testament in Greek in the "Grammarian's Corner" column that he introduced, regular Homiletical Helps and book reviews, and all the presentations to pastoral conferences and other gatherings of pastoral theologians throughout his church and beyond. His energy, his interest in both issues and the people who engage them, his willingness to go the extra mile, do the extra assignment and attend to the extra details have all been hallmarks of his life and service. Even into years now meriting retirement, he continues to devote himself to the development of a Greek course taught online; his ongoing involvement in the oral presentation of the Gospel of Mark; his continued scholarly endeavors, particularly the concluding volume of the Mark commentary; his care for his family and for countless friends and colleagues; and yes, tennis, soccer, and golf to augment his more sedentary avocation at the bridge table, where he has reached the status of Life Master. Indeed.

To Jim, we raise a glass of Richebourg and say לְחַיִּים and χαίρειν!

Bibliography of James W. Voelz
Major Publications, in Chronological Order

I. Articles

"The Language of the New Testament." Pp. 895-977 in *Aufstieg und Niedergang der römischen Welt*, 25. Band/2. Teilband. Wolfgang Haase, ed. Berlin: Walter de Gruyter, 1984.

"The Discourse on the Bread of Life in John 6: Is It Eucharistic?" *Concordia Journal* 15 (1989): 29-37.

"The Problem of 'Meaning' in Texts." *Neotestamentica* 23 (1989): 33-43.

"Biblical Hermeneutics: Where Are We Now? Where Are We Going?" Pp. 235-57 in *Light for our World: Essays Commemorating the 150th Anniversary of Concordia Seminary, St.Louis, Missouri*. John W. Klotz, ed. St. Louis: Concordia Seminary, 1989.

"The Linguistic Milieu of the Early Church." *Concordia Theological Quarterly* 56 (1992) 81-97.

"Present and Aorist Verbal Aspect: A New Proposal." *Neotestamentica* 27 (1993): 153-64.

"Semitic Influence on the Greek of the New Testament." *Concordia Journal* 40 (1994): 115-29.

"Multiple Signs, Levels of Meaning and Self as Text: Elements of Intertextuality." Pp. 149-64 in *Intertextuality and the Bible*. George Aichele and Gary Phillips, eds., *Semeia: An Experimental Journal for Biblical Criticism* 69/70 (1995).

"Why Exhort a Good Tree: Anthropology and Paraenesis in Romans." *Concordia Journal* 22 (1996): 154-63 (with Paul R. Raabe).

"Biblical Charity: What Does It Entail and How Does It Relate to the Gospel?—A New Testament Perspective." Pp. 55-92 in *A Cup of Cold Water: A Look at Biblical Charity*. Robert Rosin and Charles P. Arand, eds., Concordia Monograph Series #3, St. Louis: Concordia Seminary Publications, 1996.

"Anti-Semitism in the New Testament—Is It a Problem of Semantics?" *Concordia Journal* 24 (1998): 121-29.

"Newton and Einstein at the Foot of the Cross: A Post-Modern Theological Proposal." *Concordia Journal* 25 (1999): 264-79.

"A Self Conscious Reader-Response Interpretation of Romans 13:1-7." Pp. 156-79 in *The Personal Voice in Biblical Interpretation*. Ingrid Rosa Kitzberger, ed. London: Routledge, 1999.

"Reading Scripture as Lutherans in the Post-Modern Era." *Lutheran Quarterly* 15 (2000): 309-34.

"External Entailment as a Category of Linguistic Analysis." Pp. 223-30 in *Biblical Greek Language and Lexicography*. Bernard A. Taylor, et. al., eds. Grand Rapids, MI: Eerdmans, 2004.

"The Greek of Codex Vaticanus in the Second Gospel and Marcan Greek." *Novum Testamentum* 47 (2005): 209-49.

"The Greek of the New Testament and its Place within the Context of Hellenistic Greek." Pp. 177-96 in *Greek: A Language in Evolution: Essays in Honour of Antonios N. Jannaris*, Chrys C. Caragounis, ed. Hildesheim: Olms, 2010.

"The Characteristics of the Greek of Mark's Gospel." Pp. 137-153 in *Texts and Traditions: Essays in Honour of J Keith Elliott*. Jeffrey Kloha and Peter Doble, eds. Leiden: Brill, 2014.

"Literary Interpretation of the Scriptures (Mark 8:22-26)," Pp. 73-94 in *Listening to the Word of God: Exegetical Approaches*. Achims Behrens and Jorg Christian Salzmann, eds. Göttingen: Edition Ruprecht, 2016.

"The Greek of the Gospel of John: A Deep Sounding; Features of John's Language in John 1-6 and 18-21." *Festschrift in Honor of William C. Weinrich* (forthcoming).

II. Books

Fundamental Greek Grammar. St. Louis: Concordia, 1986, 1993^2, 2007^3, 2011^3-revised, 2014.4

What Does This Mean?: Principles of Biblical Interpretation in the Post-Modern World. St. Louis: Concordia, 1995, 1997^2, 2013.2 -revised

Mark 1:1-8:26. St. Louis: Concordia, 2013.

www.ingramcontent.com/pod-product-compliance
Lightning Source LLC
Chambersburg PA
CBHW050620300426
44112CB00012B/1584